MENTAL SUBNORMALITY

MENTAL SUBNORMALITY

BIOLOGICAL, PSYCHOLOGICAL, AND CULTURAL FACTORS

RICHARD L. MASLAND

SEYMOUR B. SARASON

THOMAS GLADWIN

A SURVEY OF RESEARCH SPONSORED BY
THE NATIONAL ASSOCIATION FOR RETARDED CHILDREN

BASIC BOOKS, INC.   NEW YORK

CONTENTS

MENTAL SUBNORMALITY

INTRODUCTION

It is unlikely that in this country there is any form of disability which equals impairment of mental ability in respect to its toll of economic uselessness and human misery. If one uses as the criterion of disability the inability to obtain gainful employment, one can say that, with the possible exception of mental illness, mental subnormality is the most significant handicap of our present society.

To be specific, of the 4,200,000 children born annually in the United States 3 per cent (126,000) will never achieve the intellect of a 12-year-old child, 0.3 per cent (12,600) will remain below the 7-year intellectual level, and 0.1 per cent (4200), if they survive, will spend their lives as completely helpless imbeciles, unable even to care for their own creature needs (Appendix I).

The United States Department of Health, Education and Welfare reports, "The mental and neurological diseases which are not among the leading diagnoses in terms of case frequency, may account for more days of disability in the younger age groups than any other kind of illness . . . and continue as the leading cause of days of disability until old age."

This is a problem which we have always had with us, but a number of factors have served recently to reemphasize its importance. The first of these is the increasing complexity of our society and the development of programs of compulsory education. Both of these have served to alter the definition of subnormality and to cause to be included within this category persons who would not previously have been considered handicapped.

An additional factor is introduced, paradoxically, by advances in medical knowledge, namely, the increase in our ability to deal with other forms of illness. As our adequacy in treating the acute infectious diseases of childhood has increased, our inadequacy in treating the disorders of the nervous system stands out in sad contrast. An increasing proportion of the patient load, especially in special diagnostic centers for children, consists of patients whose primary disability is of the nervous system.

Finally, improvement in our resources for the treatment of the acute diseases of childhood has made it possible for us to keep alive seriously handicapped persons who formerly died in infancy. Within our large state training schools the number of seriously handicapped patients of the imbecile level is constantly rising, to the point where this group, which requires the greatest nursing care, now constitutes a very large part of the over-all problem of these institutions.

3

Whether because of these significant changes in emphasis of medical practice or because of some other less tangible factors in social attitude, it is certain that the last decade has seen increasing public awareness of the problem. With this awareness has come increased pressure both for improvement of our management facilities for the subnormal and for the establishment of research programs directed toward the prevention of this form of disability.

It was against this background that the National Association for Retarded Children, under the guidance of Dr. Grover F. Powers, Chairman of the Scientific Research Advisory Board, resolved to undertake a program of research aimed at discovering the causes of mental subnormality, and ultimately at preventive measures. It is as a result of the initiative of this group that the present survey was undertaken.[1] Its ultimate objective is to provide a sound basis upon which a program of research may be developed.

It was recognized at the inception of the survey that there are two broad areas of study which relate to the causation of mental subnormality. One of these areas has to do with those factors which produce anatomical or chemical abnormalities of the nervous system and thus interfere with the ability of the brain to respond normally to environmental stimuli. The other is concerned with the study of cultural and environmental factors which, through the establishment of unhealthy or inadequate patterns of intellectual response, may prevent the optimum functioning of the mind in a person whose nervous system is basically capable of normal activity. Although it is clear that in many cases both factors combine to produce mental subnormality, it was decided at the outset to approach the two areas independently.

The two reports which comprise this volume thus represent two facets of a single survey. They reflect, however, widely differing approaches, both of which have been required in order to provide even reasonable coverage of the many areas of research which impinge upon this problem.

Their preparation and original publication as separate reports emphasizes that each approach has a distinct contribution to make to the total problem. It necessarily implies that within certain broad limits one can distinguish those mentally subnormal individuals whose disability is attributable primarily to a demonstrable defect of brain structure or chemistry from those whose

[1] The early planning and development of this program was actively fostered by the *ad hoc* Committee on Mental Retardation of the National Institute of Neurological Diseases and Blindness and the National Institute of Mental Health as part of their program development activities in this field. The National Association for Retarded Children received additional financial support from the Association for the Aid of Crippled Children, the New York Foundation, the National Institute of Neurological Diseases and Blindness, and the National Institute of Mental Health.

malfunction is the result of learning deficiencies resulting from unfavorable environmental influences.

The World Health Organization urges such a distinction, classifying the organically damaged as "mentally defective" and the individual whose mental subnormality is the result of a learning disability as "mentally retarded."

However, in considering the necessity for such a distinction it is important to distinguish between two purposes of diagnosis: research and treatment. With respect to the individual case appearing for treatment, the distinction between deficiency and retardation is often at best uncertain, and would not necessarily reflect a wise therapeutic approach even if it could be certain. Only in the most extreme cases of organic disorder can we say that psychological and environmental factors are not relevant to treatment and development, while there are equally few retarded individuals in whom we can be certain *no* biological factors (broadly conceived) are affecting their intellectual performance. The concept accepted in psychotherapy of treating the total person is equally or more important in the case of the subnormal individual. Acceptance of this concept practically forbids us to make diagnoses which will label deficits as due exclusively to biology or to learning.

With respect to basic research into the causes of mental subnormality, however, precisely the opposite is true. Research demands that we isolate each operative factor and examine it separately in order that we understand its specific nature and effects. Granting that biological and environmental factors are intertwined in each case we study, it will serve no useful purpose to pretend that they do not each make particular and different contributions to the present condition of the individual. One of the reasons for the generally discouraging state of current research in mental subnormality is the overly global way in which the problem has been viewed. A distinction between organic and learning deficits is an obviously necessary first step in dividing the task ahead into manageable and meaningful components.

In one of the reports, that of Sarason and Gladwin, the WHO terminology has been adhered to. The fact that in his report Masland instead used "retardation" throughout his discussion reflects no divergence from this point of view. Rather, he was dealing almost exclusively with identifiable biological factors and did not therefore find it necessary within his report to make a distinction. He used "retardation" rather than "deficiency" simply because the former term is at present in more common usage.

The organization of the surveys upon which these reports are based into separate reviews of research on biological factors and on psychological and cultural factors reflects a deliberate attempt to determine how much we really know about each of these broad areas of etiology. It does not imply that any of the three authors thought either area to be irrelevant. In fact large portions of the report on psychological and cultural factors are concerned with the severely organically defective child.

As we have reflected upon the form in which the two reports finally emerged, each seeming at times to brush aside the point of view central to the other, we have come to realize with some interest that what we have done is to take very different avenues to attack a single worrisome and damaging concept, that of a hereditary taint as the basis for all mental subnormality. The attempt to lay this shibboleth finally to rest is implicit in much of both reports. On the one hand the report on biological factors stresses the great multiplicity of organic disorders, most of them not hereditary as far as we know, which can depress intelligence. The other report, while not denying organic and even hereditary influences, undertakes to demonstrate the great number of psychological and cultural factors which are sufficient in themselves to explain subnormal mental development without recourse to biological explanations. It is an interesting footnote to the sociology of knowledge that two attempts to eradicate a stereotype firmly rooted in our culture should have taken such divergent pathways. At the same time it is equally significant to note that as each author pursued his findings to their conclusions he was forced ever more sharply to recognize that no case of mental subnormality could be fully understood on the basis of biological or of environmental influences alone.

In retrospect this approach to an initial survey of the field of mental subnormality still seems to be the best which could have been adopted, for it permitted at least a preliminary clarification of the subjects to be studied. At the same time it has drawbacks. If, as we hope, the survey can be repeated before too many years have passed, a different and more inclusive format would be recommended. The present approach, for example, ruled out adequate attention to the complex interplay of many aspects of organic disorder and environment with respect to family milieu, specific intellectual deficits, and the like.

Perhaps the most challenging conclusion reached by the authors, each within his own area of competence, rests upon what has been almost a truism in the field, namely that the mentally subnormal population is simply at the lower end of a continuum of intellectual ability which embraces the total population. The challenge lies in the realization which we hope is clear in these reports that the more we know about mental subnormality the more we will also know about normal intellectual processes. Study of the subnormal individual suggests subclinical organic deficits which contribute to variations in intellect within the normal range. Similarly, studies of learning in retarded children have important implications for understanding the development and structure of intellect in normals, and also focus our attention on an almost completely neglected subject, the kinds of intellectual skills which are actually needed to function in our culture, particularly outside of the school situation.

These and other research prospects fill us with a real excitement as we contemplate the research future which lies ahead. We hope we have been able to communicate in our reports some of this excitement.

RICHARD L. MASLAND
SEYMOUR B. SARASON
THOMAS GLADWIN

PART I

THE PREVENTION OF MENTAL SUBNORMALITY

———

by Richard L. Masland

I. INTRODUCTION TO THE BIOLOGICAL FACTORS

As outlined in our introduction, there is a tendency to assume that the problem of "organic" brain damage applies only to the severely retarded group and involves a relatively small proportion of the retarded. It is inferred that the question of structural abnormality or actual brain damage is relatively unimportant in connection with the large and socially important group of low-normal, borderline, or moron intelligence level. Most persons in this group are assumed to have normal brains. On clinical grounds the organically damaged or "brain-injured" child can often be segregated from among this group by psychological testing.

I consider it likely, however, that the factor of brain injury can operate throughout the whole range of intelligence, and, in fact, that minor degrees of injury are far more common than are the severe and grossly evident ones. Pathological studies of the brains of mildly retarded persons show minor developmental anomalies in a large proportion of cases (22),* although the significance of these changes has not been established by meticulous correlation with the intellectual traits of normal and retarded persons.

On clinical grounds there is adequate evidence for the existence of all grades of brain injury. For example, the occurrence of clear-cut postexanthematous (e.g., measles) encephalomyelitis is an uncommon event, which may lead to a severe degree of mental deficiency. It is now being demonstrated, however (108), that mild degrees of disturbance, demonstrable by EEG, are very common and that residual intellectual changes can frequently develop. In the past the relationship of these minor impairments of mentality to the common exanthemata has been overlooked.

In the light of the above observations, the study of severe forms of mental defect assumes a far wider significance than that of the relatively small number of severely defective persons involved. The study of these persons may provide us with an understanding of processes which are equally important in the production of minor defects or, as in the case of minor metabolic defects, minor degrees of mental retardation.

In the following report an attempt has been made to indicate the areas of research which are relevant, to summarize the state of our knowledge in each of these areas, and to point out new areas or new approaches which might be fruitful. It must be recognized that such an attempt is bound to fall short of its goal. Many of our most important advances in medical knowledge have come from research in areas apparently completely unrelated to

* Reference numbers in Part I refer to bibliographic entries listed in References, Part I, which appear on pp. 401 ff. Reference numbers in Part II refer to those listed in References, Part II, pp. 415 ff.

11

their eventual application. For this reason, it would be inconceivable that this paper could include reference to all those areas of research which may ultimately bear on the problem. The most that can be said is that the areas of research outlined here are ones which at this time are clearly related to it.

It should further be emphasized that this paper does not attempt to provide a complete bibliography of literature regarding the causes of mental deficiency. The bibliography included is primarily for the purpose of providing references to review or summary articles which are of value to those interested in a further investigation of the topic under consideration or which serve to indicate the status of research in a given field.

II. SUMMARY OF THE STUDY

A. Pathological Studies

The review of research having to do with the pathological study of mental defectives indicates that this technique has certain important contributions to offer. In the case of certain genetic diseases, pathological and histochemical study of the tissue can establish the etiological diagnosis with considerable accuracy and may also point toward pathogenesis and possible therapy. In the case of maldevelopment, such study in a given case may indicate the exact time at which the developmental process miscarried. In the case of the prenatal and neonatal destructive processes, pathological examination provides clues as to the acuteness and severity of the insult and also as to the pathogenesis of the tissue destruction. It is to be hoped that broader knowledge of function and anatomy in the nervous system will eventually make it possible to correlate the location and nature of lesions with the resultant impairment of general and specific intellectual capacities. In all of these areas, pathology in isolation is hopeless. Such studies contribute only in such measure as they can be correlated with a complete history and examination of the patient.

B. Prenatal Causes of Mental Retardation

The Recognition of the Genetic Factor in Disease

Our ability to recognize and define the genetic factor in mental retardation requires three steps. We must first define the specific characteristic which we wish to subject to genetic analysis. When this is defined, epidemiological and statistical tests can determine whether this is in fact a genetically determined trait. With this established, and through increasing knowledge of the structure and chemistry of the gene, it may eventually be possible to correlate the change in the gene with the disturbed pattern of growth and physiology with which this change can be associated.

A major stumbling block in the field of mental retardation has been our inability to define, within the great mass of the retardates, specific entities capable of being subjected to genetic analysis. Clinical, psychological, and anthropological studies in the past have made important contributions. However, at the present time, the development of new techniques in biochemistry

13

and biophysics provides us with the potential for reaching the very root of the problem, namely, the chemical changes which form the basis of genetically-produced human variation.

There are a number of avenues through which these techniques can be exploited.

1. A number of sensitive mass-screening techniques have been discovered, including chromotography, electrophoresis, and specific antigen-antibody reactions. Such tests make it possible to test a large number of chemical substances with a single analysis. Through carefully designed "loading" techniques, a single test may be able to evaluate the status of a series of metabolic pathways within the person. These techniques are being applied to normal persons in an effort to define the parameters of genetically determined human variation, and a number of inherited biochemical traits have already been defined. Such mass-screening techniques can easily be applied to persons recognized as having inherited disorders as well as to presumed "carriers" of these disorders in an effort to detect the biochemical basis of their disease.

2. In addition to the screening techniques mentioned above, biochemistry has also developed important tools for the detailed study of metabolism. The application of these techniques to the study of the metabolic processes of persons known to have "inborn errors of metabolism" can give us insight into the true nature of these errors and, in some instances, into methods for treatment or prevention.

3. Increasing knowledge of the structure and chemistry of the gene and our ability to produce genic changes through irradiation and use of other mutagenic agents provide us with a tool for the artificial production of mutations which can be studied in animals and bacteria.

The study of abnormal metabolism goes hand in hand with the study of normal metabolism. Each has its place, and each can contribute to the other. A healthy research program is one which will encourage and stimulate the parallel progress of both.

The major emphasis of this section is on the study of the biochemical variations and abnormalities which occur in association with genetically determined disorders of the nervous system. It emphasizes, above all else, the wide range of approaches and techniques which are now available for the study of normal and abnormal body chemistry. There remains little doubt that such variations exist and that they bear an important relationship to the functional deficiencies which are present in persons suffering from many forms of retardation. This review of genetic studies of disease emphasizes the expanding scope of genetics. If one is concerned solely with clear-cut hereditary disease, one deals with a relatively small problem. When one considers the problem of hereditary susceptibility to disease, the evidence suggests that one is dealing with a factor which influences a very large proportion of illnesses. The accurate definition of these diseases and susceptibilities is of basic importance.

Although in certain single-gene disorders almost every affected person shows signs of the disease, in many other instances the degree of "penetrance" varies strikingly, the factors which influence the degree of expressivity of the gene being as yet unknown. There appears to be a continuum between the clear-cut genetic disease, on the one hand, and the disorder in which there is only a constitutional susceptibility to a stressful agent, on the other. The fact that a disease is hereditary does not indicate that there is no form of therapy conceivable or that sterilization or other eugenic practices are the only hopes for modification of the problem. The modification of the stressful features of our environment, in the broadest sense of the word, may be an entirely proper and effective means of dealing with many genetic disorders. A discussion is not complete, however, without consideration of the problem of limitation of reproduction as a means of elimination of disease.

The problem in respect to single-gene dominant or recessive traits appears to be a relatively simple one. On the basis of present genetic knowledge, it is possible to predict the appearance of certain diseases and, theoretically, to reduce their incidence to that attributable to the spontaneous or induced mutation rate. There is probably little room for argument in respect to a number of clearly deleterious dominant disorders. The problem of recessive genetic disorders is more controversial.

It has been demonstrated that in some instances a gene which is harmful when present in the overt homozygous form may be protective or "advantageous" when occurring in a heterozygous combination. Especially in such common disorders as epilepsy and the psychoses, one must consider what possible "desirable" attribute might make the heterozygous or other non-overt forms of these conditions favorable to survival.

In the instance of recessive traits, prevention of reproduction in known cases can have little effect on the over-all incidence of the gene. It is unlikely that, should we develop methods for the recognition of the heterozygote, society would prevent reproduction in these apparently normal persons. Steps toward the discouragement of marriage between persons both known to be carriers of the same abnormal gene has at least a theoretical possibility of increasing the frequency of such genes in the population to intolerable levels (100).

It would seem, however, that if our methods of analysis become effective for the demonstration of the carriers, this would be a means of preventing the appearance of the overt disease, and that it would be many generations before the gradual build-up of this gene through mutation would reach significant proportions.

The problem becomes far more complex when it involves questions of differential fertility and population genetics. Principles developed as a result of experiments in practical animal breeding and fruit fly experiments become invested with political, social, and emotional connotations. Objective data are very difficult to obtain and even more confusing to evaluate.

We are still far from clear in our definition of what constitutes a "desirable" or "undesirable" trait in terms of the eventual survival and "impairment" of the human race.

Probably the extreme radical view toward eugenics was that followed by the Nazi regime in Germany. During the years 1935 to 1945, an extensive "eugenics" program was ruthlessly executed throughout Germany. It would be unfortunate if the universal disavowal of the philosophy behind this program should prevent us from obtaining an objective study to determine, if possible, exactly what was done and what result, if any, might have been achieved in this relatively short period of time.

In many instances eugenics programs have failed to distinguish between the two aspects of sterilization—namely, eugenics, on the one hand, and the social management of irresponsible persons, on the other. In addition, from a purely genetic standpoint, many such programs have failed to recognize the many factors which may contribute toward the appearance of an overt symptom, and the fact that an identical clinical picture may result from different diseases with different genetic backgrounds. In view of many variables concerned in any given instance, the importance of individual counseling is evident. There are undoubtedly many instances in which limitation of reproduction is desirable. However, the decision regarding such limitation requires the evaluation of many factors. Effective utilization of presently available knowledge requires the availability of well-trained counselors equipped to provide enlightened advice or an individual basis.

Environmental Factors in the Causation of Prenatal Pathology
of the Nervous System

The epidemiological studies outlined later are important, above all else, in indicating the extent to which the incidence of maldevelopment and retardation is capable of being influenced by environmental factors. Whatever the specific mechanisms involved, the incidence of maldevelopment and reproductive casualty is certainly lowest among mothers of the middle age group who have had a moderate number of children. The incidence is influenced by the health of the mother (or at least her social class and educational background). It is altered over a period of years by some factors operating to influence an entire population, or at least the habits of that population.

In relation to the specific field of mental retardation, further progress in the search for specific etiologies is likely to be held up until we have more information regarding the classification of mental retardation. There is every reason to believe that mental retardation is a symptom which may result from any one of a number of different diseases. The data available from such gross malformations as anencephalus and hydrocephalus indicate that different etiologies may be operative for different malformations. The correlation between etiology and defect will be difficult to measure until such time as the defects can be accurately defined.

A second *sine qua non* for the large-scale epidemiological surveys of the type outlined above is an accurate knowledge of the habits of the population and the behavior of normal or "control" groups. The carefully detailed studies from Baird, McKeown, and Roberts, in England, exemplify the advantages of having such a detailed knowledge. The study of the population and its habits cannot be a "one-shot" proposition. There is required a continuing evaluation and observation of population trends.

The U. S. Public Health Service is now undertaking a "National Health Survey Program." The purpose of this survey is the collection of data on illness and impairments in the United States. Data are to be obtained by a house-to-house survey in selected communities, and the organization of the program is such as to permit a continuing study of the pattern of illness and impairment within the country. This study will be of inestimable value, especially if care is taken to include data on incapacity from intellectual inadequacy—a disability often disguised under some more attractive heading.

One must have serious reservations regarding the accuracy of the retrospective type of survey, however conscientious the attempt to achieve accurate control. This was most bluntly stated by Worcester (323): "In the process of studying malformations one finds oneself studying prematurity, fetal loss, and all the complications of pregnancy. Presumably, the relationship between variables associated with pregnancy and delivery—the environmental factors—and malformation can best be studied in lying-in hospitals, since the relevant information will not be available from other sources.

"However, this particular approach of taking the records of malformed babies and working backwards has produced chaos. A more efficient approach, perhaps, would have been to take one of the complications of pregnancy, threatened abortion for example, and then to investigate what happened to the infants arising from such pregnancies in comparison with infants arising from uncomplicated pregnancies."

Some limitations of even this approach have been mentioned above. It would seem, however, that extensive studies involving careful observation of women throughout pregnancy, accurate recording of the data during delivery, and long-term follow-up and examination of the offspring should contribute significantly to our knowledge of these factors operative during this relatively short period of life. These must be backed up also by demographic studies of the normal and abnormal population. The need for persons willing to master the highly developed epidemiological techniques involved and to follow through on long-term studies is a significant one (225).

Laboratory Studies of Environmental Prenatal Factors

Within the laboratory, animal experimentation is also providing information regarding the effects of environmental factors in the production of fetal injury and maldevelopment. A large number of teratogenic agents have been discovered, including metallic ions, organic toxins, specific dietary deprivations, antimetabolites, oxygen deprivation, and ionizing radiations.

Important steps are being taken to discover the mode of action of these teratogenic agents. A more exact knowledge of the patterns of normal cellular development of the embryo and of the enzymatic processes underlying this development will be required for a full understanding of the nature of the interferences which lead to maldevelopment. A close similarity exists between disturbances of embryological development which result from genic changes and those produced by mutagenic agents. Often the two forms cannot be distinguished by anatomical means and can be differentiated only through a knowledge of the metabolic block involved.

In the case of the mammalian embryo, the interrelationship of mother and fetus introduces an additional factor, since teratogens reaching the fetus must pass through the mother. The mechanism of transfer of substances from mother to fetus is particularly important in the first two months of pregnancy, and recent evidence suggests that extraplacental transfer may be even more important than transfer by the placental route.

In addition to the protective role of the mother, one must also consider the possibility of endocrine or immunological maternal intolerance as a possible cause of fetal injury. Little information is yet available as to the mechanism which permits successful grafting of the "foreign" tissue of the fetus within the uterus throughout pregnancy or of those factors which lead to the termination of pregnancy. Recent studies on problems of tissue grafting and "immunological tolerance" may provide important and pertinent data in this connection.

Mongolism

The important clues to Mongolism appear to be the following:

1. There is a significant genetic factor, possibly through the mother.

2. There is a clear correlation with the age of the mother. This suggests that any of the factors discussed under "maldevelopment" may be operative as a contributory factor. Special interest has centered around immunological or hormonal maternal factors.

3. There is evidence of biochemical abnormality, as suggested by premature aging, by a disparity between intellectual performance and the so-far demonstrated anatomical defect, and possibly by an increased incidence of leukemia as well as unverified abnormalities of hormone, endocrine, nutritional, blood, and urine constituents.

The Etiology and Pathogenesis of Disease of Later Stages of Pregnancy

Prenatal infectious process.—It is an established fact that infection of the mother during pregnancy may result in infection and injury of the fetus. Fetal infections with syphilis, toxoplasmosis, rubella, salivary gland virus, and vaccinia have been demonstrated. It is probable that other pathogenic agents are also capable of causing fetal injury. The extent of the problem has not been defined. Such definition is made difficult by reason of the fact that the agents responsible are probably wide-spread, produce mild illness in the mother, and may only occasionally injure the fetus. There is evidence that a fetus has been injured by a virus which caused no evident maternal illness and that this occurred even when the mother was immune.

Epidemiological studies have so far proven negative, possibly because of the relative infrequency with which the fetus is involved. Studies having to do with the production of fetal infection in animals should parallel the isolation of new pathogenic agents. In addition, the study of maternal, placental, and fetal immunity; the development of accurate diagnostic tests for the recognition of maternal infection, and the discovery of specific antimicrobial agents are the steps toward eradication of this cause of fetal injury.

Fetal cerebral vascular disease.—Occlusion of the cerebral blood vessels during fetal life has been demonstrated by pathological examination and may play an important part in the pathogenesis of tissue damage from a number of injurious processes. Experimental cerebral embolism has been shown to produce hydranencephaly. Occlusion of the cerebral vessels may on occasion produce a pathological picture almost indistinguishable from maldevelopment. In many instances the cause of cerebral vascular occlusion in fetal life is not known.

C. PROBLEMS OF THE PERINATAL PERIOD

Prematurity

Follow-up studies of infants born prematurely have confirmed the fact that there is an increased incidence of mental retardation, especially in the case of the very small premature infant. It is probably that in some instances prematurity is the result rather than the cause of the infant's defect, but it is certain that prematurity *per se* carries the risk of retardation. The prevention of prematurity is basic to this problem. To this end, there is need for clearer understanding of the hormonal and other factors concerned with the termination of pregnancy. Preliminary studies indicate that the emotional characteristics of the mother may be correlated with the incidence of prematurity.

The management of the premature infant requires a sound basis of physiology, and recent experiences emphasize how shaky this foundation is. The problems of nutrition, oxygenation, infection, and jaundice all are under intensive investigation.

Birth Injury and Asphyxia

There exists remarkable difference of opinion as to the importance of neonatal asphyxia as a cause of mental retardation, and it will probably require a large prospective type of study to establish the extent of the problem and the specific features of the perinatal period which can be correlated with permanent injury. The discovery of some reliable index of placental adequacy would be helpful as a danger signal for potential difficulty at the termination of pregnancy.

Important for the management are studies concerned with the physiology of respiration in the newborn infant and with the pathogenesis of asphyxic injury.

Kernicterus

The immunological factors associated with kernicterus are well defined, although a few new blood groups are still being discovered. In regard to kernicterus and to jaundice in premature infants, there are important new discoveries regarding the toxicity of bilirubin and the detoxification of this compound. Especially in the premature infant, the problem of hepatic function and of a possible role of changes in hepatic circulation at birth has received little attention.

The problems of the perinatal period represent an area of overlapping interests of the obstetrician and pediatrician. The promotion of case-study conferences for these combined groups and of fetal-mortality committees similar to the maternal-mortality committees now active have proven valuable through the stimulation and opportunity for exchange of information which they provide.

D. Postnatal Causes of Mental Retardation

Cerebral Vascular Disease and Inflammatory and Degenerative Diseases of the Nervous System in Infancy

Acute and subacute encephalitis.—The general field of virus research again demonstrates the wide ramifications of even this one segment of our problem. As a result of the discovery of new methods of virus isolation and identification, rapid advances in our knowledge of the pathogenicity and the epidemiology of those agents can be anticipated. Such advances will depend upon close collaboration between the clinician and the clinical laboratory.

Progress in our ability to cope with virus infections, however, will depend upon studies concerning pathogenesis—that is, host-virus interaction—and, especially, upon greater knowledge of the nature of the infective agent.

Of particular interest are the potentialities for research relative to the basic nature of virus infection, which can be carried on with plant viruses. The tobacco mosaic virus, for example, is capable of being harvested in large amounts. It is safe to work with, since it is not pathogenic for man. There is need for more study of the chemical structure of these viruses, of their metabolic requirements, and of methods of interfering with metabolism. The resources of many departments of zoology are contributing to this important problem.

The field of veterinary medicine is also in a position to bring talents to bear on this problem. In view of the importance of animal reservoirs and vectors in respect to the virus diseases, continued survey of domestic and wild animals in respect to their resistance to various viruses and of the epidemiology of the virus diseases is important. In addition, through studies of such diseases as hog cholera, the veterinarians have derived important experience in respect to the behavior of virus diseases in immunized populations. The resources and abilities of this group could be of greater value to those in general medicine if a closer communication could be established.

The postinfectious encephalomyelitides.—There is considerable evidence to suggest that under certain circumstances an unhealthy inflammatory response of the brain to infection or trauma may play an important part in the production of permanent parenchymal damage. The "postinfectious encephalomyelitides" may represent such a situation and, as such, probably resemble the experimentally produced "allergic encephalomyelitis."

Studies are in progress to determine the antigen actually responsible for this reaction and to delineate tissues within the body which take part in the response. Efforts are being made to find ways of modifying this unfavorable sensitivity reaction.

Our ability to detect clinically those situations in which such allergic responses exist might be considerably enhanced through the development of sensitive tests to demonstrate the existence of antibodies against, or unusual sensitivities to, selected test antigens.

The primary demyelinating diseases.—Multiple sclerosis is now considered to be the prototype of a group of degenerative diseases which includes Schilder's disease, Baló's concentric sclerosis, and, in some instances, acute disseminated encephalomyelitis. The etiology is unknown.

Epidemiological studies have suggested racial, geographic, and familial factors in incidence. Such studies are difficult to evaluate because of the extreme unreliability of clinical diagnosis and the slow course of the disease, which has limited pathological follow-up.

Pathologically, the picture does not resemble the allergic encephalomyelitides. Vascular thrombosis or embolism is not a primary feature of tissue damage. The process has a striking prediliction for myelin, and, for this reason, greater knowledge of the normal and abnormal process of formation and destruction of this substance is required.

A number of toxins are known to produce demyelinization, but none bears a close resemblance to or has been implicated in multiple sclerosis. Certain nutritional deficiencies, especially relating to copper and other metallic ions, produce a similar picture in animals, but these have not been implicated in the human disease. Peculiarities of dietary fat utilization have also been suspected but remain unproven.

The leukodystrophies.—The leukodystrophies represent a group of rather uncommon familial disorders, usually having their onset in early childhood and characterized by symmetrical degeneration of the white matter. As with other hereditary disorders, primary interest is concerned with expanding our knowledge of the abnormal metabolites involved. Considerable progress has been made in the differentiation of various entities included in this group through histochemical and microchemical techniques and, in some instances, by using biopsy material. Because of the complexity and, especially, the specialized nature of these analyses, as well as the relatively infrequent occurrence of the diseases, there is need to find methods to increase the distribution of available material for study.

It is evident from this extremely cursory study of the degenerative diseases of the nervous system that research relating to this group of disorders alone extends widely throughout the field of medical research. An interesting approach to the problem of reviewing this literature has been made by the National Multiple Sclerosis Society. In cooperation with the Excerpta Medica Foundation, Amsterdam, the National Multiple Sclerosis Society is preparing summaries of research reports which have some relevancy to the problem of multiple sclerosis. Brief abstracts are provided which indicate the general area of research covered, and these abstracts are made available to investigators with an interest in problems related to multiple sclerosis.

Epilepsy

The convulsive disorders form an important factor in mental retardation by reason of their direct effect on mental performance and possibly through the actual production of brain damage by the seizure. The problem is being attacked from several angles.

1. The study of genetic and biochemical abnormalities parallels rather closely that outlined for the genetic disorders. The classification of the epilepsies is still in its infancy.

2. The understanding of the pathogenesis of brain damage from seizure involves broader knowledge of the effects of anoxia, changes in capillary permeability, and cerebral edema.

3. Knowledge of the nature and spread of the epileptic discharge is being advanced through electrophysiological and electrochemical studies of neuronal activity in the cerebrum.

4. The prevention of seizures by chemical means is at present our most effective weapon against the disability which they produce. In spite of this fact, studies concerned with expanding our knowledge of the mode of action of anticonvulsants are relatively limited in number and scope. The discovery of new anticonvulsants is being carried forward largely on an empirical basis.

E. REGENERATION OF THE CENTRAL NERVOUS SYSTEM

It is certain that, according to the present state of our knowledge, the capability of the central nervous system for regeneration must be considered very limited. However, enough evidence has been presented to indicate that alteration of the inflammatory reaction and of scar formation, and possibly the application of hormones or other inductor substances, might eventually prove capable of facilitating a significant degree of regeneration.

F. CONCLUSION

The foregoing review is an attempt to encompass in broad outline those investigations which have relationship to a search for the causes of mental retardation. Such an outline emphasizes, above all else, the tremendous ramifications of this problem and the wide range of disciplines and techniques which are applicable to it. There are few areas in medicine to which a wider range of interests are applicable and few fields in which the application of presently available techniques offers more hopes for productive discovery than this one.

Under these circumstances, it is neither profitable nor possible to point to any single approach or even to any group of approaches and to say, "This is the research which we must promote in order to achieve our objective of the elimination of mental retardation." Our interests range all the way from such direct "practical" problems as the evaluation of a specific diet for phenyl-ketonuria—a study which bears directly and almost exclusively on the problem of a specific form of mental retardation—to the study of the chemical constitution of the nuclear material and the gene—an investigation which will eventually be of significance to mental retardation and which is, in addition, pertinent to many other diseases, including not only the genetic disorders but also virus infection and cancer. One may go one step beyond this to point out that the investigator who is developing a technique for the determination of the detailed structure of ribonucleic acid is laying the type of foundation on which progress in the above-mentioned "practical" research must depend.

I am not dealing with some fields of research which are relevant to the problem of mental retardation and other fields of research which are not. Rather, I am dealing with degrees of relevancy and with degrees of immediately evident applicability.

In spite of the extent of the field, it is clear that within it certain areas are especially important. On a statistical basis, it is certain that the overwhelming majority of patients suffering with mental retardation are handicapped by reason of some prenatal factor. It is certainly not known at the present time to what extent this factor is a genetic one, to what extent it is an environmental one, and in which cases one or the other factor predominates. A clearer understanding of these factors and of their differentiation will depend upon our ability to provide a more rigid and accurate classification of the diseased states involved. Research in embryology has demonstrated the pathological similarity of genetically determined and of acquired disorders; yet, for an adequate understanding of the etiology of specific human cases, it is essential that such differentiation be possible. At the present time there is still a paucity even of meticulous pathological efforts to provide such differentiation in humans. Such pathological studies have in the past been seriously handicapped by the lack of facilities for longitudinal correlation.

An encouraging avenue of approach to this differentiation is the biochemical one. The studies of Landauer to be discussed have indicated that in those instances in which pathological examination of animals fails to distinguish between the genetically determined and the environmentally instituted abnormalities a biochemical differentiation can be made. There is every reason to believe that the same applies to human maldevelopment. The establishment of criteria for this differentiation is not likely to be developed through studies related to the retarded persons alone. Rather, what is required is the application to them of methods and techniques found to have been significant in the detection of identifiable characteristics within the different parameters of human variation.

For the development of a program, the establishment of isolated research laboratories devoted solely to the study of mental retardation will, therefore, be of limited value, although this certainly must have applicability in respect to certain specific problems. Far more productive will be those undertakings through which the problem of the mentally retarded is brought within the purview of a multidisciplinary group, whose interests encompass a wide range of approaches to the study of human disease. At the present time, our large teaching and research centers are the only institutions providing the variety of talents required for such a broad approach. If the persons within these institutions are to develop an interest in the applicability of their techniques to the mentally retarded, the mentally retarded must be brought within their jurisdiction. The establishment of productive programs thus requires that some responsibility for the mentally retarded be delegated to our university centers. It is to be anticipated that wherever this can be accomplished one will have set the stage on which research with the mentally retarded can be carried forward.

Such programs are conspicuously lacking at the present time. The lack seems to stem from two causes. The first of these is the attitude on the part of the public and the medical profession that the management of the mentally retarded is not a concern of the physician. Although many of the state programs for the mentally retarded require that the director be a physician, the position has been primarily an administrative one, and all too often the person thus concerned has been forced to operate in isolation. On the part of the profession, this attitude probably is a carry-over from the days when overtaxed medical facilities and personnel could not cope even with acute illness, when concern for chronic illness had to be relegated to second place. This attitude is also a reflection of the undeniable fact that, in the majority of instances of mental retardation, medical treatment has little to offer.

On the part of the public, this attitude is at least in part a recognition of the fact that in long-term management programs, especially those dealing with the less handicapped persons, it is the social and the educational problems which are of paramount importance. It is probable that it is for this reason that within the medical profession it has been the psychiatrists, whose interests are greater in the field of social management, who have made the greatest contribution to the management of the mentally retarded.

Certain it is that at the present time few of our large training centers for the mentally retarded are located in close proximity to our university and medical centers, and fewer still have such an administrative set-up as to encourage active participation of university personnel in their programs. The following specific steps could be important in rectifying this unhealthy situation.

1. Wherever possible, the geographical location of new training schools for the retarded should be selected with reference to the availability of the university centers within the area.

2. Medical schools should include within their activities diagnostic facilities for the mentally retarded.

3. Provisions should be made for joint staff appointments, these appointments being so designed that university personnel will have actual responsibility for patient care within the institution.

4. At the postgraduate level, resident training programs should be developed in which trainees under supervision become skilled in the diagnosis and management of the mentally retarded.

Important areas for research with mental retardation are not confined to those studies having to do with the mentally retarded person. The broad general area of the physiology of pregnancy offers an equal diversity of opportunity, especially if one includes under this heading the embryo, the placenta, and the mother. In respect to purely clinical studies, the most serious lack is represented by the paucity of longitudinal studies, especially those which are prospective in character. The formation of teams to provide continuous follow-up in special areas, such as pregnancy, neonatal, and postnatal phases, will be valuable in this regard. Programs now under development should provide valuable data and will have the important additional effect of directing increased attention toward the numerous unsolved problems under consideration. Such studies will fall short of their objectives if they are limited to an evaluation of already suspected or known factors without providing latitude for an encouragement of the search for new and presently unsuspected areas. In addition, correlation between prenatal and postnatal observations will be of questionable value unless these observations are associated with, and lead to, more accurate definition of the postnatally observed defects.

In the postnatal area, it is probable that further progress will depend upon expanded knowledge of the pathophysiology of the convulsive disorders, a more accurate evaluation of the nature and role of virus infections of the central nervous system, and a clearer picture of the role of permeability changes, of tissue sensitivity, and of inflammation in the pathogenesis of central nervous system damage.

One cannot escape the conclusion that progress in the program for the prevention of mental retardation will take place by small advances along a broad front. It is not advantageous to attempt to pinpoint isolated research projects which now appear particularly promising. Rather, efforts should be made to broaden the base of our attack by bringing an increasingly wider range of talents and techniques to bear on the problem. There are at least two ways in which this can be done in such a way as to increase the over-all research effort, rather than simply redirecting it.

The first is through the establishment of programs which provide new research positions and which will thus have the ultimate effect of keeping in research persons who would otherwise be drawn away into other fields of medicine or industry (176). The second is by making it natural and possible for men now in research to include the retarded within their thinking and within their sample populations.

III. PATHOLOGICAL STUDIES IN MENTAL SUBNORMALITY

A complete understanding of any disease requires that one have knowledge of the etiological agent which is responsible, the anatomical lesion or defect produced by this agent, and the disturbance of physiology or function which results. In the case of many disorders of the nervous system the nature of the anatomical lesion and the functional derangement may be demonstrated by the examination of the patient. Often, however, the discovery of the nature of the etiological agent is more dependent upon an accurate knowledge of the history and upon the results of specific laboratory tests.

In the case of mental retardation we are dealing with a condition which, in the majority of instances, occurs as the result of some etiological factor or agent which is operative before birth. Accurate details of the "history of present illness" are thus impossible to obtain, and what meager history is obtainable is from a retrospective report of events occurring months or years before the resultant defect is recognized. Our present knowledge of the etiology of mental retardation has therefore rested to a large extent upon the results of clinical and anatomical studies. Such studies have serious limitations. Before the review of methods of determining etiology is continued, it is therefore desirable to consider the results of anatomical and pathological study and to evaluate the contribution which such study can make to our knowledge of the etiology.

The three most extensive recent clinical-anatomical studies are summarized in Table 1.

Table 1 summarizes data obtained by Yannet (326) from a clinical study of 2000 patients at the Southbury Training School, by Benda and Farrell (25), and also by Malamud (196).

The three sets of figures are not entirely comparable. It will be noted that neither of the pathological surveys includes any persons whose brains are considered normal. By definition, persons in the "subcultural" group are considered to have normal brains by the usual anatomical criteria. It is probable, therefore, that these persons have not been included in the two surveys of pathological material. Some of the cases listed by Benda and Farrell as "oligocephaly" might have been listed by Yannet as "subcultural," assuming that Benda and Farrell have been able to demonstrate minor pathological changes in the oligophrenic group, which others have considered as normal. It is not clear, therefore, whether the group which they term "oligocephaly" should be listed under the subcultural group or whether they

29

TABLE 1

CLASSIFICATION OF CLINICAL AND NEUROPATHOLOGICAL FINDINGS IN MENTAL DEFICIENCY

	Per Cent of 258 Autopsies[a]	Per Cent of 543 Autopsies[b]	Per Cent of 2,000 Patients[c]	
			Clinical	Pathological[d]
Mongolism	21	19.5	10	16.7
Maldevelopments	14	54.5	27	45.0
Destructive processes (perinatal and postnatal)	38	22	10	16.7
Inborn errors of metabolism	7 ⎱ 12	2 ⎱ 4	13	21.6
Neoplastic	5 ⎰	2 ⎰		
Subcultural	15 (oligocephaly)		40	

[a] Benda and Farrell (25).
[b] Malamud (196).
[c] Yannett (326).
[d] Figures from Yannet's data if the "subcultural" group is excluded (other figures × 10/6).

might have been included as "maldevelopments." One can obtain roughly comparable figures from Yannet's data by excluding the subcultural group and by increasing his figures for the remaining cases by multiplying them by a factor of $\frac{10}{6}$. These figures are listed in Table 1 under Yannet as "pathological."

In essence, such a classification provides rather good evidence as to the time of occurrence of the injury of the nervous system. In the case of Mongolism, and of most maldevelopments, the pathologist can say with considerable accuracy the stage in embryological development at which the defect appears. As noted on these charts, in the case of some inborn errors of metabolism the genetic nature of the defect can be established through the demonstration of abnormal metabolites in the tissue. However, even here many of the changes observed are nonspecific. Thus, for example, Malamud reports that the brain in phenylketonuria is very similar anatomically to that in Mongolism.

Most pathologists feel that one can distinguish with considerable accuracy between genetic maldevelopment, prenatal developmental arrest, and prenatal destructive processes. Thus, Bailey and Woodward (12) have studied a series of seriously defective children with superficially similar evidences of inadequacy of brain tissue. Pathological examination has revealed three separate entities, which exemplify the general types of inadequacy of brain tissue which may be encountered. The first group of patients were those with true microcephaly—a genetically determined underdevelopment of the brain. A second group were termed "schizencephalic." Such persons showed a symmetrical maldevelopment of the brain with large areas of underdeveloped tissue. This form of maldevelopment is frequently associated with maldevelopment of other parts of the body. A third group are termed "encephaloclastic." These persons have experienced destructive lesions of the brain occurring before or after birth. Pathological examination reveals asymmetrical lesions indicating destruction of preformed tissues. There is every reason to believe that the etiologies of these three separate groups of patients are quite distinct. It must still be emphasized, however, that such studies indicate stage of development at which the insult occurred rather than the specific etiology responsible.

Hallervorden and Meyer (127) are more concerned with the pathogenesis of the cerebral lesion than with its etiology. Their classification is as follows:

	Cases, per cent
No anatomical change	31
Purely developmental	13
Developmental abnormality plus circulatory changes	3
Circulatory changes only	40
Postmeningitic	3
Miscellaneous	10

It is their belief that by careful clinical-pathological correlation much more information could be derived from the pathological study. They consider, for example, that the degree of tissue necrosis, cyst formation, and the nature of the glial scar are measures of the severity and the acuteness of the initial process. They feel that these changes differ somewhat depending upon whether the lesion is due to vascular occlusion, hypoxia, or edema. They conclude, however, that such correlations cannot be verified until we have a more accurate clinical understanding of the acute processes whose sequelae are seen by the neuropathologist often many years after the initial insult.

In the light of this observation, it is encouraging to find in the French literature (170) a study of the clinical classification and course of various types of brain disease of infancy. This study, however, is lacking in the pathological correlates.

At the Sonoma State Hospital Dr. N. Malamud is conducting a combined clinical-pathological survey of severely defective patients. It is his hope to obtain thorough clinical studies during life and to correlate these with his own meticulous postmortem examinations. His program has experienced some difficulties with personnel because of the 50-mile distance between the Sonoma State Hospital and his laboratories at the San Francisco Medical Center. At best, his data will be incomplete in many instances, owing to the inadequacy of the available history of the prenatal development and neonatal history of patients admitted to the State institution.

There has been a remarkable paucity of work reported regarding the careful study of persons suffering from minor degrees of mental retardation or specific "organic" impairment. At the present time, attempts to differentiate the subcultural or familial retardate from the organically damaged person have depended primarily upon the use of psychological testing techniques, and there has been little opportunity for pathological examination for evaluation or control of the conclusions of such studies. Our knowledge of neurophysiology is only just reaching the stage where it affords some clues as to those areas of the brain whose activity might be expected to have some "global" rather than focal effect upon intelligence. An interesting recent report by Morrell *et al.* (209) has demonstrated that lesions in specific cortical areas produced disturbances in closely correlated motor and sensory conditioned reflex learning but that lesions in the amygdala produced generalized rather than localized impairment of conditioned response.

Morrow and Mark (210) have correlated the results of psychological testing with the pathological findings in 22 autopsied adults. They found very poor correlation between the location and distribution of the lesions and the intelligence of the patient.

A review of the pathological findings of the brain in the autopsies of 110 retarded persons is reported by Crome (63). After reviewing the literature, this author reports, "The number of fully investigated cases [of mental deficiency] is small in relation to the importance of the problem, and there remains much to be learned, for example, about the rarer and less conspicuous lesions, about the constancy and frequency of structural changes in these patients, and their relation to the mental deficit."

Dr. Paul Jakolev has been conducting meticulous anatomical studies of the brains of mental defectives for a number of years, and has developed a priceless museum of specimens demonstrating the types of lesions observed.

The review of research having to do with pathological studies in mental deficiency indicates that this field has certain important contributions to offer. In the case of certain genetic diseases pathological and histochemical study of the tissue can establish the etiological diagnosis with considerable accuracy and may also point toward pathogenesis and possible therapy. In the case of maldevelopment such study in a given case may indicate the exact time during development at which this process miscarried. In the case of the prenatal and neonatal destructive processes pathological examination provides clues as to the acuteness and severity of the insult and also the pathogenesis of the tissue destruction.

It is to be hoped that broader knowledge of function and anatomy in the nervous system will eventually indicate the location and nature of lesions associated with impairment of general and specific intellectual capacities.

In all of these areas, pathology in isolation is hopeless. Such studies contribute only in such measure as they can be correlated with a complete history and examination of the patient.

IV. PRENATAL CAUSES OF MENTAL SUBNORMALITY

A. INTRODUCTION

Nowhere is the problem of the interplay of heredity and environment more clearly evident than in the relation to prenatal disorders of the nervous system and congenital anomalies.

Warkany (303) outlines this problem as follows: "It has been recognized in recent years that malformations known as clinical entities may have differing origins. A hereditary congenital malformation, such as microcephaly or cataract, may be simulated by malformations caused by prenatal diseases. The non-hereditary malformation is now called a 'phenocopy'. . . . This differentiation could be extended to histological or metabolic malformations. . . . The fact that a clinical entity appears to be hereditary in some pedigrees does not permit the conclusion that the disorder is always of the same etiology. In some clinical entities the hereditary forms prevail, in others the acquired is more frequent."

This principle has been unusually well demonstrated by Fraser (93). Fraser has been able to demonstrate that cleft palate in rats may be produced by cortisone or by drainage of amniotic fluid from the pregnant rat. The ease with which such cleft palate may be produced by these stresses is influenced by the genetic constitution of the parents. Through cross-mating experiments, he has demonstrated that the influence of genetic factors in production of cleft palate may be brought to bear either through the genetic constitution of the fetus (from both parents) or through the genetic constitution of the mother herself. In this connection, it is interesting that Murphy (212) has made a study of the occurrence of malformation among the relatives of malformed children. He observed that the incidence of malformation on the maternal side of the family is three times as great as that on the paternal side, suggesting that "the characteristics of the mother have a more pronounced influence upon the offspring than do those of the father." Pathologically the cleft palate which may occur spontaneously in animals with high genetic susceptibility is indistinguishable from that which may be produced by cortisone in similar or less susceptible strains. Fraser has demonstrated that there are several basic mechanisms which determine the development of cleft palate and which are influenced by the factors mentioned. The first of these is the time of closure of the palate, i.e., the pattern of palate closure. Animals with a genetic "resistance" to cleft palate have an early closure

34

during development. A second factor appears to depend on the amount of hyaluronidase present. Fraser points out, however, that even in closely inbred strains of animals not all the offspring are similarly affected. There is little if any knowledge concerning the "chance" factors causing this variability within a single inbred litter.

There is a suggestion that, in humans, a distinction can be made between cleft palate and cleft palate associated with harelip. MacMahon and Mc-Keown (194) have demonstrated that the incidence of cleft palate remains relatively fixed, regardless of maternal age. On the other hand, the incidence of harelip with cleft palate is strikingly influenced by maternal age, the incidence increasing progressively with increasing age of the mother. At least from this observation, there is a suggestion that the etiological factors in the two varieties of cleft palate may be distinguished on the basis of this characteristic.

Pathological examination is able to point out the phase in development during which something goes awry, but it cannot yet demonstrate the specific agents responsible in the majority of instances, although further correlations may make this possible. The following sections are thus concerned primarily with other techniques which may be useful in distinguishing the influence of various factors in the production of prenatal disorders and in a discussion of methods for demonstrating the pathogenesis of various etiological agents.

B. The Recognition of the Genetic Factor in Disease

A number of techniques are available by which the genetic characteristics of a disease entity may be determined. These techniques are capable of indicating whether a given trait is or is not genetically determined.

In the case of mental retardation, we are not dealing with a single entity or trait, but with a symptom common to many different conditions, some clearly heritable, some involving inherited susceptibilities, and some in which inheritance plays little if any part. "Inheritance" of these different diseases grouped together has no meaning. Genetic analysis thus goes hand in hand with those studies concerned with the definition of human individuality and variation as determined in normal populations as well as in specifically selected groups, including the mentally retarded. The study of the genetics of mental retardation thus includes several steps: (1) the definition of characteristics or traits which serve to distinguish one individual or group of individuals from other individuals, (2) the application of techniques of genetic analysis (usually epidemiological) to determine the extent to which the defined trait is genetically determined, and (3) the study of the mechanisms through which a change in the chromosome or gene can produce a change in the characteristics of the individual.

In the following sections, these several steps will be considered in detail. For the purposes of organization, the methods of genetic analysis are considered first. This is followed by a section discussing the study of human variation and, finally, a section in which there is a consideration of the analysis of genetically determined traits and discussion of research having to do with the interrelationship between changes of the chromosome and changes in body structure and chemistry.

Technique of Genetic Analysis

Having defined a characteristic or trait which one wishes to subject to genetic analysis, one places primary reliance on epidemiological studies, i.e., the distribution of this trait in the population, particularly the demonstration of the fact that it tends to occur in persons with similar genetic constitution.

In the case of clear-cut single-gene disorders, the family history alone may be sufficient to point out the genetic nature of a disorder. In practice, an adequate pedigree may be difficult to obtain. For this reason, the maintenance of a genic registry or of a registry of conditions often attributable to genetic factors has proven extremely valuable. There are several outstanding examples.

Probably the most extensive genetic registry is that maintained by Kemp, in Copenhagen, Denmark (161). The maintenance of this registry has been facilitated by the relatively small population of Denmark, the fact that over 85 per cent of the persons within the population die within the same community where they are born, and the fact that the country has maintained an effective system of reporting of familial disorders as well as mental deficiency and epilepsy. It is probable that Kemp's extensive files, which contain the records of 200,000 patients and their families, include most of the persons within Denmark who suffer from mental retardation, whether institutionalized or at home. There are at least two registries maintained in Switzerland. There is one at Geneva maintained by Franceschetti and Klein, and there is another at Zurich. Neither of these has the advantage of the extensive reporting system available in Denmark.

In the United States, an over-all reporting system has not been maintained. A number of centers have developed registries of families with specific diseases.

In the specific field of mental retardation, a survey of patients at the Fairbault Minnesota School for Retarded Children and of the relatives of these patients was conducted by a team set up by the Carnegie Institute and financed by a grant from the Minnesota State Legislature. A team of social workers was employed to investigate the families of the inmates of this institution. A large collection of data was obtained during the years 1911-1918, and this has been filed at the Carnegie Institute Laboratories at Cold Spring Harbor. At the present time, follow-up studies of these same families are being conducted by Dr. Sheldon C. Reed, at the Dight Institute for Human Genetics, University of Minnesota, Minneapolis (244). This study suffers from the universal problem that the disease entities involved have not been capable of definition.

The technique of analysis of pedigree has serious limitations. The first of these applies to disorders attributable to multiple genetic factors or to genes of low penetrance or producing only susceptibility to disease. In these instances, there is great difficulty in distinguishing the influence of heredity from the effects of common environment. The famous studies of Goddard (114) have been questioned because of the failure to distinguish between genetic and cultural factors, either of which can operate over several generations (251).

In cases such as this, where one is not dealing with a clear-cut single-gene effect but rather with a symptom which may result from the additive effects of a number of genes, the study of twins has great potentialities. Only in the case of identical twins can one be certain of obtaining persons with identical genetic potentialities. The study of their similarities and differences can demonstrate the results of their genetic background.

The techniques and advantages of the use of the twin-study techniques have been outlined by Kallman (155, 156). He points out that this is an ideal technique for studying variations displayed by different genotypes in the same environment and also by the same genotype when subjected to different environments. As an additional advantage of this method, he points out that it provides a helpful approach to families for study and also an opportunity for the study of traits which require a long follow-up period.

Gedda (103) also emphasizes the advantages of this technique. He goes so far as to suggest the establishment in Rome of a twin registry; the requirement of special listing of twins in birth, hospital, and employment records; the establishment of twin-study sections in departments of education and psychology within the universities; and, finally, the development of special recreational facilities for twins to provide them with special considerations which would attract them to places where they might be subjected to careful study. This latter technique has actually been used for the study of selected twins living apart (218). Further details on the application of this technique have been outlined by Allen (3).

A few studies have applied this technique to the problem of mental retardation (5). These investigators found that twins constitute 3.1 per cent of all admissions to New York State institutions for the defective. Preliminary studies provide "some indication of a gene-controlled etiology in many cases of mental deficiency." The technique has also been applied to Mongolism (4). Only three pairs of monozygotic Mongoloids were included in the series, all being concordant for this defect, while of 23 dizygotic pairs all were discordant.

The technique has recently been applied to the study of the inheritance of personality characteristics (53). Preliminary studies indicate that the technique is applicable but that effective statistics will require surveys involving the twins from at least three or four large cities. Studies of relatively small numbers of twins have also been reported by Woodworth (321) and Osborn (223).

Extensive and convincing data regarding mental illnesses are reported by Slater and Shields (265).

In respect to the study of human variation (101), chromotographic studies of the urine have revealed a genetic factor in the excretion of β-aminoisobutyric acid, threonine, tyrosine, lysine, and another undertermined amino acid. A number of other compounds showed a suggestion of genetic control.

In a study of heredity in epilepsy, Lennox (180) studied a group of 122 twin pairs affected with seizures. In twin pairs without prior brain damage, both co-twins were epileptic in 84 per cent of the one-egg and in 10 per cent in the two-egg twins. In pairs with brain damage the corresponding incidences were 17 per cent and 8 per cent. The author concludes that "a transmitted predisposition to seizures and brain damage are each (or both) important factors in the origin of a person's epilepsy."

A similar but more detailed study of a small number of twin cases of epilepsy has been reported by Lafon et al. (171), who make a sharp distinction between a group of concordant cases and others in which environmental factors seem to be the determining factor.

In addition to problems concerning the study of the defective person himself, the usual technique for the study of the pedigree is often misleading because of inadequacy of reporting. Particularly in the case of disorders with low penetrance, the occurrence of minor manifestations or "formes frustes" among relatives may be overlooked.

The analysis of pedigree is not complete unless it includes the examination of each of the persons therein. Øster's report (224) suggesting a negligible factor of inheritance in Mongolism, which has been attacked on statistical grounds, is also subject to criticism for its failure to note the incidence of the occurrence of "formes frustes" of Mongolism among the relatives of persons with this disorder.

Øster carried out an extensive study of the incidence of Mongolism in the population of Denmark and also studied the familial incidence of this disorder. Among 500 instances of Mongolism, he found 6 with a Mongoloid sibling, and he concludes that the incidence of 6 in 500 families is not statistically greater than might be anticipated on a chance basis. However, Penrose (230) reviews these data and points out that Øster failed to take into consideration the maternal age at the time of birth of the second affected offspring. Making proper corrections for this oversight, he concludes that the incidence observed by Øster is actually over three times that which might have been anticipated on the basis of chance. In this excellent review, Penrose also reviews a number of papers dealing with minor evidences of Mongolism in the relatives of patients (see pages 73-74).

Especially in diseases due to a single recessive gene, study of the relatives and presumed "carriers" of the disorder is of importance. So also is the development of techniques for the recognition of early symptoms of genetic diseases appearing late in life.

This problem has recently been reviewed by Falls and Neel (84) and by Neel (216). These authors indicate a number of areas where the search for latent, or "nonpenetrant," characteristics might be undertaken. They are as follows:

1. Instances of nominally recessive characteristics in which minor aberrations may be demonstrated in apparently normal heterozygotes. There is some suggestion that this may be the case in phenylketonuria. Jervis[1] has indicated that the administration of phenylalanine to patients with this disorder may lead to an abnormal phenylalanine-tolerance curve.

2. The search for early evidences of diseases which develop late in life.

---

[1] Personal communication to the author.

An interesting instance is reported by Fajans and Conn (83). These investigators, by using a form of stress, have developed a technique for the recognition of susceptibility to diabetes.

3. Dominant genes with varying degrees of clinical expression. Outstanding examples of such a situation are to be found in tuberous sclerosis and Recklinghausen's neurofibromatosis (33, 64). Extreme variability in the clinical expressions of these two disorders is reported by Borberg, some persons showing only a few cutaneous lesions as evidences of the presence of the abnormal gene.

4. Innocuous carriers with questionable clinical signs. Falls and Neel list 22 disorders in which carriers of a recessive gene show recognizable abnormalities. The demonstrable abnormalities include clinical symptoms, anthropomorphic variations, and irregularities in biochemical constitution.

The significance of the problem of recognition of genetic constitution may be emphasized by figures. Phenylketonuria is a rare disease whose incidence is only about one in 25,000 in the general population. However, on the basis of this figure, it can be calculated this gene exists as a recessive in one in 173 in the general population. It has been estimated that the average normal person has within his genetic make-up eight lethal recessive genes (and presumably even more "deleterious" ones) (211). Since these recessive characteristics become overt only when both the parents are carriers of the affected gene, they are more likely to appear when the parents are related. This is the basis for the study of the incidence of defect in inbred populations. The greatest incidence is most likely to be found among the offspring of brother-sister matings. Areas of geographical or cultural isolation, where there has been prolonged inbreeding, also offer opportunities for such studies.

Probably the commonest use of the factor of inbreeding is the determination of the incidence of cousin matings in instances of presumed genetic diseases. Particularly in the case of recessive genes, the overt disease is seen only in the homozygote, and the likelihood that the genes will both be present in one person is greater when there has been intermarriage in the family. If one traces the pedigrees of persons suspected of having a genetic disease of this sort, one is then likely to find a greater incidence of inbreeding, most commonly manifested as marriage of cousins, than is to be found in the normal population. This technique has found a rather wide usefulness in genetic studies.

There have been very few reports of statistical studies of incestuous matings. Reed (243) is at present keeping a registry of brother-sister matings in order to determine the incidence and character of the defects which develop in this circumstance, which is most likely to favor the expression of recessive genes.

The opportunity for the study of isolated communities is dwindling with the increasing opportunity for cultural exchange seen in modern times. In Sweden several such studies have been reported (32, 263, 264).

It has been stated by Repond [2] that there are in Canton Valais, Monthey, Switzerland, a number of relatively isolated communities in which he has personally observed a relatively high incidence of mental defect, presumably due to inbreeding in these isolated populations. The mere fact that a disease occurs in an isolated community is not proof that it is genetic in character, but there would appear to be an opportunity for study in this particular area.

Although inbreeding may serve to bring to light recessive defects, as recently pointed out by Herndon (137), the mere fact that inbreeding occurs does not of necessity lead to the appearance of overt disease, unless the genes happen to be present in the isolated community. Similar evidence is also reported by Eaton and Weil (75) from an isolated Hutterite community.

The above discussion serves to emphasize the great variety of techniques which are available for the study of a trait once it has been defined. It is important to emphasize, however, that in respect to the field of mental retardation genetic studies have been handicapped because we are not dealing with a single disease entity. Those entities which might be subject to genetic analysis have not been defined with sufficient clarity to make such analysis fruitful. Further progress in genetic analysis is thus likely to depend rather heavily upon our ability to define with greater accuracy abnormalities or traits which are specific. The first step toward this may depend upon the study of genetically determined variations within normal populations.

The Study of Human Variation

Whereas in the past the approach to this problem has been primarily through study of physical characteristics, the present attack is centered on immunological and biochemical variations. The study of blood groups has been the entering wedge of this attack, especially because of its usefulness in paternity and twin studies. The demonstration that variations in blood type, and especially in hemoglobin, may be correlated with resistance to disease has validated the significance of this approach.

There is an almost limitless range of analyses which might be applied to

---

[2] Personal communication to the author.

this problem.   The potentialities in this field are most explicitly outlined by Harris (132).

> It may be expected that research in the next few years will lead not only to the progressive characterization of the known biochemical variants, but also to the discovery of many new ones.   A large number of diseases and morphological abnormalities which are genetically determined in a more or less simple way are known in man, and we can expect that it will eventually become possible to characterize the underlying disturbance in these conditions in biochemical terms.   As happened in the case of sickle-cell disease, unsuspected causes of heterogeneity will no doubt be discovered, and the extension of such studies will perhaps lead, as it did in this case, to the uncovering of biochemical variation among apparently normal and healthy individuals.   A direct attack on the biochemical variation among randomly selected "normal" individuals may also prove profitable, though in practice the development of techniques sufficiently sensitive to cope with subtle individual differences and yet suitable for extensive population surveys and family studies is a formidable difficulty.   In the cases of rare recessive abnormalities, such as phenylketonuria, alkaptonuria, and the like, it is possible that an intensive study of known heterozygotes, that is, the parents and children of such individuals, would lead to the detection of chemical peculiarities, resulting from the presence of the abnormal gene in single dose.   Such peculiarities, though perhaps slight in comparison with the effects encountered in the homozygotes, would be of considerable importance in attempting to understand the nature of the action of the genes concerned.   Individuals heterozygous for such genes are relatively common.

One of the most stimulating discoveries in this connection is the observation by Allison (6) that resistance to malaria is associated with the carrier state for sickle-cell anemia.   This discovery stemmed from the observation that there is a very high incidence of this gene in certain parts of Africa. Because of the fact that in the homozygous state this gene has a very high mortality rate, the conclusion was inescapable that the heterozygous state must confer some advantage on the individual which, from the point of view of the survival of this gene, outweighed the disadvantage of the homozygous state.   It was possible to demonstrate a high correlation between the incidence of malaria in the population and the frequency of the gene for sickling, and supportive evidence was found to suggest that persons carrying this gene were relatively resistant to the disease.   Allison is continuing with studies to define genetically determined characteristics in the normal population.   He has demonstrated that the ability to smell a variety of odors is rather specific and is genetically determined.   He is working on the electrophoresis patterns of blood. In addition, he has shown that ability to detoxify innocuous agents, including the red dye of beet juice and the odor of asparagus, rather than to excrete them unchanged in the urine, is genetically determined.

Williams (307) has demonstrated that there is a strong inheritance factor concerned with the excretion pattern of amino acids in the urine. At the Institute for Human Variation in New York, Berry *et al.* (27) have also demonstrated that the excretion of certain amino acids is genetically determined.

Buckwalter *et al.* (48, 49) have correlated the blood types with susceptibility to duodenal ulcer, peptic ulcer, gastric carcinoma, carcinoma of the breast, carcinoma of the lungs, carcinoma of the colon and rectum, leukemia, congenital anomalies, ulcerative colitis, and pernicious anemia. A significant correlation was found between the blood type and peptic ulcer and between the blood type and pernicious anemia. There also appeared to be an association in respect to gastric carcinoma and peptic ulcer. In this series a correlation was not found with the incidence of congenital anomalies. Except for the association of the blood groups with kernicterus, a positive correlation between the blood groups and mental deficiency of any sort has not yet been demonstrated.

There is good evidence for individuality of the electrophoretic patterns of human blood serum (35, 306). By ultracentrifuge techniques, at least 10 different major groups of human serum proteins have been demonstrated. These are in addition to lipoprotein and are probably specific mucoprotein groups (111, 300). A technique for chromatographic analysis of amino acids in the spinal fluid has also been described by Logothelis (185). The technique of infrared spectrophotometry, which is very effective for distinguishing varieties of nucleoproteins, does not appear to have had extensive application to the study of human variation.

The study of the inheritance of tissue antigens is another possible line of approach to the understanding of human variation. At present, the study of tissue antigens is chiefly oriented to the problem of tissue specificity in cancer and the immune response in tissue transplantation. Recent studies have demonstrated the high degree of specificity of the tissue antigens. Outstanding work in this connection has been carried out by Billings and Medawar in London and by Snell and others at the Jackson Laboratory, Bar Harbor, Maine. The current status of these studies is summarized in a series of conferences held at the New York Academy of Sciences Second Tissue Homotransplantation Conference, on Feb. 2 and 3, 1956, and the Conference on Immunology and Cancer, Jan. 4 and 5, 1957. Tissue transplantation studies have demonstrated that the antigenic character of the nucleoprotein of the cell is specific for a given person and prevents transplantation of tissue except from the identical twin. It has further been demonstrated that there are some antigens which are specific for specific tissues within the body and some which are specific for the species or individual (248, 117). Whether the antigenic substances of tissue other than blood can be classified as the blood group antigens have been has not been determined. A limitation in such studies has been our inability to obtain pure cultures of human cells. This block may recently have been overcome by Puck (239), who has demonstrated a technique for obtaining pure strains of human cells in tissue culture. The white blood cells are presumably capable of antigenic study, but this possibility has also not been exploited.

Analysis of Genetically Determined Defects

Closely related to the study of normal variation is the study of the abnormalities which develop in persons known to have genetic diseases. The ultimate objective of such studies will be the ability to correlate demonstrable changes in the anatomy or chemistry of the chromosome with the changes in body function, structure, or chemistry which result. This may be attacked from two directions. There is required, first, a study of the chromosome itself and, second, a careful analysis of the existing abnormalities which occur.

The evidence now suggests that we must think of gene action in biochemical terms—that whatever influence the gene has on the development of the organism, this action takes place through some alteration in the enzymes which determine body development and function. It has been proposed by Garrod (99) that each gene exerts its influence on body growth and function through the action of a single enzyme for whose structure the gene serves as a pattern. It was Garrod's hypothesis that alteration in a single gene thus caused alteration in the pattern of enzyme activity within the body. There is at present some debate as to whether a single gene (or a single area of chromosome) need necessarily be the sole factor influencing the formation of a single enzyme, or even whether we should think of the genes as being entities rather than chromosomal areas. The general thesis, however, has been supported that, in the case of genetic disorders, a major area of attack should be the search for alterations in enzyme activity and biochemical reactions within the body. The study of these alterations represents an important field for exploration—one which extends widely throughout the field of medicine and into which exploration has barely begun. The nature of the physiological changes produced by mutation has been reviewed by Horowitz and Owen (143). Alteration of an enzyme may have any one of a number of effects. It may result in complete failure of a synthesis or in reduction of its efficiency, or it may result in the formation of an altered or "abnormal" product. Its effect on the body may thus express itself as a lack of a needed metabolite or as a piling up of normal metabolites due to incomplete utilization or as a synthesis of abnormal metabolites. It must also be considered that when block occurs in such places as the intestine it may lead to failure of absorption and lack of essential compounds within the body. When it involves a mechanism of detoxification, it may lead to unusual susceptibility to toxic agents and to abnormal incorporation of such substances in the body or its tissues. In the kidney, it leads to abnormal patterns of urinary excretion. The problem is complicated by the fact that, in the case of a chain of chemical reactions, an apparently identical clinical picture may result from interference at any point in the chain. Thus, for example, it was at one time considered that "cystinuria" was a disease entity. It is now recognized that several different forms of cystinuria may be defined and that they resemble each other only in respect to the finding of this particular compound in the urine (132).

The effects of enzyme lack may manifest themselves in various phases of the life cycle. Only a small percentage of genetically determined abnormalities come to our attention. The large majority are probably lethal and lead to early resorption of the embryo or to abortion.

Some of the lethal mutants in Drosophila have been studied.[3] They lead to death of the larva. Biochemical studies have demonstrated specific derangements in these organisms.

Many enzymes are probably operative only during certain phases of embryological development. Thus, for example, in humans it can be demonstrated that there is formed during fetal life a form of hemoglobin which disappears shortly after birth and is superseded by the adult form of this compound. There is a different determinant for the fetal hemoglobin and for the several varieties of adult hemoglobin which have been demonstrated. Many of the metabolic deficiencies which occur in embryological life which are not lethal must be associated with the occurrence of teratological defects.

The only "errors of metabolism" which are ordinarily recognized as such are thus those which are so mild as to be compatible with life and with normal

---

[3] Hadorn: Personal communication to the author.

prenatal development. In this group we are often under the necessity of explaining the phenomenon of progression, or of late appearance of a genetically determined disease. There are several ways in which this may occur. In the case of a general metabolic disorder, such as phenylketonuria, the fetus is protected until birth by the maternal circulation. The worsening of patients with diseases such as the lipoidoses presumably depends upon the progressive local damage produced by the presence of increasing amounts of intracellular "foreign" material. In other instances it is theoretically possible that owing to inadequacies of ingestion or metabolism the person suffers from a gradual depletion of essential substances. One must also consider the possibility that the metabolic changes of the aging process accentuate deficiencies which during youth are subclinical. Finally, it is probable that in some instances we are dealing with inability to detoxify or metabolize agents which are normally rendered innocuous.

The search for the specific biochemical abnormality in diseases presumed to be hereditary on the basis of analysis of pedigree as outlined above depends upon an intimate knowledge of the normal chemistry of the body, the development of tests to study the adequacy of the normal body reactions, and the screening of suspected persons for the detection of the presence of abnormalities of these reactions.

It follows that advances in mental retardation are based upon an understanding of the normal processes of the body, and we would be short-sighted to concentrate all of our efforts in the study of abnormal persons without this background knowledge. For example, Norman *et al.* (220) present a detailed description of the pathological changes in Gaucher's disease, with a review of the literature. From their own case material, and from the literature, they point out that in Gaucher's disease the predominant lipid is a cerebroside. It is believed that the cerebroside is stored in the form of a lipoprotein compound. Apparently from case to case there is a variation in the exact compound involved, as well as the distribution of this compound within the tissues. It is still a matter of debate whether cell destruction in this disorder is the result of the deleterious effects of intracellular storage of abnormal metabolites or whether the degenerative changes are indicative of an actual deficiency. The authors conclude, "No completely satisfactory theory of the cell changes in Gaucher's disease can be offered until we have deeper knowledge of cellular lipid metabolism and of the enzyme systems involved."

It might even be suggested that it is a waste of time to look for errors of metabolism until we have first a clear picture of the normal processes. However, important advances have occurred in a number of instances where clinical observations of diseased persons demonstrated the presence of an abnormality and this in turn was the key which opened the door to a fruitful avenue of basic research regarding metabolism.

The problem seems very formidable if one envisages a program in which every defective person is to be tested for every conceivable abnormality of body metabolism or biochemistry. Fortunately, there are several factors which make it possible to reduce this problem to manageable proportions. As outlined above, cases can be carefully selected which seem likely to show an abnormality of metabolism. The simplest approach to this problem would be to start with instances where two siblings are affected by an identical disorder.

A second factor which has tremendously widened the horizon for this field is the development of mass chemical analytical techniques. These techniques include chromotography, electrophoresis, spectrophotometry, and immunology. By these methods simultaneous analysis of many compounds and the rapid screening of large numbers of samples can be accomplished.

Finally, the administration of a single test substance as a "loading test" may serve to demonstrate a deficiency in any one of a large series of reactions, failure of any one of which may show up as a derangement of the pattern of the end-products produced. ,These several factors all serve to make biochemical studies of selected retarded persons a feasible undertaking. It has been stated (132) that the development of mass screening techniques which are sensitive is one of our most important needs at the present time.

When by some such mass screening technique the presence of an anomaly has been demonstrated, the next stage is the discovery of the specific chemical block or abnormality which is responsible and, hopefully, the discovery of some means by which the metabolic derangement may be overcome.

Discoveries relating to the problem of phenylketonuria afford an interesting example of the development of knowledge along these lines. In 1934 Følling (90) first demonstrated in a specific form of mental retardation the presence of an abnormal metabolite (phenylpyruvic acid) in the urine. The addition of ferric chloride to the urine of two children suffering from an identical picture caused the formation of a green color. On the basis of previous studies reported by Chandler and Lewis (56), Følling recognized that the abnormality was probably related to the metabolism of phenylalanine. This report was promptly taken up by other investigators. Penrose quickly demonstrated this abnormality in several families which he had previously studied because of familial forms of mental retardation. Jervis (150) was able to show that it was possible to alter the excretion of phenylpyruvic acid by altering the amount of phenylalanine in the diet. He was also able to demonstrate that the enzyme responsible for the conversion of phenylalanine is normally present in the liver and could not be demonstrated at postmortem examination in the livers of patients with phenylketonuria (151). Woolf and Vulliamy (322) projected the suggestion that "phenylalanine or one of its break-down products circulating in the blood in concentrations much higher than normal displaces the activity of the higher mental centers. If the amount of phenylalanine and the break-down products could be reduced, normal cerebral function might result."

More recently, a phenylalanine-free diet has been developed, and its efficacy is now under evaluation. Results so far afford hope that if the diet can be administered in early infancy reasonably normal development can be effected in some instances (10). In addition to the clinical results which have thus been brought about, the study of the abnormal metabolite found in this disease has provided new knowledge of the pathways of metabolism of phenylalanine and other essential compounds.

A special problem is presented by those diseases in which pathological examination has revealed the presence of abnormal chemicals within the central nervous system—deposited either in the ganglion cells or in the white matter. Analysis of the basic metabolic derangements in these diseases has been delayed for a number of reasons. Our knowledge of the normal metabolites in the nervous system is still relatively scant. The diseases are rare and, although certain general classes have been well defined, the same fundamental defects may not necessarily be present in all instances.

A brief review of present knowledge of the chemical disturbances underlying these diseases is presented by Webster (304). In Niemann-Pick's disease there occurs abnormal deposition of sphingomyelin in the brain and other tissues. In Gaucher's disease the cerebrosides accumulate, and in Tay Sach's group the retained metabolite is apparently a ganglioside.

Harriman and Miller (131) have demonstrated that in familial myoclonus one commonly finds degenerative changes with intracellular inclusion of foreign material. Chemical analysis reveals, however, that in several different families in whom the clinical and pathological pictures appear similar, biochemical study of the included material reveals them to represent different disorders of metabolism.

There are few laboratories equipped for analysis of such tissue, and, because of the lack of association between such highly specialized laboratories and those institutions dealing with large numbers of defective persons, the availability of pathological material has been poor. In addition, the material may degenerate rapidly after death, and for some analyses formalin fixation is undesirable. The use of biopsy techniques has been started in a few localities. Rapid freezing of tissues may make possible the centralization of special laboratories for such forms of study.

The study of body biochemistry, both normal and abnormal, can be carried forward both in humans and in animals. In humans, the studies are primarily concerned with the analysis of body tissues and with observations of the effects of dietary manipulation or of administration of special compounds.

In animals, the use of radioactive tracers has opened up new opportunities, as has the technique of the use of antimetabolites—drugs which by competing with normal substances may interfere with the normal utilization of these substances and demonstrate their place in the metabolic pathway. In a few instances it has been possible to study genetically developed abnormalities in animals. So far, however, the rather considerable number of "mutants" developed in the laboratory strains have not been very extensively studied (126).

The study of bacterial metabolism has also contributed. It has been demonstrated that many of the metabolic processes seen in mammals also occur in bacteria and molds. Mutation in bacteria is easily produced by irradiation of the organism. The occurrence of a desired mutation may be demonstrated by growing the irradiated organisms on media containing special metabolites and indicators. The occurrence of a deviation of metabolism in even a single colony may thus be demonstrated, and the affected organisms may be isolated for study. This technique is proving to have a number of valuable applications.

In summary, this section has to do with the study of the biochemical variations and abnormalities which occur in association with genetically determined disorders of the nervous system. It emphasizes, above all else, the wide range of approaches and techniques which are now available for the study of normal and abnormal body chemistry. There remains little doubt that such variations exist and that they bear an important relationship to the functional deficiencies which are present in persons suffering from many forms of retardation.

The time is ripe for a large-scale attack on the genetically determined defects through the application of these techniques to the study of basic metabolism and to the study of patients suffering from mental deficiency. The most effective approach will certainly occur when a multidisciplinary team can be organized for the purpose of exploring the various approaches which can be brought to bear on any given case. Such a program can be most effectively developed in those instances where there exists a laboratory or research center in which are grouped men with a variety of interests and where such a center can establish a relationship with a training school or custodial institution in which there are located large numbers of patients suffering from a variety of disorders of the nervous system. The development of such a program at the California Institute of Technology and the Pacific State Hospital in California is of particular significance in this regard. A close liaison has been established between the group at California Institute of Technology under Dr. Linus Pauling, and the staff at the Southern Pacific Hospital under Dr. George Tarjan. Within this framework, there is the possibility for developing a truly broad-scale and coordinated attack on various important forms of mental deficiency.

The Nature of Gene Action

At the same time that the studies are in progress to demonstrate the results of genetic change, parallel studies on the nature of the genes and of the process of mutation are going forward. Both advances are necessary if the ultimate correlation between genic activity and its effect on the body are to be clarified. At the present time, the biochemical study of the nucleus and the mode of action of mutagenic agents are under intensive investigation, especially by reason of their interest in connection with cancer and virus disease.

Electron microscopy has revealed the chromosome to consist of a long, coiled, thread-like structure with bead-like variation in thickness. Chemically, there is support for the thesis that it consists of a long chain molecule containing ribonucleic acid (RNA) and deoxyribonucleic acid (DNA). It is postulated that this chain in some way serves as a template for the construction of the many enzymes which in turn control the processes of body growth and function. DeBusk (69) reviews the major reactions of intermediary metabolism known to be under the control of genes. The emphasis in this review is on the metabolism of bacteria and other lower organisms. At the conclusion, DeBusk presents a model which relates the major macromolecular architecture of genic material to our present concept of enzyme formation. He states, "The principle pathway for the determination of gene-controlled enzyme and protein specificity is by the synthesis of specific RNA molecules containing linear arrays of purine and pyrimidine bases, determined by the hydrogen bonding of ribose nucleosides or nucleotides to the purine and pyrimidine bases of the chromosomal DNA."

Modifications of the chromosome and its genes may be produced artificially by a number of agents, presumably through their ability to react with the genic molecule. The mutagenic effect is most easily demonstrated through observation of the change in the structure or the chemistry of the animal possessing the altered gene. Mutagenic effect of X-ray has thus been quantitated in the fruit fly and in mice.

Its effect on human cells has been demonstrated in tissue culture[4] and has been found to be comparable with that in the tissues in other animals. Direct proof of mutagenic effects in humans is now being obtained by studies of the offspring (second generation) of radiologists and of populations living in areas of high background radioactivity levels.

Data from Hiroshima and Nagasaki have been reviewed by Neel and Schull (217). This volume contains a meticulous review of a tremendous mass of information collected in these two cities. A significant change in sex ratio, but no increase in malformation, was demonstrated. The authors point out, however, that had such changes been demonstrable as a result of this experience it would have indicated a most unusual sensitivity of the human gene—so sensitive that as little as 3 to 10 r would have been the level of dosage required to double the mutation rate, rather than the present estimate of 30 to 80 r. This volume emphasizes the many factors which still remain to be evaluated with certainty and concludes, "It is the belief of the authors that the stage is now set for very substantial advances in our knowledge of the genetics of man. Given the facilities and the investigators, great progress can be made toward a better understanding of the problem of the genetic effects of the irradiation of human populations, and, on the time scale of human evolution, within a relatively short period of time."

An authoritative review of the effects of irradiation is that recently reported by the National Academy of Sciences (214). This report includes an analysis of the mutagenic effect of X-ray of the gonads and gives an estimate of

---

[4] Puck: Personal communication to the author.

the effects of irradiation to which the average person may now be exposed as follows:

	Av. Dose of Irradiation to Gonads, r
1. From natural causes (to age 30)	4.4 to 5.5
2. From diagnostic and therapeutic procedures (to age 30)	3.0
3. If "weapons" testing continues at present level (to age 30)	0.002 to 0.5
4. Single dental survey	0.005
5. Fluoroscopic examination (general)	2.0
6. Required to double the mutation rate	30 to 80

Although, as mentioned above, direct evidence of the genetic effects of irradiation in human populations has not been ascertained, there is evidence for the direct deleterious effects of X-rays on humans—a finding which parallels that which has been demonstrated in mice. The report gives the following figures:

	Av. Age at Death, Yr.
1. Physicians having no known contact with radiation	65.7
2. Specialists having some exposure to radiation	63.3
3. Radiologists	60.5
4. U. S. Population over 25 years of age	65.6

There are no reports to indicate whether the impairment of the general health or reproductive efficiency induced by irradiation might have a teratogenic effect other than that produced by the occurrence of mutations in the germ cells or by direct action on the fetus.

In addition to X-rays, a number of mutagenic chemicals have been demonstrated, their mode of action apparently being quite similar to that of X-rays. Virus-induced mutations in bacteria, heritable in character, have also been produced, their existence being evidence that in some instances the viruses contain or consist of chemicals similar to the genic material of the host cell.

Mutations in protozoa may be produced in the nucleus by contact with aged cytoplasm. There is evidence that degeneration of the cytoplasm may have a deleterious effect on the nucleus and the genes and may actually lead to mutation (20). Sonneborn has been carrying out experiments to demonstrate that degeneration of the cytoplasm can lead to inheritable mutations of the nucleus. In Paramecium, the nuclei may be exchanged between two organisms, which can cause a young nucleus to be transferred to an old cytoplasm. Under these circumstances, mutation in the young nucleus may be produced. In humans, aging of the cytoplasm might be expected to produce mutations in the sperm, and Sonneborn is at present analyzing the figures from fetal deaths in New York City, especially those occurring in first weeks of pregnancy. Of particular interest is a recent report (C. Auerbach, *Annals of the New York Academy of Sciences* [Vol. 68, April 1958, pp. 731-749] "Mutagenic Effects of Alkylating Agents") that "incontrovertible proof for the specificity of mutagenic action has been obtained. . . . In several experiments on bacteria and molds, it could be shown that, of two genes in the same nucleus, one responded preferentially to one mutagen, the second to another." The ability to produce additional mutation for destruction selectively of a deleterious gene would represent a tremendous accomplishment.

C. Environmental Factors in the Causation of Prenatal Pathology of the Nervous System

Accurate data are not now available by which to determine to what extent maldevelopment of the nervous system is attributable to hereditary factors, to what extent to environmental factors, and to what extent to a combination of the two. The search for specific environmental factors is thus of particular importance. The problem of the detection of agents operative before birth is complicated by the fact that the results are not evident until a long time after the agent may have ceased to be operative. Although pathological examination may give some clue as to the approximate time when the injury occurred, the fact that the actual maldevelopment occurred at a specific time during pregnancy does not necessarily indicate that the primary factor responsible was operative then rather than previous to that time. Because of the great latency between the time of occurrence of the insult and the time when the diagnosis can eventually be established, the relationship between cause and effect is not often an evident one. Until such a relationship has been established, the relevant data on which to establish such a relationship may be overlooked and may not even be included in the data relative to the pregnancy or previous history of the pregnant woman. This problem is also complicated by the fact that certain factors operating in the production of maldevelopment may be operative before the pregnancy itself occurs, and they may actually be taking place throughout the early life of the prospective mother.

A second factor which complicates the detection of the causative agents in maldevelopment is the frequent interplay of factors and the difficulty of distinguishing cause from effect. It has been demonstrated, for example, that hemorrhage during pregnancy, toxemia, and prematurity are all factors which are associated with an increased incidence of mental retardation in the offspring. It is difficult to determine, however, to what extent the retardation is the result of the maldevelopment of the fetus which in itself caused the "complication of pregnancy" and to what extent the complication of pregnancy caused injury to the fetus at the time of its occurrence.

It is true that there is a strong interdependence of the factors leading to maldevelopment and, in addition, that many factors which operate in general may lead to a number of different forms of reproductive failure. Pasamanick and Lilienfeld (227) have emphasized the concept of a "continuum of reproductive failure." They point out that reproductive failure is exemplified in its most extreme degree by death of the ovum and in its mildest degree possibly by some minor defect of the central nervous system, mental retardation, or "emotional maladjustment." Within this continuum are a variety of the complications of pregnancy, all of which may be similarly influenced by factors leading to impairment of reproductive efficiency.

This concept obtains considerable support from epidemiological surveys, which are able to show a rather close correlation between the incidence of a number of such forms of reproductive failure and the general level of health of the population. However, they fail to emphasize the specificity of possible harmful factors and possible end-results. As will be demonstrated below, all forms of "reproductive failure" do not follow the same patterns, and there is some evidence at least that there are instances of a direct relationship between a specific deleterious, harmful agent and a specific abnormal developmental pattern. It is obvious, however, that the interplay of factors makes the search for such a specific relationship an extremely difficult one indeed.

Epidemiological Studies

There have been several methods of investigation relative to the search for environmental factors. The first of these is the study of the epidemiology of maldevelopment.

Several important observations have been obtained from extensive studies of vital statistics. On the basis of these data, the over-all incidence of maldevelopment in general or of specific maldevelopment may be correlated with factors influencing the entire population and operating over periods of time.

Hegnauer (134) has statistics relative to 951 malformed infants observed in 141,706 births, the data having been collected over a long period of time in several German hospitals. Correlations are made between the type of defect observed, the age of the mother, and her parity and the variations in the over-all incidence from year to year within the area included in the survey. MacMahon *et al.* (195) trace the incidence of a variety of malformations of the central nervous system during the years 1936 to 1948.

A number of reports have been published regarding the effects of mass starvation, such as that which occurred during the war time. A report of this sort from Leningrad was reported by Antonov (9), and another, by Eichmann and Gesenius (78). The effects in the Netherlands were reviewed by Smith (266).

A serious limitation in this technique is the fact that it is almost impossible to separate the various factors operative to influence an entire population over a period of years. Variations in the incidence of maldevelopment occurring during periods of deprivation might be attributable to dietary inadequacies, to an increase in maternal infection, to emotional or psychic trauma, or to excess physical activity. It is equally possible that improvements or worsening in the reproductive history occurring during or after war could be influenced by changing patterns of social custom—the age of marriage, frequency of intercourse, "fashion" with respect to desirability of large families, and the use of contraceptive techniques. The data obtained from such studies must then be subject to critical scrutiny, and interpretations made therefrom require careful evaluation.

A second type of study has been the retrospective one. For these studies lists or records of maldeveloped persons are obtained from the medical registry or hospital records and a review of the factors which may have influenced their occurrence is made. Such studies have been relevant to the evaluation of the effects of maternal age, parity, social class, and reproductive history in relationship to a variety of forms of reproductive failure. The mass surveys mentioned above have included data on age and parity.

Baird *et al.* (14) made a detailed study of social and obstetrical histories of stillbirths and deaths during the neonatal period. Their causes of death included eight categories—mature, cause unknown; trauma; premature, cause unknown; toxemia; deformity; antepartum hemorrhage; maternal disease, and others. They did not include any breakdown in regard to the type of maldevelopment involved. Malpas (197) reports the study of 294 cases of fetal malformation which occurred in a series of 13,964 consecutive births in the

Liverpool Maternity Hospital during the years 1823-1932, inclusive. His studies emphasize a correlation of maternal age, parity, and reproductive history with the incidence of malformation. A breakdown according to type of deformity is included. Record and McKeown (242) have correlated the maternal reproductive history and the family incidence. This paper is one of a long series dealing with this topic. The first paper (241) is a report of the investigation of 930 consecutive malformations of the central nervous system certified as the causes of stillbirths or first-year deaths in the city of Birmingham during the years 1940-1947. Information was obtained from the hospital records and from home visits with 742 of the mothers. This survey is also important in that a control group of 742 mothers of infants born free of malformation is included.

Murphy (212) made a similar study of obstetrical factors in the causation of maldevelopment. The affected persons were located from the birth certificates in the Philadelphia registry and from hospital records. There was no detailed breakdown of the type of malformation involved, except in that part of the survey concerned with malformation among relatives of the affected persons. A control series was not included, in some instances general figures for the over-all incidence of defects being used as controls and in other instances the sibs of the affected persons.

Pasamanick and Lilienfeld (227) have completed a series of retrospective studies which have correlated the occurrence of a variety of defects with maternal and fetal factors. Worcester et al. (324) have also made a retrospective study of the gestational characteristics of these pregnancies. Worcester (323) discusses some of the problems involved in such a survey, emphasizing particularly the value of a control series on which to evaluate the results.

Landtman (175) also made a retrospective study in which a correlation was made between the occurrence of maldevelopment and the complications of pregnancy.

The retrospective type of study suffers from several serious limitations, most of which relate to the question of obtaining adequate controls. Data obtained from the hospital records can be assumed to be objective. Information obtained by interrogation of the mother of a defective child is likely to differ from that of the mother of a normal child. It is interesting that little attention has been paid to a quantitative evaluation of the reliability of history-taking. An interesting paper by Pasamanick et al. (226) reveals that a routine questionnaire regarding infant development is found to be subject to severe error when compared with actual observations made by a visitor.

Important studies of methodology in this field have also been contributed by Yerushalmy, *et al.* (327), in which they tested the reliability of retrospective data obtained from women regarding their pregnancies.

The fullest value of such studies is obtained only when an accurate knowledge of the social habits of the population is available. This is one of the unique advantages by McKeown *et al.* in their English studies, which have been carried on over a number of years and through which a large sample control group has been established. An example of the type of problem involved is observed in studies having to do with variations of intelligence with parity. As will be outlined below, the incidence of maldevelopment increases progressively after the sixth child. The studies of Pasamanick *et al.* also indicate that the incidence of mental retardation is higher with increasing parity. It might easily be concluded (and may actually be correct) that reproductive efficiency is reduced with high degrees of parity and that this in itself is the factor responsible for lower intelligence in the later-born children. However, in respect to the question of mental retardation (as opposed to maldevelopment), there are data to indicate that mental retardation has negative correlation with family size, and there is a strong suspicion that it is the characteristics of the family of low intelligence which determine the large family size rather than the large family which determines the intelligence. Obviously, the later-born children in such a series as that reported by Pasamanick *et al.* would all be children from large families, whose average intelligence level would be anticipated to be below that of the general population. The true effect of parity can be determined only by correlation of intelligence within each individual family. Such a study has been completed in England by Fraser Roberts (247). A comparison was made of the intelligence of 622 pairs of sibs born to the same parents and separated by an average of two years. It is concluded, "Examining families of two, three, four, and five in the whole sample by family size and birth order, it is found that differences in intelligence between family sizes are highly significant and differences between birth order within the family sizes non-significant. . . . It is concluded that birth order, and hence maternal age, make no significant contribution to the correlation [of -0.224 between sib number and *IQ* found in the whole sample]."

A third limitation of our epidemiological and retrospective studies lies in the inadequacy of our present diagnostic evaluation of the defective. In respect to gross maldevelopment, such as anencephalus and hydrocephalus, it has been demonstrated that each maldevelopment has a specific pattern of occur-

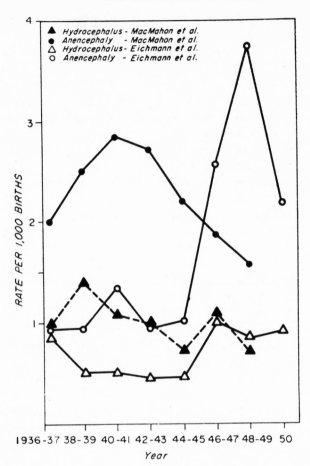

Fig. 1.—Incidence of hydrocephalus and of anencephaly in England and in Germany prior to, during, and following World War II. The English data, reported by MacMahon, Record, and McKeown (195), indicate a significant fall in the incidence of anencephaly during the war years, which the authors attribute to improved nutrition under the rationing program. The incidence of hydrocephalus was not significantly altered. The data from Germany, reported by Eichmann and Gesenius (78), show a sudden and striking increase in the incidence of anencephaly at the end of the war, presumably coincident with a period of rather severe deprivation at that time. Here also, there was no significant alteration in the incidence of hydrocephalus.

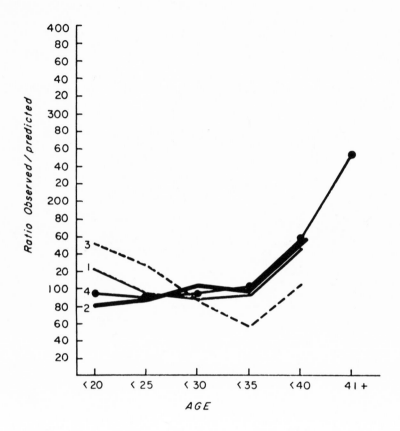

Fig. 2.—Incidence of mental deficiency, maldevelopment, and prematurity in relation to maternal age at the time of birth of the affected offspring. The figures are plotted as a ratio, the figure for each category being determined on the basis of a predicted incidence for that category, divided by the observed incidence. The predicted incidence for each category is calculated by determining the percentage of the general population or population sample which falls within the given age group and multiplying this by the total number of cases of a given defect observed in all groups. The figures of Curve *1* are for the incidence of mental deficiency reported by Pasamanick *et al.* (227). Curve *2* is the incidence of prematurity reported by Baird, Walker, and Thomson (14). Curve *3* is the incidence of maldevelopment reported by these same observers. Curve *4* is the incidence of maldevelopment reported by Hegnauer (134).

rence, suggesting that the same factors are not necessarily operative in each instance (Figs. 1, 3 and 4). It is almost certain that within the general classification of "mental retardation" we are dealing with a number of different diseases. At the present time our studies are able to demonstrate only the over-all correlation, and they leave no opportunity for correlation between specific cause and specific type of brain damage. Finally, it is also inherent in the retrospective study that it is unlikely to demonstrate the significance of a

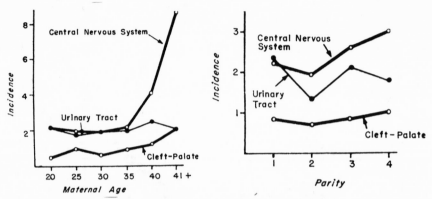

Fig. 3.—Incidence of maldevelopment of central nervous system and of other parts of the body in relation to age and to parity. Data are from Hegnauer (134). These figures indicate that the effect of age and parity on maldevelopments of the nervous system is different from their effect on maldevelopments of other organs.

factor of which we are not already suspicious. In general, a hospital record will include a report only of those details which are clearly known to be abnormal. Some additional information may be obtained from interrogation of the parents, but this is subject to the uncertainties mentioned above. If we are looking for new factors, as yet unrecognized, it is likely that prospective studies will be required and that they will involve the recording of the most minute data relative to the health and activities of the pregnant mother.

Controlled Experiments with Human Populations

The ideal method of evaluation of environmental factors is that situation in which a factor can be altered and the results of its alteration observed. It is only in the field of maternal nutrition that this has been possible; and even here conflicting results are reported. Studies of the effect of maternal diet have been extensively reviewed by Toverud et al. (293). This bulletin includes a general review of maternal and infant health and a discussion of problems of prem=aternal, prepartal, and postnatal care. These authors are able to cite studies in which the administration of dietary supplements, consisting mainly of vitamins A, D, B, calcium, phosphorus, and iron, led to a significant reduction of stillbirth and neonatal mortality rates. Controlled studies of this sort have been reported by Ebbs *et al.* (76) from Canada and by Balfour from England (16).

This type of study has recently been completed in the United States by

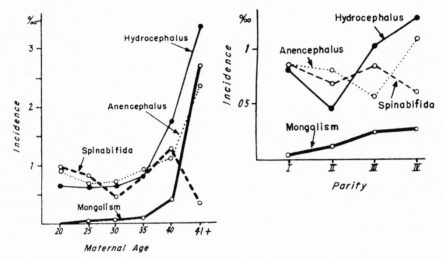

Fig. 4.—Incidence of various types of maldevelopments of the central nervous system in relation to age and to parity. Data are from Hegnauer (134). These figures emphasize that various types of anomalies are not subject to similar influences, as is also evidenced in Figure 1. It is evident that there is a striking increase in hydrocephalus, anencephaly, and Mongolism with advancing maternal age. The graph does not emphasize the more moderate increase in the incidence of anencephalus in young mothers which has been reported by McKeown and others and which is also observable on this graph.

Harrell *et al.* (130). This study involved 2400 pregnant women located in Kentucky and in Virginia. Four types of "dietary supplements" were used, these being administered to the patients as they registered in the clinics in serial order, in order to obtain four identical groups. The four dietary supplements were as follows: (*a*) ascorbic acid; (*b*) thiamine 2 mg., riboflavin 4 mg., nicotinic acid (niacin) 20 mg., and iron 15 mg.; (*c*) inert material; (*d*) thiamine 2 mg.

In no instance did the participant or the person who subsequently tested the offspring of the pregnant woman know which of the four administered supplements was involved. The patients each took one tablet a day.

In the Norfolk area, 518 three-year-old subjects (the offspring of the mothers who received the "dietary supplements") were tested individually as near their third birth anniversary as possible. Children of mothers receiving the polynutrient supplement had an average *IQ* of 103.4; the thiamine-supplemented group, 101.9; the ascorbic acid-supplemented group, 100.9, and the non-supplemented (inert material) group, 98.4. When statistically analyzed, this average superiority was found to be significant and beyond the 1 per cent level of confidence. Of these children, 370 were retested at the age of four years, and again a significantly larger mean intelligence quotient for the supplemented group as compared with the placebo group was observed.

In the Kentucky portion of the study, 811 children were tested at approximately three years of age. The mean *IQ* of the multivitamin group was 107.62; that of the thiamine group, 106.76; that of the ascorbic acid group, 105.74, and that of the "inert material" group, 107.94. These figures do not show a statistically significant difference between those who did and those who did not receive dietary supplement. The authors conclude that "the findings in the Norfolk group that supplementation of the pregnant and lactating mother's diet by vitamins increased the intelligence quotient of their offspring at three and four years of age above those obtained by children whose mothers received only a pellet of inert material is . . . statistically reliable beyond a reasonable doubt. The fact that similar differences were not reliable, found in another group living under a very different environment, with a much better diet, as far as the vitamin content is concerned (probably in other respects also), with probably less consistent intake of the vitamins and less reliable test results, does not make less valid or less credible the positive findings in the Norfolk group." The authors conclude that "this study demonstrates beyond a reasonable doubt, that vitamin supplementation supplied to pregnant and lactating women under certain circumstances . . . does increase the intelligence of their offspring, at least for the first four years of their lives."

Dieckmann *et al*. (72, 73) made a study of the dietary habits of pregnant women at the Chicago Lying-In Hospital and correlated the dietary habits of the mother with this history of pregnancy and the outcome. "A strikingly significant correlation was found between the condition of 302 babies rated by the pediatrician and the average protein intake of the mothers. The percentage of excellent babies steadily increased with increasing intake [of protein]. So large a value could occur by accident only about one in 10,000 times." They also observed a definite and striking correlation between the level of protein intake and incidence of abortions.

A number of studies have been carried out in which correlation is made between the dietary habits of the mother and the course and outcome of pregnancy. These studies suffer from the complication involved in the difficulty of distinguishing the effects of inadequate diet from the intellectual and cultural factors which may also influence the diet.

Jeans et al. (148) investigated the dietary habits of 404 pregnant women of low income. A careful analysis of the diet was made, and the mothers were divided into five groups according to their protein intakes. It was found that the lowest birth weight, low vitality and large number of deaths in the newborn infants occurred among those born to the most poorly nourished mothers. The incidence of prematurity rose sharply with the decrease in the nutritional status of the mother. Here, again, it is not possible to state unequivocally that other factors may not have been responsible both for the poor nutrition and for the poor outcome of pregnancy, and this experiment can hardly be taken as final proof that inadequate diet was the sole cause.

One of the most recent and carefully controlled studies is that reported by Darby et al. (204). This study reports the results of careful observation of pregnant women in respect to many factors, with particular emphasis on diet. On the basis of these data, the 2046 persons studied were divided into four groups on the basis of their nutritional history. Of this group, 92 persons had an intake below 1500 Cal. in the third trimester and also in either the first or second trimester. This group showed a significantly increased incidence of congenital malformations. It is pointed out by these authors, however, that it is still not possible to determine in these instances which is cause and which is effect. Certainly, in respect to toxemia, a diminished dietary intake could be considered the result of the toxemia rather than the cause. They conclude, "In our patients we were unable to indict nutrition as a major causative factor in the development of commonly encountered obstetric and fetal abnormalities." These findings are at variance with those reported by Tompkins et al. (289). These authors find an increased obstetrical risk in both the overweight and the underweight patient. It is particularly interesting that there is an important relationship between the pregravid weight status of the patient and the incidence of obstetrical complications. In addition, the hazard of premature labor for underweight patients is much greater if the gain in weight is less than the average gain in the first or second trimester. Although it is not specifically pointed out by the authors, these findings emphasize the importance of the pregravid health of the patient on the outcome of the pregnancy.

There have been few studies aimed at determining what long-term factors in the lifetime of the person may be relevant to the welfare of the offspring. An interesting clue in this regard has been reported to me by Wolf and Drillien. These investigators made a study of the correlation between the economic status of the mother and the incidence of prematurity. It was possible to demonstrate that there exists a correlation between the economic status of the family (i.e., the mother and the father) and the incidence of prematurity. There is also a correlation between the incidence of prematurity and the economic class of the mother's father. They discovered that the correlation here was even closer than was the correlation between prematurity and the economic class of the father. The interpretation of this interesting observation is difficult. It is conceivable that the nutritional status of the mother during childhood and adolescence has had an influence on her subsequent pregnancy. It is also possible that the habits of her childhood environment in respect to diet and other matters of hygiene may carry over into her married life and influence her actual nutritional status throughout the pregnancy. Long-range studies to determine the extent to which childhood health may influence subsequent pregnancies have not been reported. In the United States there have been a number of surveys made from time to time to determine the nutritional status of children within various communities. It should be possible to carry out follow-up studies of these persons, many of whom have now reached maturity and to determine whether a correlation between their childhood nutritional status and the history of their pregnancies could be determined.

Results of Epidemiological Studies

In Figure 2 are summarized the results of four different investigations concerning the effect of maternal age on prematurity, maldevelopment, and mental deficiency. In Figure 5 are summarized similar data correlating parity with these conditions. The most remarkable feature of these Figures is the consistency of the data for the several different conditions presented. The incidence of defect is high in the very young and the very old mother. It shows a slight increase (for prematurity and for maldevelopment) in primiparae, and with increasing parity after the third or fourth child.

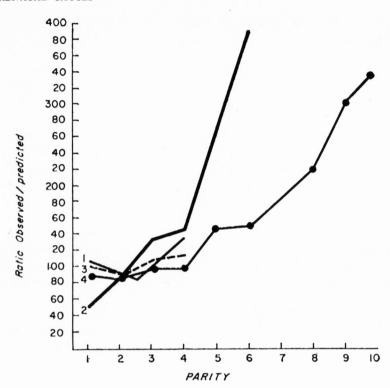

Fig. 5.—Effect of parity on the incidence of prematurity, mental deficiency, and gross maldevelopment. Ratios calculated as in Figure 2. Curve *1*, prematurity, from Baird et al. (14) ; Curve *2*, mental deficiency, from Pasamanick *et al.* (227) ; Curve *3*, maldevelopment, after Hegnauer (134) ; Curve *4*, maldevelopment, after Murphy (212).

It is interesting that the studies of Pasamanick *et al.* (227) dealing with a relatively minor defect (their cases include persons with an *IQ* of under 80) show the same types of curves in respect to age and parity of the mother as were observed in the studies reported of severe defects, such as anencephalus and hydrocephalus (Figs. 2 and 5).

In respect to maternal age, there was a high incidence among the age group under 25 and over 35, with minimum incidence at the age level of 25 to 29. In respect to parity, there was a low incidence with the first birth and a progressive increase through the sixth-plus range. Figures in Pasamanick's data do not show an increased incidence of mental retardation among the offspring of primiparae, and it would appear that this is a selective phenomenon observed only in certain specific defects such as anencephaly.

Hegnauer's data are interesting in that he shows that, whereas the incidence of maldevelopment in the central nervous system increases strikingly with age, maldevelopments such as deficiency or reduplication of the extremities do not show a correlation with either age or parity (Fig. 3). Spina bifida is also relatively unaffected by these factors (Fig. 4). Interesting information has recently been reported by MacMahon and McKeown (194), who have shown that when cleft palate occurs without harelip the incidence is little affected by age or parity but when cleft palate and harelip occur together the incidence is greatly increased by these factors. McKeown's data indicate that the incidence of congenital hydrocephalus increases progressively with increasing maternal age. McKeown's data also suggest a period of infertility preceding the occurrence of a hydrocephalic child—a phenomenon which he does not observe in respect to other forms of maldevelopment.

It would appear from these observations that in general the reproductive efficiency of women is impaired with increasing age. In addition, certain specific factors appear to be operative very early in life. It may be in respect to parity that the influence of early age is felt. McKeown's data suggest that the risk of anencephalus is a little less clear-cut, but he shows a high incidence of anencephaly in the offspring of young mothers. In general, most observers report a progressive increase in the incidence of all maldevelopments after the fourth pregnancy and in association with the first (Fig. 5).

Consistent data are also reported regarding secular changes in incidence. MacMahon et al. (195) observed a striking diminution of the incidence of maldevelopments in the British Isles during the war years. Similar results have been reported from the United States. Data from Germany, however (78), indicate a striking increase in maldevelopments in Germany during this period (Fig. 1).

Reporting from the siege of Leningrad, Antonov also observed a striking increase in reproductive failure, attributable to severe dietary restriction and physical and emotional hardships.

In all such studies concerned with correlation of prenatal factor and outcome of pregnancy, difficulties arise as a result of the grouping together of complex etiologies and complex results. The data presented above have indicated that different forms of maldevelopment show different curves and that much important information is lost if we simply deal with a general group,

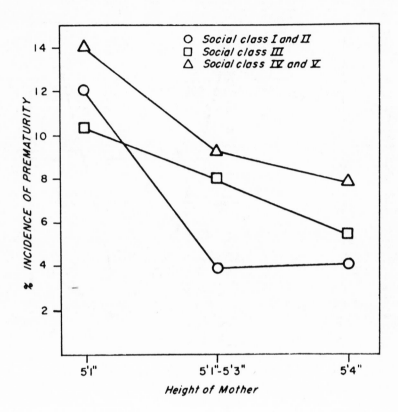

Fig. 6.—Relationship between incidence of prematurity, height of the mother, and social class of the mother. The graph shows that the incidence of prematurity is greater in the small mother regardless of social class but is also consistently higher in social Classes IV and V, which represent the least favored economic groups. (Reproduced from Baird and Illsley [13], *Proceedings of the Royal Society of Medicine,* Longmans, Green & Co., London.)

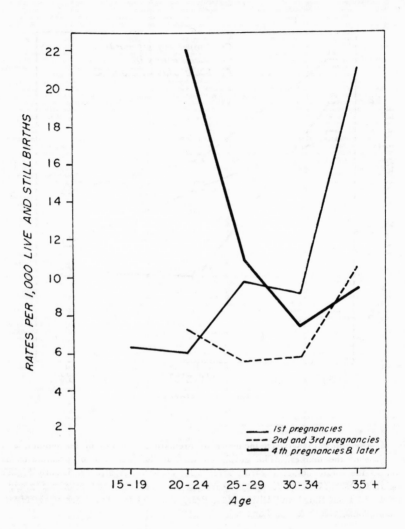

Fig. 7.—Incidence of prematurity (cause unknown) according to maternal age and parity. These data are also presented in Figures 2 and 5, as reported by Baird, Walker, and Thomson (14). The high incidence of prematurity among young multi-parae and in elderly primiparae is evident on this graph but largely obscured when the figures are consolidated.

"maldevelopment." The same is certainly true in respect to etiologies. The secular changes reported during the war years (Fig. 1) are probably the resultant of many factors, including nutritional, physical, and emotional deprivation and changes in the marriage and reproductive habits of the population. Even the raw data for maternal age may serve to obscure rather than illuminate. In Figure 7 it is demonstrated that there is an interaction of age and parity and that data in "maternal age" effects may in reality be a reflection of health of the mother at time of conception, frequency of reproduction, or age at first pregnancy.

Baird and Illsley have shown an interesting correlation between the incidence of prematurity, the height of the mother, and the social class of the mother (Fig. 6).

The studies of these investigators are particularly important in indicating the complexity of the factors operating. This Figure indicates that our graphs for age or for parity obscure some important features of the problem. In respect to prematurity, at least, the highest incidences are to be found in the very young multipara and the elderly primipara. These variations are certainly related to the physiologic process of aging, but they may also be closely correlated with the mental, nutritional, emotional, and social characteristics of the several groups concerned.

The studies of these investigators provide further evidences of the complex interactions of the many factors involved. In their culture, the young primipara is likely to be of small stature and to come from a lower socioeconomic level. It may well be this factor that determines the high incidence of prematurity in the young primipara as noted in Figure 7. There are evidently complicated factors represented by this graph—the variations are certainly related to the physiological process of aging, but they may also be closely correlated with the mental, nutritional, emotional, and social characteristics of the several groups concerned.

Although there is considerable evidence on the influence of maternal age on maldevelopment, there is relatively little regarding the influence of paternal age as distinct from the age of the mother. Sonneborn (Indiana University) has been particularly interested in this problem since he has demonstrated that in the protozoa (Paramecium) the age of the cytoplasm has an important effect on the frequency of nuclear mutation. He is undertaking an extensive statistical study to determine how significant this factor might be in human maldevelopment. Some data on this point have been reported by Penrose (231). Penrose points out that there might be anticipated two types of mutation in the human gene. One type would be the result of failure to copy the gene during mitosis. This factor would be more likely to occur in the sperm than in the ovum, since the sperm is produced as a result of a greater number of cell divisions than is the case in the ovum. The incidence of this type of mutation would thus be expected to increase with increasing age of the father more than it would increase with increasing age of the mother. In the case of achondrodystrophy, Penrose's preliminary data indicate that this is the case—a high incidence of increased paternal age with respect to maternal age is demonstrable in this disease. The other form of mutation is that which might occur spontaneously from natural causes, such as irradiation or chemical mutagens. This would affect mutation equally in mother and father and a straight-line increase with increasing age in frequency of a disease would be observed. Small increases are actually shown in Penrose's data for tuberous sclerosis (epiloia) and neurofibromatosis, both of which are believed to arise by fresh mutation in sporadic cases. Penrose emphasizes that this study is preliminary and that there is need for accurate and comprehensive inquiry into this field.

Interesting evidence that paternal age does play some part in the welfare of the offspring has recently developed from an unexpected source, namely, the influence of paternal age on sex ratio (221). It has been recognized for a number of years that the human sex ratio (males over females) decreases with increasing maternal age and with parity. It has been assumed that these changes are a reflection of some change in the maternal physiology which influences the number of males aborted during pregnancy and thus influences the birth ratio. The recent report of Novitski and Sandler indicates, however, that the decrease in sex ratio which occurs with advancing maternal age is actually a secondary reflection of a close correlation with paternal age, and that maternal age *per se,* and probably parity, is not directly related to this change. If this conclusion, which has been subjected to careful statistical analysis, should prove valid, it may have important implications relative to the influence of paternal age on the welfare of the offspring, since changes in the sex ratio have shown very interesting and rather consistent features. These features may be summarized as follows.

It has been estimated that the sex ratio at the time of conception varies from 125 to 135 males per 100 females. It is assumed that this ratio is relatively fixed (although means have not been discovered for establishing this assumption as a fact). The ratio at the time of birth is much lower, varying considerably over a range of slightly over 100:100 to 120:100. This change in ratio must represent an increased morbidity of males and probably takes place in the early phases of pregnancy, presumably more males than females being aborted. From the time of birth onward, male mortality rates are higher than female, and at some time in life (around the age of 50) more females are surviving than males.

A number of theories have been proposed to explain the higher mortality, or lower vitality, of the male. The prenatal mortality of the male might conceivably be attributed to some hormonal factor acting prior to birth in relation to the mother. It is possible that some of the glandular conditions in the male, *per se,* may be less conducive to survival throughout life. Finally, it has been suggested that the lower vitality of the male is a reflection of the fact that in humans the male has only one X chromosome. Stern (272) states, "If X chromosomes carry recessive alleles of lower viability, sublethality, or lethality, then many hemizygous male zygotes would be subjected to the influence of these alleles, while most female zygotes would be heterozygous and would not be affected." This thesis, which has had wide consideration, is unproven, however, and it must be pointed out that in chickens the female is the sex which has only one X chromosome but the male still has the higher mortality rate.

The sex ratio at birth has been shown to exhibit small, but significant, variations dependent upon a number of factors. Secular changes have been demonstrated by a number of investigators (186). A rise in the sex ratio (male over female) occurred in England and Scotland during the war years and thereafter. This rise accompanied a corresponding fall in stillbirths for this same period. In the United States the birth ratio in the white population is considerably higher than that for the Negro population. In general, it would appear that an increase in birth ratio is a reflection of general improvement of health and economic status and occurs when there is a reduction in the reproductive loss. These findings suggest that any general loss of the viability of the embryo shows up more strikingly as loss of males than as loss of females and tends to depress the sex ratio.

As pointed out by Lowe and McKeown (187), changes in sex ratio are influenced by varied and complicated factors. In their study on the effects of maternal age on the sex ratio, it was concluded that variations in sex ratio with maternal age were a reflection of the various causes of stillbirths acting at different maternal age levels.

In view of these considerations, the above-mentioned suggestion that paternal age is actually the significant factor assumes considerable importance, as indicating an influence on over-all viability of the fetus.

In regard to the constitutional factors in maldevelopment, all observers report a significant familial incidence. Murphy reports, "Of 431 subsequent pregnancies, 331, or 77 per cent, ended in the birth of full term, normally developed children. The remaining 100 pregnancies ended in 42 miscarriages where the fetal development was unknown, nine premature births, six stillbirths, and 43 live-born, malformed offspring. These unsuccessful pregnancies represented nearly one in four of those which followed the birth of the first defective child. The 43 pregnancies ending in the birth of malformed offspring represented approximately 10 per cent of the total subsequent pregnancies." (This incidence of 11.2 per cent is to be compared with a 0.7 per cent over-all incidence of malformation in the general population in Murphy's series.) Record and McKeown report, "The incidence of malformations of the central nervous system in all notified births . . . is 0.59 per cent. The incidence in *all* sibs of a malformed propositus is 1.89 per cent and that in sibs born *after* a malformed propositus is 5.18 per cent. Thus the risk for any birth following the malformation is almost nine times as great as the average risk." It is interesting, however, that the highest incidence of a recurrent maldevelopment is in the pregnancy prior to or subsequent to that of another affected person, suggesting some environmental factor tending to operate over a certain period of time in the mother's life.

There is also an increased incidence of malformation in relatives, and this involves not only maldevelopment in general, but also concordant types of maldevelopment. Murphy reports that concordance is observed three times as frequently on the maternal side of the family as it is on the paternal, suggesting that a factor of inheritance may operate through the mother. This factor may actually be disturbance of maternal physiology. As indicated above, evidences of disordered physiology of pregnancy are established through the frequency of occurrence of maldevelopment in two adjoining siblings and in an increased incidence of other complications in previous (McKeown, Fig. 8) and subsequent (Murphy, Fig. 9) pregnancies. In addition, all observers have noted a period of relative infertility immediately preceding the affected pregnancy (Fig. 10).

Landtman (175) reports that 19.5 per cent of a series of women who gave birth to malformed children were found to have had a miscarriage prior to the pregnancy resulting in the malformed child. Only 7.5 per cent of a

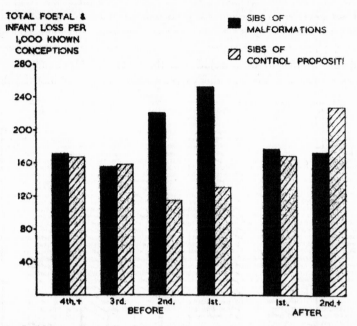

Fig. 8.—Incidence of complications of pregnancy in association with pregnancies prior to and subsequent to the birth of a maldeveloped infant. Both an absolute and a relative increase in such complications are evident when the siblings of malformed children are compared with normal controls. This increased incidence of complications is evident during the two pregnancies prior to that resulting in the birth of a deformed child. (Reproduced from Record and McKeown (242), *British Journal of Social Medicine*, British Medical Association.)

series of control women with normal children had this history. A total of 20.5 per cent of the mothers of affected children had had antepartum hemorrhage during the pregnancy which resulted in a malformed child, whereas this complication was found in only 4.5 per cent of a control series.

D. LABORATORY STUDIES OF ENVIRONMENTAL PRENATAL FACTORS

Epidemiological

Another valuable source of information relative to the environmental causes of maldevelopment is through animal experimentation. Much of our knowledge concerning specific etiological factors has been obtained in this way. It is interesting, however, that there appear to have been relatively few studies carried out in respect to the natural occurrence of maldevelopment in animals and the "reproductive loss" to be observed in wild and domestic species. Fraser (95) reports an experimental study of the fetal death rate in the white rat and reviews the literature relative to the problem. He noted a relatively high rate of fetal loss and that this varies with the age of the mother, the par-

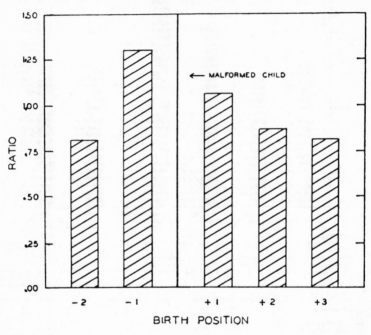

Fig. 9.—Ratio of observed, combined, miscarriages, premature births, and still-births to their "expected" frequency, arranged according to their place in family in relation to the place in family of the malformed child. The +1 position represents the first conception after, and the —1, the conception immediately preceding that which ended in the birth of a malformed child. Note the highest incidence of these abnormally ending pregnancies in the positions immediately preceding and following the birth of the malformed child. (Reproduced from Murphy (212), University of Pennsylvania Press, Philadelphia.)

ticular strain of animal, and a number of other factors, including time of year. He observed no effect of rank of pregnancy (such as might be anticipated if fetal loss were attributable to antibody reaction between mother and fetus), and he feels that the increased mortality is solely due to increasing maternal age. The author cites evidence, obtained by transferring the developing ovum

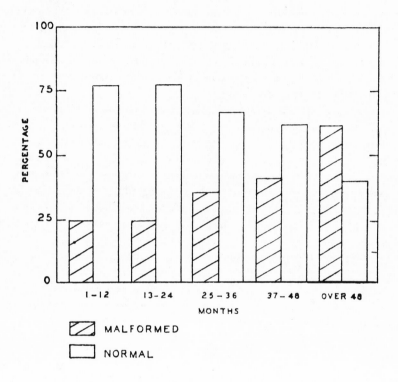

Fig. 10.—Representation of relationship of nonpregnant interval to occurrence of maldevelopment. All cases and their siblings were grouped according to the non-pregnant interval preceding the birth. The graphs indicate the percentage of cases in each category which were malformed as compared to the percentage which were normal—the total in each category would thus represent 100 per cent. It will be noted that in those instances where there was a short nonpregnant interval the pro-portion of malformed children is relatively low as compared with the high incidence when the nonpregnancy interval preceding the pregnancy had been a long one. Baseline indicates nonpregnant intervals in month. (Reproduced from Murphy (212), University of Pennsylvania Press, Philadelphia.)

from the mother to another host, to indicate that some characteristics of the mother influence survival.

Interesting evidence on the significance of season and climate on human reproduction is reported from Australia (193). MacFarlane *et al.* cite unpublished data indicating a 30 per cent reduction in human conception rate during the North Australia summer. They report animal experiments with Worcester rats indicating a fetal loss of 58 per cent when the animals lived at 35°C. When the rats were kept at the normal temperature of 20° to 28°C the fetal loss was only 7 per cent.

Pasamanick *et al.* have recently demonstrated an increased incidence of maldevelopment in pregnancies started during the summer months (227).

Attempts to alter the physiological state of animals have been reported by Wilson (312). Severe exsanguination of rats at the ninth, tenth, and eleventh days of pregnancy was found capable of producing a slightly increased incidence of malformation in the offspring (2.6 per cent). In general, such a procedure led to the death of the mother or the fetus, and maldevelopment occurred in relatively low incidence only at a rather critical phase in pregnancy (313).

The National Institute of Neurological Diseases and Blindness has established in Puerto Rico a monkey colony where reproductive processes can be studied in a free-range colony of animals as well as in a caged colony. These animals are available for controlled studies in which the effects of environmental factors during pregnancy and complications of labor and delivery can be studied.

The Discovery of Teratogenic Agents

The effects of a large number of teratogenic agents have been determined. The physical agents include X-rays and ultraviolet rays. Closely related in their effect are a large number of radiomimetic drugs, including mechlorethamine (nitrogen mustard), urethan, and other related compounds. A large number of organic compounds have been found to be teratogenic, including colchicine, ricine, trypaflavine, trypan blue, saponin, physostigmine (eserine), quinine, and many others. Among the heavy metals are nickel, cobalt, manganese, iron, zinc, lithium, and selenium.

Maldevelopments have been produced by hypervitaminoses A and by deficiencies of vitamin A, riboflavin, pantothenic acid, cyanocobalamin (vitamin B_{12}), and antimetabolites of these agents.

Disturbances of endocrine activity, including that of insulin and of corticosterone, have also been demonstrated to produce abnormalities.

Experiments have been carried on in many animals, including the rabbit, mouse, chick, amphibian, and sea urchin larva.

In general, teratogenesis has been more easily accomplished in the lower animals than in mammals, presumably because in the latter the agent must first pass through the mother and may cause maternal death before the fetus is injured. However, it has been found possible to injure the fetus in mammals through the injection of hormones, by trypan blue, by selenium, and by anoxia.

In addition to these specific agents, the deleterious effect of aging of the sperm and ova has also been evaluated. The problem of the teratogenic effects of overripeness of the egg has been extensively reviewed by Witschi (316), who cites data from human material which indicate that a high percentage of ovulated eggs obtained from endometrial scrapings show blastomic degradation and would not be capable of fertilization should this be possible. He cites his own experiments with amphibia which demonstrate that overripeness of the egg may lead to abnormalities of cleavage, twinning, deficient organogenesis, or cellular pathology. He remarks, however, that "the teratogenic effect of overripeness in mammals remains almost unexplored." In the case of his experiments with frogs, "overripeness . . . is probably composite reaction of at least three factors—endogenous aging, deficient oxygen supply, and carbon dioxide poisoning." His article is a careful review of many experiments dealing with mode of action of teratogenic agents. The question of the teratogenic effect of senescence of sperm has received less consideration.

There is also some interest in the possibility that aging of the ovary may prove responsible for damage of the ovum. Geyer (106) discusses the question in respect to Mongolism. Because the concordance of Mongoloid twins is so high, Geyer suggests that the disease-producing effect must be on the germ plasm of the egg. The emphasis of his paper, however, is in the study of "dysplastic" idiots, most of whom he felt had traits similar to those of Mongoloid children. Stieve (274) discusses the possibility that aging of the ovary may injure the cell and concludes that in the ovary of women approaching menopause or whose ovarian function has been impaired by unfavorable environment, especially in the fourth decade, there lie follicles in which the egg cell is degenerating. Possibly these injured cells may become fertilized, and from them would develop defective offspring.

A most extensive review of teratogenic agents is that by Ancel (8). In this book there are a discussion of spontaneous and induced malformations in the chick as produced by physical means, a section having to do with the determination of the "sensitive phase" of development, a section outlining the various types of malformation obtained by different chemicals, a section on the results of deficiencies of protein and various vitamins and ions, a section on the teratogenic agents active in mammals, and several sections having to do with the pathogenesis of lesions induced by these several agents. The results of maternal deficiencies are outlined by Warkany (301).

Ridgway and Karnofsky (246) have tested a large number of metallic ions on the chick. They observed maldevelopments following the administration of thallium, chromium, lead, cobalt, boron, arsenic, rhodium, barium, and selenium. Of these, only lead, cobalt, and selenium produced specific abnormalities of the central nervous system.

The original report on the teratogenic effect of trypan blue was that of Gillman et al. (109).

A number of other dyes were tested by Wilson (311). He originally found that azo blue produced maldevelopment but subsequently discovered that this was not the case. Trypan blue, Sudan IV, Bismarck brown, and Niagara blue all proved ineffective in this regard.

The screening of a large number of radiomimetic agents has been carried out in connection with studies of the effect of irradiation by Hicks (139). The effect of hormones is reviewed by Fraser et al. (94). Their paper includes a brief review of studies of other hormones, and emphasizes the nature of the effect of cortisone in mice. In this same symposium, Zwilling (328) reviews the effects of a number of endocrine and hormonal factors in the production of maldevelopment. He indicates that a variety of factors producing similar maldevelopments may act through a common influence on carbohydrate metabolism. This effect, of course, is most strikingly exemplified by the teratogenic effects of insulin.

The effects of oxygen lack have also been reported by Ingalls et al. (147). A very small number of their animals developed anencephaly. Animals subjected to anoxia by decompression on the ninth and tenth days showed a rather high frequency of vertebral abnormalities. Of those treated on the fifteenth day, cleft palate was common.

The Pathogenesis of Maldevelopment

Equal in importance to the recognition of the etiological agents in maldevelopment is the expansion of our knowledge of the mechanisms through which such agents interfere with the normal development of the embryo. This requires, first, a knowledge of normal embryogenesis and, secondly, an observation of the alterations of this process which occur when the deviation is produced. The two steps are increasingly overlapping—observation of the alteration produced by a teratogen being useful as an explanation or demonstration of some normal process and actually contributing greatly to the knowledge of it.

The first attack on the study of embryogenesis has been the anatomical one. The gross pattern of development has been well worked out. Increasingly, the need is now for detailed knowledge of cellular changes which occur during the development of the embryo. Such detailed knowledge requires accurate mapping of the neurons and of their precourses, their source of origin, their migration, and their eventual function.

The development of cell growth in the central nervous system of the chick has been outlined by Hamburger (128). A similar study in vertebrates is reported by Berquist and Källen (26). Stroer (276) has recently reported a detailed study of the nuclear differentiation in the diencephalon of the rat.

In the human embryo, studies of the embryological development have been reported from the Carnegie Institute by Streeter (275). The early process of development of the human embryo has been reported by Hertig et al. (138). It is interesting that of 34 specimens studied 13 showed abnormalities and would not have been capable of development even if pregnancy had been permitted to continue. They observed that the abnormal ova were most frequently found on the anterior wall of the uterus. The problem of implantation and the early development of the vertebrate embryo is reviewed by Boving (36). This paper contains, in addition to a discussion of the development of the blastocyst, a consideration of those factors influencing implantation, the adhesion of the blastocyst to the uterine wall, and the invasion of the tissue during the process of implantation.

Although there are still many details of histology and anatomy to be worked out, attention is turning to the development of our knowledge of the biochemical processes which parallel the anatomical ones.

Increasingly, this will require an interdisciplinary approach. Brachet (38) states, "The main task of the future will be to find a common ground between experimental embryology and chemical embryology." Boyd (37) states, "It is from the neural tube that the brain and spinal cord arise. The early neuroplate arises in the ectoderm overlying the invaginated prechordal material, and the chordal-mesoderm. . . . There is much evidence that can be adduced in support of the concept, that the induction of the neuroplate is due to a chemical substance (possibly substances) produced by the cells of the invaginated material. . . . Later stages in the developmental story are more complicated. To the processes of proliferation, morphogenetic movements, and cell degenerations are added those of histodifferentiation, migration, and complex interaction between center and periphery. . . . The central canal of the neural tube shows quite remarkable differential expansion, of which the three primary brain vesicles are only the first manifestation and about the mechanism and production of which we are effectively ignorant. Later, blood vessels grow into the wall of the neural tube, and at an undetermined stage, cerebrospinal fluid begins to be produced. We know almost nothing about the physical, chemical, and histochemical factors involved in all of these processes."

Increasingly, the methods and resources of physics and chemistry are being applied to these difficult problems. Oppenheimer, in a section on methods and techniques (222), states, "It is indisputably by the application of these resources [of physics and chemistry] that the greatest advances are being made at the present time. The results of current investigations of structure and ultra-structure by phase-contrast microscopy, and cinemicrography, and by electron microscopy; of molecular arrays by polarization optics; of chemical constitution and activity by histochemical and immunological techniques, by microspectrography, and microspectrophotometry; of the localization, constitution, and genetics of enzymes and enzyme systems, and of other antimetabolites and other specific poisons, by modern nutrition studies, and by the use of both radioactive and stable isotopes as tracers; of genetic effects of ionizing radiations—all of these will be discussed in ensuing chapters of this book.

"Continuation and elaboration of such physical and chemical descriptions of the embryo, of its cells, and of their compounds, are an underlying *condito sine qua non* for further embryological progress." Oppenheimer points out, however, that, in spite of these advances, we are still dealing with a structural rather than functional analysis and that "structure, in embryonic material, is not yet adequate to 'explain' process."

The last ten years have seen a rapid expansion of the research effort using these techniques. Only a few examples could be included in this review.

A whole series of experiments are in progress to observe the appearance and modification of the chemicals involved in the normal development of the embryo. A number of techniques are being applied. The standard method of histological staining still is being used and expanded. Brachet's (39) report on the use of basic dyes and ribonuclease for the cytochemical detection of ribonucleic acid might be cited as an example of modification of standard techniques for the study of complex chemicals. Another approach to the study of this same agent is reported by Hughes (144). He reports that the ultraviolet microscopic technique has also proven valuable for the demonstration and analysis of ribonucleic acid within the cell and its nucleus.

Radioactive tracers have found increasing utilization. These techniques are reviewed by Dent and Hunt (71). A number of elements may be administered to the developing embryo, and their site of utilization may then be demonstrated by radioautographic techniques. The application of this technique is illustrated by Sirlin *et al.* (262). These investigators cultivated tissue in glycine C^{14}, methionine S^{35}, or adenine 8 C^{14} and then cultured the labeled tissue in juxtaposition to other unlabeled tissue. Through this technique, the transfer of the labeled substances and the movement of the "organizer" substance were demonstrable when the tissue was analyzed by the radioautograph technique.

The use of antigen-antibody reactions has also proven very valuable in the study of embryological development (77). Antibodies can be prepared against specific substances known to be present in the developing embryo. The time of appearance of these substances can then be established by permitting the embryo to be acted upon by the antibody. Such an antigen-antibody compound may be demonstrated by injury of the developing fetus when a specific antigen appears or by labeling the antibody with a tracer (238) or by using a fluorescent-labeled antibody and demonstrating its fixation to the specific antigen within the embryo.

The study of the damaging effects of teratogenic agents involves a close coordination of chemical and anatomical observations. Thus, Bruemmer *et al.* (46) observed changes in the DNA content of rats injured as a result of deficient diet. Anatomically, these animals frequently developed hydrocephalus, and this late effect was attributable to gliosis occurring in the affected animals. In general, the emphasis of present research is in the use of specific blocking agents or antimetabolites and on efforts to alter their effects by the administration of the blocked or lacking agents in order to verify the specificity of their actions. A number of these experiments are summarized in the symposium on effects of radiation and other deleterious agents on embryonic development (139).

In respect to radiation, Hicks (139) reports that the primitive differentiating cells of the nervous system are probably the mammalian cells most easily destroyed by ionizing radiation. "Radiomimetic" drugs such as mechloretha- mine and triethylene melamine and certain sulfhydryl reagents selectively de- stroy the radiosensitive neuroblasts and spongioblasts. Aminopterin mimics this radiation effect. Hicks points out that the primitive neuroblast is con- cerned with rapid nucleic acid and protein synthesis, and seems to accomplish this, at least in part, in association with its system of sulfhydryl enzymes. Such enzymes are believed to be vulnerable to radiation because radiation pro- duces oxidizing agents in the cell water.

Landauer (173) considers the maldevelopments produced in the chick by the administration of insulin, boric acid, or pilocarpine. He observed that the maldevelopment produced by these agents could be prevented by the simultaneous administration of nicotinamide and also noted that these malde- velopments were similar to those produced by riboflavin deficiency. This author makes the observation that the same types of congenital abnormalities are seen very commonly in the chick on a genetic basis. No fewer than eight out of seventeen genetic lethal conditions have associated abnormalities of the beak and extremities similar to those produced by insulin. However, whereas nicotinamide was able to prevent the malformation produced by in- sulin and other agents, it was ineffectual against the genetic variety. He be- lieves that "alterations of the normal phenotype are due to changes in or complete suppression of the elaboration of specific enzymes and, more spe- cifically that the protein part of these enzymes (apo-enzymes) is involved. . . . In the case of our experimental syndromes on the other hand, we have definite reason to conclude that interference with co-factors rather than with enzymes is responsible for the deviations from normal morphogenesis. . . . We are led to the inference that the complex chain of events which leads to the normal phenotypic trait is, in the two instances, broken in different places. This interpretation of other observations helps to explain the simi- larities as well as the discrepancies in behavior of our mutants and their phenocopies."

A great variety of teratogenic agents are capable of analysis by these and other techniques. Hermann (136) has observed the disturbances of develop- ment which occur from amino acid analogues which serve to interfere with development. The use of labeled teratogenic agents has had relatively little application. Lallier (172) has demonstrated the teratogenic effects of nickel, cobalt, manganese, iron, and zinc. In addition to observing the maldevelop- ment, he has localized the area of invasion by the toxin through histochemical techniques. An interesting extension of this technique is reported by Ficq (86). In her experiments, Ficq has taken advantage of the fact that lithium is a teratogenic agent and, in addition, is available in radioactive form. By the injection of the radioactive lithium, she has produced the teratogenic pattern and has been able to localize the site of action of the agent by the radioautograph technique.

Experiments such as those outlined above are providing insight into the mechanism of normal development and the ways in which this can be impeded by noxious agents. It has been demonstrated that many different agents may interfere with the same metabolic cycle. Their effects are modified somewhat in accordance with the phase in the cycle during which they act. These studies have reaffirmed the time-honored concept that during each phase of development certain types of cells may be more susceptible to damage than others and that, in general, the nature of the maldevelopment will be significantly influenced by the time during development at which the injury occurs. In general, susceptibility to maldevelopment increases as differentiation proceeds: "As development of the embryo proceeds, its parts acquire more specific vulnerability to treatment with particular teratogenic compounds." The recent studies indicate, however, that the nature of the defect is significantly influenced by the nature of the specific agent involved and that timing is not the sole factor which determines the nature of the defect.

The question of teratogenesis is reviewed in *The Analysis of Development* (310). Zwilling summarizes the following principles laid down by Stockard.

"1. Every type of developmental monster known in the literature may be produced by one and the same treatment.

"2. The same structural abnormality may be induced in the embryos of various species by a great number of experimental treatments.

"3. In all cases the initial effect of the experimental treatment is a lowering of the developmental rate, and the resulting deformity is always secondarily due to this slow rate of development.

"4. The type of monster or deformity is determined by the developmental period during which the slowing in rate is experienced."

Zwilling indicates that these time-honored concepts must be accepted with reservations. He points out the following facts:

1. The "critical period" for the same maldevelopment is different for different substances.

2. Careful study will demonstrate that there are differences in the detail of apparently identical maldevelopments.

3. Most embryologists have abandoned the idea that retardation of development *per se* is the cause of specific defects.

4. Although there may be a common denominator for a number of agents producing similar effects, the pathway of action of such different agents as the genetic factor and the environmental one may be quite different.

In regard to the so-called "sensitive period," Zwilling remarks, "In view of the fact that indistinguishable end results may be mediated through more than one developmental pathway (e.g., limblessness or taillessness, either by degeneration of normally formed structure or failure of the structure to be elaborated), only the most limited conclusions about sensitive periods can be obtained from the appearance alone of the fully developed organism. . . . Instances where the same terata have been produced by a variety of treatments have led to the emphasis on stage of treatment and neglect of specific action of the agent. However, there is evidence which indicates that the specific nature of the substances used is of considerable importance." Zwilling concludes, "This chapter has shown that aberrant development results from a distortion of normal developmental processes; that both genetic and environmental factors may be responsible for producing anomalies; that the same development principles are involved in both. Terata may follow treatment of embryos with highly toxic foreign substances, but also may result from dietary imbalance, blood factor incompatibility, irradiations and action of disease-causing agents. The reaction of the embryo may depend not only on the stage at which it is subjected to the abnormal influence, but on the nature of the teratogenic agency, the length of time which it is exposed, the physiological condition of the embryo, and its resistance or susceptibility as determined by its genetic constitution. Similar anomalies may result from more than one developmental aberration. Teratology is still in the stage where it is most concerned with the visible effects which are the expression of prior physiological disturbances. The next big step in studies of the etiology of anomalous development must concern itself with the details of these physiological processes."

In order for a noxious agent to be operative during pregnancy, it must either injure the fetus secondarily by damaging the mother's supporting mechanism or it must itself reach the fetus. The mechanism of exchange of substances between the mother and the fetus is of importance in this connection. In the past, emphasis has been placed on the placenta as the medium for maternal-fetal exchange. Only recently has the importance of the passage of substances through the uterine fluids in the early stages of gestation been emphasized. Studies of maldevelopment indicate that most of the severer disturbances occur in the earliest stages of embryological development, possibly even at a time when the placenta has not yet developed. The passage of fluid into the uterine cavity, into the interstitial fluids, and directly into the yolk sac is probably of greater importance in the early stages of pregnancy than is the mechanism for exchange of materials through the placenta.

Ferm (85) has made a study of the passage of trypan blue into the yolk sac of the guinea pig. By a rapid freezing technique it has been possible to "shell out" the yolk sac fluids and to analyze the substances within these fluids without permitting any postmortem transfer. He has been able to demonstrate rapid passage of trypan blue into the yolk sac fluids by this technique. Lutwak-Mann (191) has injected various sugars, sulfonamide compounds, and amino acids into pregnant rabbits and has made analysis of the blastocyst to see whether penetration has occurred. It was demonstrated that these substances passed freely into the fully implanted (eight-day) blastocyst, but except for small amounts on the surface did not significantly enter prior to implantation. The passage of antibodies into the fetus has been studied by Brambell et al. (42). The passage of immune globulins, and presumably other protein molecules, to the fetus may be accomplished through the amniotic fluid, these substances entering the fetus by being swallowed. In reviewing their work, Brambell reports (41), "The transfer of passive immunity occurs before birth in man. The late human conceptus is bounded by the placenta and by the chorion laeve, consisting of the allanto-chorion to which the amnion is fused. Transmission of antibodies from the maternal circulation to the fetus must occur through one or both of these membranes. Transmission through the placenta, which is a very vascular organ, presumably would be direct to the fetal circulation. Hitherto, this has been generally assumed to be the route, and it appears at first sight to be the more obvious one, but so far as we are aware, there is no evidence to support this assumption." Brambell's experiments suggest that transfer may occur through the chorion laeve into the amniotic fluid, whence it is swallowed and absorbed by the embryo from the gut.

The question of interchange of substances from the mother to the fetus is important in regard to external toxins. It is also significant in relation to the possible influence of endogenous substances which might pass from the mother to the fetus. The first such possibility is that of immune bodies. The importance of fetal-maternal interaction in this respect has been established as a result of the discovery of the importance of blood group incompatibility in the etiology of kernicterus. This entity has clearly demonstrated that the presence of circulating antibodies of the mother can have a deleterious effect on the fetus—in this instance, in the last stages of pregnancy, and presumably through exchange of substances through the placenta. There have been a few experiments to suggest that in early pregnancy the presence of specific immune reactions of the mother against other tissues of the fetus besides blood may be capable of injuring the fetus and, in this instance, may lead to maldevelopment.

Penrose (229) subjects this possibility to statistical analysis, pointing out that a low consanguinity rate can be demonstrated in Mongolism, anencephaly, and spina bifida. Although there are other explanations for the low consanguinity rate, this finding suggests the possibility of antigenic incompatibility as a cause of these maldevelopments. Penrose makes no mention in this article of the question of increasing incidence with increasing parity. If one might draw a parallel with the observations of Rh incompatibility, an increasing incidence of the disorder with increasing parity would be anticipated.

A few animal experiments have been attempted to verify the possibility of this antigenic incompatibility. The first such experiments were reported by Geyer and Smith (107). These investigators injected lens extract into pregnant rabbits in an effort to immunize these animals against crystalline lens. They observed abnormalities of the lens in the offspring and considered that they were an indication of mutation produced in the germ plasm. They further reported that inheritance of this defect to subsequent generations had been demonstrated. These experiments were repeated in rabbits by Huxley and Carr-Saunders (146) and in mice by Finlay (87). Both of these observers had negative results. The experiments have again been repeated more recently by Flickenger *et al.* (89). These investigators immunized female rats against crystalline lens antigen over a two-month period. The degree of immunization achieved by the intraperitoneal injections used was not known. These animals were impregnated, and normal offspring were produced. In other experiments dealing with frog and chick embryos, the authors demonstrated that antibodies against lens extracts could be produced and that these reacted specifically with substances extracted from the anterior half of the frog larvae. They further observed that the antigenic material did not appear in the developing animal before the stage of the beginning development of the lens.

These experiments have more recently been repeated by Wood (318), who immunized rabbits by the injection of crystalline lens with Freund's adjuvant. The offspring of the immunized animals showed lens and eye abnormalities similar to those reported by Geyer and Smith.

Several experiments have also been reported relative to the immunization of pregnant animals with brain extracts (182). Lipton and Freund, in connection with another series of experiments, attempted to produce injury of the fetus by immunization of the mother with brain tissue and adjuvants. No abnormality of the offspring was observed. However, in these experiments, the immunizations were given during pregnancy rather than before, and antibody formation may not have occurred until rather late during the pregnancy. Furthermore, the pregnancy was permitted to go to term, and those animals that were injured might have died and have been reabsorbed.

Clayton[5] has had an opportunity to look for maldevelopment in the offspring of immunized mothers and has observed none. Here again, the observations were incidental to another experiment, which was not specifically designed to test this hypothesis.

Gluecksohn-Waelsch (113) carried out experiments in which female mice were immunized by the injection of brain tissue with adjuvant. She was able to demonstrate the occurrence of anencephaly in a significant proportion of the offspring. Her experiments, which were carried out with several different strains of mice, showed a striking variation in susceptibility, depending upon the genetic constitution of the individual animal used, but the maldevelopment could be produced even in strains with a high resistance to the anomaly.

On theoretical grounds one might question whether antibodies produced in the mother against adult brain would be injurious to fetal brain. Myelination of the central nervous system is a phenomenon which occurs rather late in embryological development. In experiments conducted so far, extracts of fetal brain have not proven effective in the production of allergic encephalomyelitis in adult animals. It would appear unlikely that the injury of fetal nervous system produced in Gluecksohn-Waelsch's experiments can be attributed to the same antigen and antibodies which are responsible for the allergic encephalomyelitis in adults. One would have to assume that the brain extracts used in these experiments contain other substances injurious to the fetal nervous system, existing in addition to those which produce demyelinization in adults.

---

[5] Personal communication to the author.

The possibility of antigenic incompatibility between the mother and the placenta also deserves consideration. Murray (213) demonstrated the existence of maternal antibodies to placental antigens during the second and third months of pregnancy. In view of this observation, it is interesting that little attention has been paid to the important question of what makes it possible for the fetus and the placenta to receive its nourishment from the maternal uterus without being rejected by that organ. Experiments with transplantation of tissues indicate that transplantation of tissue from one animal to another of even slightly different genetic strain will result in early rejection of the transplant except in very unusual circumstances. In many respects the implanted embryo must be looked upon as a "tissue transplant." As such, its persistence in the uterus for a period of nine months represents a unique situation. The mechanism through which the natural immunological response of the mother is modified in this situation has not been described.

In addition to the effect of maternal antibodies on the fetus, one must also consider the possible influence of endocrine factors occurring in the mother on the fetus. This question has been reviewed by Jost (152). In this article there is first a discussion of the influence of hormonal factors within the mother on the growth of the fetus. In addition, there is a brief discussion of the effects on the fetus of extraneous hormones. The most striking effects are those produced by injections of sex hormones during pregnancy, which may lead to permanent intersexuality of the fetus. A few clinical cases of such abnormalities in the offspring of patients with adrenal hyperplasia have been described. It has been demonstrated that cortisone can produce abnormalities of the offspring.

Estradiol and diethylstilbesterol produce injury of the embryo, presumably by mitotic arrest (291). Jost states, "Extraneous hormones may either enter the fetus via the placenta under normal and experimental conditions or be introduced directly into the fetal organism. It seems that proteic hormones are more or less unable to cross the placental barrier during the largest part of pregnancy, but systematic studies of this question are needed.

"One of the most important points raised by the observations presented in this section is whether a fetal or maternal endocrine imbalance may be responsible for prenatal abnormalities. Pseudohermaphroditism as a result of adrenal-cortical hyperplasia before birth is well known; . . . but many facts remain to be discovered or explained; the case of abnormal infants born of diabetic or prediabetic mothers, for instance, remains an acute question."

E. Mongolism

Mongolism represents a particular form of maldevelopment which is of special interest because it represents a clearly defined entity and because it is a common problem—probably accounting for approximately 20 per cent of severely handicapped children. It is believed that the morphological pattern of Mongolism results from some interference with embryological development occurring prior to the eighth week of pregnancy. The degree of mental defect varies from that of the imbecile probably to a normal level, and other stigmata of the disease vary in the frequency of their occurrence. They include abnormal formation of the palpebral fissures, with the presence of an epicanthic fold; brachycephaly, with the flattening at the bridge of the nose; exaggeration of the iris pattern, with white flecks in the iris, and irregularities of the palmar creases (23).

Congenital heart disease is frequently present, there being a failure of normal junction of the endocardial cushions separating the right and left sides of the heart—a process which is normally completed during the eighth week. The fact that the cardiac malformation is not more widespread lends some support to the thesis that the agent responsible for this maldevelopment acts over a relatively short period of time at approximately this stage in development. However, it should be emphasized that the noxious factor responsible for this maldevelopment could theoretically be operative at any time prior to the eighth week.

Through studies of the relatives of children with Mongolism, through reports from study of identical twins, and from extensive statistical analyses of incidence, Penrose concludes that there is a significant genetic factor in this disorder. The most clearly established fact regarding Mongolism (which it shares with other forms of maldevelopment) is the increasing incidence of this condition with increasing maternal age. This points to, but does not prove, some environmental factor which operates in addition to the genetic one on the causation of this genetic disorder.

Penrose (230) presents a review of data regarding the etiology of Mongolism. Statistics show that maternal age bears a close correlation with the incidence of Mongolism whereas paternal age does not. They show absolute concordance in monozygotic twins but marked disagreement in dizygotic twins (an observation suggesting a multifactorial influence rather than single-gene inheritance). Penrose presents data demonstrating the presence of minor traits in the relatives of patients with the overt disease and concludes that the "combined evidence of the data on maternal age and familial incidences suggests the conclusion that some mothers, by virtue of an inherited disposition, are likely to have affected offspring. This increased susceptibility is expressed by a partial suspension of the defensive effect of young maternal age which is normally present." Penrose suggests as a profitable approach the systematic quantitative examination of mothers (and controls of the same age) for hormone activity of all sorts. Benda (24) reports studies to determine the environmental factor responsible and concludes that Mongolism occurs when there is a "borderline condition of hormonal sterility" in the mother.

Until recently, it has been generally held that a Mongol woman is herself sterile and unable to become pregnant. However, this has proven to be false. It is of great interest that among reported instances a very high (almost universal) incidence of Mongolism in the offspring has been observed. Reliable figures are not available due to probable bias in reporting, but if it is true that the child of a mongol is almost always also a mongol, one has to postulate either the existence of some transmitted reproductive aberration, or the occurrence of spontaneous mutation of very high frequency. There are no reported instances of a Mongol male reproducing.

An additional point of interest relative to Mongolism is the suggestion, not well documented, that there occurs a progressive retardation of the patient's development, even after birth. In most maldevelopments growth proceeds in a linear fashion in its later stages, and the occurrence of deterioration is suggestive of some continuing deleterious factor. The suggestion has been made that the original maldevelopment results in hormonal or trophic inadequacies which in turn lead to a secondary deficiency. Another possibility is that Mongolism is actually associated with some chemical or metabolic error which, in addition to leading to antenatal maldevelopment, may also predispose to continuing damage of the nervous system. There is some suggestion of premature aging in the Mongoloid person.

An abnormally high incidence of leukemia among Mongoloids may possibly be correlated with this phenomenon.

A few biochemical studies have appeared to suggest some metabolic abnormality in Mongolism. An abnormally high level of β-aminoisobutyric acid excretion has been reported. There are unconfirmed reports of abnormalities of the blood lipoprotein fractions. An irregularity of vitamin A absorption has also been suggested. In view of the extent of the problem of Mongolism, it is surprising that more definitive data on these observations are lacking.

It is also remarkable that, in spite of the frequency of this condition and the fact that numerous autopsies have been carried out and reported, marked differences of opinion exist relative to the character of the pathological changes of the brain which can be demonstrated in this disease. Benda (23) reports, "Histological studies of the nervous system reveal certain remarkable patterns that seem to explain the slow mental development and hypotonia of the Mongoloid infant. Myelination of the brain is greatly retarded and myelin sections reveal—at an age of five to six months, for instance—that the Mongoloid brain shows a stage of myelination comparable to the normal brain of the newborn of one or two months. Thus, the brain itself reveals a decelerated maturation. The nerve cells are often undersized and show severe degrees of cell degeneration, or at least vacuolization."

Malamud [6] reports, however, that, in his experience, the changes observed in Mongolism are relatively nonspecific. He also has observed some disproportion in the relative sizes of various portions of the brain—the frontal lobes being frequently underdeveloped. He points out, however, that in other conditions, such as phenylketonuria, rather similar changes may be noted. Bailey[7] emphasizes that the changes reported in Mongoloid brains are remarkably minor in degree. In his own studies, he has been impressed with the very minor changes which he has been able to demonstrate in Mongoloid brains. In respect to the problem of delay in myelinization, many observers have pointed out that the normal rate of myelination has still not been thoroughly investigated.

A careful analysis of the rate of progress of myelination of the human central nervous system in fetal and neonatal life is reported by Fleischig (88). Although this is a careful analysis of rates of myelination in brains at different ages, it still deals with a limited number of specimens and provides no indication of the degree of variation in rates of myelination which may occur within the normal population. The most authoritative works on human cerebral development are those by Conel (60). This study involves a relatively small number of brains. Bailey emphasizes that there is a remarkable disparity between the minor pathological changes demonstrable in the Mongoloid and the relatively severe degree of mental impairment which may exist. This disparity would suggest that the area of maldevelopment is a very crucial one or that something in respect to its distribution causes severe impairment or that we are dealing here with some more generalized toxic or metabolic disorder

---

[6] Personal communication to the author.
[7] Personal communication to the author.

which leads to impairment not only through anatomical lack but also through interference with physiological activity.

F. The Etiology and Pathogenesis of Disease of Later Stages of Pregnancy

Prenatal Infectious Processes

In contradistinction to the maldevelopments, which have their primary emphasis in the early phases of pregnancy, the destructive processes of the fetus have been most clearly evident in the late phases of development. No sharp line of distinction can be made between the two processes, a fact which is most strikingly evidenced by the results of rubella infection. The virus of this disorder, attacking the fetus in the early trimester of pregnancy, produces a selective injury of certain structures and an interference with their development as well (292). It is the infectious diseases which have received the greatest attention in this connection, these including syphilis, toxoplasmosis, and the virus diseases. The significance of syphilis as it relates to maldevelopment has been recognized for many years, and the means for its elimination are available. Prevention of this disorder at the present time is entirely a matter of education—education of the public and continued education of the profession. Recognition of the significance of toxoplasmosis is a more recent development, but a definite relationship between infection with this organism and the occurrence of hydrocephalus and destruction of the central nervous system has been established. The significance of rubella was first demonstrated by Gregg (123), who demonstrated the occurrence of congenital cataract in a number of children following an epidemic of German measles in the community. The causal relationship between other viruses and maldevelopment has been far more difficult to establish (129). However, the virus of cytomegalic disease has also been implicated.

The problem lies in the fact that it is likely that a number of viruses which produce little or no symptomatology in the mother may attack the fetus and cause injury of the nervous system, which serves as a more suitable medium for growth than does the adult system. In view of the large number of viruses of low pathogenicity for adults which are encountered in the average community each year, the potentialities of injury of the fetus from this source would seem to be considerable, and the problem of determining which virus may be responsible for injury of the fetus is particularly complex.

A number of serological surveys of populations have indicated the extensive involvement of large proportions by viruses, in the majority of instances without there being a clear-cut history of the acute infection. Jensen *et al.* (149) have reported on the serological evidence of experience with pneumonitis virus in 40 per cent of a U. S. population. The virus has not yet been isolated in this country, and the possibility exists that there may be some cross immunization with the influenza virus. LaVeck (178) made a similar study with the Western equine encephalitis virus and found antibodies present in over 10 per cent of the U. S. population. Southam conducted a similar survey in connection with two overt cases of encephalitis occurring in a Japanese school (267). He concluded that among the groups studied there were 500 to 1000 inapparent infections with the Japanese B virus for every overt case of this disease. In respect to the Newcastle virus, a survey of laboratory workers and chicken farmers was carried out by Bang and Foard (17), who showed that a large proportion of those persons who had presumably been exposed to the virus had positive serological tests without ever having been known to have experienced the acute disease.

That the fetus can be infected in the course of a very mild maternal illness is reported by Schinefield and Townsend (253). These investigators report the case of twins who developed encephalitis with antibody titer rise immediately after birth. The mother was known to have been exposed to mosquitos eleven days prior to delivery and had had a mild febrile illness before. Schick (252) reports on infection of the fetus occurring in spite of immunity of the mother. He reports ten cases from the literature in which mothers known to be immune to smallpox were exposed to the disease and subsequently were delivered of a child who suffered from the disease. They themselves were not sick. He also gives references to reports of injury of the fetus due to German measles in which no apparent sickness of the mother was recorded.

The methods of determining the role of prenatal infection in the occurrence of maldevelopment and fetal destruction are similar to those concerned in relation to other causes of maldevelopment. They include epidemiological surveys, both retrospective and prospective. Methods used include modifications of maternal environment and actual maternal infection (vaccinia) and also the use of animal experimentation.

The original demonstration of the significance of rubella in maldevelopment by Gregg was presumably retrospective in character, depending upon the establishment of a correlation between the occurrence of eye difficulties and an epidemic of rubella. Following this, retrospective studies of persons in institutions were carried out in an effort to determine how often a history of maternal infection during pregnancy could be obtained.

Kirman (165) made a survey of 791 institutionalized defectives and found that in 0.9 per cent of these persons a history of maternal infection during pregnancy could be obtained. Lande (174) examined sixteen institutionalized patients whose clinical picture resembled that seen following rubella infection of the mother during pregnancy. In retrospect he found that in seven of these there was a history of maternal rubella, in five the mother had suffered from a "common cold" during pregnancy, and in one there had been an attack of influenza.

With the demonstration by retrospective methods of the significance of rubella infection in maldevelopment, a number of studies have been reported of the follow-up of women known to have suffered from infection during pregnancy. Initial studies suggested a very high incidence of maldevelopment in these cases. Bass (18) suggests a possible incidence of 20 per cent to 50 per cent. Similar figures are reported by Swan (278). This author estimated that the chances of maldevelopment following maternal rubella are about 83 per cent during the first month of pregnancy and 61 per cent during the second month of pregnancy and then fall to from 11 per cent to 29 per cent during the last five months.

More recently Greenberg and Pellitteri (120) have made a prospective study relating to this problem. They made a follow-up examination of women of child-bearing age reported to the New York Public Health Bureau as having been sick with German measles. There were 104 women subsequently found to have been pregnant at the time that German measles was reported. Of these 104 women, 48 had therapeutic abortions and ten cases were lost from the study due to unavailability. Of the 46 women whose pregnancies went through to completion, three had children with congenital defects, three were stillborn, there were twelve other fetal deaths and 28 delivered normally.

The actual incidence of congenital deformities among the liveborn babies of women with rubella during the first trimester of pregnancy was 9.7 per cent. This figure is much lower than those of other cities. There is some suggestion from others in New York City that the higher incidence of rubella occurred during an epidemic summer—sporadic cases did not seem to have as high an incidence of congenital malformation.

Another approach has been through epidemiological studies attempting to correlate the incidence of maldevelopment with the occurrence of virus infection. A number of studies have indicated a seasonal variation in the incidence of maldevelopment, although the variation has been rather small and has not always been the same in different surveys. On the assumption that the majority of virus infections occur during the winter months, an effort has been made to demonstrate an increase in the incidence of maldevelopments in the instances of pregnancies where conception occurred in the fall and the critical phase of fetal development would occur during the winter, when the presumed infections would be in the highest incidence.

Buck (47) found no convincing evidence that seasonal and annual fluctuations in congenital malformation are associated with variations in maternal exposure to German measles, mumps, measles, chicken pox, influenza, or poliomyelitis in the first trimester of pregnancy.

This approach would appear to be of highly questionable validity, since it is not yet established what types of viruses are likely to be responsible for such developments and what is the actual time of year when the incidence of these viruses is highest. In view of the frequency of central nervous system involvement in the adult in relation to mild enteric virus infections, it would seem entirely possible that injury of the fetus could occur either from viral gastroenteritis or in association with respiratory infection. The highest incidence of such viruses as the enteric cytopathogenic human orphan (ECHO), the Coxsackie, and the poliomyelitis viruses is during the months of June to October (142).

In a few instances an effort has been made to correlate an increase in the incidence of maldevelopments with the occurrence within a community of an epidemic of some specific virus, such as influenza A, poliomyelitis, or the acute exanthemata of childhood. Clear-cut correlations do not appear to have been established at this time. However, Bland (30) reported a 58 per cent incidence of interruption of pregnancy after influenza at the time of the great epidemic, but he was concerned primarily with complications of pregnancy rather than maldevelopment.

The recent epidemic of "Asian influenza" has provided a unique opportunity to correlate prenatal infection with maldevelopment. This organism is "new" in our population, and the occurrence of infection can be proven through the demonstration of specific antibodies in the blood of the infected individual. In a number of research centers, serological specimens have been obtained from pregnant women during this epidemic. Their children will be examined specifically for congenital defect. If the Asian influenza virus is actually pathogenic to the fetus, a correlation may appear.

Even such careful epidemiological surveys as those mentioned above may fail to detect a significant relationship between maternal infection and maldevelopment if the occurrence of fetal infection is a relatively rare event. This fact is most clearly demonstrated in respect to experiences with vaccination of pregnant women. A number of series have been reported in which an attempt was made to correlate vaccination of pregnant women in association with epidemics of smallpox with the subsequent incidence of maldevelopment. The results are contradictory. Greenberg et al. (121) made a follow-up of pregnancies during which the mother was vaccinated and found no increased incidence of maldevelopments in the offspring. MacArthur (192) made a similar study and found a high percentage of abnormal pregnancies occurring in women who were vaccinated during the first twelve weeks of pregnancy. The occurrence of abnormal pregnancy in this group was much higher than was the case in women vaccinated during the third month of pregnancy. It is interesting in connection with MacArthur's paper that there was only a single incidence of overt vaccinia occurring in the offspring of a large number of vaccinated women. A number of instances of such infection have been reported by Shuman (254) and by Marsden and Greenfield (199).

The study of virus infection of animals has proven entirely practicable and certainly should serve as a screening test for presumptive significance of similar infections in man. A number of human viruses have now been proven capable of producing maldevelopments in animals.

Cohlan and Stone (59) were able to produce malformations in the rat by rubella virus. Hamburger and Habel (129) demonstrated the ability of influenza A and mumps viruses to produce maldevelopments when injected directly into the chick egg. Adams et al. (1) showed that infection of the hen's egg with influenza virus or injection of this virus into pregnant albino mice caused an increased mortality of the offspring and an increased incidence of maldevelopment. Williamson et al. (308) studied the teratogenic action of Newcastle disease virus in the chick. A variety of maldevelopments were produced, the nature of the defect depending upon the time of infection of the embryo. They demonstrated that this virus attacks the cells in rapidly differentiating and proliferating tissues. There have not been re-reported systematic experiments in which pregnant animals have been subjected to a series of viruses for the demonstration of possible fetal involvement by these agents.

In addition to determining the specific agents which may be responsible for fetal injury, there are a number of approaches which are of value regardless of the nature of the specific infective agent. These involve the study of the infective agent itself, the search for routes of infection and the epidemiology of the disease, and the development of methods of treatment. These problems are considered in detail under the section of infections of the central nervous system (see below).

Of particular concern in respect to prenatal infections is the development of effective diagnostic means of recognizing the presence of maternal infection. The ability to diagnose syphilis during pregnancy has been a powerful factor in reducing the incidence of congenital defects due to this disease. Since the discovery of the significance of maternal rubella, termination of pregnancy has been carried out in a number of instances, and examination of the fetuses in these instances has provided evidence that many of the infants would have been severely defective.

Clinical and laboratory diagnosis of toxoplasmosis is becoming increasingly more feasible (see below) and may eventually be useful in preventing infection of the fetus.

In addition to the study of viruses and of virus disease in the mother, it is also of importance to determine the mechanism of spread of the infectious agent to the fetus and ways in which such spread might be influenced. This is of particular concern in view of the evidence to suggest that the virus may reach the fetus in an immune mother without the mother's becoming sick in the course of this infection. There is remarkably little evidence regarding the method of spread of virus to the fetus and the ease and frequency with which this may occur. In 1942 Goodpasture (118) made a study of virus infection in tissue cultures of placenta. He discovered that the human chorionic epithelium is rather resistant to most of the viruses which he tested on it. He remarked at that time, "It is surprising to find little knowledge concerning placental infection and the relative specific resistance of placental and fetal membranes." Although there is considerable work in progress relative to the passage of chemicals and immune bodies to the placenta and other fetal membranes, there appears to be little active work regarding the passage of infective agents through these structures.

The final factor of importance in respect to prenatal infection of the fetus is that of fetal immunity and resistance to disease. The work of Brambell and of others has demonstrated the pathways through which passive immunity of the fetus may be obtained from the mother. It is now well established that the fetus does not develop immunity of its own until some time after birth. Of particular interest has been the recent discovery that the fetus is actually incapable of an immune response to antigens presented early in fetal life and, in some animals, probably even after the time of birth. An even more startling discovery is the demonstration that when an animal has been treated with an antigen during fetal life it is also incapable of developing immune bodies against this antigen later in life (40).

It was originally suggested by Medawar (205) that this "immunological tolerance" might be related to the development of the fetal adrenal gland. However, this suspicion has not subsequently been proven or clearly disproven. The fact that immunological tolerance may develop in animals who show no hypertrophy of the adrenal gland during fetal life would appear to militate against this possibility.

The question of immunological tolerance has important implications in regard to the subsequent resistance of the fetus to infections of later life. In this connection, interesting data should be available from follow-up studies of persons whose mothers were vaccinated during pregnancy. A number of series have been reported in which studies have been made of the immediate immune responses of infants of vaccinated mothers (297, 162). In Urner's series, none of the infants of mothers vaccinated during pregnancy developed an "immune" response on subsequent vaccinations. It is interesting, however, that of those infants whose mothers were vaccinated prior to pregnancy, 91.6 per cent had a subsequent satisfactory vaccination, whereas in the case of those whose mothers were vaccinated during pregnancy the figures were from 66 per cent to 71 per cent positive.

Knox (167) has reported the results of infection of mice with murine poliovirus during pregnancy. There was an extremely high mortality during this infection. The surviving offspring were temporarily protected by the antibodies from their mother's milk but had no immunity when tested at 119 days. It is not clear, however, whether these animals were incapable of developing antibodies or whether they simply had not been infected during pregnancy.

There is an interesting report by Freudenberg et al. (96). These observers report the case of an infant who suffered from congenital fractured hip with myositis of the thigh. A Coxsackie virus was cultured from the infant, but the child never showed an antibody against this virus. The mother showed a minimal neutralizing antibody.

Regardless of the significance of the few above-reported studies, it is certain that the fetus shows little resistance to disease if it is infected. The studies of Töndury (290) of the pathology of German measles in the fetus suggest that this virus produced a chronic infection which may persist almost throughout pregnancy, with only minimal responses on the part of the fetus.

The most certain proof of fetal infection is the demonstration of the virus in the abortus, or stillborn child, or possibly the early appearance of antibodies in the child with a maldevelopment. Systematic attempts to culture virus from such material by the newer techniques have not been reported.

The problem of toxoplasmosis presents an interesting example of research in the various areas outlined above. It is now well established that infection of the mother with toxoplasmosis may lead to fetal infection and to maldevelopment or death. Serological studies have indicated that the population is widely infected. Epidemiological studies and examination of domestic and wild animals have indicated that the organism is also widespread in nature and that a large proportion of domestic and wild animals may be infected. The method of spread of infection is still uncertain, although there are recent interesting studies to suggest that the ingestion of uncooked meat may be one means for the spread of the organism (305). Comparison of the incidence of trichinosis and toxoplasmosis has shown a parallelism, suggesting a common means of transfer through inadequately cooked pork.

The clinical picture is only gradually becoming more clearly recognized. Confirmation of the diagnosis by serological studies or by isolation of the organism from affected lymph nodes is helping to clarify the clinical picture (261). It is probable that in the adult the disease is most commonly manifested simply by low-grade fever and generalized lymphadenopathy. Increased use of lymph node biopsy during pregnancy, greater general awareness of the possible significance of these mild symptoms, and the development of serological studies of increasing sensitivity and reliability should improve the diagnostic accuracy.

Studies are in progress relative to the biochemical make-up and metabolic requirements of the organism.[8] These are being paralleled with efforts to develop specific agents which will be capable of inhibiting the growth of the organism (82).

Fetal Cerebral Vascular Disease

An important mechanism which appears to be significant in relation to fetal injury in the later stages of pregnancy is involvement of the cerebral blood vessels. The pathological studies of Hallervorden and Meyer (127) indicate a high frequency of involvement of cerebral blood vessels in the case of mal-

---

[8] Summers: Personal communication to the author.

development, and in many instances their figures suggest that the primary lesion is a vascular one. Such gross lesions as hydranencephaly show a distribution strongly suggestive of occlusion of cerebral arteries, and it is presumed that it is the vascular occlusion which is responsible for this pattern. In the majority of instances no reason for such an occlusion is evident. Although there is considerable emphasis on this problem in the German literature, one finds few references to the study of the cerebral blood vessels in cases of maldevelopment reported in the American journals.

Meyer (207) reports on the study of 385 brains of feeble-minded persons. Of these, 153 had circulatory changes and 30 had localization in the distribution of a cerebral vessel. Meyer observed that there was a high concentration of lesions in the parieto-occipital area, where all three major superficial arteries join. He observed these changes in cases of brain injury secondary to asphyxia at birth and secondary to fevers, convulsions, or gastrointestinal infections in infancy. However, similar changes were observed in persons suffering from prenatal defects. It is his belief that the distal portions of the cerebral arterial tree are especially vulnerable to circulatory disturbances. In ontogeny there appears to be a lack of capillary anastomosis through which the blood stream might be adequately maintained in these areas. Under pathological conditions with a fall in systemic blood pressure, the morphological and hemodynamic characteristics of this area permit a disproportionate fall of pressure in the distal cerebral vessel, leading to a diminished circulation in this area and to tissue hypoxia and destruction.

It has been demonstrated by Becker (21) that occlusion of the cerebral vessels will cause hydranencephaly. This "anomaly" was produced in animals by the injection of paraffin emboli into the carotid artery. The pathological findings have been reviewed by DeMorsier (70), whose studies indicate that agenesis of the corpus callosum may be produced by two entirely different mechanisms—by failure of closure of midline structures or by interference with the circulation in the anterior cerebral artery. Similarly, agenesis and malformation of the cerebellum may result from failure of closure of the midline structures as well as from lesions in the different territories of the cerebellar arteries. Pathological findings of hydranencephaly are presented in which the only remaining structures are those supplied by the anterior cerebral artery, the remaining arteries presumably having been occluded.

V. PROBLEMS OF THE PERINATAL PERIOD

The major problems of the perinatal period are prematurity, jaundice, birth injury, and asphyxia. The relative importance of these various factors has been subject to considerable dispute. In view of the fact that each is unquestionably deleterious in nature and to be prevented as much as possible, discussions as to the frequency with which each of these factors may lead to subsequent mental retardation may be considered largely of academic interest. However, when one is concerned with evaluating specific obstetrical procedures, medication, and anesthesia, some means for the evaluation of outcome is necessary. For this reason, studies carried out in an effort to determine the outcome of various complications of pregnancy and of the newborn period are of importance in promoting our ability to prevent complications which may prove damaging to the infant.

A. PREMATURITY

One of the most extensive studies of the effects of prematurity is that by Alm (7). This author found that among the prematurely born there was a statistically significant number of persons who required institutional care and a statistically significant increase in spastic paralysis, epilepsy, and educable mental deficiency. There was also a statistically significant diminution of the average height and weight at the age of 20 years. It is the conclusion of the author that "Among those prematurely born children who survived the first two or three years of life, there is a moderately higher incidence of such disorders as are usually considered to be associated with birth injuries, than among the controls." The author did not define any statistically significant difference in the number able to do military service or in the general social adaptations of the two groups. Knobloch et al. (166), in a follow-up study of 500 premature and 492 control infants, demonstrated that at 40 weeks of age 50.9 per cent of infants with a birth weight of less than 1501 gm. suffered defects ranging from minor neurological change to severe intellectual damage.

Centeno et al. (55) were able to complete a five-year follow-up of 218 children from among 536 prematures who survived to this age (this is a 40.7 per cent follow-up). Of the children followed, 18 were found to suffer from severe handicaps—8.5 per cent of the survivors. In four cases the handicap was due to congenital anomalies; in two others it was probably due to infec-

101

tion. Six had retrolental fibroplasia as a major handicap, and in seven mental retardation was the presenting problem. It was the authors' impression that in 12 of these 18 persons the prematurity itself was presumably responsible for the defect. These authors emphasized the great value obtained from routine review of all cases of neonatal deaths and of stillbirths. Participation by obstetricians, pediatricians, pathologists, nurses, and at times internists, psychiatrists, and geneticists was recommended.

The importance of such conferences has also been stressed by Bundesen (50).

The British social organization and system of medical care provides an unusually favorable environment for follow-up studies of prenatal and neonatal complications. Studies have been reported there with respect to prematurity, birth injury, asphyxia, kernicterus, and *Rh* incompatibility.

Because there appears to be a close affiliation between those factors responsible for prematurity and those concerned with maldevelopment, the epidemiological approaches to these problems have been considered together in the previous paragraphs. Of more specific concern, relative to prematurity, is that reasearch having to do with specific factors responsible for the initiation of labor or premature delivery. It is certain that in many instances abortion or prematurity is the result of actual disease or injury of the fetus. Pathological examination has proven considerable evidence of the factor of placental disease in cases of miscarriage (236).

There is some evidence that disorders early in pregnancy may have a prolonged effect leading later to prematurity. Turnbull and Walker (295) made a follow-up study of 46 patients with threatened abortions early in pregnancy. Of these, 19 per cent subsequently aborted. Of those whose pregnancy was complete, the incidence of prematurity, obstetrical death, and antepartum hemorrhage was three times as great as in a normal control group. The babies were in general small, and there was an increased incidence of abnormalities. The authors conclude, "Whether our findings can be explained by persisting or recurrent maternal defect . . . or whether damage to the deciduo-placental site caused permanent impairment" is uncertain. Studies of oxygen saturation, however, did indicate impairment of oxygen transfer in this group of patients when compared with normal subjects.

Of fundamental importance to the problem of prematurity is the question of the factors which precipitate labor. This question is extensively reviewed in the most recent Josiah Macy, Jr. Foundation Conference on Gestation

(298). In connection with this conference, Dr. Pincus remarks, "As far as I am concerned, the endocrine factors concerned in the precipitation of parturition are still as mysterious as ever." This same point is stressed by Zarrow, who emphasized the striking species differences in serum progesterone levels. Other studies (285) have shown that there is some correlation between hormone levels and uterine activity.

There is considerable interest also in the emotional factors relative to activity of the uterus and, especially, prematurity. A series of papers from Aberdeen report studies of the personality of women during pregnancy and a correlation of their social, intellectual, and emotional traits with the outcome of pregnancy (255-258). It is concluded from these studies that "the trends described . . . point to a relationship between uterine action and some fundamental aspect of personality not likely to be altered by such short and superficial psychotherapy as might be undertaken during the course of pregnancy. The methods of investigation used so far do not afford means of predicting uterine dysfunction in the individual case, and there is no immediate prospect of preventing this condition. Further research is obviously needed." The authors feel that difficulties in parturition are most likely to occur in the persons with repressed anxiety rather than those in whom overt evidences are present. The studies reported above place primary emphasis on the duration and complication of labor rather than miscarriage and prematurity. Similar studies are in progress in several clinics in the United States. It would appear that efforts to define personality during pregnancy and to correlate these findings with endocrine function and with the outcome of pregnancy should be productive.

It is probable that a considerable reduction of mental retardation secondary to prematurity has resulted from improved management of the premature child. Studies of the physiology of the premature should continue to contribute to this reduction of mortality and injury. The outstanding problems for investigations in the premature are control of infection, maintenance of nutrition and oxygen supply, liver function and the prevention of jaundice, and temperature control. It is interesting that in each of these areas therapeutic measures for which there appeared to be good rationale have proven to be dangerous. Thus, the addition of vitamin K to the diet has been proven a significant contributory factor in jaundice. There is some suggestion that the use of certain sulfonamides has contributed to the occurrence of kernicterus. Overenthusiastic use of oxygen is a cause of retrolental fibroplasia and may also contribute to "hyaline membrane." The maintenance of

mperature may be harmful to the anoxic premature infant by
oxygen requirement.

m of jaundice of the premature infant is one of the most serious
which there appear to be several interesting lines of approach.
The͟ ͟een little emphasis on the significance of circulatory readjustments
on liver function. It has been demonstrated that during fetal life the left
lobe of the liver receives its blood supply directly from the mother, whereas
the right side has ordinarily a blood of lower oxygen content. The situation
is rapidly changed at the time of birth, with the closure of the ductus venosus.
The evidence suggests that closure of the duct depends upon vasoconstriction
within the vessel. Failure of closure might permit considerable shunting of
blood around the liver and could very well contribute to failure of function
of this organ. There have been no reported studies to determine the relative
efficiency of the mechanism for closure of this duct in premature infants.

A second line of attack on the problem of neonatal jaundice has to do
with the demonstration of the specific toxic agent and the development of
methods of detoxification. There is reasonably strong support for the thesis
that it is actually the indirect-reacting bilirubin which is the toxic agent. In
a rapidly progressing series of experiments it has been demonstrated that
conjugation of the bilirubin with glycuronic acid leads to the formation of
the direct-reacting bilirubin and that this agent is nontoxic and capable of being
excreted. The enzyme responsible for this conversion has now been isolated.
Jervis has unpublished data in which he has demonstrated a lack of this
enzyme in a patient with congenital jaundice. Such a lack has also been
found to exist in a strain of mice afflicted with this disorder. The basis has
now been established for further studies to determine the significance of this
enzyme in relation to jaundice in the premature infant and possibly toward
the development of rapid methods of conversion of the indirect-reacting to the
direct-reacting bilirubin.

B. Birth Injury and Asphyxia

A special problem is presented by those attempting to evaluate the effects
of birth injuries and neonatal asphyxia. In many instances it is extremely
difficult to evaluate the severity of the insult. Studies now under way, therefore, involve two aspects—one is the attempt to recognize the immediate
effect of presumed injury; the other is to assess the results of this injury at
a later date. It is most likely that sound data regarding these problems will

be obtained only when longitudinal studies of a single person can be carried forward over a period of years. A few centers are now undertaking such studies. The most extensive report is probably that by Thomas and Dargassies (287). These authors have concentrated on meticulous examination of the newborn infant and have correlated these findings with biochemical studies of the blood and tissues, with the electroencephalogram, and with the subsequent development of the child. In the English literature, the problem of the psychological testing of small infants has been reviewed by Griffiths (124).

Hartmann *et al.* (133) are attempting to demonstrate anoxic injury of the newborn infant by observing the responsiveness of the child to a standard electrical stimulus of the lower extremities. The responsiveness of the child to this stimulus, or the lack of responsiveness, is being correlated with the history of neonatal asphyxia and with the subsequent developmental history of the infant.

Considerable differences of opinion exist relative to the late effects of asphyxia neonatorum. Darke (66) did follow-up examinations of persons whose hospital records had shown evidences of severe asphyxia neonatorum. Cases were selected from the hospital records of infants who were known to have had a severe degree of asphyxia but who were considered to have been normal at the time of the end of the neonatal period. Psychological examinations (Binet-Simon) were carried out on these children and on parents or siblings as controls. The mean *IQ* of the children (tested at ages two to eleven) was 88.05. That of the controls was 100.47. This difference was considered highly significant. Keith and Norval (160) made a follow-up study of 57 infants presumed to have suffered from birth injury or asphyxia. Of these infants, only 22 lived beyond the age of eight months. Of these 22 infants, 13 were evidently maldeveloped. In the rest it was difficult to demonstrate that the birth injury was relevant to any subsequent disability. The authors conclude, "Difficulties during birth had comparatively little to do with persistent neurological abnormalities in most of the infants who survived. Prolonged labor appeared to increase the risk of intracranial injury and death. . . . However, if the infant survived, there was little or no abnormality in subsequent development, and no increase in neurologic disturbances, at least during the first few years of life." It was evidently the impression of the authors that the infants died shortly after birth or, if they survived, were relatively undamaged. Courville (61) presents a brief historical review of data relative to the effects of anoxia on the nervous system. It is his impression that a variety of pathological changes of the brain may be the result of anoxic injury.

Working with monkeys subjected to controlled asphyxia at the time of birth, Windle (314) has demonstrated the subtle pathological changes which are produced. Brains examined several weeks after asphyxia show diffuse ganglion cell degeneration. Although these are easily observable during the acute stages of cell death, it is probable that following recovery the results would consist only in a "falling out" of cells, with reduction in total cell populations. Such changes would be demonstrable in later life only by cell counts on brain sections—a technique not yet developed. At present, such brains of adults would be classed as "normal."

The prevention of physical injury of the brain depends upon knowledge of the mechanism of labor. There is also a need for data regarding the anatomy of the cerebral vessels and the way in which they may be affected by deformations or pressure changes involving the head and body. As mentioned in the section regarding disorders of the cerebral circulation in the fetal period, episodes of hypotension may lead to inadequacy of cerebral circulation, with characteristic areas of softening in the distal regions of arterial supply of the brain.

Measures to reduce infant injury from asphyxia fall into two categories, namely, measures to prevent asphyxia and measures to increase the infant's tolerance to it. One must question our ability to improve the established natural adaptive mechanism of the infant sufficiently to increase his tolerance to any significant degree. More significant advances will probably depend on our ability to prevent the occurrence of asphyxia. The prevention of asphyxia depends upon early recognition of fetal distress, the completion of rapid nontraumatic delivery, and the maintenance of adequate aeration of the lungs. Studies have indicated that toward the end of pregnancy the adequacy of the placenta progressively diminishes and, especially in instances of prolonged gestation, may reach a critically low level. Methods are not now available for assessing placental adequacy during pregnancy, but such would contribute significantly to our ability to terminate labor before fetal embarrassment develops. Attempts have been made to facilitate recognition of fetal distress during labor through the use of electrocardiographic studies, but the techniques have still proven too cumbersome, and in general the clinical signs still appear the most reliable indices.

The second major factor is the refinement of methods of the safe, rapid delivery of endangered infants.

Prevention of asphyxia rests to some extent upon the development of methods for the stimulation of natural respiration and for the establishment and maintenance of adequate gas exchange in the infant who fails to breathe spontaneously.

In regard to the resuscitation of newborn infants, the Special Committee on Infant Mortality of the Medical Society of the County of New York (268) reports, "Because of the incompleteness of basic physiological information, lack of adequate standards for equipment and the poor training of personnel using methods for resuscitation of the newborn, a cooperative research project should be formulated which will approach the various phases of the problem in a well organized and scientific manner.

"This project should have qualified individuals engaged in research in pediatrics, anesthesia, obstetrics, respiratory physiology, public health, pathology, and pharmacology study the various phases of the problem."

A number of methods are now available for the study of the physiology of respiration in the newborn, and the mechanism of pulmonary expansion and circulatory readjustment at the time of birth is now under reexamination. The use of sensitive methods for recording pressure changes in the trachea and thorax and the new technique of cineradiography and angiography have been utilized. Studies reveal that there is a close interrelationship between the expansion of the alveoli and the establishment of blood flow through the lungs. Histological examination has demonstrated that prior to expansion the alveolar capillaries are coiled and tortuous. Immediately after birth and with expansion of the lungs these vessels elongate. It has been assumed that this elongation is the result of alveolar expansion, but it may be that it is the circulatory adjustment which comes first and which itself aids in expansion of the alveoli.

An important factor in respiratory distress of the neonatal period is the occurrence of "hyaline membrane" in the lung. For some time it was suggested that the presence of this membrane in the lungs of neonates was attributable to prenatal inspiration of amniotic fluid. It has been demonstrated that the protein-containing membrane actually contains antigens from the baby's body, and it is presumably an actual exudate (112). Stevenson and Laufe (273) have demonstrated that the inspiration of amniotic fluid, combined with variations in oxygen saturation, may produce this picture in animals. It is probable that the hyaline membrane results from a variety of factors interfering with adequate gas exchange in the lungs, and its development may be associated with changes in capillary permeability. Such changes in the lung have been demonstrated by Aikawa.[9] It is of interest that both in the lung and in the brain the problem of vascular integrity and permeability change is of importance, relating the problem of asphyxia very closely to that of "shock." The significance of vascular changes in head injury has recently been demonstrated by Brierly (43). This investigator produced experimental brain injury by freezing an area of the brain with liquid oxygen. Subsequent to the injury the permeability of the cerebral vessels in various areas was tested by the use of radioactive-labeled phosphate and diiodofluorescein. Changes in capillary permeability were demonstrated both in the area of the injury and in distant portions of the central nervous system, and these changes were observed to persist for as long as 40 days after the injury. Studies relative to the mechanism of anoxic injury, as well as the evaluation of its after-effects, have recently been reviewed (314). Present evidence indicates that the newborn infant is capable of tolerating a relatively severe degree of oxygen deprivation. Studies are presented to suggest that lowering of metabolism may occur during anoxia, possibly associated by hypothermia, the lowered temperature being a protective mechanism. Important changes in the chemistry of the body occur during conditions of asphyxia, and evidence is presented to suggest that some of the secondary changes occurring during asphyxia are of more serious concern than is the oxygen deprivation *per se*. Some evidence regarding the pathogenesis of anoxic brain damage may be obtained from the pathoanatomical study of the brains of injured animals or persons (61, 62).

C. KERNICTERUS

It is estimated that kernicterus is responsible for approximately one per cent of severe institutionalized defectives. It is still not established with certainty which cases are attributable to blood-type incompatibility and in which other factors are paramount. However, blood group incompatibility is known to account for a large proportion of the cases of neonatal jaundice. Continued extension of our knowledge of the blood groups and their distribution and antigenic character may establish an exact figure. Not all patients who have such incompatibility will develop an unfavorable immunologic response. Placental exchange may be an important determinant, and there is needed a definition of those factors which influence leakage of fetal red cells into the maternal circulation.

---

[9] Personal communication to the author.

This topic has recently been reviewed by Chown (58), who reports the case of an anemic child born to an *Rh*-negative mother and different from its mother in having antigens Cw and D. Careful testing of the mother's blood gave proof of the presence of fetal blood mixed with it. The estimate of the amount of fetal blood present agreed very well with the state of the baby and the baby's degree of anemia. The author suggests that "this mechanism of feto-maternal transfusion may cause, in addition to nonhemolytic anemia of the newborn, fetal death, atypical toxemia, and rarely, jaundice of pregnancy."

VI. POSTNATAL CAUSES OF MENTAL SUBNORMALITY

A. Cerebral Vascular Disease

The frequency with which occlusion of a major blood vessel occurs during infancy has not been reported, but it is probable that vascular occlusions are responsible for some of the cases of hemiplegia occurring in infancy and childhood. Pathological studies also suggest that in many instances hydranencephaly and porencephaly are due to occlusion of the cerebral vessels during intrauterine life. The causes of the sudden infantile hemiplegias have not been well established. It has been suggested that hemiplegias occurring during the first few days of life may be attributable to embolism, as, for example, from the umbilical vein, and may be associated with persistent patency of the cardiac septa. In other instances actual disease of the blood vessels leading to thrombosis has been implicated. The new techniques for study of heart and circulation having to do with the mechanism of vascular occlusion and the control of the cerebral circulation are also contributory.

B. Inflammatory and Degenerative Diseases
of the Nervous System in Infancy

The term "encephalitis" has been used loosely to describe a number of disorders of infancy and childhood in which varying degrees of inflammation of the central nervous system exist. These disorders are differentiated with difficulty, and clinical diagnosis is frequently impossible. Because of this fact, the clinical symptoms have not been well defined, nor has a close correlation between the clinical picture and the pathological finding been established. Furthermore, in many instances the clinical pictures presented by diseases in which gross pathological distinctions are possible may be approximately identical. The classification of diseases within this group has therefore developed largely on the basis of pathological findings. In Table 2 is presented the classification prepared by Lhermitte (181). This outline, prepared in 1950, is incomplete, especially in respect to a number of viruses (e.g., herpes) which may rarely produce direct invasion of the central nervous system. However, the general classification is in keeping with that published more recently by Poser and van Bogaert (235).

TABLE 2

CLASSIFICATION OF INFLAMMATORY AND DEGENERATIVE DISEASES OF THE
NERVOUS SYSTEM[a]

Encephalitis	Meningoencephalitis	Lymphocytic choriomeningitis Mumps meningoencephalitis	Virus
	Polioencephalitis	Anterior poliomyelitis Borna's disease Rabies Encephalitis lethargica Type A Inclusion-body encephalitis (Dawson)[b]	
	Panencephalitis	St. Louis encephalitis Japanese B encephalitis Russian tick encephalitis Pette-Doring panencephalitis[b]	
	Leukoencephalitis	Sub-acute sclerosing leukoencepha- litis (L. van Bogaert)[b]	

		Acute hemorrhagic leukoencephalitis
		Perivenous encephalitis
		  Postexanthem, postinfluenzal,
		    postrabies vaccine
		  Spontaneous encephalomyelitis
			Allergic
			mechanism?
			(exogenous
			allergic)

		Multiple sclerosis group[c]
		  Acute multiple sclerosis
		  Multiple sclerosis
		  Neuromyelitis optica (Devic)
		  Schilder-Foix disease
		  Concentric sclerosis (Baló)
			Possibly due
			to allergic
			mechanism

Degenerative disorders	Demyelinating without inherent inflammatory reaction	Progressive familial leukodystrophy Pelizaeus-Merzbacher disease Lipodystrophies	Degenerative process, often familial and heredi- tary
		Carbon monoxide myelopathy Edematous necrosis Others	Divers processes

[a] Adapted from Lhermitte (181, p. 188).

[b] Virus etiology suspected but unproven.

[c] Myelonecrosis, sometimes associated with an inflammatory reaction capable of interpretation as an expression of encephalitis.

Acute and Subacute Encephalitis

The first group comprises those diseases due to virus infection and in which brain damage is presumed to be a direct result of invasion of nervous tissue by the organism. Probably mumps meningocephalitis is the commonest of this group. However, included in it is a large number of virus diseases, apparently varying in their site of predilection in the body, the frequency of invasion of the central nervous system, and the severity of damage produced. Presumably closely related to the "acute encephalitides" is a group of three forms of subacute encephalitis. In none of these has an infective agent been isolated, but they are considered to be infective in nature because of their sporadic nature, subacute course, and marked evidences of inflammation. It has been demonstrated that these three diseases produce a rather characteristic electroencephalographic pattern. It is interesting that none was described prior to the epidemic of encephalitis lethargica (1918-1920), and the suggestion is made by Lhermitte that they may represent a modified form of this infection.

No effort will be made here to review the many viruses which have been implicated in the acute encephalitides. There are, however, a number of important generalizations relative to these diseases. First is the fact that, with a few important exceptions (e.g., rabies), these agents are rather common in the population, produce many inapparent infections, and only rarely lead to recognized encephalitis. Experience, for example, with the virus of poliomyelitis, which has been capable of extensive study, has indicated that invasion of the nervous system occurs only occasionally in the course of infection—that many hundred persons may have mild or inapparent infection with the virus for each person who experiences symptoms of invasion of the nervous system. It is probable that a number of other viruses—agents which are either relatively infrequent invaders or which produce extremely mild illness—may from time to time invade the nervous system with the production of an encephalitis picture. Probably the majority of these agents, when they do invade the central nervous system, lead only to the occurrence of a relatively benign "aseptic" meningitis (163). However, reports have been published of encephalitis occurring in association with a variety of other virus disorders (51, 208, 250) and in a number of cases of aseptic meningitis. Thus, Godenne and Riordan (115) found that the poliomyelitis virus could be isolated from 90 per cent of a series of 49 patients with paralytic disease. In cases of aseptic meningitis, in contrast to the paralytic group, only 13 of 41 patients were found to be harboring a poliomyelitis virus. In a few instances cyto-pathogenic agents, as yet unidentified, were also encountered. A few have subsequently been identified as Coxsackie viruses; others, pending their iden-tification, have gone under the name of orphan viruses, or enteric viruses (299).

It is becoming evident that a large and varied group of agents may be responsible for this picture. Until such time as the causal relationship be-tween a given virus and the encephalitides of childhood has been established, almost any of the known viruses must be considered suspect. Because isola-tion of the virus from a given case of encephalitis is often difficult or impos-sible, the diagnosis in these instances may depend upon our ability to demon-strate the appearance of specific antibodies within the afflicted person. In addition to evidence obtained from the direct isolation of viruses from pa-tients, our ability to demonstrate the causal relationship between a given virus and involvement of the nervous system will depend also upon a program in-volving, first, the isolation and accurate classification of a large variety of known viruses and, second, the demonstration of the appearance of antibodies against these viruses in patients with the encephalitides.

Efforts to isolate the virus are closely allied with epidemiological surveys. They involve isolation of the virus from patients, from normal and diseased hosts, and from animal vectors. One approach has been through mass survey techniques.

The results of such a survey of a population are reported by Honig (141). Stool culture revealed a high incidence of infection with ECHO, Coxsackie, and poliomyelitis virus during the summer months.

The search for viruses within animal populations has produced a number of "new" infectious agents, some of which are already known to be infectious for man. The frequency with which wild animals are subject to encephalitic disease has been emphasized by Frauchiger and Fankhauser. These investiga-tors have made routine examinations of the brains of wild animals dying in Switzerland and studied in their laboratory. They report that approximately 20 per cent of the wild animals whose brains they examined show lesions of the central nervous system, a large proportion of which are inflammatory in character.

The problem of transmission of viruses is largely unexplored. Day (67, 68) reports that studies with the arthropod-borne viruses have indicated that these agents may be transmitted by a wide variety of hosts, that some may actually be maintained in plants during phases of their development, and that the agents are capable of a considerable degree of adaptation and genetic variation, depending upon the particular host.

In general, studies of the serologic reactions of populations have been useful primarily in demonstrating the prevalence of involvement of that population by the infective agent. In some instances, because of the possibility of cross agglutination, the possibility has presented itself that large segments of the population are involved by a virus not yet isolated. Karzon (159) shows that almost 100 per cent of adults have an antibody in their sera which neutralizes the canine distemper virus. He points out that the infection actually responsible for the production of this human antibody has not yet been proven. Similarly, Jensen *et al.* (149) found serological evidence of experience with pneumonitis virus in 40 per cent of the U. S. population although the virus has not yet been isolated in this country. The possibility of cross agglutination by an anti-influenza-virus antibody is a possibility in this situation.

One of the major difficulties in the establishment of the prevalence and significance of virus diseases is the complexity of the present diagnostic procedures for these diseases. Isolation of the virus is possible and, as mentioned above, is being carried out in a number of centers throughout the country. The effectiveness of these laboratories will depend upon the acumen of the general practitioner as well as of the specialist and upon the willingness of the physician to provide the laboratories with the specimens for accurate diagnosis. The detection of specific antibodies is, unfortunately, also a relatively slow procedure. Antibodies may not develop for a period of several weeks during the illness. Because a large proportion of the population shows antibodies against many of the suspected viruses, the mere demonstration of antibodies is not proof that the concurrent illness is responsible unless progressive changes in antibody titer can be demonstrated. For this reason, serial blood specimens may be required in order to ascertain the diagnosis. The clinician is frequently frustrated because of the delay in establishing the diagnosis and the difficulty in keeping track of his patients during those periods of time required for the obtaining of serial blood specimens. Close rapport between the laboratory and the clinic is vital.

The present status of diagnostic procedures in virus infections has recently been summarized by Rhodes (245). In this article are outlined a number of presently available procedures, as follows:

1. Examination of smears or scrapings. In a few of the virus diseases the organism can be demonstrated under the oil-immersion lens. In other in-

stances characteristic giant cells or inclusion bodies may be demonstrated by scrapings from the cutaneous lesions.[10]

2. Use of suckling mice. The Coxsackie viruses may be demonstrated by injection into these animals.

3. Tissue culture technique. A number of viruses, especially those of the poliomyelitis group, can be grown on tissue culture of a variety of cells. The so-called "orphan" viruses have also been isolated by this technique.

There is still some difficulty in being certain of the "cytopathogenic effect," since some viruses produce no visible damage to the culture. However, the ability to demonstrate the growth of viruses in tissue culture is developing rapidly at this time. This topic is also reviewed by Enders (79). Enders has reviewed the developments in the field of virus research over the past 25 years. His review emphasizes the extent to which progress has depended upon the discovery of new techniques and methods. It is evident that, at the present time, the ability to propagate viruses in tissue culture represents a major opportunity for greatly broadening our knowledge of these numerous agents.

At the same time that there is increasing knowledge of the agents which may be responsible for viral diseases, there is also increasing knowledge of the nature of the virus and its reaction to the host cell. The new techniques of electron microscopy have contributed considerably to the knowledge of the nature of the virus and the virus-cell reaction (11, 98). Biochemical techniques are also providing useful tools (79).

Considerable interest rests in the antigenic character of the virus and the degree to which this characteristic may change in the process of adaptation. In this connection, ontogenic classification of viruses is desirable. Casals (52) has carried out an analysis of the relationships between various viruses in the arthropod-borne (Arbor) group of animal virus. It has been demonstrated that these organisms can be assembled in sharply defined groups on the basis of serological interreactions detected specifically by hemagglutination-inhibition tests. Three groups of viruses are listed. Although the capacity of an agent effective against one virus to protect against another virus of the same group was demonstrated, the degree of this protection and the ability of resistance to one virus to protect against infection with another awaits further experimentation.

---

[10] Recent studies by Liu and Coffin (184) have indicated that it is possible to stain cells in conjunctival smears with a fluorescent-labeled antibody, this technique being sufficiently sensitive to be useful as a diagnostic procedure.

Evidence exists that the viruses themselves may be capable of modification. That this can occur has been clearly demonstrated in mice (45, 105). Serial passage of the influenza A virus through mice which had been immunized produced a progressive change in the antigenic characteristics of the virus such that eventually animals immunized with the parent virus were not protected against the variant strain. Experience with the hog cholera virus has suggested that this process can interfere seriously with the effectiveness of immunization programs. Animals inoculated against the standard cholera virus strains may occasionally become afflicted with a similar virus with different antigenic properties. Culture of this virus in the laboratory at first indicates that it is different from the standard strain; however, over the course of time, when cultured in the laboratory, it reverts to its original characteristics. The ability of viruses to mutate when exposed to an immune population represents a serious problem with respect to immunization programs.

This question has been studied by Shope (259). The author uses four hog diseases known to be due to viruses as examples, namely, hog cholera, swine influenza, vesicular exanthemata, and transmissible gastroenteritis. Data are presented to indicate that these are "new" diseases, presumably resulting from the appearance of a new organism, or at least from the introduction *de novo* of this organism into animals. In respect to hog cholera, reference is made to a report by Williamson (309) which indicates that a new variant strain of hog cholera has shown ability to produce virus disease in presumably protected animals but that the new virus produces immunity against the standard cholera virus. Shope also mentions experience with a "tamed" rabies virus, which when used as a vaccine in animals proved lethal, presumably because of some unpredicted change in the virus. This article emphasizes the fact that "at the present time our knowledge of virus ecology is fragmentary and limited to but a few agents." It offers a striking example of the valuable experience with viruses in veterinary medicine, which can be referred to similar problems in the human.

In view of the possibility of genetic changes in the antigenic characteristics of these agents, there may be some limitation of the efficacy of immunization programs for their elimination. One must seriously consider, then, whether there may be other ways of influencing the resistance of the population. This approach should have considerable potentiality, especially in view of the fact that with many viruses the general level of resistance is high. Interest thus centers around the question of those factors which determine the occurrence or lack of occurrence of involvement of the nervous system in association with virus disease. This question has had considerable attention in connection with poliomyelitis. A number of attempts have been made to associate the occurrence of paralytic poliomyelitis with excess activity or fatigue during the phase of the acute illness or with antecedent operations, especially tonsillectomy. It is interesting that in poliomyelitis some influence of genetic susceptibility has also been demonstrated, but no clue as to the chemical or metabolic nature of this susceptibility is available.

Considerable data on susceptibility are available from animal studies. Factors influencing the rate of protein metabolism have been shown to influence the rate of virus multiplication (158). The injection of testosterone, which increases the rate of protein metabolism, causes an increase in virus proliferation. Castration, which reduces protein metabolism, delays virus proliferation, as does the administration of corticotropin (ACTH) or cortisone. The studies relative to this factor do not provide evidence, however, as to whether the alteration in rate of virus proliferation is correlated with the degree of resistance to the disease or to ultimate survival.

Similar studies have been carried out to demonstrate the effect of alterations in oxygen tension on virus proliferation (157). Here, again, anoxia has been demonstrated to slow the proliferation of influenza virus and mouse encephalomyelitis virus, and there is a possibility that this delay is associated with a slowing down of tissue metabolism.

Another factor which has been shown to influence susceptibility to virus infection is malnutrition (270). During a period of starvation fluctuations of susceptibility can be demonstrated, again suggesting a complex interplay of factors influencing host-virus interaction.

One of the most striking factors in variations in resistance is that of age (260). The sensitivity of young mice to infection has been particularly striking in respect to the equine encephalitis and the Coxsackie viruses. The degree of susceptibility of young animals varies, depending upon the particular virus involved. Although changes in metabolism and hormonal factors appear to be important, a variety of mechanisms which influence virus-host relationships are probably operative.

This question has been studied by Boring, Angevine, and Walker (34). These investigators made a comparison of the spread of the Coxsackie virus in young, adult, and adult cortisone-treated mice. In all three groups rapid spread of the virus was demonstrated. However, in the young animal widespread multiplication and tissue destruction occurred. In the untreated adult the only change was minor damage in the pancreas. In the adult cortisone-treated animal, however, multiplication and damage occurred in numerous sites, although these were still not identical with the areas of destruction in the four- to five-day-old animals. It was the belief of these investigators that the varying patterns of tissue destruction depended upon developmental changes in cells and tissues and were related to changes in cellular metabolism, alterable by cortisone. Spread of the virus did not appear to be the determining factor in these instances.

A great deal more needs to be known regarding the specific factors responsible for immunity and the relationship of the immune response itself to tissue injury. It has been demonstrated that in the case of poliomyelitis in the monkey the rate of virus multiplication can be influenced by pretreatment of the animal with cortisone or, more especially, with cortisone and X-rays. These procedures, which reduce the immune response, permit rapid multiplication of the virus in this animal (282). In mumps infection in humans, however, there is at least some clinical evidence that treatment with adrenal hormones may reduce the severity of the disease (232). The administration of cortisone or other hormones has been followed by a rapid defervescence and reduction of testicular swelling and pain in a group of 23 patients with mumps orchitis.

In addition to the question of over-all resistance of the organism to virus infection there exists the more specific problem of factors determining invasion of the central nervous system. In this connection, the question of permeability of the "blood-brain barrier" to infective agents is relevant.

In addition to new techniques of electron microscopy, the study of the barrier is being advanced by physiological techniques. Bakay (15) is working with radioactive tracers to determine permeability under normal and pathological conditions. Mayer and Bain (201, 202) have made some interesting observations of the localization of a fluorescent-labeled convulsant drug within the nervous system. This drug, when applied locally to the brain, has a powerful convulsant effect. However, following intravenous injection no convulsions occur. The drug is concentrated in the nuclei of the brain capillary endothelium—the tela choroidea and the neurohypophysis. The chief barrier lies between the outer wall of the capillary endothelium and the glial plasma membrane.

The present concept of the blood-brain barrier has recently been summarized by Dobbing (74), who emphasizes that the static concept of a barrier which would permit the passage of some molecules and prohibit the passage of others must be accepted with considerable reservations. He remarks, "Very few if any small molecular weight substances are totally unable to pass from blood to brain, and between these and those like heavy water for which there appears to be no barrier, there exists an infinite gradation. It is possible that for some substances, e.g., the acid dyes, such a barrier exists in the capillary endothelium; but much more acceptable is King's concept of some sort of 'tissue affinity' for dyes, the barrier being a system consisting of blood, endothelium, and the nervous tissue rather than a single structure. Broman's list of possible components of the barrier system includes the specific permeability of the vascular endothelium, and the metabolic activity of nervous tissue, and the permeability of the nerve cell membrane. The observed phenomenon are to be regarded as the results of an almost infinite number of variables existing in a three compartment system, consisting of more than a kilogram of nervous tissue with its cells and intracellular fluid; about 125 ml. of cerebrospinal fluid with some sort of circulation, being formed and reabsorbed in normal conditions at a rate of between 0.03 ml. and 0.3 ml. per minute in the resting state. Most workers are now tending to think of the subject in these more complex and dynamic terms, and the concept of a mechanical blood-brain barrier, as such, is therefore declining in importance."

In this more dynamic concept the nervous tissue itself must be considered to play an active part in the spread of virus. Wright (325) has reviewed the evidence relative to spread of viruses and toxins in the nervous system, especially in relation to such agents as tetanus toxin, which has been demonstrated to travel the peripheral nerves. He concludes, "The general problem of the invasion of the brain and spinal cord by neurotrophic viruses and their remarkably rapid dispersion within their substance is of great importance in neurology. Fortunately, its experimental analysis is becoming easier than it was formerly, for there are now available several viruses with strains which have been highly adapted by selection, both for the nervous system and for the animal species commonly used in the laboratory. Through their employment and by the application of acceptable physiological principles, it should become possible greatly to enlarge our knowledge of the pathogenesis of infections in the central nervous system under both natural and experimental conditions."

In this connection, the availability of the technique of radioactive isotopic or fluorescent labeling of viruses should lend itself admirably to the study of the passage of these agents into the nervous system.

An example of such techniques is that reported by Rubin and Franklin (249). These authors have used a labeled virus to study the relationship between the antibody and the virus molecules.

This technique has also been used by Liu and Coffin (183). These authors were able to trace the spread of the virus following intranasal inoculation by the use of fluorescein-labeled antibodies.

The development of specific antiviral agents is another important and promising area. Francis (91) states, "The fact is clearly established that effective chemoprophylaxis can be anticipated. One can visualize materials of a nature which may become part of a daily diet, having a broad protective effect in the general population."

The study of virus metabolism and the chemistry of the virus may provide the basis for the development of antimetabolites capable of producing specific inhibition of virus growth. Here, again, the use of radioactive labeling is proving valuable, e.g., Franklin, Rubin, and Davis (92) have studied the incorporation of small molecular phosphorus-containing material in viruses and have been using this technique of labeling to study the metabolic requirements of this organism.

A number of specific and nonspecific inhibitory chemicals have been tested against various viruses. Hollinshead and Smith (140) report the testing of a series of 44 compounds, some of which showed inhibitory actions against three different types of viruses tested. Quinacrine (Mepacrine) has been demonstrated to have marked inhibitory activity against equine encephalomyelitis in mice but not in other species (145).

Tamm and Overman (283) have attempted to correlate the structure of the agent with its antiviral effect. The field of chemotherapy of viruses has been reviewed by Mathews and Smith (200). This review discusses methods of testing antiviral agents, the structure and multiplication of viruses in relation to chemotherapy, the effects of purine and pyrimidine analogues on viruses, virus inhibition by other types of compounds, and incorporation phenomena in relation to antimetabolite action. Their report emphasizes the large number of agents which are available for testing, pointing out that "for many of the substances showing some virus inhibitory activity, there are large numbers of related compounds already available. Only in a few instances do the potentialities of such compounds appear to have been assessed adequately from the practical point of view."

Some efforts have been made to isolate antiviral agents from other organisms (119). In addition, there is some evidence to suggest that other living organisms may be capable of destroying viruses (125). Certainly the fact that a number of agents have been found to exhibit antiviral activity should encourage intensification of the search for an agent which may prove clinically effective.

The Postinfectious Encephalomyelitides

Although the actual invasion of the nervous system and the tissue destruction produced by the virus are of fundamental importance, the "defense" reaction of the central nervous system and the process of the inflammation which may occur under certain circumstances may be an important factor in determining the degree of permanent injury which results from the disease. Studies in respect to tuberculous meningitis have indicated that measures to reduce the inflammatory response may ameliorate the symptoms and, where effective antibiotic therapy is available, improve the possibility of cure. In the case of mumps orchitis, cited above, there is clinical evidence to suggest that relief of the inflammatory reaction may minimize the permanent damage produced by the disease, especially in its late phases. In view of these considerations, an understanding of the nature of the cerebral inflammatory reaction, and of its modification, is of considerable importance. At the present time, particular interest centers around the problem of the so-called "allergic" encephalomyelitis (54, 188, 317). It is now clearly established that under proper conditions the repeated subcutaneous injection of brain tissue extract (proteolipid A and B) with adjuvants may lead to an inflammatory reaction in the nervous system and that histologically the picture so produced is very similar to that observed in the so-called "postinfectious encephalitides." Emphasis of the present studies is in the direction of determining more exactly the nature of the antigenic substance and, especially, the degree of specificity of the response to extracts from various parts of the nervous system. It is presumed that the inflammatory response is the result of a "tissue immunity." In many ways it is similar to the type of reaction which occurs on attempted tissue grafting. In this instance, the immune response may reside in the plasma cell of the immune person. There is little available information at the present time regarding the exact site of action of the antigen and the cells within the nervous system which take part in the response.

An interesting approach to determining the nature of the immune response is that of Lumsden, who is observing the response of sensitized tissue in tissue culture in response to the specific antigen. Under these circumstances a remarkably prompt alteration in the sensitive tissue can be observed. The responses involve the ground protein within the cell, and effects on the mitochondria appear to be secondary. There is shrinkage of the nuclei, suggesting a liberation of material from within the nucleus into the cytoplasm.

It would be very valuable if some reliable means of diagnosis of the allergic state could be developed. At the present time it is considered very likely that the post-infectious perivenous encephalomyelitis is to be considered an allergic manifestation. There is evidence suggesting that certain forms of peripheral neuropathy may develop on a similar basis. However, the extent of the problem has not been defined, and the extent to which this reaction may contribute to other forms of degenerative disease of the central nervous system has not been established. The development of a test to establish the presence of autosensitization would be extremely valuable in this connection. Freund (97) has been able to demonstrate the existence of a circulating antibody through crossed circulation experiments in parabiotic animals. Lumsden et al. (190) have demonstrated the presence of complement-fixing antibodies in monkeys having the experimental disease. However, this was a variable finding, which did not appear to correlate closely with the activity of the destructive process.

The demonstration of antibrain antibodies in multiple sclerosis has been reported (240). With use of antibodies prepared from the brains of patients with multiple sclerosis and with schizophrenia and of normal persons, complement-fixation tests were carried out against the blood sera of patients with multiple sclerosis and of a control group. Normal persons showed a considerable frequency of occurrence of antibodies against these antigens, but higher titers and a greater frequency were demonstrated in the case of the patients with multiple sclerosis.

Some efforts have been made to find an effective means of modifying the destructive and inflammatory reaction occurring in experimental encephalomyelitis. Sodium salicylate and p-aminobenzoic acid have been shown to have some prophylactic and therapeutic effect (116). In the case of post-measles encephalomyelitis, the incidence of this complication of measles is reduced by the prior administration of immune globulin. These preliminary findings are sufficient to encourage the hope that a really effective means of blocking this destructive reaction may be developed.

An interesting development with respect to research in lupus erythematosus might conceivably be pertinent to the problem of other forms of sensitization (169). In this disorder it has been demonstrated that the rapid aging and destruction of cells, which leads to an allergic response, is associated with abnormalities in deoxyribonuclease (DNase) and DNase inhibitor levels. Encouraging results have been reported by the use of DNase inhibitor in this condition. This report is interesting in suggesting that, at least in this disorder, it is not the sensitization reaction which is primary, but the tissue destruction which leads to sensitization.

The Primary Demyelinating Diseases

A second group of diseases in which the primary lesion involves the white matter of the brain is that of which multiple sclerosis is the commonest form. This group includes acute diffuse encephalomyelitis, multiple sclerosis, Schilder's disease, and Baló's concentric sclerosis. In general, these disorders are characterized by recurrent episodes in which areas of myelin are selectively destroyed, with minimal destruction of the axis cylinder and inflammatory reaction of minor and secondary degree. Unlike the postinfectious lesions, the lesions in this condition are not perivenous but tend to lie along the blood vessels and around the wall of the ventricles—adjacent to these structures but not within the distribution of any particular vessel. Although for a number of years Schilder's disease was considered a separate entity from multiple sclerosis, it is now being suggested that the fundamental process is similar in the two forms and that the difference in appearance depends more upon the age of the person afflicted and possibly some constitutional characteristic of the nervous system. Thus, Lhermitte (181) points out that multiple sclerosis is uncommon before the age of ten years and suggests that this is an indication that the younger person reacts more violently to develop a severer form, namely, diffuse sclerosis. However, he points out that it would be unwise to affirm that Schilder-Foix disease is only an infantile form of multiple sclerosis and that age represents only one of the factors which determine the distribution, extension, number of foci, and evolution of a disorder which, in spite of its diverse aspects, results from the same morbid process. He concludes, "In the final analysis, it seems to us that Schilder-Foix disease should take its place in the large group of multiple sclerosis along side of the typical form with successive episodes, the chronic and the acute forms." This problem is also discussed by Poser and van Bogaert (235), who state, "Demyelination, of course, is a completely nonspecific reaction of nervous tissue to any number of injurious agents (Scheinker). The role of allergy is not well known, yet some phenomena which are loosely spoken of as allergic may produce in the brain a pathological picture very similar to diffuse sclerosis; certain cerebro-toxins may also have the same effect (Ferraro, Verhaart). The way in which age, racial background, endocrine phenomena, previous exposure to neurogenic disease, or circulatory factors may effect the response of cerebral tissue to a given injury is still not clearly understood. It is, therefore, not illogical to assume that the same disease may represent itself in somewhat different forms in different individuals, depending upon the interplay of the above mentioned factors. On the other hand, it is quite as conceivable that different diseases may have the same clinical picture and provoke similar pathological changes."

Several excellent recent reviews of research concerning the demyelinating disorders are now available, including a book on multiple sclerosis by McAlpine et al. (203), reviews of the demyelinating diseases by Lhermitte (181) and by Poser and van Bogaert (235), and articles by Greenfield (122), by Wolf (317), and by Bertrand and van Bogaert.[11]

Epidemiological studies have provided some very interesting observations. The disease is very common among the Nordic races and almost unheard of in Japan. In the United States it is said to be commoner in the northern portion of the country than in the southern.

Several reports are available suggesting a familial incidence of disseminated sclerosis. Estborn (81) has found reports of 33 families in each of which there were three cases of multiple sclerosis, five families with four cases each, and one family with five cases. A somewhat similar series is reported by Pratt et al. (237). These investigators obtained case records of families in which more than one person had had multiple sclerosis, compared this with a calculated incidence for the disease in the area under observation, and concluded that there was an appreciably higher likelihood of occurrence of the disease in the families of afflicted persons than in the control population.

A similar study is reported from Scotland by Sutherland (277). This observer noted that multiple sclerosis is commoner in the northern than in the western islands, suggesting a greater vulnerability in the Nordic than in the Celtic stock. There was observed a family incidence of 11.0 per cent.

Kurland et al. (168) have reviewed a number of epidemiological studies and have reported their own, in which they demonstrated an incidence six times higher in Winnipeg than in New Orleans. Their patients and controls appeared similar in respect to national origin in the two cases. The clinical picture and course of the disease were similar in the two groups.

Studies of the geographical distribution of multiple sclerosis and of its

---

[11] Reference 28, p. 682.

familial incidence are subject to serious sources of error. In the case of the
search for a familial incidence, the disease is easily confused with disorders
such as Friedreich's ataxia, Marie's cerebellar ataxia, and familial spastic
paraplegia. The inclusion of a few families with such disorders in the series
may significantly alter the figures. In respect to population surveys the difficulty with diagnosis is also a serious stumbling block. One may often
suspect that the reported incidence of the disease in any community is more
closely related to the diagnostic enthusiasm of the physicians than to the
actual incidence of the disease. Multiple sclerosis is easily mimicked by
intoxications, familial vascular diseases, and a host of systemic diseases which
may produce intermittent diffuse injury of the central nervous system. Without pathological control the level of diagnostic accuracy in this particular
disorder is likely to be very low.

There is at this time a great need for accurate data relative to these two
features of the demyelinating disorders. It is my opinion that such data
must be viewed with considerable distrust until we have improved our diagnostic acumen, unless reported studies include a very careful and extensive
pathological control of the diagnostic criteria used.

Repeated efforts to culture an infective organism from patients with multiple sclerosis have failed, and at the present time there are few who feel
that this disease is directly attributable to infection.

The majority of present investigators do not believe that the lesions of
multiple sclerosis are the result of vascular thrombi or embolus. The lesions
are not distributed in the area of distribution of the cerebral vessels. The
clinical and pathological picture observed in multiple sclerosis is not identical
with that which may be produced by experimental embolism or thrombosis.
The latter lesions are necrotic in character, involving not only myelin but
axis cylinders, whereas the lesion in multiple sclerosis is selective for the
myelin.

Attempts have been made to relate multiple sclerosis and related diseases to
postinfectious allergic encephalomyelitis. However, the character of the reaction and the distribution of the lesions differ in the two instances.

Of particular interest are basic studies concerned with the mechanism of
formation, metabolism, and replacement of myelin. The occurrence of areas
of demyelination might be attributable to some factor interfering with the
formation or replacement of this substance or to the blockage of some normal
process for its nutrition or maintenance. The distribution of the lesions
around the wall of the ventricle or in juxtaposition to the blood vessels has

suggested the possibility that some myelolytic agent may pass into the tissue and produce its destructive lesions. Efforts to find such a myelolytic substance in the blood serum, urine, or spinal fluid of patients with demyelinating disorders have failed. Efforts have been made to study enzyme levels in the plaques of multiple sclerosis, but in these instances it is difficult to distinguish cause from effect—abnormal metabolites or enzymes found in the plaque may simply be the result of tissue degeneration rather than the cause.

The injection of myelolytic substances, including saponin and lecithinase from cobra venom or from Clostridium welchii, has produced lesions not entirely dissimilar to those of the disease.

The injection of ergotamine in large doses and, occasionally, of lead may produce degeneration of the white matter, bearing considerable resemblance to Schilder's disease. Carbon monoxide poisoning leads to degeneration of the gray and white matter, especially in the region of the basal ganglia. In some instances the disorder produced has appeared to be a progressive one, with worsening of the clinical and pathological picture for a long period of time after the toxic agent has presumably ceased to operate. Potassium cyanate has also been shown capable of producing destructive lesions of the white matter. In this connection, Lumsden (189) has made some interesting observations on the effect of this toxin. Large single doses produced necrotic lesions of the cerebral cortex and cerebellum. Repeated small doses, however, appeared to produce a suddenly developing disease characterized by degeneration of white matter. This condition is remarkable by reason of the occurrence of a sudden reaction following a repeated small dose, the initial injection of a similar dose having provoked only a minimal effect.

There are several conditions of animals, presumably due to intoxication, which bear some resemblance to the human disease. Because these animal diseases have had rather limited study, it would be difficult to say with certainty how close the resemblance is. There is a disease of horses called "moldycorn poisoning" (leukoencephalomalacia). The most extensive studies of this disorder are those reported by Biester et al. (29). The specific agent responsible for this disorder has not been determined, but it is known to result from ingestion of corn which has been permitted to lie on the ground under damp conditions, and the experimental disease has been produced by administration of moldy corn. In this disorder the pathologic process is primarily characterized by gross and microscopic lesions of the brain tissue, consisting of numerous hemorrhages and edema, frequently leading to liquefaction necrosis. These lesions are confined to the white matter of the brain and, occasionally, of the cord.

Probably the most interesting demyelinating disease of animals is "sway back," a demyelinating disease of lambs. Investigators in Australia and in Great Britain have demonstrated that this is associated with abnormalities of the metallic ion content of the soil and that levels of copper are extremely important in respect to this disorder. A low level of copper in liver and blood of the pregnant mother, the liver of the affected animal, and the forage have been demonstrated. Degeneration of the nervous system in these animals may actually take place prior to birth, and in the severe cases the white matter of the centrum ovale may have degenerated into a gelatinous mass with cystic cavities. Histopathological examination reveals degeneration of the myelin sheath accompanied by serious changes in the axones.

Efforts to demonstrate abnormalities of copper metabolism in patients with demyelinating diseases of the central nervous system have not been successful (198). No difference was detected between patients with disseminated sclerosis and normal subjects either in the blood copper level or in the urinary excretion of copper in response to injected dimercaptol (BAL). It was observed that the urinary copper level in the absence of injected dimercaptol appeared to be somewhat lower in the diseased than in the normal group, but this difference was considered a possible result of the conditions of invalidism of the diseased group. The relationship of the disease of lambs to the human demyelinating disorders is thus not established.

Another disorder of nutrition which has been suspected in multiple sclerosis has to do with lipoid metabolism and the ingestion of fats. There is a form of nutritional encephalomalacia of chickens which may bear some relationship to this problem (154). It occurs in animals which are retained on a diet high in fats and low in vitamin E and may be prevented by the addition of vitamin E to the diet. The lesions produced in the nervous system are primarily vascular in origin—they consist of areas of ischemic necrosis followed by reparative organization. However, a variety of neuropathological forms have been demonstrated, the reason for these variations being uncertain. Certain chicks on the deficient dietary regimen develop typical ischemic necrosis. Others present only large, sharply punched out areas. Vacuoles may be seen in the white matter of the cerebellar folia, in the medulla, or in the posterior commissure. In some phases the pattern is one of exudation. Capillary proliferation is a striking feature in most instances, although in the late

phases the picture is one of glial scar formation. In regard to these pathological changes Jungherr *et al.* report, "While all neuropathological expressions of nutritional encephalomalacia in chicks seem to be initiated by circulatory disturbance the end results of the degenerative and reactive processes
involved differ markedly, thereby widening the pathologic spectrum for this
disease more so than for any other neurologic entity in the fowl. Variations
in predominant changes are believed to be brought about by differences in
the individual host and by differences in the reactive capacity of the particular neuroanatomic portion involved."

Swank has been the chief proponent of the thesis that multiple sclerosis in
humans may be related to ingestion of large amounts of fats, particularly in
relation to dairy products. Swank's original observations stem from the fact
that the incidence of multiple sclerosis is high in those populations which have
a high fat intake (279). A further study along these lines was reported in
1952 by Swank *et al.* (281). This survey of the distribution of multiple
sclerosis in Norway demonstrated that, whereas the incidence of the inland
areas was 4.1 per 100,000 per year, along the coastal area this incidence was
only 1.2 per 100,000 per year. It was the author's impression that this remarkable difference in incidence could be correlated with the level of dairy
product utilization in these two groups. These authors have reported on
seven years' experience with a low-fat diet and feel that the results are encouraging, although a control series was not available (280).

The Leukodystrophies

Closely related to multiple sclerosis and its related demyelinating disorders
is a group of familial disorders also characterized by loss of myelin. In contradistinction to the above diseases, these familial leukodystrophies are characterized by symmetrical diffuse degenerative changes and by a steadily progressive course. According to the classification of Poser and van Bogaert (235),
included in this group are Pelizaeus-Merzbacher disease, the leukodystrophies
with "glial insufficiency," the globoid-cell type, and the type characterized by
spongy degeneration of the neuraxis. These diseases have in common a degenerative change in the myelin. In some instances there is a suggestion
that the primary disorder has to do with the glial cell. These structures
are deficient, and it is assumed that this deficiency leads in turn to a failure
of myelin formation with which they are concerned. In other instances the
primary disorder appears to be the myelin degeneration itself, and interest
centers about the presence of abnormal break-down products of myelin and

lipids. The major emphasis in the differentiation of these poorly defined dis-orders has been on the development of histochemical techniques for dis-tinguishing the abnormal metabolites present. Biochemical studies of these disorders are in their infancy. The problem here is closely related to that of the lipoidoses. In each, the emphasis is on disorders of lipoid metabolism in the central nervous system. It would appear that there may be a large number of closely related entities, each involving some separate aspect of metabolism in the central nervous system.

Cumings (65) reports a study of various lipids of the brain in several of the demyelinating diseases. It is his suggestion that it might be possible with less than 1 gm. of cerebral biopsy material obtained during life to suggest tentatively the diagnosis of any of these cases, with the possible exception of the metachromatic type of diffuse sclerosis. In Table 3 are indicated the findings reported in these diseases.

TABLE 3

LIPID ABNORMALITIES IN DEMYELINATING DISEASES

Disease	Cases, No.	Total Phospho-lipid (White)	Choles-terol Esters (White)	Cerebro-side (White)	Neura-minic Acid (Cortex)	Phospho-protein Phos-phorus (White)	Hexo-samine (White)
Amaurotic family idiocy	6	Normal or reduced	Absent	Normal or reduced	Increased	Reduced	Increased
Multiple sclerosis	5	Reduced	Present	Reduced	Increased	Reduced	Normal or increased
Sudanophilic	2	Reduced	Present	Reduced	Increased	Reduced	Variable
Spongy	1	Reduced	Absent	Reduced	Increased	Reduced	Normal for age
Pelizaeus-Merzbacher	1	Reduced	Absent	Reduced	Increased	Normal	....
Krabbe, or globoid-cell	1	Reduced	Absent	Increased	Normal	Reduced	Normal for age
Metachromatic	1	Reduced	Absent	Reduced	Increased	Reduced	Increased

There is still a great deal to be learned from the study of the normal metabolism of the central nervous system. It is probable that systematic bio-chemical analysis of abnormal tissue is also an important measure. At the present time there is considerable difficulty in carrying out the latter type of study. There are certainly relatively few laboratories which are equipped and prepared to carry out this particular type of analysis. The complexity of the situation is such that even in these laboratories the analysis may be limited to certain specific components of the many with which one might be concerned. The diseases involved are relatively uncommon, and postmortem specimens are not easily available. The problem of obtaining the right specimen for the right laboratory is thus a very difficult one. For some types of analysis fixed tissue is satisfactory. In other instances there is some question as to whether the chemical reaction may be modified by the process of formalin fixation. The development of freezing techniques should obviate this concern, but only if the laboratories carrying out postmortem examinations in these cases will save some material by this technique. It would appear that some type of coordinated program will be required if adequate amounts of material from this type of case are to be made available to those laboratories specifically concerned with special studies.

C. Epilepsy

It is reported by Yannet that approximately 15 per cent of institutionalized ·defectives may have convulsions. In possibly 2 per cent the convulsive disorder seemed responsible for the patient's retardation.

In Tarjan's series (284) epilepsy was present in 536 of 2000 patients studied for mental deficiency and was considered the primary cause of the patient's deficiency in 138. In any patient having both convulsions and mental retardation there are several possible explanations for the association of the two. Both symptoms may be the result of a disease which has injured the brain—in this case, the seizures might simply be considered a coincidental finding. In other instances very frequent minor seizures may themselves lead to impairment of mentation, producing a mental retardation on a physiological basis rather than on an "anatomical" basis. Finally, the occurrence of severe seizures may produce irreversible brain damage. Whichever of these may be the case, the extension of our knowledge of the convulsive disorders is a step toward the prevention of mental retardation.

Since epilepsy is a symptom bearing close resemblance to mental retardation in its etiologies, the program for recognition of the etiological agent is the same for each. In addition, in the case of epilepsy one must search also for certain special types of local cortical injury. The frequent occurrence of foci in the temporal lobe has centered interest on common mechanisms for the injury of this area. The study of the mechanics of acute head injury has indicated that the temporal lobes are particularly vulnerable to certain types of displacement. This area may also be peculiarly subject to pressure by head molding during delivery—swelling and distortion leading to compression and ischemia of the medial aspect of the lobe by impingement on the tentorium. This same mechanism may operate to produce permanent injury as a result of febrile illnesses during childhood, some investigators suggesting that swelling of the brain may be common and may cause temporal lobe compression and injury in some instances.

It is not clear to what extent and through what mechanism the seizures themselves may lead to further permanent brain damage (286). Degeneration of cells in Ammon's horn is a frequent finding in "deteriorated" epileptics and is claimed by some to be so specific that the entity can be diagnosed by pathological examination. Presumably such changes might be produced by anoxia, by ischemia, or by edema. The further evaluation of vasomotor changes and of tissue swelling in association with seizures is pertinent to this problem.

It is probable that, in this, changes in cerebral capillary permeability may play an important role (as they do in connection with head injury and virus infection; see pages 108 and 118). Bauer and Leonhardt (19) are making an interesting study of changes in permeability which occur during convulsions induced by pentamethylenetetrazol (Cardiazol). Capillary "leakage" is demonstrated by staining with Geigy blue—an agent which they have found superior to the trypan-blue usually employed. Ordinarily, the induction of seizures through the injection of pentamethylenetetrazol is associated with increased capillary permeability. The previous injection of the proprietary phenothiazine derivative Megaphen can reduce this permeability change, although it has no effect on the convulsions.

Until such time as the knowledge of etiology leads to prevention, the treatment of seizures remains the best method of prevention of disability and further damage. Studies to this end include the following topics: (1) the normal activity of the cerebral neurons and ways in which this activity is altered in epileptics, during "normal" or induced seizures, and in response to anticonvulsant drugs; (2) the function of the excitable membrane—the physical and chemical changes which occur under the above conditions and in the area of epileptogenic "foci"; (3) the nature and spread of the epileptic discharge and its modification by drugs; (4) the evaluation of anticonvulsants, especially including the correlation of the clinical features of the epileptic disorder with response to therapy.

Recent advances in electrophysiological techniques have made it possible to record the electrical activity of the brain not only from diffuse leads, which provide records of diffuse or synchronized activity, but also from needle electrodes, which make it possible to record the activity of single neurons, even within the highly complex organization of the cerebral cortex. Because of the organization of the cortex into layers, it has been possible to distinguish between the activity of the nerve cell body and its dendrites. With these newer techniques it is also possible to record not only rapidly shifting (A. C.) potentials but also steady-state potentials with direct coupled amplifiers. These techniques have greatly advanced our knowledge of the electrical activity of the nervous system (233). Recent studies throw increasing emphasis on the importance of slow potentials and nonconducted activities of neurons. It is certain that the electrical activity of the brain cannot be explained solely on the basis of conducted waves of depolarization such as those which accompany the passage of the nerve impulse in the peripheral nervous system. It has been demonstrated that the cell layers of the cortex are in a constant state of polarization, in general the cortex being positive with respect to the deeper layers. Nonconducted or at least decremental potential changes are an important feature of the activity within the dense network of the cortex, especially in the dendritic layer. The potential gradient within the dendrite and between it and the cell body can be influenced by afferent impulses. It is postulated that the brain rhythms recorded by electroencephalograms depend on a number of processes, including D. C. potential fields, presynaptic and local potentials, electronic spread, and/or decremental conduction in the neuropil and dendritic plexus in connection with interneural activity.

Within this network the occurrence of a focal cerebral seizure is associated with abnormal bursts of very rapid discharges of cortical neurons (200 to 1000 per second) (2, 153). Potentials of similar frequency have been observed under normal conditions, but in these instances the bursts are of very short duration. It is postulated that in the case of the epileptic state some inhibitory mechanism which normally prevents a continuation of this rapid discharge is lacking.

The nature of the epileptic discharges and the action of the anticonvulsants has recently been reviewed by Toman and Taylor (288). The authors state, "The transition from normal to seizure activity represents a qualitative change in neuronal behavior involving slow as well as fast elements. Within limits, the cerebral cortex appears to be capable of handling excessive stimulation by means of an inhibitory counter process which appears in the EEG as a slow potential. . . . Repetition or excessive stimulation may disorder and overwhelm the counter process, permitting a self-sustained new and increased state of reverberation, which is brought to an end ultimately by a process akin to fatigue and related to an increase in threshold. The self-sustained discharge may remain delimited or may spread to involve the entire brain." These authors review the presumed mode of action of convulsant and anticonvulsant drugs. The major effect of diphenylhydantoin (Dilantin) and many other anticonvulsants is to reduce the lowering of threshold which ordinarily occurs after a period of activity within the nervous system (80). It has been shown that diphenylhydantoin deepens depression following transmission of a single impulse and hastens fatigue during repetitive stimulation. Post-tetanic potentiation is strikingly reduced by diphenylhydantoin.

Another approach to the problem of the epileptogenic focus involves the search for biochemical abnormalities of the involved area (234). Epileptogenic areas produced experimentally in the monkey cortex have been shown to contain a moderate increase in acetylcholine esterase activity. In addition, the production of bound acetylcholine during incubation of slices of focal epileptogenic cortex is lower than that of normal tissue (294).

Experiments have further indicated that anesthetics and anticonvulsants have the property of enhancing the capacity of normal cerebral cortex to bind acetylcholine. It was also demonstrated that glutamine and asparagine added in vitro proved effective in restoring to normal the ability of epileptogenic cortex to bind acetylcholine.

A number of studies have been carried out in an effort to determine the biochemical mechanism through which anticonvulsants limit neuronal overactivity. It has been demonstrated that diphenylhydantoin and a number of barbiturate anesthetics may interfere with neuronal activity without altering oxygen uptake (177). It has been suggested that these agents interfere with the energy supply of the neurons by blocking phosphorylation (234).

Another attack on the question of the mode of action of anticonvulsants has had to do with its influence on hormonal control of brain excitability (319, 320). In an extensive series of investigations Woodbury observed that the electroshock threshold in experimental animals varied directly with the plasma sodium concentration and inversely with the ratio of extracellular to intracellular concentration in the brain. These parameters might be altered by adrenal hormones, and these in turn were influenced by diphenylhydantoin. The author pointed out that the mechanism through which these various agents influence sodium metabolism is not known and that further work in which the effects of hormones on brain metabolism are correlated with electrolyte movement is necessary for elucidation in this interesting and fundamental problem. Another similar approach has recently been reported by Bonnycastle *et al.* (31). These authors were concerned with the mechanism through which diphenylhydantoin might mediate its inhibitory effects on the pituitary-adrenal system. They studied the levels of 5-hydroxytryptamine (a neuroaffector drug) and observed that the levels of this substance were reduced after the administration of diphenylhydantoin. Reserpine is an agent which lowers the level of this compound, but it appears sensitive to a few other agents.

A major problem having to do with our understanding of the convulsive disorders lies in the fact that these do not represent a single entity. The complexity of the clinical and electroencephalographic manifestations of these disorders is outlined by Gastaut (102). On the basis of a number of clinical and electroencephalographic observations of seizures induced by pentylentetrazol (Metrazol), Gastaut has attempted a classification and analysis of epileptic disorders. The manifestations of epilepsy vary strikingly, depending upon the locus of origin of the seizure. Further understanding of these phenomena is to be anticipated from further clinical studies such as those reported by Gastaut, from depth electrode studies of epileptic patients, and from observation of the spread of the epileptic discharge in artificially induced lesions in animals.

There has been little emphasis on the fact that the anatomical or chemical agent responsible for the actual production of the seizure may not necessarily be the same in every instance. Experimentally it is possible to produce an "epileptic state" by numerous agents, including electric shock, alteration in water balance and ions, hormonal therapy, and convulsant drugs, such as strychnine, caffeine, and pentylenetetrazol, as well as by alteration in metabolism produced by changes in oxygen supply and by metabolic blocking agents and antimetabolites. It is not known to what extent the actual mechanism of initiation of the seizure produced by these different agents may vary. This fact is well recognized and forms the basis for the animal testing procedures for new drugs. At the present time new anticonvulsants are tested both against electric shock and against chemical agents. It has recently been demonstrated (320) that the seizure patterns produced in animals by a variety of convulsant drugs vary in accordance with the different agents used and that the response of these seizures to anticonvulsants may be grouped into three categories—mephenesin-like, barbital-like, and diphenylhydantoin-like. There has been little, if any, attempt made to classify patients with epilepsy on the basis of the etiology of their seizure pattern or to correlate these various parameters with responses to medication.

Without accurate knowledge of mode of action the development of new, effective anticonvulsant drugs is largely on an empirical basis, with primary emphasis on testing large numbers of drugs related to the barbiturates. There have been no recent publications attempting to determine the nature of the anticonvulsant action of bromide, whether or not this is identical with that of the barbiturate group, and whether its anticonvulsant and its depressant effects are inseparable. The recent suggestion that meprobamate has an anticonvulsant action may open a new avenue for study, since this drug appears to differ, structurally at least, from the barbiturate group.

VII. REGENERATION OF THE CENTRAL NERVOUS SYSTEM

Interest in the possibility of at least limited regeneration within the central nervous system has recently been revived as a result of experiments demonstrating the fact that it is possible for regeneration of axons to take place within the severed spinal cord. An extensive series of experiments reported by Windle and others (315) has demonstrated clearly that at least in lower animals functional connections can be reestablished within the severed cord. In their volume are summarized experiments having to do with evidences of restoration of function in animals and man, including studies of the anatomy and pathology, physiological experiments indicating regeneration, and detailed case reports. The studies reported provide conclusive evidence that, under certain circumstances, regeneration can occur in the central nervous system of animals. Analysis of several of the human case reports lends at least some support to the thesis that regeneration has also been shown to occur in clinical instances.

The degree of effective regeneration is dependent to some extent upon the density of the scar through which the regenerating fibers must grow and can thus be influenced by the administration of agents which impede scar formation. These include steroid hormones, a Pseudomonas polysaccharide (Piromen), and X-rays. There is a considerable species difference in respect to the ease with which regeneration can occur, and experiments carried out in monkeys have been less encouraging than those carried out in lower animals. Controlled experiments in which alternate human cases have been treated with Piromen have not been reported.

Tissue culture studies have also demonstrated growth of axons in excised tissue.[12] These studies suggest that the pial membrane may be an important factor in facilitating the growth of axons and suggest that the regeneration of axons may be influenced by their proximity to other tissues, especially those from the meninges.

Husby, Bassett, Noback, and Campbell have recently been experimenting with use of a Millipore filter to encourage regeneration across gaps in peripheral nerves and more recently in the spinal cord. They have discovered that if the severed nerve is surrounded with a Millipore filter, the ingrowth of scar tissue is prevented, a bridge is provided over which a more normal delicate pial membrane is encouraged to regenerate, and the axons are permitted to re-form through the viable clot which is interposed.

---

[12] Pomerat: Personal communication to the author.

136

Experiments with regeneration of tissue are being continued, efforts being made to determine those factors which will influence regeneration and to find out whether by nerve grafting or other techniques artificial bridges can be obtained. These techniques to date have had little application to the central nervous system itself, although experiments have been carried out in which the distal end of a peripheral nerve was actually grafted into the cortex, and a functional connection appears to have been established.[13]

Even greater uncertainty surrounds the question of the possibility of regeneration of neurons within the central nervous system. It has been accepted as a rule for many years that the neurons of the central nervous system do not show mitosis and are incapable of reduplication under any circumstances. Recently, one investigator (104) showed that it is possible to demonstrate multiplication of adult neurons in tissue culture. This observation has not been confirmed by a number of other investigators who have attempted to make similar observations, and at the present time the question of whether or not multiplication of neurons does occur in the adult nervous system is still a matter of dispute.

A new light on the potentialities for regeneration within the central nervous system has been reported by Sperry (269). This investigator has been studying regeneration of injured nerve fibers within the central nervous system of amphibians. In a series of observations of the regeneration of the optic nerve in the newt it has been possible to demonstrate that in some astonishing fashion the myriads of regenerating fibers which grow into the cut optic nerve are capable of reestablishing connections with their proper endings within the sense organ. Experiments in which the eye was rotated, or in which the nerve was cut and rotated, have indicated that if incorrect connections are established there is very little capability of reorganization of the pattern within the central nervous system. Sperry's experiments show, however, that if the nerve is simply cut and resutured correct regeneration of fibers does take place—those intended for the upper portion of the eye going to that area and similarly with other fibers.

> It follows that optic fibers arising from different points in the retina must differ from one another in some way. . . . Each optic fiber must be endowed with some quality, presumably chemical, that marks it as having originated from a particular spot of the retinal field. And the matching spot at its terminus in the brain must have an exactly complementary quality. Presumably an ingrowing fiber will attach itself only

---

[13] Freeman, L.: Personal communication to the author.

to the particular brain cells that match its chemical flavor, so to speak.
. . . Such chemical matching would account for recognition on contact,
but how does a fiber find its way to its destination? There is good reason to believe that the regenerating fibers employ a shotgun approach.
Each fiber puts forth many branches as it grows into the brain, and
the brain cells likewise have widespread branches. Thus the chances
are exceedingly good that a given fiber will eventually make contact
with its partner cells. . . . Eventually the growing tip encounters a
type of cell surface for which it has a specific chemical affinity and to
which it adheres. A chemical reaction then causes the fiber to stop
advancing and to form a lasting functional union with the group of cells,
presumably roughly circular in formation, which constitutes the spot in
the brain matching the fiber's source spot in the retina.

The experiments on vision have been found to apply equally to other
parts of the central nervous system. Normal function can be recovered
through regeneration by general sensory nerves in the spinal cord, by the
vestibular nerve in the ear mediating the sense of equilibrium and by
other sensory and motor nerve circuits.

All the experiments point to one conclusion: the theory of inherent
chemical affinities among the nerve fibers and cells is able to account
for the kinds of behavior tested better than any hypothetical mechanism based on experience and learning. There is no direct proof of the
theory, for no one has yet seen evidence of the chemical affinity type of
reaction among nerves under the microscope. But an ever-growing
accumulation of experimental findings continues to add support to the
chemical theory.

These data are of extreme importance in relation to potentialities for regeneration within the central nervous system, for they indicate that, at least in
lower forms and in relatively simple organization patterns, there is the ability
of regenerating fibers to reestablish themselves in an orderly fashion, even in
a relatively complex structure. The extent to which these findings will be
demonstrated to carry over to higher forms is, of course, debatable. It also
remains to be seen whether ways can be found for modifying the chemical
milieu in such a way as to impede or retard regeneration in its elective fashion.

VIII. SURVEYS FOR INCIDENCE OF MENTAL SUBNORMALITY

Figures for the incidence of mental retardation vary in accordance with the definition used. The basic question is "Retarded for what?" The problem is most clearly outlined by Penrose (228) in *The Biology of Mental Defect,* 1954: The distribution of intelligence in the population forms a continuous "Gaussian" curve. This curve is slightly skewed, with a higher incidence on the low side. The curve has a very steep slope at the 70 to 80 *IQ* level, and the incidence of "retardation" reported will be strikingly influenced by variations in the criteria established, especially if these criteria are at this marginal level of intelligence. It should be noted that it is at this level that methods of testing are most likely to be influenced by cultural and environmental factors. The tests used at this level have been validated to a large extent on the basis of academic performance. It is this fact which probably accounts for the observation that the highest incidence of retardation, as determined by population surveys, is found at the ten- to fourteen-year age level.

It is at this age that the school child is being most critically evaluated by academic standards. Many persons thus judged retarded subsequently adapt effectively into our culture in nonacademic pursuits.

It is also at the upper border of retardation that the amazingly high incidence of rejection by the Army is involved. The figures show great variations in incidence, depending upon social, geographical, and cultural background (Ginzberg and Bray [110], *The Uneducated*).

The most recent survey in the United States, that carried out at Onondaga County, New York, concludes with the following summary:

A special census of children believed to be possibly retarded was conducted through local child care agencies in a New York State metropolitan area. One percent of all children under 18 years of age were reported as retarded, measured by an intelligence quotient less than 75. Two-tenths (0.2) percent were severely retarded, with an intelligence quotient less than 50. Including children known to have intelligence quotients greater than 75, a total of 3.5% were referred as "possibly retarded."

Reported suspected prevalence rates were observed to vary markedly with age, sex, color, and place of residence. Rates increased to a peak at ages 10-15 years, then fell off sharply. The reported male rate was nearly twice the female, and non-whites higher than whites. Residence in the economically depressed central area of the city was accompanied by higher rates for all colors.

These data strongly suggest that behavior leading to the social sus-

139

picion of "mental retardation" is not necessarily a fixed characteristic of individual children, but is rather a complex set of manifestations of some children's relationship to their immediate environment.

The question of the incidence of moderately severe mental retardation, i.e., the "trainable" child—mental age approximately four to seven years—has recently been reviewed (164). On the basis of a small local survey, it is concluded that the incidence of this group in Michigan is 0.33 per cent— a figure which compares with others in the country, ranging from 0.234 per cent to 0.5 per cent.

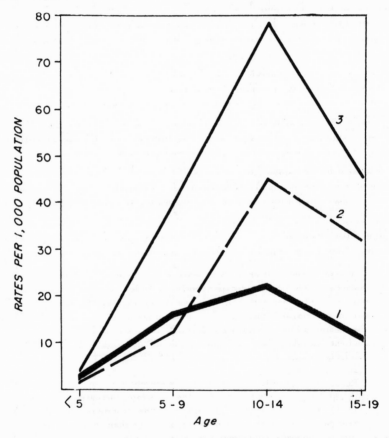

Fig. 11.—Incidence of mental retardation in different age groups as reported from three different surveys. (1) Data from Reference 206; (2) data from Reference 179; (3) data from Reference 219.

Figures for prevalence of severe degrees of retardation are also difficult to establish, and they are certainly influenced by the survival rate of the severely defective persons, which at the present time is increasing. The figure of 0.1 per cent for the most severely retarded level is derived from recent U. S. figures indicating that during the year 1954, 2158 persons classed as "idiot" were admitted to institutions in the United States (215).

PART II

PSYCHOLOGICAL AND CULTURAL PROBLEMS IN MENTAL SUBNORMALITY

———

by Seymour B. Sarason and Thomas Gladwin

IX. INTRODUCTION TO THE PSYCHOLOGICAL AND CULTURAL FACTORS

Part II of this volume was written by a psychologist and an anthropologist.[1] The participation of an anthropologist in this undertaking reflects a conviction on the part of both authors that real understanding of the nature and implications of subnormality can only be approached by paying more than lip service to the fact that this is a social and cultural as well as a biological and psychological problem. In our society the problem looms large—statistically, financially, and emotionally; in most non-European societies it is inconsequential, confined to cases of severe pathological defect who are cared for, as long as they live, with a mimimum of distress or dislocation. The difference lies in culturally determined attitudes, behaviors, and criteria of social acceptability, as we shall endeavor to make clear. Therefore, although we shall be concerned primarily with the sources of retardation rooted in the individual and his environment, we must pay equal attention to the way in which society defines, perceives, reacts to, and attempts to cope with mental subnormality regardless of its origin. Even a child with a severe defect must be viewed as deficient *relative to* cultural standards of acceptability; the cause of his deficiency may be organic, but its magnitude is dependent upon social criteria.

Viewed in a different light, the study of mental subnormality can make important theoretical and substantive contributions to our understanding of the nature and development of normal intellectual functioning, in much the same way that we have enriched our understanding of normal biological and psychological processes through the study of pathologies in those spheres of functioning. In this way, for example, we can relate deficits in childhood learning to failures and successes in later adjustment and thus obtain a clearer picture of those aspects of learning (the acquisition of culture) most essential for social living, and at the same time isolate cognitive or intellectual components from the totality of demands a society makes on its members. One of our primary objectives in writing this report is to present the prob-

---

[1] We cannot properly present this report without mentioning our gratitude to two persons without whose help it probably would never have been able to reach completion: Mr. Roy J. Jones who in an early phase of the survey helped us greatly in a preliminary review of the literature, and Mrs. Iris Keim who was of inestimable value to us in countless ways in the preparation of this report.

lem in terms which we hope will encourage social scientists, who have thus far been almost totally uninterested, to view mental subnormality as an important research area. We also hope to lure more psychologists, psychiatrists, and others whose disciplines are already somewhat represented in the field, to join our ranks, and perhaps provide them with a few fresh perspectives. There are undoubtedly many reasons for the lack of interest by competent researchers in subnormal mental ability, but we believe few if any of these reasons have a realistic basis. We are convinced that the result of this disinterest has been a serious loss in the development of the science of human behavior as well as a failure by our society to come to grips with a problem it has itself largely created.

Our primary concern is necessarily with etiology. The fact that subnormality can only be meaningful with reference to some external criterion of normality is important, but from a practical point of view it would be unrealistic to hope for a change in the cultural standards of mental normality sufficient to resolve the problems with which we are here concerned. We must therefore take as our point of departure the realization that only a minority of the population falls into that end of the distribution we label "subnormal." In seeking the causes of the misfortunes of this minority we immediately discover the multiplicity of factors operative within individuals and within groups which culminate in a diagnosis of subnormality, and we find that this diagnosis itself is highly variable and dependent upon shifting criteria. Under these conditions it is not surprising that the field at present has some of the attributes of chaos, particularly from the research point of view. No matter how determined our intentions we cannot hope with two reports to bring all the issues into orderly focus, and will be satisfied if we can clarify the range of questions which must be answered before such order can be achieved.

We begin by attempting to indicate in a general way the major cultural and psychological research problems which mental retardation presents. Before taking up in detail the variety of factors subsumed under the term cultural, we consider it necessary to discuss two problems. The first concerns the criteria, reviewed in Chapter XI, by which one judges the significance of test results, more specifically, the failure to study systematically the relations between problem-solving behavior in test and non-test situations. The second problem concerns some recent contributions to conceptions of intelligence and their implications for the measurement or evaluation of intellectual functioning (Chapter XII). In Chapter XIII we discuss the implications of widespread belief in the heredity of mental subnormality; the lack of a demonstrable basis for this belief with respect to mental retardation leads us to a closer examination of environmental factors, particularly those which are culturally determined. Chapter XIV therefore constitutes a critical review of existing research relevant to the cultural determinants of both normal and subnormal intellectual performance as this is expressed in intelligence test results, while Chapter XV suggests the questions which must be explored with reference to the broader implications of intellectual performance in social living as a whole, including the later adequacy of persons who were judged retarded while of school age or on the basis of test scores.

Chapters XVI and XVII primarily concern the severely defective child. Because misconceptions about these cases are fairly extensive—both in terms of varieties of behavior which may be observed and the importance of the research problems which such behavior presents—we have more than elsewhere in this report quoted rather extensively from the clinical literature.

In Chapter XVIII our discussion concerns the so-called higher grades of mental deficiency. The research we shall be discussing primarily is of two kinds: it either concerns certain diagnostic groupings (e.g., minimal brain injury) or characteristics (e.g., rigidity) which have almost exclusively been studied within the high grade portion of an institutional population—a restriction to generalization which is not always recognized. There is no doubt that the high grade segment of an institutional population is largely made up of what is traditionally called the familial defective. As will be indicated in different parts of this report, we think it to be a source of confusion to label such cases as mentally defective when they are institutionalized and as mentally retarded when they remain in the community—as if the act of commitment is a valid criterion in the consideration of etiology and diagnosis.

Finally in Chapter XIX, we attempt to pull together in summary form the research implications and suggestions which have emerged from our survey with the hope that many more researchers than at present will see and take up the challenge offered by this rich but largely unexplored field of mental subnormality.

X. THE UNEDUCATED

A. MILITARY REJECTION FOR MENTAL DEFICIENCY

In 1953 Ginzberg and Bray (87) published a book entitled "The Uneducated." This book contained a searching and illuminating analysis of men who were rejected on the ground of mental deficiency for military service in World War II. It also contained a study of a sample of men who had been accepted by the armed services but who were illiterate or semi-illiterate. The men in this sample had been through a special education training program set up by the military. We shall discuss this book not only for the data it contains but also because we feel that it can serve as a basis for raising some of the most important research problems in the area of mental retardation.

From the beginning of selective service until the end of the war, there were 716,000 individuals who were between 18 and 37 years of age and were rejected on the grounds of mental deficiency. Some of the problems associated with the interpretation of this figure may be seen from the following quotation (87, p. 41):

> Relatively little research has been devoted to ascertaining the number of individuals in the population who cannot meet a minimum performance criterion as workers and citizens. Some authorities estimate that approximately one per cent of the population can perform even unskilled work only under close supervision in a protective environment. It is believed that another one per cent of the population are able to work effectively only if they have some type of special supervision. According to these estimates the percentage of persons who would not meet a minimum performance standard because of intellectual deficiency would be 2 per cent. The more than 700,000 men rejected for military service under the general heading of "mental deficiency" amounted to about 4 per cent of the men examined. On the surface this might be taken to mean that the screening standards used were somewhat tight but approximately correct. Again, however, a national average obscures the truth, for nearly 14 per cent were rejected in some states and only one-half of one per cent in others. The fact that the national rejection rate was only a little higher than the theoretical rate of true mental deficiency cannot be taken as an indication that the screening validly assessed either mental deficiency or ability to give satisfactory performance. The regional patterning of the rejections indicates that the screening assessed primarily the individual's educational background.

148

TABLE 1
REJECTION RATES PER THOUSAND REGISTRANTS, BY REGION AND RACE
[From Ginzberg and Bray (87)]

Region	Total	White	Negro
Total U. S.	40	25	152
New England	17	16	65
Middle Atlantic	15	11	67
Southeast	97	52	202
Southwest	60	54	107
Central	14	12	61
Northwest	14	13	40
Far West	10	9	50

The regional patterning of rejections is indeed striking as can be seen in Table 1. Ginzberg and Bray (87, p. 43) comment:

Several striking facts are revealed by this table. First, the rate of rejection in the Southeast is almost ten times as large as that in the Far West. All of the regions of the country except two have a total rejection rate between 10 and 17 per 1,000 examined; the Southeast and the Southwest have rates of 97 and 60, respectively. Although the range is less for the white population, it is still striking. The Far West has a rejection rate of 9 while the Southeast and the Southwest each have a rate of more than 50. The Negro rate is so much larger in every region that it might appear to be a different population; the over-all Negro rate is just over six times the white rate. However, there is evidence within the Negro distribution to suggest that the population is basically parallel. One finds, for instance, that the rate of rejection for Negroes in the Northwest and the Far West is actually below the white rate in the Southeast and the Southwest. Even in the other three regions—New England, Middle Atlantic, and Central, the Negro rate is only slightly above the white rate in the South. The sixfold difference in total rates between Negroes and whites results from the exceptionally high rejection rate for Negroes in the Southeast and the lower but still high rate in the Southwest. The most extreme regional and racial differences are between the rejection rate for whites in the Far West of 9 per 1,000, or less than one per cent, and the rate of 202 per 1,000, or more than 20 per cent, for Negroes in the Southeast. Unless there were evidence that there are gross differences in mental capacity among various racial and ethnic groups, here is an overwhelming demonstration that the results of the screening examination reflected primarily differences in the educational and environmental opportunities in different regions.

Although similar rejection rates have been tabulated 'and analyzed by various experts, all of the analyses to date have been limited either to national totals, regional comparisons, or state comparisons. These comparisons shed considerable light upon the problem of the illiterate and the poorly educated youth of the country, but a more thorough understanding of the problem awaits an analysis of smaller geographic units which might bring out the range of specific factors likely to contribute to high or low rejection rates.

On the basis of Selective Service sample data, we prepared two detailed maps. The first presents the rate of rejections for mental deficiency for white registrants in each of the more than 3,000 counties throughout the United States. The second map is necessarily less extensive; it shows the Negro rejection rates for Eastern counties having at least 100 Negroes in our sample. Nearly all other counties in the nation had too few Negroes examined to compute a rate. Exceptions were a few large urban counties.

The most general finding that emerges from the study of rejection rates on a county basis is the general gradation from low to high rates rather than abrupt changes. In a large number of cases this gradualness ignores state boundaries, suggesting that local factors play the predominant part in determining the differential rates. There is, however, contrary evidence which suggests that in some instances state policies are determining. Sharp differences are conspicuous between Mississippi and the bordering states, and between the western and northwestern counties of Texas and the much higher rates in the neighboring states. Much the same contrast is observed between the higher rates in West Virginia and those in the border counties of Ohio and Pennsylvania, and in the border counties of Kentucky and Virginia.

The map of county rejection rates for Negro registrants in the Southeast helps to bring certain generalizations to the surface. An outstanding fact is that every county in South Carolina, without exception, had a Negro rejection rate of 175 per 1,000 or more. The situation in Alabama was a little better. The counties in which the cities of Birmingham and Mobile are located show, however, relatively low rates. The other states show greater variation between high, medium, and low county rejection rates. There is no doubt that the degree of urbanization is a major factor related to lower rejection rates of Negroes, just as for whites. On the basis of sample studies, the other two factors which seem frequently to be connected with relatively low rejection rates for Negroes are the economic prosperity of the county and a relatively low proportion of Negroes in the total population. There are, however, a considerable number of counties where such specific factors as local white or Negro leadership, or special efforts by outside groups, such as foundations interested in Negro education, apparently are important. Such factors may be at work where the rejection rate for a particular county or group of counties is low in

comparison to others which are broadly similar on an economic and
demographic basis.

We have presented but a small fraction of Ginzberg and Bray's analysis
and comments. From what we have presented above, in addition to the
wealth of other data contained in the book, it seems justified to conclude
that rates of rejection for mental deficiency were affected by *at least* three
factors: regional-cultural differences, minority group membership, and rate
of expenditure for educational facilities. Let us now turn to the interpretation and research problems which such a conclusion suggests.

B. The Diagnostic Criteria of Mental Deficiency

A cursory review of the literature in mental deficiency will quickly reveal that one cannot at all be sure that different researchers employ similar criteria in the diagnosis of mental deficiency (225). The criteria which
probably have received most acceptance—if only a token acceptance—are as
follows:

1. The mentally defective individual is one whose mental defect existed
at or shortly after birth.

2. The mental defect manifests itself in intellectual and social deficiencies which prevent the individual from solving problems to the degree
that other individuals of similar age are capable of doing.

3. Because of the social and intellectual deficiencies, manifestations of a
basic central nervous system defect, the individual is and always will be in
need to some degree of the guidance of others.

4. Mental deficiency is essentially an incurable condition.

The diagnosis of mental deficiency clearly requires the presence of central
nervous system pathology. Within this group, however, there is tremendous
variation in degree and site of pathology and, of great practical importance,
in the degree to which normal intellectual and social development are
possible. For purposes of this report we shall use the term mental deficiency
or mental defect to refer to those individuals who have demonstrable central
nervous system pathology of a kind and to a degree which probably rules
out normal social and intellectual functioning. This, of course, involves in
young children the prediction of status at maturity, which in some cases it
is difficult to do. It should also be explicitly stated that although the diagnosis of mental deficiency implies irreversibility of the condition, it clearly
does not rule out that in the future we will learn how to prevent entirely

certain types of mental deficiency or bypass the drastic effects by early detection (e.g., galactosemia, phenylketonuria).

We feel it is important to differentiate between mental deficiency and mental retardation. Mentally retarded individuals—the majority of Ginzberg and Bray's "uneducated," the majority of those in special classes, and the majority of our "high grade" institutionalized cases—these individuals presumably do not have any central nervous system pathology.[2] They almost invariably come from the lowest social classes. In fact, the frequent practice of labelling these individuals "subcultural" reflects the fact that their functioning reflects cultural rather than constitutional variables.[3] The low test scores of these individuals cannot be considered a reflection of intellectual *potential*. The bulk of them are capable of leading an independent social existence, as many follow-up studies well indicate. The need to differentiate between what we have called mental deficiency and mental retardation has been recognized by many workers in the field. Kanner (146) has put it in the following way:

> 1. *Absolute feeblemindedness.* One variety consists of individuals so markedly deficient in their cognitive, affective, and constructively conative potentialities that they would stand out as defectives in any existing civilization. They are designated as idiots and imbeciles. They would be equally helpless and ill-adapted in a society of savants and in a society of savages. They are not only deficient intellectually but deficient in every sphere of mentation. They are the truly, absolutely, irreversibly feebleminded or mentally deficient in every sense of the word. The most carefully planned therapeutic and education efforts will not succeed in helping them to function self-dependently, without the need for protecting supervision. They continue throughout their

---

[2] The familial defective (variously called the Kallikak or garden-variety, or subcultural defective) represent the bulk of the "high grade" cases in our institutional population. They differ in no fundamental respect from the bulk of the mentally retarded in the community. We think it misleading to label, as is traditionally done, the institutionalized mentally retarded as mentally defective. This problem is discussed further in Chapter XVIII.

[3] The use of the term "subcultural" in referring to the mentally retarded as a group is not strictly in accord with anthropological usage because these individuals, found as they are in places varying both geographically and culturally, do not and cannot share common cultural experiences. Reference to the mentally retarded as "subcultural" does at least direct attention to the most important aspect of the problem. However, one sometimes gets the impression that a value judgment is implied in the use of the term, i.e., the subculture is inferior to our own middle-class one. The danger in such a value judgment is that by branding the subculture as inferior, one is likely to misperceive or misinterpret the behavior of individuals in the subculture, that is, it becomes difficult to understand the subculture in its own terms (see Chapter XIV).

lives in need of custodial care, the custody being carried on by relatives or in appropriate institutions.

Even in this group, the assumption of irreversibility has recently been challenged. Disregarding the sensational claims made in newspaper reports and popular magazine articles, one must still await further and more conclusive results of experiments with glutamic acid. So far, sporadic additions of a few points to the intelligence quotient have not managed to lift even the most responsive patients out of the absoluteness of their defects. At least for the time being, the enthusiasm about glutamic acid is a little too reminiscent of the promises made not too long ago with regard to the "brightening" effects of cortin in mongolians.

2. *Relative feeblemindedness.* Another, larger variety is made up of individuals whose limitations are definitely related to the standards of the particular society which surrounds them. In less complex, less intellectually centered societies, they would have no trouble in attaining and retaining equality of realizable ambitions. Some might even be capable of gaining superiority by virtue of assets other than those measured by the intelligence tests. They could make successful peasants, hunters, fishermen, tribal dancers. They can, in our own society, achieve proficiency as farm hands, factory workers, miners, waitresses, charwomen. . . .

The members of this group are not truly and absolutely feebleminded or *mentally* deficient. Their principal shortcoming is a greater or lesser degree of inability to comply with the *intellectual* requirements of their society. In other respects, they may be as mature or immature, stable or unstable, secure or insecure, placid or moody, aggressive or submissive as any other member of the human species. Their "deficiency" is an *ethnologically determined phenomenon* relative to the local standards and, even within those standards, relative to educational postulates, vocational ambitions, and family expectations. They are "subcultural" in our society but may not be even that in a different, less sophisticated setting.

It is for this group that the suggested designation of intellectual inadequacy seems more appropriate than any other existing term.

From the standpoint of etiology, diagnostic clarity, prognosis, social implications, educational orientation, and research planning, it can only be a source of confusion if mentally defective and mentally retarded individuals are not differentiated from each other.

Stating the above criteria is far easier than describing the procedures, technical and interpretive, which would allow one to assess validly each of the criteria. Perhaps the most incisive (but too succinct) discussion of this problem is that by Jastak (38, 130, 132). He points out the limitations both of the social and conventional statistical criteria and presents a schema which, while not as yet substantiated by published research, has the definite virtue of focussing on and clinically illustrating the most significant problems: (a) the development of more pure measures of intellectual factors which are more numerous than conventional tests suggest; (b) similarly, the development of better measures of personality variables; (c) the absolute necessity of considering the relation between intellectual and personality factors. What is unique in Jastak's approach is the significance he attaches to the highest score an individual obtains on a particular factor *regardless of his scores on other tests*, i.e., even if the score on the particular factor is far above all other scores, it is regarded as an approximation of the individual's capacity. As Jastak puts it (130, p. 372):

> In agreement with most psychologists, we regard intellect as a capacity, potentiality, or latent power. Webster defines capacity as "the power of receiving, containing, or absorbing; extent of room or space, content, volume; maximum output." Concepts of capacity incorporate the idea of use to the fullest extent or maximum potential. This notion of capacity is as useful in psychology as it is elsewhere in science and in daily life. To determine the capacity of a water tank, its maximum volume is obtained. It would be senseless to take repeated measurements of water actually contained therein, average them, and regard the average as the capacity of the tank. The analogous procedure in psychometrics in the form of *IQ* is equally misleading as a measure of capacity.
>
> Fortunately, there is in every psychometric record an ability through which a person's latent intellectual power may be adequately approximated. It is the ability which yields the highest score. . . .
>
> Intellect is not what is, but what could or would be if everything else were normal. As everything else is rarely normal, intellectual power remains incompletely consummated in nearly all people. Some individuals function close to their capacities, others far below them because of abnormal character traits, personality disturbances, and environmental deprivations. We call this index of latent potential the altitude quotient. Even though it is a maximum score, the altitude quotient underestimates rather than overestimates the potentialities of a great many people suffering from severe personality abberations or from lack of educational opportunities.

In Jastak's approach the significance of an individual's pattern of intellectual abilities—in terms of present or future social, vocational, or educational functioning—depends on their relationship to personality variables. Once this relationship is understood, it will be possible to formulate an appropriate program for the individual. Jastak's approach, which is really an outline for research, deserves the strongest support. Jastak is rare in that he has taken seriously in his writing and research the lethal criticisms which over the years have been made against conventional tests and *IQ* scores—in addition, he has been bold enough to make suggestions about tests and diagnostic criteria which, if they are not correct in all respects, are of a most constructive nature.

It is probably entirely justified to assume that the above criteria were not employed in the large bulk of the 716,000 "uneducated" men who were diagnosed as mentally deficient. First, the evidence is rather compelling that many research workers in the field, who presumably should know better, base their diagnoses either on narrow criteria (e.g., test scores) or on a superficial evaluation of the several criteria (225). Second, the large majority of selective service physicians were undoubtedly not trained and experienced in making such diagnosis and the few who were undoubtedly did not have time to evaluate the above criteria. It is not surprising, therefore, that the number of rejectees was 100 per cent more than would be expected.

To the student of mental deficiency what we have thus far presented and discussed is neither terribly new nor surprising. In addition, the relevance of the Ginzberg and Bray study for an understanding of the rôle of psychological and cultural factors in the causation of subnormal functioning has, at this point at least, not been made clear. We have begun our report in the way we have in order to make the following point: since we are dealing with a problem which is defined and assessed differently by different people (i.e., between and within the different disciplines), it is not only extremely difficult to evaluate certain aspects of the problem but it forces one to be very pessimistic about the fruitfulness of future research. This condition is certainly not peculiar to the field of subnormal functioning, witness the diversity of opinion which existed, and to a somewhat lesser extent still exists, in psychiatry concerning the descriptive and etiological aspects of adult and childhood schizophrenia, hysteria, and various so-called borderline and latent psychotic and neurotic states. But whereas these problems in psychiatry occupy the interest both of the trainee and practitioner in the field, and have given rise to a good deal of research, the complexity of the problem of subnormal functioning nowhere receives such attention. It is our opinion that until the nature and standards of training in subnormal functioning are formulated, and implemented in our university and research centers, our basic knowledge about subnormal functioning will not increase perceptibly. It is also our opinion that until such a development takes place the importance of the field of subnormal functioning for such disciplines as anthropology, psychology, and psychiatry will not become apparent. It is our hope that by the end of this report the importance of such a rapprochement will be a little clearer.

C. The Cultural Factor

It will be remembered that on the basis of their detailed analysis, Ginzberg and Bray concluded that "The regional patterning of the rejections indicates that the screening assessed primarily the individual's educational background." It is, of course, impossible to determine for how many of the rejectees this generalization holds. It is probably justified to assume that a fair proportion of the 716,000 rejectees for mental deficiency would clearly meet comprehensive criteria for such a diagnosis. Our concern here is with that proportion where educational retardation was the important, if not the sole, factor in the diagnosis.

We might approach the problem by asking a deceptively simple question: What accounts for the somewhat fantastic differences in rejection rate between different sections of the country? Concretely, why should the rejection rate be 97 per thousand registrants in the Southeast and 10 per thousand in the Far West? Omitting the Negro registrants the figures are 52 for the Southeast and 9 for the Far West. The fact that these regions differ strikingly in expenditure for educational facilities tempts one to the conclusion that the rejection rates are *caused* by differences in educational opportunities. In a broad sociological frame of reference such a conclusion has meaning, although even in such a frame of reference it is dangerous to use correlational data as a basis for determining causation. As soon as one realizes that the two areas differ in many respects other than the quantity and quality of educational resources, the possibility arises that we are dealing, generally speaking, with people who differ culturally in some important respects. To be more concrete, we put the following questions:

1. How do these people differ in their view of the function of education? Are there differences in conception of the relationship between schooling and later adjustment in the society in which they live?

2. Are there differences in the kind and extent of personal rewards which are available through education? What are the differences in the punishments which go with the avoidance of or failure in schooling?

3. Are there differences in how these people conceive of "success" and "achievement"?

One could raise many more questions, and in connection with other problems where cultural differences exist we shall find it necessary to do so. On the basis of the few questions posed above, we wish to suggest that the relationship between educational opportunity and educational (and intellectual) attainment or level is a very complex one in which the quantity and quality of educational resources may be symptomatic of a cultural constellation which is primary in the sense that it gives rise both to the educational resources and to the attitudes toward education. One might pose the question in this way: Would educationally retarded individuals in the Southeast and Far West react to or conceive of their retardation in similar ways or would there be marked differences reflecting the different cultural contexts in which they have developed? One could, of course, ask the same question in terms of how educationally retarded are viewed and reacted to by the non-retarded individuals in each region.

We should reiterate at this point that we are concerned with that indeterminable group of rejectees who could not enter the armed forces because their degree of educational retardation was so extreme as to be labelled mentally deficient by people in their own regions. There is every reason to believe, as the data presented by Ginzberg and Bray suggest, that a large number of men with similar or somewhat less educational retardation were inducted into the armed forces. We are, obviously, dealing with a staggering national problem. How this problem is met and handled will, of course, depend in part on our scientific knowledge. On the assumption that we are dealing with a complex problem—one that cannot, for example, be explained simply in terms of genetics—we have to guard against our tendency to oversimplify. For example, we earlier raised questions concerning the relationship between regional differences in educational retardation and possible cultural differences in conceptions of education. (On the basis of Ginzberg and Bray's data one could pose the problem in terms of intra-regional differences.) Let us assume that an anthropological study would reveal significant cultural differences in conceptions of education. We would then be faced with at least three problems: How does a distinctive cultural factor affect the psychological development, content, and motivational structure of the individual? What are the differences between individuals in the different subgroups of each area? In the sphere of educational achievement, how does one explain those who are atypical for their group?

It should be clear by now that we are dealing with the problem of the relationship between performance level and capacity, a problem of tremendous import in such fields as genetics, psychology, anthropology, psychiatry, and education. It seems also clear that the problem cannot be adequately handled by any one of these disciplines.

D. THE EFFECTS OF SCHOOLING

It is our opinion that one of the implications of the Ginzberg and Bray study—an implication which we have attempted to elaborate above—is that educational retardation is not likely to be significantly decreased by building new and more schools and hiring more teachers. If future research should establish that educational retardation and quantity and quality of educational resources are in fact symptomatic of prevailing attitudes and experiences in a particular subculture, then sheer expenditure of money for buildings and personnel should not be expected to have a marked effect. Unless such expenditures reflect some kind of cultural change, and take into account the cultural setting in which changes are hoped for, a good deal of time and money may be wasted. We are not saying that better and more adequate educational facilities *per se* have no effect on the population concerned; there is no evidence that such an effect takes place. For example, Wheeler (290) reported a study in which group intelligence tests were administered to over 3,000 children in 40 mountain schools of East Tennessee and the results compared with those obtained with children in the same areas and largely of the same families similarly studied 10 years earlier. Wheeler found that the children tested in the second study were superior at all ages and all grades to those tested 10 years earlier.[4] He pointed out that in the decade (1930-1940) between the two studies "there has been definite improvement in the economic, social and educational status of this mountain area." It is deserving of reiteration in light of our previous discussion that improvement in educational status seemed related to, if not a function of, more widespread cultural changes. Without knowledge of the details and dynamics of cultural change, it is difficult to assess the significances of a general increase in test scores in terms of psychological structure, varieties of problem-solving situations, and the range and explanation of individual differences. For example, in Wheeler's study we have little real understanding not only of the apparent increase in test scores but

---

[4]This increase in scores has been reported by others and Anastasi (5) presents an excellent discussion of some of the problems involved in explaining such increases.

of the finding that in 1940, as in the first study, there is a steady and dramatic decrease in *IQ* as one goes up the grades—a finding which is not completely explicable by the nature of the test, and which is similar to that found in other studies of educationally backward areas (5).

That the influence of schooling, even when viewed from a narrow psychometric approach, is not a simple one can be seen by a Swedish study reported by Husén (125) as well as in an earlier one by Lorge (172). In Husén's recent study, his subjects were a group of 613 boys in a Swedish town to whom a group intelligence test had been administered in school when they were approximately 9½ years of age. At the time of the first test all subjects had received the same amount of school training. Ten years later this sample was retested at induction to military service. Husén found (*a*) the mean *IQ* scores were found to be slightly lowered for those that had not gone beyond primary school while they were raised for others in proportion to four levels of additional academic training; (*b*) when the data were analyzed according to levels of ability (using test scores at CA 9½) it was found that those with the highest scores retained their level, even if the effect of schooling was excluded, while those with the lowest scores regressed downward in the statistical sense. Husén points out that the calculated regression effect in the case of those with the lowest scores should have been upward. In analyzing the effect of secondary schooling, which automatically excluded those with initial below-average scores, Husén found positive gains in test score whereas the calculated regression effect was in the downward direction.

Although Husén's study suggests that amount of schooling has important effect, we do not know how a variable like "amount of schooling" is reflected in the psychological structure of individuals differing in intellectual status—nor do we know how amount of schooling and intellectual status interact with or are reflections of certain cultural factors. For example, it may be that the failure of low-scoring individuals to show expected gains is due to factors other than amount of schooling. It may also be that the problem-solving behavior of low-scoring individuals outside the testing situation is significantly better than in a testing situation. There is fair agreement in the research literature that the adult level of non-test problem-solving behavior of individuals who as children received "retarded" scores is frequently better than predicted (8, 14, 40, 70, 151, 173, 189).

When one views the problem of the relationship between capacity and functioning in terms of the interaction of psychological processes and cultural settings, one soon realizes the inadequacies and dangers of conclusions based on test scores. This, of course, is a banal conclusion. But when one reviews the literature on the nature and causes of mental and educational retardation, it becomes apparent that at least *four* assumptions are implicitly made about intelligence tests: (*a*) intelligence is *a* thing; (*b*) this thing can be measured by *a* test or tests; (*c*) the testing situation is a representative sample of all problem-solving situations; (*d*) that we know enough about psychological processes and development in relation to broader cultural variables to guard ourselves against the drawing of invalid conclusions concerning capacity and functioning. With the hope that we will not, at best, be considered rank pessimists and, at worst, nihilistic and destructive critics, it is our opinion that the first assumption is untrue, the third probably untrue, and the fourth likewise untrue. Insofar as the second assumption is concerned we do believe that a more comprehensive theoretical formulation of intellectual functioning than we now have will be capable of being evaluated by testing procedures, a problem which will be discussed in a later section. Suffice it to say at this point that recent studies on the nature and varieties of intellectual capacities strongly suggest that much of our present conceptions, and more of our practices, will have to be scrapped if our understanding is to be extended.

Two Dutch studies by de Groot (61, 62) are suggestive of the rôle of cultural disruption on educational and intellectual status. In one study his subjects were 13-14-year-old candidates of a boys' industrial school, one group from the pre-war years and the other from the years 1944 and 1945. He found a significant drop in mean intelligence test score from the pre- to post-war groups and attributed this to the disruption of educational facilities during the war. He also found that tests closely related to school training showed more decline from 1944 to 1947 than tests unrelated to schooling, supporting his contention that lack of training was responsible. In a second study de Groot found that the average *IQ* for classes of applicants for the years 1948, 1949, and 1950 had already achieved prewar level. We have presented de Groot's studies not only because they suggest that educational deprivation is related to discrepancy between potential and functioning but also because it is clear that the educational deprivation was one aspect of widespread cultural disruption in which many spheres of an individual's behavior were affected.

E. The Uneducated in the War

In order to amplify some of the points raised above, and to make concrete some of the directions that future research might take, we turn to Ginzberg and Bray's study of a group of men who had been accepted by the armed services but who were illiterate or semi-illiterate. These men had been through a special education training program set up by the military, a program that became increasingly larger as the standards for acceptance into the armed forces became progressively lower. The men sent to the Special Training Units were of two kinds: those who were formally classified as illiterate and those who scored low (Group V) on the Army General Classification Test. Re the latter Ginzberg and Bray state: "These men were considered 'slow learners' but in reality were mainly those who had had only a little more education than those called illiterate." The problem of illiteracy confronting the military can be seen from the following (87, p. 77):

> More than 400,000 illiterates served within the Armed Forces during World War II. The combined group of illiterates and poorly educated who saw active duty totaled almost 700,000. To this must be added more than 700,000 additional persons, the vast majority of whom were rejected outright for military service because of serious educational deficiencies. In short, the findings which emerge are directly relevant for appraising a group of almost one and one-half million persons out of a total of 18 million registrants who were screened. Clearly we are dealing with a significant sector of the nation's manpower resources.

In setting up the Special Training Program certain specific goals were sought (87, p. 69):

> 1. To teach the men to read at least at a fourth-grade level so that they would be able to comprehend bulletins, written orders and directives, and basic Army publications.
> 2. To give the men sufficient language skill so that they would be able to use and understand the everyday oral and written language necessary for getting along with officers and men.
> 3. To teach the men to do number work at a fourth-grade level, so they could understand their pay accounts and laundry bills, conduct their business in the *PX*, and perform in other situations requiring arithmetic skill.
> 4. To facilitate the adjustment of the men to military training and Army life.
> 5. To enable the men to understand in a general way why it was necessary for this country to fight a war against Germany, Japan, and Italy.

The maximum amount of time that an individual could remain in the course was 120 days. "Approximately 40 per cent of the men graduated in less than 30 days. Almost 80 per cent graduated in less than 60 days. Only a very few, less than 11,000 out of 255,000 graduates, remained in a Special Training Unit more than 90 days" (87, p. 70).

Let us make the following assumptions: (a) more than a few of those formally classified as illiterates were not intellectually retarded; (b) more than a few of the "slow learners" were diagnostic errors—their true *IQ* was above that indicated by Army test scores; (c) more than a few of the graduates did not reach the goals previously indicated and did not in fact pass the examination in reading and arithmetic required for graduation. Making the allowances indicated by these assumptions we think it not unreasonable to make the further assumption that the above figures suggest that the *rate of learning* of more than a few men was far beyond that which one would expect from their potential as inferred from test scores. Put in another way: the performance of more than a few was better than an evaluation of the potential or capacity had indicated. Here again one cannot avoid inquiring about the possible factors which can produce an apparent discrepancy between capacity and functioning. In order to do so it would be helpful if one described some of the background characteristics of the sub-sample of 400 men whose Army records were scrutinized by Ginzberg and Bray (87, p. 80):

> Our sample, it will be recalled, consisted of 400 men: 200 white and 200 Negro, half drawn from the deep South and half from the border states and the North, half inducted in the latter part of 1943, and the other half in the last six months of 1944.
>
> All but three of the 400 men were born in the United States. Since, at the time of the 1940 Census, almost three-fifths of the 1.5 million draft-age men with less than four years of schooling lived in small communities or on farms, it is not surprising to discover that most of our group also came from rural backgrounds. Almost three-fourths were born in communities of under 5,000 population. More than one-third, however, had migrated from their birth places. When inducted, 56 per cent lived in communities under 5,000 population; a little more than a fifth were inducted from cities of more than 100,000.
>
> Slightly under half, 179, were 20 years of age or less when inducted; 275 were 25 or less; and just under 85 per cent of the entire group were 30 or less. Thirty-nine were between the ages of 31 and 35, and 14 between 36 and 38. The median age for the entire group was 21.5 years. The median age of the Negroes, however, was 2.4 years higher than for the whites.

There were no conspicuous differences between the years of school completed by the whites and the Negroes, but the "northern" group (Camp Atterbury, Indiana) showed a higher average than the "southern" (Camp Shelby, Mississippi, and Fort Benning, Georgia) group. The men inducted in 1944 also had a higher average number of years of schooling than the group inducted in 1943. The most striking fact about the educational background of the group is that 55 per cent had completed more than four years of schooling. Only 3 per cent had never attended school. Almost 5 per cent had more than eight grades of schooling, and more than 25 per cent had reached at least the seventh grade. In light of these facts, it is surprising to find that of the men for whom information was available, 228 were designated as illiterate, while only 69 were classified as literate and sent to special training because of a low score on the Army General Classification Test.

More than half of the group, 226 men, had once been farmers, although less than half were farmers when inducted. Just more than two-thirds of the whites had farming backgrounds, but less than half of the Negroes. Only about a third of the Northern Negroes but almost 80 per cent of the Southern whites had been farmers at some time.

Not only is it clear from the above that these men came from rural areas where educational resources are generally inferior, but also that many of these men either learned nothing or little from their schooling, or that whatever they did absorb during school was of no significance in their later lives and consequently was "unlearned." That an individual can go through eight grades of school and then at the age of 20 appear to be illiterate may be explained in different ways; that the same individual at age 20 can in a very short period of time demonstrate a fair amount of educational progress increases the complexity of the problem. We feel that we do not have a basis for choosing among different explanations. We do feel, however, that it is justified to suggest that we are not dealing primarily with an educational problem in the narrow sense of the word but one of motivation and attitude both of which cannot be understood unless studied in the cultural matrix in which they arise.

Also deserving of discussion is the fact that a fair number of the men had migrated from smaller to larger communities. In terms of tested intelligence and educational status it would seem from this study that the larger urban centers tend to attract inferior individuals, but as will be discussed in Chapter XIV, this generalization is not supported by all studies of the problem. In terms of the intellectual capacities of these migrants we feel such a conclusion to be premature. It may be that the capacities of these individuals are not essentially inferior. It may also be, for example, that their capacities are inferior but that the discrepancy between performance level and capacity need not be as large as it is. That the problem of selective migration is by no means a simple one can be seen when one realizes that we do not know either why the migration or the effects of it. Further characteristics of the 400 men studied by Ginzberg and Bray (87, p. 81) follow:

> About 55 per cent of the group were single when inducted. Just under 40 per cent were married. Fourteen men were separated, seven were divorced, and three were widowers.
>
> In 94 per cent of the records there was no evidence that the men had ever run into any trouble with law-enforcement authorities.
>
> In summary, almost all were native-born, and the majority were in their early twenties and came from rural backgrounds. At least one man in four had migrated to a larger community before induction into the Army. Very few had failed to attend school at all, and the majority had gone at least to the fifth grade. One is forced to conclude that the education received was poor and that the men had retained only a small amount of what they had once been taught.
>
> Although more than half of the group were employed as farmers or common laborers at the time of induction, a considerable number were holding semi-skilled jobs, and a few were employed at skilled work. With very few exceptions, these men were self-supporting. Considering their background and education, their earnings were about what might be expected for the kinds of jobs they held.
>
> The fact that almost half were married or had been married reflects the tendency among the rural population of the Southeast toward early marriage. It also indicates, however, that the men earned enough to assume the responsibilities of the head of a household. It is particularly noteworthy as far as we could tell, that only 6 per cent had police records of any kind.
>
> It would appear, then, that the vast majority of these men had made a reasonable adjustment to civilian life. They were economically self-sufficient and socially responsible. This does not deny that the group might have contained a few "floaters." But if account is taken of the background from which they came, the type of education which they received, and the kinds of employment open to them, the civilian adjustment of most of the group must be considered adequate. At least there is no evidence to the contrary.

Table 2 contains information concerning the occupational status of the men at induction. Since we know that these men were either illiterate or low scorers on an intelligence test, it is not surprising that they had the

TABLE 2

OCCUPATIONS AT INDUCTION OF MEN ASSIGNED TO SPECIAL TRAINING UNITS
[From Ginzberg and Bray (87)]

Occupation	Total	White		Negro	
		North	South	North	South
Farmer	173	43	60	22	48
Non-Farm:					
Laborer	90	22	13	29	26
Janitor, porter, busboy, etc.	36	3	4	21	8
Truck driver, chauffeur,					
auto mechanic, etc.	44	12	6	15	11
Factory operative	26	11	8	5	2
Coal miner	13	7	2	4	0
Craftsman	7	1	3	0	3
Other	11	1	4	4	2
Total non-farm	227	57	40	78	52
Grand total	400	100	100	100	100

kinds of jobs they did. However, it is one thing to say this is expected and another thing to provide an explanation. In one sense it is perfectly correct to say that these men held the jobs they did *because* of their intellectual and educational status—these are the kinds of jobs available to them. But this brings us back to the recurring question: What are the factors determining the intellectual and educational status of these men? Again leaving this question aside—primarily because our current knowledge only permits us to suggest, as indicated earlier, what some of these factors and their interaction might be—we would like to pose another question: How does one evaluate an individual's problem-solving behavior outside of a test situation? Throughout the course of the day in the life of any individual he is presented with problems the solutions to which vary in the complexity of response they require for resolution. Not only may we commonsensically assume variation through the course of a day but also among problem-solving activities in different spheres of functioning, e.g., educational, vocational, sexual, etc. Although more often than not there is a fair degree of variation or "scatter" within an individual's own test performance, it is surprising how frequently we assume that the level of problem-solving behavior outside the test situation is fairly even. When it is remembered that our discussion concerns those men whose performance in the Special Training Units suggests a capacity beyond that indicated by their test scores and educational status, we think it justified to raise the possibility that the previous non-test problem-solving behavior of these men was in some spheres or activities better than their test scores or educational status suggests. Unfortunately, there have been no systematic investigations of this problem. It is apparent that there are extremely thorny problems involved in the observing, sampling, and recording of non-test problem-solving behavior— aside from the problem of quantifying samples of behavior obtained in situations over which we have no control. But if problem-solving behavior in test situations cannot be assumed to be representative of all problem-solving, the lack of research in this problem can no longer be excused.

In the context of the present discussion it is important to report briefly the results of the analysis of the military records of the subsample of 400 men.

> To check on the reasonableness of our evaluation of the military performance of the uneducated, the graduates of the Special Training Units were compared with a control group consisting of average soldiers whose education and mentality were sufficient to enable them to enter basic training immediately after induction into the Army. This control group was constructed by selecting the man of the same race whose serial number was next higher than that of each man in the Special Training Unit group. If the man with the next higher number had also been assigned to a Special Training Unit, the man with the nearest higher number was selected. The control sample was not representative of the Army as a whole, but permitted a comparison between men inducted from the same localities who differed primarily with respect to their level of education.

> While 26 per cent of the 400 Special Training Unit men had less than four years of schooling, this was true of only one per cent of the control group. Only 2 per cent of the whites and 8 per cent of the Negroes in the Special Training Unit group, but 55 per cent of the control group had attended high school. Five per cent of the control group had attended college. Obviously, there was a significant difference in the educational background of the two groups. With respect to occupational background, the size of the communities in which they had been born, the extent to which they had migrated, and their place of residence at the time when they were inducted, however, the differences between the two groups were not substantial. . . .

> In order to judge the relative over-all performance of the Special Training Unit and control groups, a summary card was prepared for each man. Care was taken that the cards would contain no hint whether the case was a Special Training Unit graduate or a control case, or whether the man was white or Negro. These cards were then shuffled and sorted into the five groups: very good, good, acceptable, not acceptable, and non-chargeable. . . .

This objective comparison showed that just under a quarter of the men of the control group were very good, a third were good, another third were acceptable. Only 7 per cent of this group were not acceptable, and 3 per cent were non-chargeable. Only 9 per cent of the men of the Special Training Unit group were very good, but slightly under a third were good, and almost half were acceptable. Twelve per cent were not acceptable, and 3 per cent were non-chargeable.

This comparison demonstrates conclusively that, granted our criteria, the control group contained many more very good soldiers than the Special Training Unit graduates. One of our criteria, however, was rank, and it is to be expected that those with more pre-service education would more often qualify for higher non-commissioned-officer assignments. It was, in any case, not expected that the Special Training Unit graduates would include a great many outstanding soldiers. The question was rather whether any appreciable number would perform adequately and represent a clear gain to the Army. This question is answered unequivocally. Eighty-five per cent of the graduates performed acceptably or better as compared to 90 per cent of the control group. Clearly, at a time when the Armed Forces needed men badly, they were able with a small investment to turn many illiterates and poorly educated men into acceptable soldiers.

It should be noted that Ginzberg and Bray were quite aware of the many problems involved in utilizing and categorizing military records. Even if one were to assume that the "true" picture of the records of the men from the Special Training Units was not as favorable as Ginzberg and Bray describe, it would still be reasonable to conclude that the problem-solving behavior of many of the men was better than objective educational and test data indicated. It would repay the reader to study the 22 case records which Ginzberg and Bray present in one of the chapters in the book. In more than a few of these cases the discrepancy between problem-solving behavior in and outside the test situation is marked.

We have previously noted that the rate of learning of many of the men in the Special Training Units was surprising. Unfortunately we do not have the data or observations with which to evaluate such a conclusion. However, the following partial description of the Training Unit has some important implications for future research on this problem (87, p. 71).

A "cadre" or staff of enlisted personnel form the basis for all instruction in the Special Training Unit. Each man has been selected for the position on the basis of his academic background as well as being a capable military instructor. With but few exceptions, all of the instructors are college graduates, many of them possess Master's degrees and a few holding various Doctor's degrees. Formerly they were connected with civilian school systems, ranging from the elementary through the college level. The unit is staffed by 26 officers qualified both academically and militarily.

Experience has shown that men of the calibre that are received in the Special Training Unit learn more and faster if they are allowed to absorb the training given with the same group of men for the entire period they are here. For that reason, men are assigned to barracks and remain there until they leave. One classroom is set up on each of the two floors of the building and provided with tables, chairs, blackboards, and other instructional aid pertaining to the type of work being covered. For a short period of time after entrance into the barracks, some men are prone to exhibit shyness due to the fact that they have never associated closely with other men.

Gradually the spirit of teamwork and coöperation are developed and within a few days the men have made an adjustment sufficient to enhance learning. Since changing from one group to another would tend to prolong the period of adjustment, that method is not employed. The military instructor, a Corporal or Sergeant, lives in the barracks with the men, eats with them and works with them and it is rare that he fails to gain the complete confidence of his men almost immediately. The instructor's job lasts 24 hours per day. During the off duty hours much of his time is taken up writing letters for the trainees or giving them advice on their personal problems. Also he will devote considerable time to additional instruction for men who are learning slower than others.

The implications of this excerpt might be put in a series of questions: What significance did these men attach to being sent to the Training Unit? Did they view the education they were now receiving differently than when they had previously been in school? What were the kinds and strengths of motivations engendered in these men by this experience? To what extent was their progress due to the fact that instruction was specifically geared to their needs? Were the attitudes of the instructors to the men different from those of the teachers they had in their previous school experiences? Was there a change of attitude on the part of these men toward education as a result of experiences after leaving school?

The above questions bring us back to a question raised earlier in the report: Both between regions which differ in cultural outlook and organization and within a particular cultural region, how are differences in attitude toward schooling related to kinds and strengths of motivations as well as quality of problem-solving behavior? Within recent years increasing recognition has been given to the rôle of middle-class values and aspirations in determining public school curricula and "climate." In addition there is now general acceptance of the conclusion that our achievement and intelligence tests contain types of items and information which unfairly penalize the lower-class child, giving us a distorted, or what may better be termed an unreliable, estimate of such a child's potentialities (55, 56, 58, 68, 106). While these broad generalizations are probably true we are far from an understanding of several aspects of the problem. For example, and as we have several times indicated, while it is important to know that certain groups differ culturally, the significance of such differences is not clear until we understand how they are reflected in such psychological variables as motivation, attitude, and problem-solving behavior. It is also important to bear in mind that any particular cultural group—however distinctive it may be from other groups—is made up of individuals who differ widely among themselves on important psychological variables—a conclusion rather well illustrated by the study of the Trukese (90). This conclusion is also supported by Lemkau in his discussion of the epidemiological aspects of mental deficiency (165):

> The social class structure of a society presents many epidemiological problems that are still far from solved. One of these that is now attracting a great deal of attention is the "nesting" of diseases of widely divergent types in a small group of families of a community. This has been illustrated most clearly, perhaps, by the St. Paul study which showed that social and health problems, including mental deficiency, were concentrated in that 6 per cent of the population which absorbed 50 per cent of the social, health, and recreational services available in the community. Similar "nesting" of diseases, including mental diseases, has been reported by Downes on the basis of sickness surveys, and by Plummer and Hinkle in surveys of industrial health problems among telephone operators, though in the last study mental deficiency does not appear to have been a factor.
>
> Although it remains clear that mental deficiency is distributed more heavily in the lower socio-economic group than in the higher, it is also clear that the defectives are not evenly distributed within the lower socio-economic group, but are concentrated, along with other diseases and social defects in particular groups of persons. More defined studies of local distribution are greatly needed and offer a challenge to epidemiologists.

From the standpoint of future research it would seem that greater attention should be given to individual differences in problem-solving behavior within distinctive cultural groups. To illustrate the direction of this suggestion: Let us take a geographical area which contributed a disproportionate number of mentally defective or mentally retarded individuals. This area may be either urban or rural. Within this area let us take a representative school where we shall focus on those children who will be entering school for the first time. Our first problem is to attempt to evaluate each child, before he begins school, in terms of those variables (psychological, familial, physical) and experiences which our current knowledge of child development indicates as important in determining the content and organization of personality. Our focus would be on the ways in which the child behaves in various spheres of his activities, the rôle of external factors in such behavior, and the developmental factors to which such behavior might be related. On the basis of such information it would be important to attempt to predict each child's response to schooling in terms of the kinds of problem-solving demands which the particular school will make and also in terms of the kinds of interpersonal relationships that are established with teacher and peers. Such a prediction would have to be based in part on intimate study of the kinds of values, restrictions, and adult personalities (e.g., teacher, principal) to which he will be exposed. The final steps in such a study would involve direct and sustained observations of the child in the school environment and the relationship of such data to the family's response to the child's new experiences.

The above is obviously not a research design in the technical sense. Each step in the above problem involves many thorny problems of a methodological and theoretical nature. We presented the illustrative problem in order to emphasize several things. First, within any distinctive cultural grouping there is much variation and our understanding of any particular form of behavior (e.g., problem-solving) will depend on our knowledge of the factors related to such individual differences. Not all children in such a study would show, for example, the same kind and level of test behavior even though as a group they would be rather different from other groups of children that could be studied. We are here asking a question which has been raised and studied with much profit in another problem area (91): Why does one child in a particular geographical area become a delinquent while another does not?

A second reason for presenting the above research problem is to reiterate a point which while obvious when stated seems not to be fully comprehended by researchers in the behavioral sciences: understanding the mentally retarded child presents problems no different than those involved in understanding other children, problem or so-called normal. The complete absence of intensive, longitudinal, psychological studies of the mentally retarded may well be a reflection of the inability of the behavioral scientist to identify himself with the problems of that large group of individuals from whom he differs so markedly intellectually and culturally. Interest in a human problem presupposes a personal identification with it. If these kinds of speculations have some degree of merit, they suggest the situation in which the cultural narrowness of the behavioral scientist prevents him not only from a proper understanding of a particular group but, as a result, of a better understanding of his own cultural background. We may be in a situation analogous to that which Davis (55) has described in his discussions of children from what he calls our "slum culture"—a culture which contributes a great number of mentally retarded individuals. He points out that the middle-class psychiatrist, working primarily with individuals in his own class and utilizing theories based on such a narrow clinical foundation, not only is prone to misinterpret the significances of the behavior of people from another class background (e.g., the slum child) but is also prevented from seeing in true perspective the ways in which his own class background has determined his theory and practice.[5]

It may well be that for many of the crucial problems in child development focusing on the mentally retarded child might be methodologically easier and ultimately more fruitful for theory than focusing either on the so-called normal or on other varieties of atypical children. For one thing such children can at least be very reliably diagnosed, even though our testing procedures can tell us little about etiological factors or the degree of discrepancy between functioning and capacity. Also, the fact that the mentally retarded are a very large group makes it likely that one can get respectable numbers of cases to fit most research designs. Finally, and perhaps most

---

[5]In this connection mention might be made of the series of studies by Redlich, Hollingshead, Myers, *et al.* (120, 121, 190, 210, 211, 215, 216, 234) of the relationships between social stratification and psychiatric disorders. In several of these studies there was found a significant relationship between social class of the patient and the type of therapy administered—psychotherapy definitely not being the treatment of choice for lower-class individuals. As these authors suggest, such findings require serious discussion because they suggest that decisions about type of therapy with lower-class individuals reflect more the cultural biases of the middle-class therapist than they do any empirical evidence concerning amenability of such people to the psychotherapeutic process. It might be added that similar biases long prevented the recognition that both the mentally retarded and defective individual could benefit from psychotherapy (225).

important, the fact that the mentally retarded come from a cultural milieu, probably rather different from that of most researchers and the experimental populations they tend to study raises the possibility that the rôle of cultural variations in producing between and within group differences will become a more integral part of theory and practice in the behavioral sciences. It is fashionable today to believe that cultural factors are important for understanding behavior and it is even fashionable to assume that our theories and practices are influenced by such factors. Unfortunately, however, since most behavioral scientists have an intimate knowledge of but one, their own, sub-culture, it is not surprising that when talking about other classes or groups we overgeneralize from our findings and never get to the point of testing conclusions which are, so to speak, class based.

In this chapter we have attempted to indicate in a general kind of way something of the extent and significance of the cultural aspects of mental retardation. We have done this not only to emphasize that the cultural factor is important but also to suggest that we are dealing with a too-long-neglected research area which should be central rather than peripheral to the social sciences. In Chapters XIV and XV we shall return to a more detailed consideration of the rôle of cultural factors in mental retardation.

XI. PROBLEM-SOLVING BEHAVIOR IN NON-TEST SITUATIONS

In a real sense part of the previous discussion has begged a question which, while central to any analysis of the problem of subnormality, has received surprisingly little attention. We refer here to the question: What do our available intelligence tests measure? From the previous chapter one could conclude that these tests to a marked degree measure educational opportunity and achievement. While it is encouraging to know that these tests are significantly correlated with these variables, the implications of such correlations are both far reaching and disturbing. Since the contents and goals of our school curricula are extremely narrow in terms of the skills and contents encompassed, we are faced with the possibility that our intelligence tests measure a very restricted range of problem solving stimuli and intellectual activities.[6] Let us put the problem in cross-cultural terms: if one were to observe daily learning activities of an urban American 10-year-old and his counterparts among the Navaho or the Alorese, one would be struck by the differences in the kinds of problem-solving stimuli and intellectual activities which would be observed. Although the differences on the stimulus side would probably be greater than on the response side (i.e., the kinds of thinking sequences required for problem solution), the important point is that any conclusion about the "intellectual performances and capacities of 10-year-olds" would be limited and even misleading if based on the observation of any one of these cultural groups. In this connection it should be recalled that in the previous chapter it was pointed out that for many children in our culture, particularly those that have been labelled mentally retarded or slow-learners, there is reason for raising the possibility that the kinds of intellectual stimuli and activities which one observes in a test or school situation may be of a different level and/or kind than one would observe outside of such a situation. In other words, there is no *a priori* basis for rejecting the possibility that the range of differences we observe cross-culturally may be found, to a lesser degree, between and within certain groups in our own culture *if a representative sample of their problem-solving behavior was obtained.* It should perhaps be made explicit that we are not equating problem-solving with all intellectual activity or thinking

---

[6]Wertheimer (288) presents some observations of problem-solving behavior in the classroom which suggest how pedagogical technique can limit the kinds of intellectual processes which the child can employ and, perhaps more important, even interfere with the learning of more productive ways of thinking.

behavior. We stress the problem-solving situation, be it a standardized one as in a test or one observed in a free situation, not only because of what we learn about the adequacy, level, and varieties of problem-solving behavior but also because it allows us to make inferences about kinds and characteristics of thought processes. Equally important is the fact that the problem-solving situation, being a clear instance of goal-directed or motivated behavior, gives us the possibility of studying the relationships between intellectual and personality variables.

That intelligence tests may be excellent indicators of educational achievement and poor indicators of non-test or non-academic intellectual activity is something to which the practicing clinician, particularly the one who has worked in an institutional setting, will readily attest. Some examples follow:

Case 1

Ginzberg and Bray (87, p. 89) describe the case of a man who was either a low scorer on the Army General Classification Test or illiterate—or both. In any event, he was one of the many who after induction was sent to one of the Special Training Units. This man subsequently received the Silver Star, one of the infrequently given medals during war. This man's behavior during combat is given in the following citation:

> At this time PFC E.S.M. was a member of a squad whose mission was to clear an enemy position of a delaying force of Germans in order to permit the remainder of the platoon to advance. PFC E.S.M., by his intrepid action, quick thinking, and deliberate coolness under fire, killed three and wounded three of the enemy, led to the capture of 20 prisoners, and paved the way for the balance of his platoon to attain their immediate objective. Suddenly he came upon a group of three Germans and quickly fired three shots. The result was two enemy killed and one wounded. Although it was daylight and there was no cover whatsoever, and the Germans in the area had opened fire upon him from all directions, he deliberately exposed himself to those dangers and with determination and boldness moved forward. Three more Germans tried to stem this individual advance, but PFC E.S.M. fired three more well aimed shots and three enemy met the same fate as their comrades. Still under fire of enemy riflemen and machine guns, he surged forward never losing sight of the fact that he had a squad in back of him. PFC E.S.M. encouraged them to move forward as he personally removed each obstacle from their path. This unusual display of outstanding individual initiative and courage so startled the surprised Germans, that the 20 remaining enemy defending this particular terrain threw up their

hands and surrendered. PFC E.S.M.'s heroic and courageous action on this occasion reflect great credit on himself and become the highest traditions of the American soldier.

If one views the described instance as a sample of problem-solving behavior, it seems not unreasonable to conclude that this soldier was capable of a completely adequate degree of sustained problem-solving activity, his previous level of performance on intelligence or achievement tests notwithstanding. That this soldier's behavior suggests that "personality" factors were probably not irrelevant to his problem-solving behavior, as indeed they never are, goes without saying.

Case 2

The second case is also from Ginzberg and Bray (87, p. 122):

E.H., a white soldier, born and still living in rural Kentucky when inducted, represents perhaps the clearest case of a man who should be classified as a very good soldier. He was inducted at the age of 19 in the summer of 1943. While being examined for registration a year previously, he fainted and fell and suffered a simple fracture and a lacerated wound, for which he was hospitalized at the local Air Force Station Hospital. Shortly after induction, he was sent to the Special Training Unit at Camp Atterbury, Indiana, where he spent two months. He had attended school for four years. The date is not given, but when E.H. took the Army General Classification Test, probably prior to his assignment to the Special Training Unit, he received the very low score of 42. After completing the special training, he was sent to the Infantry Replacement Training Center at Camp Blanding, Florida. Although many men received ratings of excellent for character and efficiency during basic training, E.H. was graded very good in character and only satisfactory in efficiency. He was trained as a rifleman. Immediately after "D Day" he was en route to the European Theater as a member of the 8th Infantry Division. He received the Combat Infantry Badge, which made him automatically eligible for the Bronze Star Medal. Moreover, he earned three Bronze Service Stars for the Campaigns in Northern France, the Rhineland, and Central Europe. But his most important achievement was the award of the Silver Star for gallantry in action, which carried the following citation:

Sgt. H., a squad leader, exposed himself to enemy small arms, mortar and artillery fire to work his way within 25 yards of an enemy machine gun position which was holding up their advance. He threw two hand grenades and then overran the positions, killing one of the enemy and wounding two others. Later, during the attack, his squad accounted for more than 30 Germans. Sgt. H.'s great courage, coolness under fire, and devotion to duty were an inspiration to his men.

Although we do not know the kinds of intellectual activities or problem-solving behaviors involved in being a squad leader, more particularly, a successful squad leader under conditions of stress, it again seems not unreasonable to conclude that this man's intellectual activity is not predictable either from his meager educational achievements or very low test score.

Case 3

Another case (224) describes a girl who had been institutionalized when she was 15 years of age. On a battery of tests several years later her mental age ranged between 10 and 11 years, and on achievement tests her grade placement in reading was 3-9, in spelling 3-0, and in arithmetic 4-9. At the time of psychological testing this girl had been working for some time in the hospital laboratory. After one year of such work she was able to perform the following tasks:

1. Sterilization and chemical cleansing of glassware used in bacteriology and quantitative chemistry.

2. Preparation of bacterial media, physiological and chemical solutions used in bacteriology, hematology, and qualitative chemistry.

3. Cleansing of volumetric, graduated, and hematological pipettes and special chemical filters.

4. Complete urinalysis, except for microscopic including qualitative and quantitative sugars, albumin, acetone tests, and specific gravity.

5. Streaking and plating of bacterial cultures with aseptic technique.

6. Assistance in quantitative blood and tissue chemistry as in total proteins, lipids, sodiums, and potassiums.

7. Staining of hematology and bacterial slides.

8. Taking stool culture and finger blood tests alone.

9. Keeping daily record of work performed.

10. All blood typing (all work is, of course, checked by the head of the laboratory).

We presented the above not because it unequivocally demonstrates a surprising degree of problem-solving behavior (although this is likely) but because it illustrates (a) that much more attention should be given to non-test behavior, and (b) that the problems involved in describing the intellectual processes at work in non-test behavior are probably far more difficult than in the formal test situation where we have more control over the presentation of the stimulus problem.

Case 4

The next example concerns an institutionalized woman of 30 who obtained an *IQ* of 49, her problem-solving behavior in any situation never seeming to be out of line with such a score. This case has been described by Schaefer-Simmern (232, 233) in great detail and the reader is urged to consult his full description. Selma was one of the "children" with whom Schaefer-Simmern worked in order to study the nature and development of artistic activity in the efforts of defective individuals. In choosing children for the study Schaefer-Simmern (232) did not select on the basis of ability to draw but rather on the basis that the child's drawing did *not* reveal a tendency to copy or imitate nature or to represent objects schematically, e.g., stick figures. The initial drawing of the children would be considered most primitive by conventional artistic criteria. Selma (as did the other participants) came to a workshop one day a week. When she was requested to show her first drawing:

> Her feelings of inferiority, her shyness, and even a certain anxiety gripped her. Turning her face away, she submitted her drawing with trembling hands. She obviously feared attention and criticism. Selma's first picture—according to her own statement, the only one she had ever done—indicates that even a mentally deficient person can create in a modest degree an ordered pictorial whole. It was astonishing that she was able to accomplish even so simple a pictorial result, and the writer praised her for her work. Her reserved attitude disappeared at once and a big smile spread over her face; apparently a word of encouragement was what she needed. Another fact was still more astonishing. While the writer was engaged in supervising the work of the other girls belonging to the same group, Selma took some drawing paper from the desk and started a new picture. She repeated almost the same subject. . . . Except for a little more careful execution of her drawing, there is no further development in the organization of form. But two essentials must be noted: the smaller trees show a different application of the stage of variability of direction of lines, a variation of form invented by herself; and furthermore, the fact that she drew this picture spontaneously indicated the possibility of an unfolding of energies that no one expected (232).

Language is an inadequate means for conveying to the reader what becomes evident from a study of Selma's artistic development—a development which can be labelled creative in that the content and structure of each of her drawings reflected her own decisions, her own way of solving the problems which such activity presents. Unfortunately, little interest in or research about the intellectual and problem-solving aspects of artistic activity is reflected in the psychological literature, although there can be no doubt that such activity is in large part of a problem-solving nature. The significance of Selma's case is not only that she was capable of a degree of sustained effort and achievement which was not predictable from her test or school behavior but also because it emphasizes how a particular kind of intellectual activity is not sampled by our tests. In addition, as a reading of Schaefer-Simmern's case description would clearly reveal, the problem of the content and structure of intellectual activity cannot be considered apart from that of motivation and the nature of the stimulus conditions (i.e., the pedagogical procedures and goals employed).[7] We have singled out the case of Selma only because of our focus on mental retardation. Schaefer-Simmern's book contains many instances of individuals of differing test-score status where the development of a high degree of problem-solving behavior is indeed dramatic. It is difficult to avoid the conclusion that conceptions of the nature of intelligence underlying the development and use of our conventional tests give one a rather limited sample of intellectual activity.

Thus far we have been discussing the possibility that our intelligence tests measure a restricted range of problem-solving stimuli and intellectual activities, and we have focused on the suggestion that these tests may be excellent indices of educational achievement and poor indicators of non-test intellectual activity. Support for the conclusions drawn has been largely observational, a fact which reflects not only the absence of systematic research but, more important, the tendency to view intelligence from the perspective of our current tests. The often heard statement that "intelligence is what intelligence tests measure" may have the virtue of being an operational definition but it may also have the vice of being scientifically nearsighted to a degree where one cannot see the forest for the trees.

At this point mention should be made of a large body of research, spear-

---

[7]When Schaefer-Simmern's procedures are contrasted with those ordinarily employed in the occupational therapy units in institutions for defectives— for that matter, in art classes in our ordinary schools as well—one has a rather clear example of how the content, procedures, and goals of our schools restrict the range of problem-solving behavior which one can observe. This conclusion is identical to that which may be drawn from Wertheimer's (288) observation of conventional procedures of teaching geometry. It is important to emphasize that both Schaefer-Simmern and Wertheimer discuss and describe intellectual processes (i.e., the creative, the productive) which are neither reinforced by pedagogical technique nor in any way reflected or measured in tests of intelligence. The implications of Schaefer-Simmern's work for recent studies of rigidity among subnormal individuals are discussed later.

headed by Davis and Havighurst which rather clearly indicates that our conventional intelligence tests consist of materials and problems to which lower-class children are exposed in the course of their lives to a lesser degree than in the case of middle- or upper-class children.[8] In other words, our conventional tests tell us more about non-school problem-solving experiences of middle- rather than lower-class children—perhaps a reflection of the fact that teachers and psychologists come largely from middle-class backgrounds.

Because of the findings in regard to cultural bias in intelligence tests, in addition to the fact that most intelligence test items present the child with problems which he infrequently meets in real life, Davis and Eells (56) standardized a test of problem-solving ability in which they attempted to reduce cultural bias and to include items more clearly reflecting problem-solving situations met in everyday life. The following quotation, which concerns why certain items were eliminated from the final form of the test, gives one a succinct but partial picture of Davis and Eell's approach (56, pp. 48-50):

> One item will illustrate the way in which several lines of evidence frequently contributed to the ultimate decision to eliminate an item. One Analogy item required the pupil to report that a horse bears the same relationship to a horse's hoof as does a boy to a boy's foot. The item was relatively easy, being answered correctly by 77 per cent of the six-year-old children, 88 per cent of the eight-year-old children, and 98 per cent of the 10-year-old children. This item also showed a very substantial socio-economic difference at the six-year-old level. Of children from high-status homes, 93 per cent of the six-year-old children answered correctly, while only 78 per cent of the low-status children answered correctly. This socio-economic difference was more than twice as great as the average for Analogy items at this age level. This socio-economic difference would not, of itself, have been grounds for eliminating the item, unless examination of the item led to the conclusion that the difference was due to bias in the nature of the item rather than to basic differences in the problem-solving ability of children in the two groups.

---

[8]It will be recalled that thus far in this report we have been discussing that large group of low test-scoring individuals who conventionally have been regarded as representing the low end of the normal distribution curve of intelligence—individuals in whom there is no apparent central nervous system pathology. These individuals we have labelled for purposes of discussion as mentally retarded, in contrast to the mentally defective in whom there is some central nervous system pathology (e.g., mongolism, phenylketonuria, convulsive disorders, metabolic disfunction, etc.). The significance of the researches we are discussing above resides in the fact that the large bulk of the mentally retarded are of lower social class status.

In the case of this particular item, it seemed clear that in order to answer the item correctly, the child must be able to recognize that the drawing of the third term in the analogy was of a horse's hoof and not of a dog's or a cat's paw. Since the item was tried out in a large metropolitan city, it seemed unlikely that many of the six-year-old children had had much firsthand experience with horses. Recognition of the picture as that of a horse's hoof would probably be dependent, almost totally upon familiarity with children's books which contain pictures of horses. Books of this sort would, of course, be much more frequently found among high-status homes than among low-status homes. It appeared likely, therefore, that the higher proportion of correct answers from children of high socio-economic background reflected, not a basic superiority in problem-solving ability, but merely greater familiarity with the particular subject matter of this item. The reasoning involved here may be made clearer by thinking of this item as it might be answered by rural and urban children. If rural children should be found to do better on the item than urban children, as seems quite likely, this would probably be due to the greater opportunity which rural children have to be familiar with horses' hoofs and not to any genuine superiority in problem-solving ability on the part of the rural children. It was decided, therefore, that the item should be eliminated in favor of one dealing with materials more likely to be equally familiar to children from different cultural backgrounds.

Incidentally, the distribution of wrong responses on this item bears out the interpretation just suggested. Almost all the errors made by low-status children on the item involved checking the dog instead of the horse. For a child unfamiliar with the details of a horse's hoof, this seems an "intelligent" response, since the drawing more nearly resembles a dog's foot than that of a cat.

Because of the importance of this question for proper interpretation of the scores on the present test, it must be stressed that *no item was eliminated simply because it showed a large socio-economic difference.* Only if such difference served to call attention to a previously unnoticed bias in the content of the test item (as in the case just described) was the item eliminated. As a matter of fact, four other Analogy items which showed socio-economic differences larger than this one were not eliminated, and appear in the final test, since examination of the items did not reveal any obvious reason for believing the items to be biased.

It is important to point out that the test devised by Davis and Eells is the only one where an attempt was made to choose problems on the basis of observation (and interviewing) of children in such areas of activity as school, home, play, stories, and work. In addition, this is the first widely used test where the validity of the instrument is not evaluated by correlations with school grades or other standardized tests.

 A general intelligence test is valid if it measures over-all capacity to solve mental problems. Since scientists have discovered no objective criterion of intelligence, previous test makers have tended to rely on the correlations of test scores with school grades, and upon the fact that their problems proved more difficult for lower-age groups than for higher-age groups, as evidence that their tests were actually valid measures of intelligence. But, as many, including Binet, have pointed out, school grades are greatly influenced by work habits, attentiveness, conscientiousness, home training, desire to compete, and many other aspects of the pupil's work. Therefore school grades are not satisfactory as a criterion of validity for a test of general mental capacity. Secondly, the fact that a problem shows an increase in the percentage of pupils passing it at increasing ages does not at all validate the problem as an index of intelligence. Large increments in percentage of pupils passing a problem at successively higher chronological ages may result simply from the fact that increasing instruction and practice are given pupils on similar problems, as the pupils advance through school and become older.

 The fact is that there is no satisfactory objective criterion of true mental capacity, and therefore no possibility, at least at present, of constructing a satisfactory test of intelligence by purely objective means. It is necessary for the makers of intelligence tests to construct items which appear to require the main types of intellectual problem-solving behavior. The keenest insights of psychologists and students of culture are called for in this process.

 It follows that the validity of the *Davis-Eells Test* necessarily must rest, as does that of any other intelligence test (as distinct from a "scholastic aptitude" test), on the reasonableness of the problems as indicators of general problem-solving ability (56, pp. 6-7).

A recent study by Zweibelson (302, 303) lends support and corroboration to Davis and Eell's rationale and findings. To 258 fourth-grade public school children, Zweibelson administered the Otis-Alpha, Otis-Beta, Davis-Eells, and Stanford Achievement tests. Previous to these tests the children were given the Test Anxiety questionnaire which concerns attitudes toward and experiences in test-taking situations in school (226).

1. In Table 3 are given the correlations of the three standardized intelligence tests with the achievement test. As one would expect from Davis and Eell's rationale and findings, their test is least correlated with a criterion of academic achievement—although it is itself significantly correlated

TABLE 3

CORRELATION OF SCORE ON MENTAL ABILITY AND ACHIEVEMENT TESTS
[From Zweibelson (302), $N = 258$]

Stanford achievement	r with mental ability		
	Otis-Alpha	Otis-Beta	Davis-Eells
Paragraph meaning	.56	.77	.50
Word meaning	.53	.77	.43
Spelling	.50	.73	.44
Language	.59	.69	.49
Arithmetic reasoning	.57	.72	.48
Arithmetic computation	.48	.54	.38
Mean achievement	.62	.81	.52

with such a criterion. If the three mental ability tests were placed on a continuum on the basis of content, format and similar factors, the Otis Alpha could easily be estimated to be in a position between the two other mental tests—an estimate congruent with the size of correlations found in Table 3.

2. When scores on the three tests were correlated with teacher opinion about whether a child was or was not a reading or arithmetic problem, the Davis-Eells was least related to teacher opinion, the Otis Beta was most related, and the Otis Alpha again in between. These results suggest that the problem-solving abilities measured by the Davis-Eells are less related to what may be called problem-solving in reading and arithmetic than is true of the other tests. The above findings were most clear in the case of reading.

3. Test Anxiety was significantly less related to Davis-Eells score (—.14) than in the case of the Otis Alpha (—.28) or Otis Beta (—.24). In other words it would seem that anxiety is less of an interfering factor in the Davis-Eells than in the other tests—a finding predictable from the rationale and administration of the Davis-Eells.

Because the Davis-Eells test reflects a different and refreshing approach to the problem of the measurement of intelligence, it is important that it be critically scrutinized.

1. The final forms of the test consist of four types of problem-solving items. As we shall see in the next section, it is extremely doubtful that four types of items are in any way representative of the range of human abilities, either of adults or children. Consequently, it would seem unjustified to interpret scores on this test as reflecting intelligence or problem-solving ability *in general*—a limitation not peculiar to this test. While the various criteria for inclusion or rejection of types of items could be justified in a clinical sense (e.g., mode of administration, de-emphasis of time limits, real-

ism of problem situations, etc.), they nevertheless resulted in a test with a very restricted range of problem-solving situations. There is nothing inherently wrong with a test of restricted range of items. But it would seem unwarranted to call such a test one of general intelligence or problem-solving ability.

2. Although Davis and Eells attempted to reduce the usually obtained differences between social classes in test score, such differences still obtain with their test. This finding is susceptible to a variety of interpretations, as discussed in Section VI. We wish only to point out that until the relationships between social class and motivation for achievement are studied and clarified, the differences in intellectual performance between individuals in different social classes cannot properly be evaluated, as the writings of Davis (55) and the work of Haggard (101) suggest. In comparing the test performance of a group of Americans and Australian Aborigines, one would hardly be justified in attributing the poorer performance of the Aborigines to poorer general intelligence or problem-solving ability, although ultimately this *may* be found to be the case. This, of course, is an extreme example but it does serve to illustrate that differences in test performance between groups of differing experiences (i.e., culture background) are associated with other kinds of differences (non-intellectual) which *a priori* cannot be considered effects rather than causes of the test differences. There are two limitations of the Davis-Eells as well as other more conventional tests. First, as already suggested, there is no evidence or justification for the assumption that the problem-solving tasks sampled by these tests are representative of problem-solving behavior in everyday life. Second, whatever theoretical rationale underlies these tests has not come directly to grips with the problem of the relation between motivation and abilities, a problem to which Bray (26) has recently called attention.

3. As we indicated earlier, Davis and Eells made a deliberate attempt to observe children in various spheres of life activities as a guide in selecting items for their test. Unfortunately, in terms of the point of view we have presented, these workers never seemed to consider the problem of the relation between problem-solving in and outside of the test-situation, although the importance of this problem is implied in much of Davis' writings. For example, when one finds, as Davis and Eells did with their test, that there are pervasive differences between certain social class groupings, are there similar differences when the everyday problem-solving behavior of these groups is studied? Put in another way: are the differences in level of problem-

solving behavior in the test situation observable in *all* problem-solving behavior outside of the test situation?   While it should be indispensable in
constructing a test to observe non-test behavior as a guide in selection of
items, it should also be essential that one demonstrate that the level of problem-solving which is elicited by these test items is highly correlated with behavior to these items when they are met with in everyday life.   In constructing a test to select certain machine operators, one selects items which
clearly reflect what these operators actually do or will be required to do,
and one endeavors to construct the test so that it will differentiate between
levels of actual performance.   Similarly with our intelligence tests: implicitly and explicitly they have been validated on the basis of scholastic
achievement and the content of these tests reflect such an aim.   If one's goal
is to construct a test which will predict problem-solving behavior outside of
school-like situations—then it would seem necessary to study and demonstrate the relationship between performance in such situations and in response to the test.   Although Davis and Eells correctly maintain that their
test cannot be validated by the usual criteria of academic achievement or
degree of correlation with other tests (which themselves employed the academic achievement criterion), it does seem that their own theoretical position requires that they employ, in part at least, the criterion of problem-
solving behavior observed in everyday life situations.

In this as well as in the previous section we have centered our attention
on some aspects of the logic of intelligence test construction, paying particular attention to the limitations of the criteria most frequently employed.   In
doing so we have attempted to indicate that these limitations are as much of
a problem with a test designed to reduce the effects of culture bias as with
the more conventional ones.   The specific ways in which cultural and social-
class factors may influence test performance are discussed in Chapter XIV
which also contains an evaluation of culture-fair or culture-free tests in light
of existing studies.

XII. "THE STRUCTURE OF INTELLECT"

Although the recognition that cultural bias pervades our conventional tests of intelligence represents an important advance in our knowledge, it does not in any explicit way consider the problem of the nature, range, or organization of intellectual abilities. In the previous discussion, however, we have had occasion to raise this question: how adequate are our tests for describing or evaluating the various human abilities? The most succinct answer to this question has been given by Guilford (99) in his penetrating discussion of the "structure of intellect":

> The advent of multiple-factor analysis has done something to broaden and enrich our conception of human intelligence, but factor theory and the results of factor analysis have had little effect upon the practices of measurement of intelligence. We do have a great variety of tests in such intelligence scales as the Binet and its revisions and in the Wechsler scales, to be sure. Too commonly, however, a single score is the only information utilized, and this single score is usually dominated by variance in only one or two factors. There is some indication of more general use of part scores, as in connection with the Wechsler tests, but each of these scores is usually factorially complex and its psychological meaning is largely unknown as well as ambiguous. The list of factors that is to be presented in this article should clearly demonstrate the very limited information that a single score can give concerning an individual, and on the other hand, the rich possibilities that those factors offer for more complete and more meaningful assessments of the intellects of persons (99, p. 267).

It cannot be too strongly stated that most of our tests are woefully inadequate for the evaluation of the various human aptitudes, a point of which more than a few clinicians have long been aware. To give some idea of the complexity of the problem as well as an indication of the progress which has been made we present below a portion of Guilford's discussion of but one (the cognition or discovery factors) of the three groups of factors which seem to fall under the general heading of thinking:

> The cognition factors have to do with becoming aware of mental items or constructs of one kind or another. In the tests of these factors, something must be comprehended, recognized, or discovered by the examinee. They represent functions on the receiving side of behavior sequences.
> The cognition abilities can be differentiated along the lines of two major principles. For some time we have been aware that thinking factors tend to pair off according to the material or content used in the

185

tests. For each factor of a certain kind found in verbal tests there seemed to be a mate found in tests composed of figures or designs. We found, for example, a factor called *eduction of perceptual relations,* parallel with a factor called *eduction of conceptual relations;* a factor called *perceptual foresight,* parallel to one called *conceptual foresight;* and a factor of *perceptual classification,* parallel with one of *conceptual classification.* Only recently there has been increasing evidence for a third content category. Factors were found in tests whose contents are letters, or equivalent symbols, where neither perceived form or figure nor verbal meaning is the basis of operation. Factors based upon this type of material have been found, parallel to other factors where the test content is figural or verbal. Thus a third content category seems necessary.

A second major principle by which cognition factors may be differentiated psychologically depends upon the kind of things discovered; whether it is a relation, a class, or a pattern, and so on. Thus, for each combination of content and thing discovered, we have a potential factor. The cognition factors can therefore be arranged in a matrix as shown in Table 4. The third and fourth rows seem to be complete at the present time. There are vacancies in the other four rows. With each factor name are usually given two representative tests by name to help give the factor operational meaning. A word or two will be said in addition regarding the less familiar tests.

It should not be surprising to find the factor of *verbal* comprehension, the best known, and the dominant one in verbal-intelligence tests generally, in the first row of the cognition factors and in the conceptual column. The fact that the cognition factors sometimes come in threes leads us to look. for parallel factors for the perceptual and structural columns. One candidate for the perceptual cell in this row would be the well-known factor of *perceptual speed.* This factor has to do with discriminations of small differences in form rather than in awareness of total figures, hence it does not quite fill the requirement of parallel properties with *verbal comprehension.* A better factor for this purpose is the one Thurstone called "speed and strength of closure," called *figural closure* (Table 4). For this factor, awareness of perceived objects from limited cues is the key property. The limitation of cues is necessary to make the test sufficiently difficult for testing purposes. . . .

Two factors involving ability to recognize classes are known, one in which the class is formed on the basis of figural properties and the other on the basis of meanings. It was interesting that the Picture Classification test had more relation to the *perceptual-classification* factor than to the *conceptual-classification* factor in spite of the fact that the things to be classified were common objects, the basis for whose classification was intended to be their meaning. This might mean that the

TABLE 4
COGNITION (DISCOVERY) FACTORS
(From Guilford, 99)

Type of thing known or discovered	Type of content		
	Figural	Structural	Conceptual
Fundamentals	*Figural closure* Street Gestalt Completion Mutilated Words		*Verbal comprehension* Vocabulary
Classes	*Perceptual classification* Figure Classification Picture Classification		*Verbal classification* Word Classification Verbal Classification
Relations	*Eduction of perceptual relations* Figure Analogies Figure Matrix	*Eduction of structural relations* Seeing Trends II Correlate Completion II	*Eduction of conceptual relations* Verbal Analogies Word Matrix
Patterns or systems	*Spatial orientation* Spatial Orientation Flags, Figures, Cards	*Eduction of patterns* Circle Reasoning Letter Triangle	*General reasoning* Arithmetic Reasoning Ship Destination
Problems			*Sensitivity to problems* Seeing Problems Seeing Deficiencies
Implications	*Perceptual foresight* Competitive Planning Route Planning		*Conceptual foresight* Pertinent Questions Alternate Methods *Penetration* Social Institutions Similarities

perceptual-conceptual distinction is a somewhat superficial matter, pertaining only to how the material is presented. It is possible, however, that in many of the items in this test the general shapes and sizes and other figural properties are an aid in classification. For example, there are cleaning implements, containers, etc. in some items, where similarities of appearance may serve as clues. . . . For the discovery of problems, there is only one factor—*sensitivity to problems,* which is in the conceptual column. The appearance of this factor parallel to *general reasoning* in the row preceding, emphasizes the well-known observation that it is one thing to be aware that a problem exists and another thing to be aware of the nature of the problem. The titles of the tests are quite descriptive. A sample item from the test Seeing Problems asks the examinee to list as many as five problems in connection with a common object like a candle. The test Seeing Deficiencies presents in each item the general plan for solving a given problem, but the plan raises some new problems. What are those problems?

Whether we shall ever find parallel factors for seeing problems or deficiencies of figural and structural types remains to be seen. Problems of a figural type are faced in aesthetic pursuits such as painting and architecture. Problems of a structural type might be faced in connection with spelling or the development of language. Tests pertaining to the seeing of problems have thus far provided no figural or structural bases for problems. It should be relatively easy to test the hypothesis that such factors exist. If they do exist, their possible implications for everyday performance need further study. . . .

Porteus has maintained that his series of maze tests measure foresight. He can well claim support from the factor-analysis results just mentioned. The type of foresight measured by maze tests, however, is of a concrete variety. This ability may be important for the architect, the engineer, and the industrial-lay-out planner. It may not be found related to the abstract type of planning that we find in the political strategist and the policy maker. So far as our results go, the maze test should by no means be offered as a test of general intelligence. This statement might need modification, however, after the maze test is factor analyzed in a population of lower general intellectual level (where general intelligence is defined operationally as an average of all intellectual abilities). In a population of "high-level personnel," we can say that a maze test measures most strongly the factor of *perceptual foresight* and, incidentally, to some degree the factors of *visualization* and *adaptive flexibility.*

The appearance of a factor called *penetration* . . . , along with *conceptual foresight,* calls for comment. A factor of penetration was hypothesized in the first analysis of creative abilities and was not found. An unidentified factor found there might well have been *penetration.* A factor has been so identified in a more recent analysis that emphasized creative ability tests. It is strongly loaded on a test called Social Institutions, which asks what is wrong with well-known institutions such as tipping. It was designed as a test of *sensitivity to problems,* and it has consistently had a loading on that factor. In the first creativity analysis, two scores were based upon this test; one being the total number of low-quality or obvious defects and the other was the total number of high-quality or "penetrating" defects—defects that can be seen only by the far-sighted person. As a matter of fact, the two scores had much to do with effecting a separation of the seeing-problems tests into two groups, one of which might have been identified as the *penetration* factor.

In his article Guilford also presents and discusses two other broad thinking factors: production and evaluation. Several things should be said or emphasized or concluded from his presentation.

1. The identification of a factor involves consideration of at least two things: (*a*) the kinds of thinking sequences that a problem presumably engenders in or requires of the individual and (*b*) the content of the stimulus task. The significance of Guilford's research in this connection is that he has demonstrated that the number of different intellectual factors is probably far greater than had been previously thought or is contained in existing tests of intelligence.

2. Guilford has described factors, the production and evaluation ones, which previously either had not been systematically studied or had not at all been considered as intellectual processes. Guilford describes these two groups of factors as follows:

> The second large group of thinking factors has to do with the production of some end result. After one has comprehended the situation, or the significant aspects of it at the moment, usually something needs to be done to it or about it. In the analogies test, for example, having seen the relation between the first pair of elements of an item we must then find a correlate to complete another pair. Having understood a problem, we must take further steps to solve it.
>
> Evaluation factors have to do with decisions concerning the goodness, suitability, or effectiveness of the results of thinking. After a discovery is made, after a product is achieved, is it correct, is it the best that we can do, will it work? This calls for a judgmental step of some kind. It was our hypothesis in the project that the ability to make such decisions will depend upon the area within which the thinking takes place and the criteria on which the decision is based.

Guilford's description and discussion of these factors represents a systematic attempt to observe in a test situation intellectual processes which heretofore had been noted as important in the non-test problem-solving behavior of people. It seems to us, in fact, that the discrepancies that too frequently are found between test and non-test problem-solving behavior (the latter being better than the former) would perhaps arise with less frequency if the tests had included what is in part subsumed under Guilford's production and evaluation factors.[9] In other words, what we observe outside of the test situation cannot be gleaned from test behavior because of a narrow conception and inadequate sampling of intellectual abilities.

3. Regarding the large number of factors reported we can do no better than again to quote Guilford:

> A theory or a method should be judged by its fruits. If the results that have been reported here contribute to psychological understanding and, through that, to useful psychological practice, factor analysis has passed this kind of test. The mathematical model that has been applied, which conceives of individual differences in intellectual performances as being represented by a coordinate system of n dimensions, has served certain purposes. While it may be shown at some future time that the model is not the best that could be applied, its power to generate new psychological ideas and to extend considerably the conception of the realm of intellect has been demonstrated.
>
> The average reader will no doubt be surprised by the large number of dimensions that seem to be required to encompass the range of intellectual aspects of human nature. Some 40 factors are reported as being known and a great many additional unknown factors are forecast. This would seem to go against the scientific urge for parsimony.
>
> The principle of parsimony has led us in the past to the extreme of one intellectual dimension, which everyone should now regard as going too far in that direction. There is actually no fixed criterion for the satisfaction of the principle of parsimony. In science we can satisfy the principle to some degree whenever the number of concepts is smaller than the number of phenomena observed. Forty, sixty, or even a hundred factors would certainly be a smaller number of concepts than the number of possible tests or the number of observable types of activities of an intellectual character. In this sense the principle of parsimony has been satisfied.

---

[9]We emphasize the situation where level of non-test problem-solving behavior is better than in the test situation because we think there is sufficient clinical and research evidence that among the mentally retarded such a discrepancy is by no means infrequent. The reverse situation—where level of problem-solving in the test situation is markedly above the individual's actual achievements—is certainly not a rare occurrence among the non-retarded, as the observant reader can attest. Here, too, the "discrepancy" and reaction of surprise are probably a function of the implicit but unwarranted assumption that the sample of behavior observed in the test situation is a representative sample of problem-solving behavior.

The number of the factors is less unattractive when we find that they can be subsumed within a system that is describable by a smaller number of categories or principles. Some readers will ask whether, since there are many probable intercorrelations among the factors, a small set of second-order factors will not suffice. Granting that we can make sufficiently accurate estimates of the intercorrelations among the factors, which the writer doubts that we can do at present, to use only second-order-factor concepts would lose information. This follows from the fact that where n linearly independent dimensions are necessary to describe a domain geometrically, no one dimension can be entirely accounted for by combinations of the others.

It may be asked whether some of the factors listed are not really specific factors rather than common factors. This is a legitimate question. It is not uncommon experience in factor analysis to find what was formerly regarded as a single common factor appears later to split up into two or more factors. The "splitting up" description is not completely accurate. It applies best to the fact that a group of tests having a "factor" in common later divide into two or more groups each defining its own common factor. In clear thinking about this phenomenon, we must keep in mind the distinction between "factor" as a mathematical concept and "factor" as a psychological concept. The immediate results of a factor analysis are in terms of mathematical factors. Whether each mathematical factor represents a single psychological factor or a combination of psychological factors has to be determined by interpretation and by further experimental work applied to the designing of new factor analyses. Eventually we reach the stage where further efforts to "split" a factor fail. Whether this has brought us to a specific factor in any particular case can be decided on the basis of a single criterion. Are the tests defining this factor essentially just different forms of the same test? This cannot always be decided with certainty, but there is usually little difficulty in doing so. If we suspect that any factor is a specific, a new analysis that includes more obviously different tests, but tests that should measure the same *common* factor, should be done.

4. Guilford's research is based on studies of the superior human adult. Although it is probably true, as Guilford indicates, that in studying such individuals one can "investigate intellectual qualities and functions in their greatest scope and variety," one can only hope that similar studies will be done with those in the lower end of the distribution curve. At this point mention might be made of Satter and McGee's (229, 230, 231) studies of a group of retarded adults who showed an unexpectedly good level of vocational behavior (i.e., unexpected in terms of initial testing on admission to the institution) and also showed test score increases beyond the age of fif-

teen or sixteen. "This group was then matched with one of equal size and composition on the basis of IQ earned on the 1916 Stanford-Binet at the time of admission, its length of residence, chronological age and its etiological background." A variety of tests was given to the subjects and a factor analysis was done with the 27 variables which had been found discriminating between the two groups. Three factors were extracted: a general one, a perceptual motor one, and a substitution one.[10] Although Satter and McGee's studies are worthy of note because they illustrate the fruitfulness of attending to non-test problem-solving behavior, they also exemplify an important limitation in a factor analytic approach. We refer here to the fact that the kinds of factors which will emerge in such a study depend in large part on the kinds of tests employed. For example, Satter and McGee used the more conventional psychological tests and because of this many of the factors described by Guilford could not appear. It is also obvious that to sample the varieties of intellectual processes would require many more tests than the relatively few used by Satter and McGee. Jastak (130, 131), who has thought most penetratingly about the usefulness of factor analysis in relation to mental subnormality, concluded on the basis of his research and clinical experience that "from 20 to 50 different mental functions will have to be tested before a truly scientific diagnosis of feeblemindedness can be made." In fact, both from a clinical and theoretical standpoint Jastak's approach—which unfortunately for the field has never been systematically and comprehensively presented by him— goes beyond Guilford's in that he emphasizes the absolute necessity of viewing the intellectual factors in terms of the personality ones. His illustrative presentation of individuals with an identical low IQ, differing psychometric patterns on 12 intellectual factors, and radically different "personality genotypes" effectively directs attention to what is perhaps the most important research in the field. Equally important is Jastak's emphasis (supported, we think, by his unpublished research) that it is only on the basis of this approach and the research to which it gives rise (a) that more sensible therapeutic and educational programs can be developed and (b) that the frequently found "discrepancies" between level of conventional test scores, on the one hand, and level of social and vocational performance, on the other hand, can be seen as artifacts of conventional test scores.

---

[10]In a non-factor analysis study of two retarded groups who also differed in level of problem-solving behavior outside the test situation, Sarason and Sarason (227) also obtained significant differences in the perceptual-motor sphere.

It could be argued that many of the factors that Guilford obtained with his superior group would not be applicable to or simply would not be found among the mentally retarded. This *may* be so but it would be a scientific mistake of no small proportion if such assumptions were considered as facts and prevented the kind of systematic research which is so desperately needed in this area. It would be our opinion that unless such research is done we not only may be kept from a better understanding of the retarded but we may also be misled in some of the conclusions drawn about the significance of and interrelationships among the various factors in the superior individual. One could point to several problems—such as amenability to psychotherapy or level of social and vocational competence—where unjustified and untested assumptions about what the retarded could do prevented the acquisition of new knowledge, to the detriment both of practice and theory.

5. One of the intriguing and important problems suggested by Guilford's research may be put as follows: What is the relation between variety and relationships of intellectual factors, on the one hand, and cultural differences, on the other? Put in cross-cultural terms: What would likely be obtained if we were to attempt to replicate Guilford's findings (on superior American males) with the Eskimo? Having posed the question we could predict at least two things: (*a*) we would probably not know how to begin such a study, and (*b*) many of the tests used by Guilford would clearly make no sense to the Eskimo (even taking the language barrier into account). To do such a study would require a most intimate knowledge of Eskimo culture in the hope that such knowledge would allow us to construct meaningful tests for the different factors. It may well be that such intimate knowledge would lead us to conclude that some of the intellectual factors we find in certain groups of our culture do not manifest themselves in Eskimo culture. Is it that the brains of Eskimos are different or is this a reflection of the fact that their culture is quite different from our own? If it turns out, as we think likely, that the great bulk of the mentally retarded in our own culture come from or constitute a different sub-culture, we would be faced with the same kinds of questions that arise when one compares drastically different cultures, e.g., Eskimos and Americans. The important result of such a study would be to illuminate the kinds of cultural settings which inhibit or facilitate the development of particular intellectual factors. It is difficult to see how without these kinds of studies a really comprehensive general theory of human intelligence—its nature, development, and relationships or interactions with motivation and life experiences—can be de-

veloped. At the present time we have knowledge of the nature of some of the intellectual processes. One can only hope that such knowledge, based as it is on a very restricted sample (culturally and intellectually), does not result in premature theory building about *all* people. The study of individual differences, between and within cultures, may well give us the kinds of data necessary for a general theory of human intelligence. We strongly feel that psychological theories built upon data obtained without explicit and systematic regard for the factor of cultural differences are likely to be either incomplete and/or misleading. In such instances much talent and time are wasted and not until the rôle of the cultural variable is demonstrated does one see the inadequacies of past practice and theory—a good example of this being the lack of recognition of the cultural bias in our conventional tests of intelligence (see previous section). Perhaps a better example of this is the status of social science research before and after the development of modern anthropology.

Thus far in this and previous sections we have discussed the problem of the measurement of intelligence in terms of a few propositions which might be summarized as follows:

1. Conventional tests sample a very limited number of intellectual processes, for the most part those kinds of processes which are required in scholastic achievements.

2. Conventional tests, by virtue primarily of their content and means of validation, contain a large element of social class or cultural bias.

3. There is no evidence that the level and kinds of problem-solving behavior signified by scores on conventional tests are highly correlated with non-test problem-solving behavior.

4. It appears that the bulk of the mentally retarded are found primarily in the lower social classes and that the cultural matrix in these classes is different in important respects from that of other groups. Because of the cultural bias in conventional tests, the intellectual potential of this group, as well as its level of functioning outside the test situation, cannot be assumed to have been adequately assessed.

5. It is becoming more and more apparent that the variety of intellectual processes is far greater than had been thought previously to be the case and that the continued use of conventional tests and test scores *in practice and research* is likely to be, at best, non-productive. Whatever new knowledge we have (or will obtain) in this respect is due less to a particular method (e.g., factor analysis) than to changes in conceptions about the

nature, organization, and variety of intellectual processes. This statement perhaps requires some elaboration. Although factor analysis has been around for some time and has long influenced or given rise to theories of intelligence, its fruitfulness has been reduced by the failure of many workers to realize that the conventional tests they used immediately and drastically reduced their sample of intellectual activities. Put in another way: one's conceptions (i.e., theory) about the variety of intellectual functions should dictate the tests devised and employed rather than one's conceptions being dictated by tests which happen to be available. It is difficult to avoid the conclusion that some workers have been uncritically dependent on tests because they have no theory concerning the structure of intellect. We have been impressed with Guilford's work less because he employs factor analysis than because he seems to have started out with a rather broad conception of the varieties of intellectual functioning. It is not surprising, therefore, that Guilford discusses and attempts to measure activities which are not found in our conventional tests. This is not because Guilford uses factor analysis but because of his conception about what is "intellectual." When the clinical psychologist has to evaluate an individual's intellectual capacity and performance, he almost always finds himself taking into account so-called qualitative factors which are either not at all or inadequately sampled by conventional tests, so that his final judgment reflects more than test scores. It is our impression that Guilford has come closer to recognizing these qualitative factors than previous factor analysts. The reader unfamiliar with the nature, usefulness and limitations of factor analysis might profitably read Anastasi and Foley (7) and Bray (26).

6. Unless research in this area explicitly takes account of cultural variations we will be robbing ourselves of an important source for the understanding of the factors which determine the nature and organization of different patterns of intellectual processes.

XIII. HEREDITY AND ENVIRONMENT

In 1912 Henry H. Goddard (92) published *The Kallikak Family, a Study in the Heredity of Feeblemindedness*. He was by no means the first to propose that feeblemindedness was an inheritable characteristic, but his study was accepted as confirmation so conclusive that it was scarcely questioned for at least 10 years after publication of the book. Although at the present time practically all responsible workers in the field recognize that conclusive proof of the heritability of mental ability (where no organic or metabolic pathology is involved) is still lacking, the assumption that subnormality has a genetic basis continues to crop up in scientific studies. This undoubtedly results in some degree from the general failure to observe a distinction between "simple" retardation on the one hand, resulting presumably from inadequate learning and stimulation, and true deficiency of probable organic origin on the other. But it must also be recognized that an assumption of inferior heredity can provide an appealingly simple explanation for a condition which to the average person is both very disturbing and quite incomprehensible. The most recent example which has come to our attention is an article by McGurk (181) in a national magazine, purporting to demonstrate the inherent inferiority of Negroes. This irresponsible product employed seductively plausible but scientifically spurious reasoning to fuel the fires of an explosive national issue. It need concern us here only insofar as it underlines the dangers inherent in giving any serious weight to genetic factors until—and unless—they can be demonstrated to be relevant.

As we review in this section a selected few studies bearing on the effects of heredity versus environment in the etiology of mental subnormality and as we discuss the research implications of these studies, it will be our thesis that a hereditary determinant of mental capacity must not be assumed to exist unless proven. Furthermore, proof should be sought in terms of our present knowledge of human genetics and of the nature of human intellect, rather than, as is commonly done, through the administration of routine intelligence tests to a variety of different "racial" and other groups. We do not propose to *deny* that heredity is a factor, particularly in mental deficiency, but rather that we should leave it out of our accounting until it is supported by more than speculation and bias. Although scientifically we must retain an open mind, we must also recognize that among laymen and among many physicians and other professionals the assumption of a genetic determinant is customarily accepted. A considerable educational effort will therefore be necessary before they can even share our state of open-mindedness. The belief is widespread that even moderate subnormality results from a defect in heredity and is therefore irreversible. This belief carries with it a sense of hopelessness which not only prevents doctors and others from encouraging people to look for means of rehabilitating the mentally handicapped, but also discourages most researchers from entering the field. In the broader context of our society it implies biological as well as social support for the concept of segregation, and helps keep alive the idea of sterilization as a means to reduce the numbers of retarded and problem children. These trends would at best not be healthy if they were founded on known facts, but resting as they do on an assumption which, despite repeated efforts, has as yet to receive scientifically acceptable proof we can only view them with distress.

Goddard's (92) study of the two Kallikak families, with its fairly obvious methodological weaknesses, is too well known to require review. Very few later researchers followed Goddard's lead in applying the genealogical method in large-scale studies of mental subnormality, except as applied to cases of clearly identifiable pathology. The method itself can be valuable and has been used to good effect by Kallmann (140), in conjunction with statistical prediction procedures, in the study of schizophrenia. It does not, however, appear applicable to research in mental retardation due to the virtual impossibility of obtaining reliable diagnoses or even adequate behavioral descriptions of people who are dead or cannot be located. This difficulty exists in addition to those we shall discuss later which apply to almost any type of research in the heredity of mental capacity, and virtually precludes genealogical research in this field.

Interest in the heritable factors in subnormality took a new turn with the availability after the first World War of the results of large-scale intelligence-testing of draftees. Among the first things to be observed in these data were the significantly lower test scores attained by Negroes than by whites. Although subsequent analyses of these same data revealed regional and other factors which were at work in determining test outcomes,[11] the fashion was established of applying intelligence and other types of performance tests uncritically to a wide range of ethnic groups. Typically in many studies the averaged *IQ*'s and other indices of two or more groups

---

[11]For a review of these data, see Montagu (186).

were compared, with the explicit or implicit assumption that these comparisons were somehow descriptive of "racial" characteristics. Not infrequently
the researcher, having watched the test subjects wrestle with language and
other problems in the tests, would conclude with the hesitant suggestion
that there were perhaps factors of environment, schooling, or the like which
affected the results. However, these afterthoughts were not enough to dis-
courage further research of the same order. Without any attempt to track
down all studies of this sort we uncovered several dozen which fit this description during our survey of the literature. Although most of these date from
the 1920's and 1930's, they continue to appear in diminishing numbers to
the present time. In later studies various attempts were made to use tests
which the researcher believed would hold constant the cultural and environmental factors; in the next section we discuss some of these tests and point
out that none we have discovered control environmental factors in the hoped
for manner.

We shall not attempt to review these studies in any detail, although a
number of them are discussed elsewhere in this report as they have bearing
on particular problems. It is, however, important to note the persistence
of this research approach over time, in spite of the doubts which it so often
engendered in the minds of the researchers and in the face of other research
and theoretical criticism which demonstrated in a variety of ways the in-
validity of any "racial" or ethnic IQ. With the problems attendant upon
the gradual rise in the social and economic status of the Negro as a background, it was probably not merely the availability of subjects which led
so many researchers to focus particularly upon Negro-white comparisons.
Nor is it surprising that, in spite of evidence to the contrary, we find Henry
E. Garrett (80), having reviewed some studies, writing in 1947 that "the
regularity of this result [i.e., lower Negro IQ] from babyhood to adulthood
makes it extremely unlikely, in the present writer's opinion, that environmental opportunities can possibly explain all the differences found" (p. 333).
Although Garrett does admit that these are not true "racial" comparisons,
it is disturbing to observe a person in his professional position making the
bland assumption that he has in fact explored all possible explanations other
than that of constitutional inferiority. It is also significant to note that in
the 14 studies which we culled from our review in which Italian IQ's or
mental retardation rates are compared with those of a variety of other
ethnic groups, the Italians consistently fall near or at the low end of the
continuum (sometimes below the Negro groups selected for comparison),

yet nowhere did we find a claim that Italians are constitutionally inferior to other persons of European origin.

As early as 1921 Artlitt (13) published a study in which she determined Stanford-Binet *IQ*'s and ranking on the Taussig Socio-economic Scale of 191 native-born white, 87 Italian, and 71 Negro primary school children. She concluded that "the difference in median *IQ* which is due to race alone is in this case at most only 8.6 whereas the difference between children of the same race but of Inferior and Very Superior social status may amount to 33.9 points" (p. 182). Because of the early date at which this research was conducted it is only to be expected that the assumption of a racial factor remained, but she appropriately titled her paper "On the Need for Caution in Establishing Race Norms," a warning which was unfortunately widely disregarded. Had she taken into account other factors such as language handicaps, length of residence in the United States, or educational level of the parents she would undoubtedly have found even less of a residual difference to be accounted for on "racial" grounds.

Only three years later Bere (17) conducted an even more sophisticated study which is relevant even today. She administered the Stanford-Binet and the Pintner-Paterson Performance Tests to boys of immigrant Hebrew, Bohemian, and Italian parents, 100 of each ethnic group, and all having been at least two years in the New York City public schools. Through comparisons between the various tests and subtests she attempted to identify the types of thinking process associated with the differing cultural backgrounds and experiences of the boys, concluding that the Hebrew boys did best in problems involving abstraction whereas the Italians thought in more concrete terms, with the Bohemians falling between. This attention to qualitative differences in problem-solving thought processes learned in different cultural settings was true pioneering. It is only in quite recent years that additional serious work had been undertaken in this area, yet it is increasingly clear that this is the direction in which we must travel if we are truly to understand the mechanisms which produce cultural and ethnic differences in problem-solving behavior, to say nothing of quantitative *IQ*'s.

In the years following, along with the continued outpouring of naïve comparisons of "racial" *IQ*'s, a variety of increasingly sophisticated critiques and critical research was undertaken. In 1927 Mead (184) compared a group of 160 American children with 276 children of the same grade in whose homes Italian was spoken, utilizing *IQ*, social status measures, amount of English spoken in the home, and length of parental residence in the

United States, concluding among other things that "classification of foreign children in schools where they have to compete with American children, on the basis of group intelligence test findings alone, is not a just evaluation of the child's innate capacity" (p. 468). In separate articles published in 1928 Thompson (269) and Viteles (279) reviewed a number of comparative studies of Negro and white *IQ*'s and concluded that existing tests appeared to measure only acquired, not innate, ability and were therefore worthless for interracial comparisons. In 1932 Daniel (51) compiled a checklist of factors which must be taken into consideration in attempting interracial comparisons of mental ability, including statistical considerations, sampling, norms, test artifacts, educational opportunities, and the like. Subsequent work would suggest a further expansion of his list, but acceptance even of his criteria would be sufficient to invalidate virtually all extant comparisons of racial intelligence. Franzblau (73) in 1935, rather ingeniously administered the nonverbal National Intelligence Test to groups of girls in Copenhagen and in Rome, and then to Danish-American and Italian-American girls of similar age in the United States. Confirming the results of other studies, it was found that in the United States the Danish girls scored higher than the Italians, but the differences between the Danish and Italians girls tested in their home countries were not statistically significant. Because of the possibility of selective migration or other intervening factors one cannot accept this study as proof that native Danes and Italians are in fact identical in intelligence, but it does place the burden of proof on those who would contend that cultural background has no effect on the ability to adapt to and profit from the American educational system.

Also in 1935, Nissen, Machover, and Kinder (195) attacked the problem somewhat differently. They compared, on the basis of performance tests, groups of Negro children in West Virginia, St. Helena Island, and West Africa, the last from an area from which the slavers drew most of the slaves who were the ancestors of the present Negro population of the New World. As might be expected the West African Negroes scored lowest, while the New World Negroes were higher but below the white standardization norms. The differences, as might also be expected, were greatest on those subtests which the authors considered to have the greatest amount of Western cultural content. More important here than their research results are the conclusions they drew from their research experience, which are worth citing at some length.

In most reports of psychometric test findings with "racial" groups, whether civilized or primitive, the purpose, either expressed or implied, is that of affording an objective basis for the determination of "racial" differences. If test results are interpreted as reflecting differences only in specific, immediately present abilities which are closely related to those involved in the tests, there is little room for disagreement. If, however, differences in test results are generalized and considered as indicative of differences in *general* ability or adaptability, we encounter difficulties. Leaving aside the question of the significance of various traits and abilities for diverse cultures and environments, we cannot even be sure that the correlates of a given test performance are the same for all "racial" groups. Interpretations become even more speculative when the attempt is made to adduce from observed differences in test results evidence of inherent "racial" differences in specific or general native potentiality, potentiality for differential development being maximum at birth and never the same thereafter. Even assuming perfect analysis of the test, it would be virtually impossible to trace, not to say measure and make proper allowance for, all the subtle and elusive factors which contribute to the development of the associative abilities.

The difficulty of determining the degree of racial homogeneity of any given group, consideration of the mobility of races, which raises the issue of the fairness of temporal sampling, and the necessity of securing adequate geographic samplings for experimental purposes, complicate the problem immeasurably.

The sheer accumulation of test scores, then, whether or not they consistently point in the same direction, must leave us with the essentially inseparable variables, viz.: race and environment. The test which will eliminate or measure the effect of either element alone has not yet been devised, nor can we accept speculation as a substitute for the scientific differentiation of these two factors (pp. 309-310).

Starting in the late 1920's Otto Klineberg of Columbia University, both through his own research and through reviews of the work of others, has been one of the most continuous critics of comparative studies of "racial" intelligence. He has considerably extended the number of factors which must be considered as affecting test performance, including such matters as culturally determined attitudes toward speed of performance in any context or toward excelling in a test. In 1941 (158) he summarized "some of the factors in the social environment which may be responsible for the observed ethnic differences in test scores, and which should be controlled before any direct comparison between two different ethnic groups can legitimately be made. These include the factors of motivation, rapport, schooling, socioeconomic status, and language, as well as the background of interest, attitudes, and point-of-view which collectively we may call 'culture'" (p. 293).

Various aspects of Klineberg's work are discussed in more detail at several points in this report. He is one of the few psychologists concerned with this problem who has had anthropological research training.

An extensive research program at the University of Chicago, conducted by Allison W. Davis and Robert J. Havighurst and their colleagues, also handled social and cultural factors with sophistication. Because their primary focus was on the influence of social class factors in urban areas of the United States, rather than on ethnic factors, the results of this research are more appropriately discussed elsewhere. Davis and Havighurst (59) succinctly summarize their basic orientation as follows: "The crucial problem raised by the attempt to compare scientifically the capacity of any two individuals to learn is that of finding situations with which the two individuals have had equal experience" (p. 301).

Although ethnic comparisons undoubtedly form quantitatively the largest bulk of research relevant to heredity factors in mental ability, there have been other more direct approaches to the problem. One of the more obvious lines of attack is to administer intelligence tests to the children of persons who, in their earlier years, were adjudged retarded. Recent examples of such studies are those of Reed, Reed, and Palm (212) and of Charles (40). In the former, 37 people institutionalized as children at the Faribault (Minnesota) State School and Colony during the period 1910-1918, with an average *IQ* of 48, had 80 children who could be located and tested in the 1950's. These children had a mean *IQ* of 71. Charles, as part of a larger study, tested 73 children of parents adjudged in an earlier survey to be retarded on the basis of *IQ* and poor performance in the Lincoln, Nebraska, school system. He found their *IQ*'s to average 95.4, with only one-sixth of the group below 80. This rise in the *IQ* of children compared to their retarded parents, which is confirmed in other studies, is not capable of clear-cut interpretation. In the first place, the parents themselves when retested after living in the community for some years generally show higher *IQ*'s than they did as children (cf. Fairbank, 70; Muench, 189); this was true in Charles' sample and immediately raises the question whether we are viewing the parents' genes as having been determinants of their earlier or their later *IQ*'s. Furthermore, it is rarely possible to test the other parents, that is, the spouses of the persons originally judged retarded, and patently impossible to determine what their *IQ*'s would have been had they been tested at the earlier time, so at best we knew only half the genetic picture. Finally, we have ample evidence (e.g., Skeels and Harms, 246) of the effect of a more or a less stimulating environment on the development of intelligence of the sort measured by tests. Unless we have detailed data on the environments in which both the parents and the children were reared we can say nothing about the effects, if any, of heredity as the determinant of the children's higher *IQ*'s.

Herndon (114) addressed himself to a particular aspect of the folklore of the genetics of retardation, to wit, the belief that inbreeding, presumably by "weakening the strain," produces an increase in retardation. It is of course well known that inbreeding is more likely to permit expression of pathological and other characteristics determined by recessive genes, but the popular belief appears more general in nature and implies that inbreeding of itself has a weakening effect on intelligence as well as other characteristics. It was this belief which Herndon undertook to test. He administered the Wechsler-Bellevue to 223 persons in 86 inter-marrying families who lived in isolated pockets in the Blue Ridge Mountains of North Carolina, comparing these results with those obtained on other rural, but not isolated, North Carolina populations. He found "a range of *IQ* scores within normal limits for a rural population, occurring in a population with an unusually high cousin marriage rate and with presumably small size of mating isolates" (p. 57). The mean *IQ* was 94.5. This result is the more notable when viewed in relation to an earlier study by Sherman and Key (240). These authors administered a battery of tests to people in four of these "hollows" in the Blue Ridge Mountains somewhat north of the locale of Herndon's study, as well as to a group of people who had left the mountains to work in a sawmill in a Virginia town. The environment was similar but there was no evidence of a high rate of inbreeding. They found that, by ranking the communities on degree of isolation from day-to-day contact with the outside world, greater isolation appeared to correlate with a lower *IQ*. However, with more isolation there was also a lower socio-economic status, this latter having been shown in many studies to correlate with *IQ* also. Thus we cannot with assurance blame the environmental effects of isolation alone in the Sherman and Key study, but we *can* say that Herndon's inbred group lived in an environment at least no more conducive to developing a high *IQ* than their unisolated rural neighbors. Similarly, the study by Eaton and Weil (65) discussed more fully in Section VII of the inbred Hutterite population showed the morbidity rates of mental deficiency to fall within a normal range, while in the non-defective population at large there was no evidence of depressed intelligence.

Researchers concerned with separation of the effects of the seemingly inseparable factors of heredity and environment in humans have long been intrigued with the possibilities inherent in studies of identical twins. It requires more than mere superficial similarities in appearance to determine with certainty that such twins actually originated with a single fertilized ovum, but once such a determination has been made it is safe to assume that the two twins have identical hereditary endowments. From this it follows that any differences which appear between them are due to environment alone. It is then deceptively easy to slip into the next step of the argument, that if a pair of twins are reared apart all the differences between them can be ascribed to identifiable differences in their respective environments, and conversely any similarities which exceed those shared by other persons respectively in these two environments can be attributed to heredity. This line of reasoning has caused a great deal of interest to be focused on studies of identical twins reared apart, but alas, few firm answers have emerged from such studies.

There are a number of reasons for this, one being that relatively few cases are available for study. In 1941 Woodworth (300) reviewed the literature on the subject and was able to report only 22 seemingly valid cases of identical twins who were raised separately. More have come to light since, but when one considers that some attempt must be made to match at least approximately the respective environments of the twin pairs it is evident that the number of subjects available for valid comparison is very small. It would not be very meaningful to compare one pair of twins placed in middle class and lower class rural homes with another pair placed in middle class and lower class urban homes. If one further takes into account educational factors in both foster parents and children, number of foster siblings, language factors, regional characteristics, and the host of other things known to have bearing on the development of mental ability, each twin pair becomes practically unique.

Another problem arises in identifying the environmental factors responsible for the differences observed. We know that their respective foetal positions in the womb, birth order, and probably other factors create differences in genetically identical twins even by the time of their birth, so we cannot say their relevantly different environments are in their foster homes only, nor that they were born identical. Assuming they are not separated on the day of their birth, we have also to take into account the effects of coexistence with each other, for the immediate presence of another identical infant creates an environment significantly different from that of the single baby (cf. Burlingham, 33). This environment probably even differs, particularly with respect to adult responses to the baby, in important ways from that experienced by fraternal twins, but on this point we have no data. Furthermore, once they have grown up and we wish to make statements as to the relative effects of heredity and environment in determining their similarities and differences, we have to have some idea of how similar they would have been had they not been twins. Here again we run into the great multiplicity of factors which affect the development of intellect, personality, etc. A valid basis for estimating environmental differences calls for comparison groups comprising for each twin persons of the same age and sex, from the same or a very similar neighborhood, who are also adopted into foster homes with a similar number of children in them, where the same language and ethnic backgrounds obtain, of the same social class, and so on. It is obvious that it would be extremely difficult if not impossible to locate such comparison groups of sufficient size to average out the individual genetic factors in each group. We cannot just go out and find such groups, but rather have to look for them in the area where we happen to have located one of a pair of twins. It is perhaps by now clear why precise answers to questions as to the relative effectiveness of heredity and environment are not likely to be found in twin studies. Unless we can define the environmental forces we cannot say how much effect heredity really has, nor in what ways it is effective. Conversely, even though we know heredity is identical in a pair of twins, we must pinpoint just which environmental factors produced the observed differences in each twin. Otherwise we know no more than we did before about environmental influences except to say with assurance what we have said before, that genes alone do not determine intelligence or behavior. We cannot say, however, that we have proven that they have no effect.

Similar conclusions can be reached from studies of children placed in foster homes or actually adopted. Probably the most conclusive among these are the follow-up studies done at the Iowa Child Welfare Station (cf. Skeels and Harms, 246; Skodak and Skeels, 248) of children born to occupationally and intellectually inferior families and adopted into average or superior homes. The IQ's of these children conformed quite consistently to the norms of their adoptive parents, with averages substantially higher than those of their own parents. This confirmed the findings of earlier but less well controlled studies (e.g., Wells and Arthur, 284, and Speer, 257.)

However, Skeels and Harms did find in one of their groups that despite the higher level of performance of the children (mean IQ 105.5 vs. 62.7), their IQ's correlated (.23, significant at the five per cent level) with the IQ's of their mothers, implying strongly that the foster home environment was not the only determinant of intellectual ability. This correlation is higher than that found in any earlier studies (cf. Snygg, 255). This relationship might be explained in a number of ways, including the possibility of selective placement of children from better true parents in the better foster homes, but in the absence of a positive causal explanation it forces us again to leave open the question of how much or little influence heredity has in determining mental ability.

The uniformly negative conclusions we have reached in this synoptic review of research on the effects of heredity versus environment in mental retardation might lead to the presumption that we feel no research at all in this area should be undertaken. Rather, however, we would say that the moral to be drawn from the vast amount of relatively futile effort which has gone into the subject is that research should only be contemplated if it can proceed without the help of unjustified theoretical assumptions, building only upon the foundation of known facts and relationships. Unfortunately, this second statement, although more optimistically phrased, at present says virtually the same thing as the first. It is our conviction, which we shall try to document below, that the scientific tools to work with are simply not yet available, and that the undeniable pressures from society to do something will not justify the substitution of conceptual tools derived from folklore.

An instructive analogy can be drawn from the field of physical anthropology. One of the earliest and most enduring orientations in this field was toward race, starting with the three major divisions of Caucasian, Negroid, and Mongoloid, followed by the gradual definition of a variety of subtypes within each. These distinctions were refined on the basis of a large number of reassuringly objective and quantitative scales of observation and measurement of external morphological features—head form, skin color, body build, and the like. (We might note in passing that all of these were more constant and more verifiable than the IQ.) The validity of these racial criteria, and of the research in race mixture, etc., which utilized them, rested of course upon the assumption that they were determined by genetic factors which ultimately would be identified. Over a period of many years literally millions of painstaking measurements and observations were made on both skeletal material and living subjects, many anthropologists devoting their entire professional lives to this line of endeavor. Washburn (281) has described the situation in words which might provide food for sober thought by many psychometricians: "The efforts of physical anthropologists have been to get agreements on how to take measurements and observations. Introductions to physical anthropology are largely instructions on how to take measurements, with little or no indication of what it is that the measurements are supposed to mean. International congresses have ended with pleas for uniformity, so that the classification might continue" (p. 717).

Finally, questions began to be raised as to the actual genetic and developmental significance of the measures selected as racial criteria. A series of investigations led to increasingly discouraging conclusions. Then, after the war, a group of younger physical anthropologists who had taken the time to obtain a thorough training in embryology, developmental anatomy, serology, genetics, and other relevant fields, began the serious study of the concepts so long in vogue, each from the standpoint of his own additional specialty. Within a very few years the work of lifetimes was discarded (except as the data were useable by anatomists, human engineers, and the like) and a completely new start was made, based upon a few characteristics (especially blood groups) whose genetic determinants were known, and upon the growing understanding of population genetics. It is interesting to note, parenthetically, that the breeding populations tentatively defined on a world-wide basis through serology bore practically no resemblance to the classical groupings of racial types so long assumed to be real entities.

Research in the genetics of mental subnormality—and we must emphasize again that we are *not* talking about identifiable pathologies—appears to be following a similar path, although the effort expended thus far is not nearly as great. There are two differences which should be noted, neither of them encouraging. First is the fact that the *IQ* and other measures of mental ability are far more unstable and indeterminate than any used by traditional physical anthropology. Second is the far greater social significance of any research results in this field, particularly in the context of racial issues in the United States and elsewhere in the world, a significance approximated by physical anthropological research only during the Nazi era. In this situation science bears a moral as well as a professional responsibility to be highly critical of the validity of the assumptions it uses.

The most crucial assumption in any genetic investigation lies in the identification of a true genotype, that is, a characteristic which can be observed and which reflects the influence of genes. No possibility exists at present of being able, through microscopic or other means, to determine by observation of reproductive cells the characteristics they will help to create in the organism. Studies in genetics therefore must depend upon the observation of characteristics of the organism known or presumed to have certain determinants in the genes, followed by deductions concerning the manner in which such genes are transmitted and reach expression. It is not necessary that we be certain that a characteristic is genotypic—that is, that it represents the result of genetic rather than environmental forces—in order that we examine its distribution. Kallmann, for example, in the study of schizophrenia cited earlier, simply assumed that a tendency toward schizophrenia was inherited in certain ways, calculated predicted frequencies of distribution of the disorder among twins, siblings, and other classes of relatives, and then successfully compared his predictions with actual frequencies of occurrence. His research has been criticized on several grounds, but there appears to be little argument as to the soundness of this type of genetic research as such.

However, although we do not have to *know* that we have an observable genotype, we do have to have a basis for making such a presumption. The first requirement for establishing a presumption of genetic determinism is that the characteristic in question be relatively constant over time and be reliably observable by independent observers with similar results. Mental retardation without detectable pathology does not even approach these requirements. The recent survey of persons under 18 referred as mentally retarded in Onondaga County, New York (New York State Department of Mental Hygiene, 193), provides eloquent refutation of both points. With regard to constancy, the age-specific curve rises to a peak at age 15, and thereafter drops off sharply. Unless one wishes to make the preposterous assumption that the majority of retarded children do not live beyond 16 or 17 one is forced to conclude that retardation means different things to different people, and that the criterion changes at about 16 (which happens to be the upper limit of compulsory education in New York State). Furthermore, it did not prove possible to isolate any one diagnostic criterion which was applicable to all cases; for example, although it is often customary to set the cut-off point for mental deficiency at IQ 70, almost 25 per cent of all referred cases in Onondaga County had reported IQ's of 90 or over.

It is equally unsatisfactory to presume that the IQ alone is a genotypic characteristic. There is in the first place abundant evidence that the IQ as determined by intelligence tests is not constant in the individual over time, and that its variation does not follow a uniformly predictable pattern such as one would expect of a hereditary characteristic which changed along with the biological maturation process. In different individuals the *IQ* may increase or decrease over time. Also, *IQ*'s are derived from a variety of different tests and most psychologists now require knowledge of the test used before attaching any real significance to an *IQ*. This of course means that the *IQ* is not a reliable and absolute measure of over-all intelligence. Finally, much of this report is devoted to documenting the various ways in which environmental experiences determine mental ability and therefore *IQ* level. Most psychologists recoil in alarm over the implication that the *IQ* be taken as a measure of inherent—as against learned—mental capacity, yet this presumption must be made if the *IQ* is to be considered genotypic.

This assumption, when accepted, can lead to remarkably devious reasoning when an attempt is made to account for the known environmental variables. It is for example well known that retardation and a low *IQ* are more common in lower socio-economic levels of society, whereas so-called idiots and imbeciles are randomly distributed through all social classes. It is customarily concluded that most of the retardation in the lower classes results from lack of stimulation, poor schooling, and various motivational factors, while idiots and imbeciles represent pathologies (some probably genetic in origin) which occur fortuitously. Yet one finds persons with a genetic point to prove (e.g., Moore, 187, or Halperin, 103) stating that the idiots and imbeciles are indeed pathological, but that the morons are of genetically inferior stock which cannot compete successfully in the framework of *laissez faire* capitalism and therefore sinks down the social scale. This oversimplified application of the principle of natural selection and survival of the fittest would fit more appropriately into the intellectual climate of the 19th Century than of today, for students of biological evolution have come to realize that in altering the characteristics of large populations natural selection operates in highly complicated ways and only over long periods of time (Snyder, 254). Even if one were to assume that the *IQ* reflects true genetically determined mental capacity, the concentration of a pool of inferior genes in the lower classes would require many generations of breeding, coupled with a relatively complete lack of intermixture between social classes. These conditions obviously do not exist in our society. The opportunity, and actuality, of vertical social mobility is almost a byword, with many persons in each generation marrying outside of the social class into which they were born, assuring a flow of genes up and down the social scale. Furthermore, in the United States at least, very few generations have elapsed since the population reached approximately its present size, not nearly enough time to stabilize even an isolated breeding population.

Even if it were possible to determine the actual inherent mental capacity of various ethnic and socio-economic groups, the differences observed would not lead necessarily to a genetic explanation. Pasamanick (202) has demonstrated that, in addition to gross defects, more minor brain damage sufficient to affect intellectual functioning can result from both complications during the mother's pregnancy and premature birth of the child. In his study of these factors in Baltimore, Pasamanick found that Negro infants run a 50 per cent greater risk of prematurity than white, presumably because of dietary and other cultural influences. Similarly, he compared the incidence of complications of pregnancy in upper class whites with that found in lower class whites (on the basis of a five-class scale) and in Negroes. They showed an incidence respectively three times and 10 times greater than the upper class whites. From the standpoint of the heredity versus environment controversy, these findings simply point up yet another environmental influence on intelligence which must be controlled before it can be maintained that a purely genetic component has been isolated.

If one examines further the requirements of genetic research it becomes apparent that most research approaches require not merely the presumption of a genotype, but also the presumed identification of a single gene or a specific combination of genes which determines the genotype. This applies to the genealogical method, to most twin studies, and to the determination of gene frequencies in population genetics. Again it should be emphasized that it is not necessary to *know* such a relationship exists, but it must be possible to provide at least an a priori justification for an assumption of this order, if only as a basis for predictive hypotheses to be tested. Yet if we look to researchers in the field for an indication of where to look for aspects of intelligence which might have such unitary determinants, we find Lawrence H. Snyder in genetics and J. P. Guilford in psychology, each outstanding in his field, agreeing that intelligence is multifactorial. After reviewing some sorts of human pathology whose genetic bases are isolable, Snyder (254, p. 397) concludes that intelligence and indeed most of "those genetic differences which are involved in [the] non-pathological range of human variability are most probably contingent upon multifactorial inheritance." Approaching the problem from a different angle, Guilford undertook to determine by factor analysis the components of intellect. His research is discussed in detail in Chapter XII and we may simply note here that, having identified 40 factors and believing that his list was not yet complete, Guilford stated (99, p. 287): "The question 'Is intelligence inherited or is it acquired' makes less sense than it ever did. Such a question must be asked regarding each and every factor."

We must therefore conclude that the *IQ* is unstable over time, cannot be reliably measured by any agreed-upon single instrument and has strong environmental determinants, and that its genetic determinants are sufficiently multifactorial that they do not lend themselves to existing techniques of genetic research. Therefore, genetic studies based on the test *IQ*, or upon the even vaguer concepts of mental deficiency or retardation, do not present a very promising avenue for research.

If, however, we turn to mental defectives with identifiable pathologies or to variations in blood chemistry or physiology which appear to be related to mental functioning we can undertake valid and fruitful genetic studies. Recent research in phenylpyruvic oligophrenia, galactosemia, and cerebral palsy are cases in point. Twin studies are particularly useful in determining whether a hereditary factor is involved and, often in combination with other techniques, can reveal much of the nature of the genetic process involved. With this knowledge one can predict the likelihood of occurrence, and furthermore be fairly explicit as to the certainty with which such predictions are made. On the other hand, these genetic studies may conclude with some assurance that heredity is not involved and thus point research more positively in other directions. Either outcome is productive and will fully justify the genetic approach, provided only that a sufficiently determinate factor is fed into the genetic equation in the first instance. Rather than continuing to devote money and talent to genetic studies based on the elusive *IQ*, it would appear sensible to wait upon the biochemists, physiologists, and others who are increasingly turning up suggestive leads based on factors which experience has taught us are likely to have identifiable genetic determinants. There may be a single enzyme, determined by a single gene, which has an important effect on mental capacity, but this enzyme appears more likely to be discovered in the laboratory than through the administration of intelligence tests to persons of differing ethnic origins or social classes, or to various relatives of institutionalized subnormal children or adults.

XIV. CULTURAL BACKGROUND FACTORS AFFECTING
TEST PERFORMANCE

A. SCHOOL PERFORMANCE

In our discussion of the hereditary versus the environmental factors in the etiology of mental retardation we concluded that, except for certain identifiable pathological conditions, a hereditary determinant of intelligence has yet to be isolated and demonstrated. Even if, however, it should ultimately prove possible validly to estimate the effects of heredity in a given case this will not eliminate mental retardation. This knowledge will make possible some preventive measures but it will do little or nothing to resolve the problems of defective or retarded persons already born. It will, furthermore, contribute only very indirectly to improving the lot of those whose environment, as children and adults, limits their opportunity to develop the full use of their inherent intellectual capacity. It is this latter group with which this report is primarily concerned.

A vast amount of research has gone into the effort to elicit the social and cultural factors which affect intellectual functioning. Almost all of the research in this area has accepted an intelligence test of one kind or another as the primary criterion of level of intellect, with the derived intelligence quotient providing a measure of advancement or retardation. In this section we shall therefore be summarizing the major findings of research on the environmental antecedents of test performance as such, working backwards from the test situation in search of explanations for differences in performance. In the next section we will reverse the order of our inquiry and widen its scope, focusing upon the kinds of thinking processes to which children in various social and cultural groups are exposed and attempting to relate this to the intellectual demands made by society upon its members through life, recognizing intelligence tests only as an incidental factor important in a few cultures.

We cannot, however, defer consideration of one kind of intellectual demand which our own society imposes upon practically all of its members, the school situation. Two facts force us immediately and constantly to be aware of the intellectual problems presented by school. First is the fact that school is the principal, and often the only, context in which many children of borderline intelligence are labelled and treated as mentally retarded. Reference has already been made to the survey of Onondaga County, New York (N.Y. State Department of Mental Hygiene, 193), which shows the prevalence of identified retardation rising with age until, with the years of compulsory schooling behind, from age 16 onward the age-specific rates drop off dramatically. Earlier studies have demonstrated the same thing elsewhere (e.g., for England and Wales, Mental Deficiency Committee, 185, and Baltimore, Md., Lemkau, Tietze, and Cooper, 166, p. 280). In other words, many children who through their final year of schooling are still labelled "retarded" immediately thereafter merge into the "normal" population with at least sufficient completeness no longer to be reported statistically. The compulsory school experience may therefore be viewed for many people as in effect the most difficult intellectual hurdle which will confront them throughout their entire lives, although later in other settings they may perform tasks of substantial complexity.

The second fact which forces our interest in intelligence tests to focus also on the schools is that school performance is the criterion to which the great majority of intelligence tests predict and against which they are validated. Furthermore, as Davis and Havighurst (59, p. 307) have pointed out, the problems presented in intelligence tests are essentially academic problems. Yet they will probably be with us for a long time. Budd (32), commenting on the efforts of Davis, Eells and others to develop culture-fair tests, observes:

> Teachers and administrators feel they know the "good" students in their schools and present day intelligence tests largely corroborate their judgment. It is therefore difficult to envisage the time when the present tests will be replaced in a very practical way by such newer and theoretically more valid instruments (p. 334).

Stenquist (263) expresses the same dilemma in a slightly different way:

> If in this study the purpose is merely to discover new techniques ... to try to salvage individuals who have already shown that they cannot compete with the scholastically minded, I fear that the harvest will be meager. Through efforts to recognize and respect status differences we may establish that a few more individuals actually possess the type of ability that is reflected in the traditional I.Q. concept if we extend these crutches to them and thus help them a little up the ramp. But I fear this is meeting only a part of the problem. It seems clear to me that if we are to guage our measuring stick to the whole range of mental ability we must have a broader criterion than success in present-day schools (p. 187).

Although it is our purpose in this report to consider some ways in which the broader criterion of which Stenquist speaks may be established, in this chapter we limit ourselves to existing research and are thus largely bound to the conception of school as the proving ground of intellect, and therefore of intelligence tests.

Often in the pages which follow our discussion will focus on the factors affecting test performance in a wide variety of "normal" groups and in the population as a whole rather than being confined to the problems only of retarded persons. The reason for this is simple. Within any social or cultural grouping there is a distribution of intelligence, and of test scores if the people are tested. There are high scorers and low scorers and all grades in between but the majority of people usually have scores near the mean or median for the particular group in question. These average scores, we will see, differ quite markedly from one social class or subculture to another, even in our own society. But at the same time in this culture of ours, as represented by the school systems, occupational placement policies, etc., there is defined through the *IQ* or other criteria a level below which a person, whatever his origin, will be considered inadequate. It is therefore apparent that if the distribution of test scores around a mean is for any reason pushed downward within a given group, more of its members will fall below the level of socially-determined adequacy and be considered retarded. Consequently, the more we know about the factors which produce high or low average scores in groups as wholes the more we will know about the sources of retardation in those who fall below the line defined for our society at large. We cannot say that every retarded child from a subcultural group is retarded solely because of his group membership and experience, for there are others who perform adequately among his fellows, but we can say that the handicap which affects them all has contributed also to his misfortune. If this particular handicap can be alleviated he can very possibly improve to a point of social adequacy. For this reason, then, we must examine the factors affecting the test performance of all members of a given segment of society, not merely of those who are retarded.

Although, as we have seen, researchers who are concerned with demonstrating a hereditary component in intelligence occasionally make fairly naïve assumptions about the *IQ* as a measure of inherent capacity, the great majority of psychologists recognize that there are both cultural and individual differences in experience which predispose a person toward a good or a poor test performance. This realization in fact goes back practically to the inception of intelligence tests themselves. As Allison Davis (55) pointed out so effectively, Alfred Binet himself explicitly recognized as early as 1908 that cultural and social class differences existed, but he was unable to resolve the difficulty.

For some years thereafter little attention was given to the problem. As in the case of investigations of heredity of intellect, the first real stimulus to environmental studies came from the results of testing World War I recruits with the Army Alpha and Beta. Soon after it was determined that Negroes had lower average scores than whites, it was further discovered that the average scores of Negroes from several Northern states were higher than those of rural white persons in some Southern states. From this initial finding of broad regional differences the focus sharpened down during the 1920's to isolate for study most of the areas which have concerned researchers ever since—socio-economic and social class factors, ethnic differences, language handicaps and bilingualism, rural-urban differences, sex differences, and cultural and subcultural factors. We shall review the major findings in each of these areas. It may be well, however, first to anticipate in general terms a criticism which will be levelled repeatedly at studies in all of these categories. With a few notable exceptions far more effort has been expended on establishing that the *IQ varies with,* for example, social class than has been devoted to finding out *why* lower-class people test lower. Even where reasons have been sought, the focus has commonly been upon the test situation—motivation, speed, competitiveness, comprehension, and the like—rather than upon the kinds of thinking which on the one hand are necessary to solve test problems and on the other are likely to be learned in various environmental contexts. We thus find available for both retarded and standard populations a wide array of correlations between *IQ* and almost any other factor imaginable, but in these studies one finds very few hints as to specific causal relationships.

If we are to have the understanding of subcultural mental retardation necessary for training, rehabilitation, and prevention we must know the "why" of the correlations. The early research which established that *IQ* varied with social class was of great value, but we cannot stop there and wait for the problem of subcultural retardation to be solved on the utopian day when over-all class differences cease to exist. Nor, as Stenquist observes, will the construction of special tests judged *a priori* to be more "fair," but of uncertain predictive value, erase the fact that the school performance to which standard tests predict is no longer merely preparation for adult life but has become a crucial end in itself. Failure to surmount the hurdle of school and intelligence tests brands the child as subnormal, implying, at least, that he is unfit not only for school but also society at large. Kanner (146) comments with some bitterness on the stigma of retardation to which a child is vulnerable when "scholastic curricula demand competition in spelling, history, geography, long division, and other preparations deemed essential for the tasks of feeding chickens, collecting garbage, and wrapping bundles in a department store" (p. 10).

The introduction of special classes in school systems provides ever increasing opportunity for the training and education of retarded children, but helps little with the stigma. Since we cannot reasonably expect, nor indeed desire, that over-all scholastic standards be overhauled to fit the limitations of marginal students, it would appear more fruitful to seek out the particular aspects of the social or cultural experience of these students which were inadequate or detrimental to the development of the intellectual skills required to do well in school (or on intelligence tests). With these more specific relationships established correction and prevention can have more clearly defined targets.

Consider for example arithmetic and sentence diagramming. These certainly involve abstraction and symbolic logic. But are the intellectual processes in both essentially the same, so that a child who is equipped for one is also equipped for the other? And how does this skill relate to the skill required for example on the digit-symbol subtest of the Wechsler-Bellevue? And again, how severely handicapped in this regard is the lower-class Italian child who is expected to do his daily tasks around the house in response to concrete instructions, without bothering his elders with abstract questions about the how and why of things?[12] If we knew the answers to these questions we could perhaps plan to give Italian children certain kinds of special training when they first enter school, training designed to correct their particular deficits. In this way they could cope from the beginning with the gradually rising level of abstraction in the curriculum in later years, rather than fumbling and bluffing in the lower grades and failing outright later on.

The most ambitious effort to explore the environmental determinants of school and test performance in this country thus far has been that conducted by Allison Davis and his associates at the University of Chicago. Although they have concentrated their research primarily on social class differences their interests have ranged more widely to embrace almost all aspects of the prob-

---

[12]This statement, as well as others concerning the living patterns of lower-class Italian children to be discussed in Section VII, is based only upon impressions and conversations with a (middle class) Italian acquaintance of one of the authors. It is an unhappy commentary on research in this area that despite the consistently low test scores obtained by Italian children over the years no one has, to our knowledge, undertaken any systematic study of the reasons for this deficit.

lem. Some of their more general conclusions will serve as an introduction to a more detailed review of the field. Haggard (101) has this to say of the intelligence tests themselves:

> In terms of our present knowledge, the standard-type intelligence tests are inadequate on several counts. Among other things, (a) they have measured only a very narrow range of mental abilities, namely those related to verbal or academic success, and have ignored other abilities and problem-solving skills which are perhaps more important for adjustment and success—even in middle-class society; (b) they have failed to provide measures of the wide variety of qualitative differences in the modes or processes of solving mental problems; (c) they have ignored the influences of differences in cultural training and socialization on the repertoire of experience and the attitude, motivation, and personality patterns of sub-groups in our society, and the effect of such factors on mental test performance; and (d) they have considered mental functioning in isolation, thus ignoring the interdependence of the individual's motivational and personality structure on the characteristics of his mental functioning, as seen, for example, in the differences between rote learning and the ability to use previous experiences creatively in new contexts.
>
> A re-evaluation of the purposes and problems involved in the appraisal and description of mental abilities is necessary before adequate mental tests can be developed. But before this can be done, it will first be necessary to conduct anthropological, sociological, and psychological studies to learn how representative children in our society live. For lower-class and ethnic children, for example, information is needed concerning their value, attitude, and motivational systems, the nature of their daily experiences, and the range of mental behaviors and modes of thinking used in finding solutions to their life problems. It will also be necessary to consider the growing body of evidence that mental functioning does not exist in a vacuum, but that the individual's motivational and personality structure, his attitudes, interests, needs, and goals are intimately related to, and in a large measure determine, his mental processes (pp. 180-181).

Allison Davis, in his Inglis Lecture (55), stresses repeatedly the way in which both intelligence tests and school curricula are rooted in middle class values and standards:

> Fundamentally, the cultural bias of the standard tests of intelligence consists in their having fixed upon only those types of mental behaviors in which the higher and middle socio-economic groups are superior. . . . They do not use problems which are equally familiar and motivating to all . . . groups. . . . By choosing a limited range of mental problems, notably scholastic problems, the present tests very likely bias our mental ratings of even the middle-class child (pp. 47-48).

Davis points out that 95 per cent of all teachers are middle class, and discusses the values they therefore share:[13]

> From his middle-class culture, learned from his parents, teachers, and friends, both the teacher and the professor of education have learned to regard certain mental interests and skills, certain moral values, as the "best," or "most cultured," or "most intelligent." Granted that, for this society, the basic *moral* values of middle class people may be the most adaptive for survival, it does not follow that present-day middle-class academic skills and goals are most effective in developing the intellectual, imaginative, and problem-solving activities of human beings (pp. 89-90).
>
> The present curricula are stereotyped and arbitrary selections from a narrow area of middle-class culture. Academic culture is one of the most conservative and ritualized aspects of human culture. Its formalization, its lack of functional connection with the daily problems of life, has given a bloodless, fossilized character to the classroom which all of us recognize. For over a generation, no basically new types of mental problems have been added to intelligence tests. . . . What proportion of the *basic mental problems* met by children (and by adults for that matter) in their daily life can be solved by having a large standard vocabulary, or skill in reading, or skill in arithmetical process? (pp. 97-98).

To these comments of the University of Chicago group we should add only the observation of McCandless (177, p. 675) that "many authors have failed to see that the construction of an intelligence test is actually a definition of 'intelligence.' " At present there is really no other available way operationally to define intelligence than through the IQ or its equivalent. This is readily seen if one observes persons who work regularly with retarded children. They will watch or work with a child and then, even though they may never have seen his test results or records, will often phrase their estimate of his capability as "probably IQ so-and-so" or the like. This tendency to define the level of retardation in terms of the IQ is, of course, reflected also in many of the attempts to arrive at a legal definition for purposes of institutionalization, sterilization, etc. Therefore, however great our dissatisfaction with the IQ measure, we must recognize the importance of finding out all we can about the factors which contribute to intelligence test performance.

At the same time we must not err in the other direction and conclude that

---

[13]Warner (280) cites the proportion of teachers who are middle class or higher as 97 per cent in "Yankee City," 100 per cent in "Midwest," and 97 per cent in "Deep South." All of these are cities studied under the auspices of the Committee on Human Development of the University of Chicago.

an examination of test performance will tell us all we need to know about the etiology of subcultural mental retardation. The Onondaga County, N. Y., survey found that one out of every four children referred for suspected mental retardation had *IQ*'s of 90 or above. The label of mental retardation spreads wide, and is applied for many reasons. We can agree that everyone who bears the label has a problem, but scientifically we cannot be satisfied with the criteria established by either the *IQ* or community referral.

With these words of caution in mind, we may proceed to the examination of factors which have been explored in the search for the social and cultural determinants of intelligence test performance.

B. Socioeconomic Class

Studies demonstrating the correlation between social class status and *IQ* vie with research on ethnic and racial factors for first place both in the early date of their beginnings and in the number of replications. Clear-cut and significant relationships between *IQ* of children and the social and occupational level of their parents were obtained in separate studies by Mead (184) and Stoke (266) as early as 1927. By 1938 Neff (191) was able to survey the numerous studies by then available and, in connection with a reanalysis of data collected by Terman and Merrill, conclude that:

> (1) the standardized tests are far from constant, particularly when the retest interval is large; (2) continued residence in a very poor environment brings about a considerable loss in *IQ*, often from the "normal" level to that of "dull" or even "borderline;" (3) translation from a poor to a good environment brings about large increases in *IQ*, which, at the extremes, may amount to 30 or 40 points; (4) there is a strong possibility that the positive relation between age and social status does not exist below a certain age level; (5) some evidence from identical twin studies indicates that there is a correlation of about .50 between social status and intelligence even where heredity is held constant; (6) the inequality of social and economic opportunity renders suspect one of the major assumptions basic to the construction of the test; namely, that knowledge and information are a direct function of native ability and that the former may be used to measure the latter (p. 754).

Although the bulk of studies in this area are concerned with white groups in the United States, there is ample evidence that the relationship between socioeconomic status and *IQ* is not confined to this population.[14] We may in

---

[14]Similar results have been obtained for Negroes in the United States by Canady (36), Tomlinson (273), Edmiston and McBain (66), Jenkins and Randall (137),

fact safely endorse the statement of Eells (in Eells, Davis, Havighurst, Herrick, and Tyler, 68):

> In view of the large number of research studies which have shown the existence of sizeable and statistically significant *IQ* differences between pupils from different social-status backgrounds and in view of the almost total lack of any contrary indications from any of the research to date, it seems abundantly clear that there is no need for further research aimed merely at establishing the existence or nonexistence of such differences (p. 4).

Granted that such a relationship exists there is, as pointed out above, little that we can do with the information. A number of different approaches have therefore been tried in an effort to come closer to identifying more specifically the relevant aspects of middle class versus lower class experience. One line of attack has been to seek other factors which correlate more closely with *IQ* than does the father's occupation or the other commonly accepted measures of socioeconomic status (family income, size of house, etc.). One reason for adopting this approach has been the realization that the correlations usually employed are, although statistically significant, not nearly high enough to permit of prediction in the individual case—that is, there are still a lot of high-*IQ* lower class children, and vice versa (cf. Wellman, 282). Loevinger (169) reviewed several studies and concluded that average income was the poorest predictor of intelligence available, and father's occupation little better; the *IQ* and educational level of the parents (which are also a function of social class status, of course) showed substantially higher correlations. A rather careful study by Honzik (122) of California school children produced similar conclusions, except that she found that the *IQ* of the mother was a substantially better predictor than the educational level of either parent. She also found that these correlations (including that with social status) became higher with advancing age (up to 8 years in her study). It will be remembered that Neff reached a similar conclusion in the study cited earlier; we shall return later to a fuller discussion of these and similar findings regarding age effects. Focusing on a population heavily weighted toward the lower end of the occupational scale, District of Columbia Negroes, Robinson and Meenes (217)

---

and undoubtedly others. Robbins (214) reported the same trend on the basis of a 10-year study of 9956 fourth grade children in the public schools of Ottawa, Canada. A sampling of studies from Europe follows a similar pattern: Kuiper (161) on Holland and Germany; Sandels (223) on Sweden; Forbes (71) on Northern Ireland; and Heuyer, Piéron, and Sauvy (116) on France are examples. Also consistent are the findings of Ginnsberg (86) in Brazil, and Kirahara (153) in Japan.

found very little relationship between IQ and father's occupation, but a substantially higher correlation than other studies have shown with economic factors, particularly the average rent in the area and the ownership of radios. In interpreting this outcome it should be borne in mind that, as the University of Chicago and other studies have pointed out, the relationships between lower class parents and children tend to be less close than in the middle class and therefore involve less transfer of intellectual stimulation between generations within the immediate family. Furthermore, lower class Negro fathers tend to drift in and out of the family relationship more casually and frequently than other groups. We may therefore speculate that whatever stimulus value (or lack thereof) the father's occupation may have in the general case is more diluted in this population of District of Columbia Negroes. Concomitant with this, we would expect the children to receive a greater proportion of their stimulation from the neighborhood around them, and that therefore measures of the socioeconomic status of the neighborhood would be more relevant than father's occupation as correlates of IQ.

In the studies just described a relationship has been sought between certain aspects of the social and cultural background of individuals and the IQ's of the same individuals. Another way to approach this problem consists in seeking relationships between, on the one hand, the average test scores of groups of people in a large number of communities and, on the other, characteristics of these communities as wholes derived from census data. Thorndike (271) utilized in this manner Pintner IQ's and Metropolitan Achievement scores[15] available on half a million children in 300 communities. Correlating average test scores for each community with a variety of other measures, he found the following correlations with IQ to be significant (in decreasing order of significance): educational level of the adult population, proportion of persons owning their own homes, quality and cost of housing, proportion of native-born white persons, rate of employment of women (a negative correlation), and the proportion of professional workers in the population. Correlations with achievement scores were significant only for the proportion of professional workers and educational level of adults. The tests were administered exclusively in public schools and, where schools were segregated, only in white schools. Utilizing a similar approach, Davenport and Remmers (53) utilized mean test scores by states of young men who were candidates for officer training under the wartime A-12 and V-12 programs and found sig-

---

[15]The testing was done in connection with the standardization of a revision of the Metropolitan Achievement Test.

nificant correlations with number of telephones per 1000 population, per capita income, and the value of school property in each state. These officer candidates of course represented a selected population of college graduates. In both these studies it is immediately apparent that the items which correlate with intelligence are either actual indices of or closely related to the general socioeconomic level of the community or state, and as such serve only to verify what we already know. However, it is of importance to note in Thorndike's findings that the most significant correlate of IQ was the educational level of adults—i.e., with the parents of the children being tested. This provides additional support for the identical finding in Loevinger's research on individuals. It would be interesting to know whether, if adult $IQ's$ were available from these communities, they would support Honzik's further conclusion that the mother's IQ is an even more crucial determinant of children's intelligence than parental education. Since adults are seldom tested routinely once they are old enough to have school-age children this would probably be very difficult to test on a mass basis.

The closeness of a child's relationship with his parents as well as the intellectual content of the relationship is probably a factor in determining the degree to which the child can find intellectual stimulation in the home. Skeels and his associates at the Iowa Child Welfare Research Station conducted a number of studies exploring the effects of intellectual stimulation. Most relevant here are those concerned with the adoption of children born into lower class families (cf. Skeels and Harms, 246; and Skodak and Skeels, 248). They found that these children, whose mothers often had borderline $IQ's$, themselves developed $IQ's$ averaging well in the normal range in middle class homes, while those adopted into superior homes had correspondingly superior $IQ's$. Haggard and others at the University of Chicago attempted to produce similar effects experimentally. In a carefully controlled study, over 600 11-year-olds divided into high and low social status groups and matched for school grade, age, and IQ, were given a variety of standard and special intelligence tests and then retested with various combinations of these tests four days later. One group, comprising both high and low status children, received three days of concentrated training on the tests between test and retest, whereas a similar control group did not. Although a preliminary analysis of these data (Haggard, Davis, and Havighurst, 102) appeared to indicate that the low status children had profited more from the training than the high status ones, and some class differences did emerge under some of the controlled conditions, Haggard (101) concluded after full analysis, "When the effects of all such treatments and conditions were thrown together, there was no significant difference between the two groups of children in their ability to learn to solve intelligence test problems" (p. 184). This outcome suggests that the intellectual void created by the lower class environment is not one which can be filled through intensive but brief training. Skeels' children had years in which to build their intellectual foundations; lacking such foundations Haggard's children did not score major gains even when the training was very specific to the tasks at hand. Haggard's findings, incidentally, make it appear unlikely that the improvement in Skeels' children could have been attributable to the practice effect of retesting after a period of years.

In an effort to explore some of the causes of differences in personality as well as intellectual functioning associated with social class differences, Davis and Havighurst (57) conducted interviews with 200 mothers in Chicago, largely on the South Side. They interviewed 50 each from the middle and lower classes, Negro and white. The found, among other things, that the lower class parents, both Negro and white, tended to permit their children more freedom earlier, in effect often turning them loose to find their own entertainment and activities as soon as they were able to take care of their basic physical needs through the day. In contrast the middle class parents were more protective and more strict in training, but at the same time were more likely to assign the children definite responsibilities at home and outside at earlier ages than in the lower class. It is clear that, aside from the consequences for personality and emotional development, this difference is important for intellectual development. Both groups of children are presented with problems for solution, but whereas the lower class children can seek solutions only on a trial and error basis, with their equally inexperienced peers as mentors, the middle class children are supervised in the discharge of their responsibilities and are guided in their selection and execution of solutions along lines of known effectiveness, solutions which also fit into the accepted patterns of middle class culture. Not only is this training and responsibility well adapted to preparing the child to cope with the problems presented by middle class teachers, but by virtue of its early inception it begins to equip the child for the school experience before he starts school. The responsibilities assigned to a lower class child come later in his development, often after he has started off his school career at a disadvantage from which he will never fully recover.[16]

---

[16]The findings of this study, although probably in the main valid, must be viewed with caution because the data are derived only from mothers. Fathers might have

The impoverishment of a lower class child's opportunity for intellectual development is by no means confined to his lack of early assigned and supervised responsibility; we must recognize, although we have very little firm knowledge in this area, that there are many other facets of the intellectual climate of the home environment of a child in the lower class (or other disadvantaged subculture) which leaves him ill-prepared to cope with school and its associated intelligence testing. We are forced to this conclusion by the consistency of the relationship found in a variety of cultural settings between social class and *IQ*. However, if it is true that home environment operates across the board to stimulate or depress intellectual development, we should then expect the inadequately *prepared* lower class child to *perform* inadequately from the time he first enters school. This turns out not to be so, at least if we accept the intelligence test as a measure of the ability of a child to do school work—and if it does not measure this it measures nothing.

---

a different perception, and both might differ from the perceptions of an independent observer, as Havighurst and Davis (107) themselves later pointed out. Sears, Maccoby, and Levin (238) conducted a study in the Boston area which in part paralleled the Chicago interviews, again confining their attention to mothers, and arriving at somewhat different conclusions. We cannot attempt here to judge the soundness of the over-all findings of either study, but inasmuch as both were concerned primarily with aspects of the emotional development of children, and only secondarily with intellectual factors, most of the differences are irrelevant here. The important findings of Davis and Havighurst that middle class children were assigned tasks and responsibilities under parental supervision earlier than lower class is largely confirmed in the Boston study. With respect to the second conclusion of Davis and Havighurst we have stressed, that lower class children have more unsupervised freedom than middle class, Sears and his colleagues believe their data point in the opposite direction. However, it appears that whereas Sears is referring to the amount of restriction to which the child is subjected as long as he remains in the house or near his mother, Davis and Havighurst are concerned with the amount of time spent away from this supervised environment. For example, in our opinion one cannot equate in terms of parental guidance the middle class mother permitting her child to go down the block to visit with a child of well-known neighbors on the one hand, with the lower class mother letting her child go off with his friends unescorted to the movies on the other. Furthermore, whereas the children studied in Boston were all five years old, the median age of the lower class children in Chicago was six, an important factor in determining the amount of freedom they might be allowed. Finally, Sears and his coworkers attempted to obtain a balanced sample of mothers of children in various ordinal positions—only children, and first, middle, and youngest children. Inasmuch as the number and spacing of children varies significantly with social class (as shown in the sample, random with regard to this factor, studied by Davis and Havighurst) the sample used in the Boston study *must* be unrepresentative of at least one if not both of the social classes, since the middle class families in their study averaged 2.7 children, as against 2.5 in the working class—an insignificant difference, and opposite to the expected direction. (In the Chicago study the figures were 2.2 and 3.2 for whites, 2.2 and 3.7 for Negroes.) In view of these considerations we do not consider the studies comparable, and because of the sampling bias introduced into the Boston study we do not at present see any basis for questioning the validity of those findings of the Chicago study with which we are concerned in this report.

It will be remembered that the mental age equivalents of intelligence test performance are so standardized upon a "normal" population that they will coincide on the average with chronological age, with the intention that the average *IQ* of groups of "normal" children will fall fairly close to 100 at any given age level, and thus hopefully remain essentially constant. Turning to children of lower class or culturally marginal groups, however, we find quite consistently that during the first two or three school years, although they obtain scores somewhat lower than those of middle class white children, they deviate far less from the normal *IQ* than they do later. Often the early differences do not even reach statistical significance. This phenomenon has been demonstrated in testing of Negroes of various ages enrolled in the schools of Atlanta, Georgia, by Graham (96) and in Oklahoma and Texas by Garth, Lovelady, and Smith (83). Tomlinson (273) obtained better control of the home environment by testing only siblings. He administered Forms *L* and *M* of the 1937 Stanford-Binet to 75 pairs of Negro siblings from age 4 to 9 and found that whereas their over-all average fell 10.4 below the white norm, most of this difference was contributed by the older siblings. Furthermore, the correlation of *IQ* with the Sims index of socioeconomic status increased with increasing age, thus showing rather clearly that despite the presumed continuity of home environment its depressing effects are delayed for several years, at least in their expression in test performance.

A similar decline of *IQ* with age of children in marginal groups was found by Sherman and Key (240) in the isolated "hollows" of Virginia, by Skeels and Fillmore (245) in orphanage children, by Garth and Johnson (82) among the Mexican population of Texas and New Mexico, by Haught (105) in Indians of the Southwestern United States, and by Nissen, Machover, and Kinder (195) among the Sousou tribe of West Africa. Finally, it will be recalled that Neff and Honzik, in separate studies referred to earlier in this section, also found their correlations of *IQ* and socioeconomic status increased (negatively) with age among lower class American white children. Eells, Davis, Havighurst, Herrick, and Tyler (68), in an extensive study of almost 5000 white children in the age groups 9-10 and 13-14, reached similar conclusions, although with an interesting additional point of difference. In the 9-10 year group, which it should be remembered had already had a few years of schooling, test performance did correlate with socioeconomic status up through lower middle class, but thereafter there was no correlation. In the 13-14 year group the correlation of test performance and socioeconomic status was maintained throughout the social class range. This means in effect that in the lower age group the lowest class children were already suffering from their inadequate preparation for schooling, but the tests were not discriminating differences among the children of more privileged background. After a few more years of schooling, differential environments were showing their effects at all social class levels.

A very different, but equally interesting, outcome was reported by Estes (69). She administered the Wechsler Intelligence Scale for Children (*WISC*) to 80 children, half of high socioeconomic status and the other half low (using, as in the study of Eells, *et al.,* above the Warner Index). Each status group was further divided by age and grade into two groups; one group was clustered closely around age 7½ and in the second grade, while the other was 10½ years and in the fifth grade. (The subgroups were further divided equally into boys and girls, but this does not concern us here.) What should be noted about this sample is that it is not defined on the basis of age *or* grade, but age *and* grade. In other words, the children tested included only those who were keeping up with their grade and therefore were, by this definition at least, not retarded. If we bear in mind this difference in sampling from other studies, it is perhaps not surprising that whereas she found a significant difference in average test scores of the two socioeconomic groups at the younger age, this difference was not significant in the older group. It is encouraging to find that the *WISC* can discriminate in at least one study as early in school as the second grade, although this may be accounted for by the fact that the socioeconomic groups were selected from near the two extremes of the Warner scale. But it is far more interesting to find that it does not discriminate later. One is forced to conclude that in the particular community studied the great majority of children who were not equipped to cope with schooling on a par with their fellows had already dropped back a grade or more before reaching the fifth grade. One immediately wonders what it was in the background of the lower class children who did stay in grade (and who performed adequately on the test used in this study) that permitted them to do this whereas their fellows fell by the wayside (cf. p. 157). On the basis of the massive contrary evidence we cannot assume that this particular school system was able to build up the intellectual skills of all its deprived students to a par with the higher class children, so there must have been many children 10½ years old who did not get into the fifth grade on schedule and therefore were not tested. Unfortunately, Estes did not investigate the special characteristics of her lower class fifth graders in this way, but perhaps the greatest value of her study lies in pointing up this possible avenue for future research. Due to the highly selective nature of her sampling, the study is not comparable to the others we have reported and cannot of itself provide much insight into the mechanisms whereby lower class children become scholastically handicapped, and upper or middle class children aided, by their cultural backgrounds.

If we accept the assumption, as indeed we must, that the intellectually deprived child is ill-prepared for schoolwork from the time he enters the first grade, it appears that we can only explain the paradoxically late manifestation of his disability by making the further assumption that the intelligence tests themselves present different *kinds* of problems at higher age levels, problems progressively less appropriate to the nature of intellectual preparation the subculturally handicapped child has had. All intelligence tests, of course, become more difficult as they reach each mental age criterion level, but the evidence presented here suggests strongly that along with increasing difficulty, the tests begin to move into new sorts of intellectual processes at higher levels. This discontinuity in what the tests are testing is not apparent in the performance of the middle class child who is doing adequately in school, but shows up in the deprived child who can "get by" at first and then stumbles more and more as new intellectual dimensions assume increasing importance. Evidently the child who is well equipped to profit from schooling derives from his first years of study the skills necessary to handle the later hurdles, but the lower class or culturally marginal child, although seemingly performing fairly adequately on the basis of test results, actually lacks the intellectual and doubtless also verbal foundation upon which his schoolwork should be building in order that he can handle the different kinds of tasks which will come during the following years. Viewed from a different standpoint, the intelligence tests fail in the lower school grades to measure the capabilities which will later become of critical importance, and thus do not detect intellectual deficits at the very time most appropriate for remedying them. They also cannot be expected to take into account the progressively increasing discouragement experienced by many marginal children through the school years.

It is interesting to note that the failure of intelligence tests to identify potentially retarded children in the lower grades of school extends also into preschool years. Kirk (154) attempted for a research project in Urbana, Illinois, to find a group of children three, four, and five years old who would have Stanford-Binet *IQ*'s between 45 and 80. He had great difficulty in finding any children who were not either grossly deficient with an organic diagnosis or else had *IQ*'s over 90. His conclusions follow:

> Apparently, children with low intelligence are not detected at the pre-school ages by social workers, doctors, or other agencies dealing with children. This, coupled with the small number of cases located, suggests that many children later placed in special classes or institutions are not mentally retarded in terms of intelligence test scores at the ages of three, four, or five. Some children, whose older brothers and sisters were in special classes, tested approximately normal at the preschool ages. This raises the question as to whether children from low cultural levels who are approximately normal at an early age may later become mentally retarded because of their cultural environment or other unknown variables (p. 698).

We still lack the careful research necessary to determine the precise nature of the thinking processes the growing importance of which progressively handicaps the deprived child, and sooner or later often results in his being labelled "retarded." Some efforts have been made to analyze the performance of lower class children on various subtests of the standard intelligence tests in order to see which subtests are relatively more difficult for them than others. The research of Haggard, Havighurst, and their associates referred to above is probably the most exhaustive in this area. Although a scattering of statistically significant differences have been discovered, the results are very difficult of interpretation. One reason for this is that in the process of standardizing these tests on a "normal" population it is customary to eliminate or modify those items and subtests which do not intercorrelate fairly well with the overall test scores; this means that the subtests generate variables which depend not only upon social class (or some other independent variable chosen) but also upon the indeterminate weighting created by the original statistical screening of items in the subtests. Another, and more crucial, difficulty arises from the fact that the subtests are not designed and validated to measure some particular and explicit type of intellectual process as such, but are rather justified for inclusion because of their intercorrelation with total test score. The test as a whole is in turn justified on the basis of its correlation in a standardization population with performance on the Stanford-Binet or some other well established instrument. This interlocking mesh of correlations avoids examination of just what the various tests and subtests measure, and thus makes it almost impossible to reach more than inferential *post hoc* conclusions as to the real meaning of consistent variations in subtest scores in various subcultural groups. Guilford's (99) factorial studies of the components of intellectual process discussed in Section IV hold great promise for the future, but his findings are as yet far from being applicable to studies of subcultural differences in thinking patterns.

Some clues to the nature of various subculturally determined differences may perhaps be found in the following formulation of the levels of intelligence proposed by Sir Cyril Burt (34, p. 71): "(i) the level of simple sensory and simple motor processes; (ii) the level of complex perceptual and complex motor processes; (iii) the associative or reproductive level (imagery, mechanical memory, and habit formation); and finally (iv) the relational level, including generalization by concepts (abstraction), generalization by propositions (judgment), and rational inference (reasoning)." It would appear reasonable to assume that it is in the last, or highest, of these levels that we should look for significant differences in the thinking of various social class groups when faced with academic-type problems.

Although the evidence to be considered later in this chapter with respect to the effects on intellectual process of ethnic and cultural differences is perhaps a little more conclusive than that for socioeconomic status, some suggestive studies do exist in the latter area. However, in order to arrive at conclusions of the order with which we are here concerned, additional inferential interpretation is necessary. Thus we find in two related studies by the Chicago group (Havighurst and Janke, 109, and Janke and Havighurst, 129) a large array of tests administered to all the available 10-year-olds and 16-year-olds respectively in a Midwestern community. Among other things they reported at age 10 a high intercorrelation between all tests, and a consistent correlation of test performance with socioeconomic status, including the results of the Minnesota Mechanical Assembly Test. At age 16, however, although the other tests (Stanford-Binet, Wechsler Performance Scale, Iowa Silent Reading, and Minnesota Paper Form Board) correlated significantly with socioeconomic status, the Minnesota Mechanical Assembly Test did not. If we make the not unreasonable assumption that mechanical ability is learned as a part of living in the American culture irrespective of school experience, whereas the other tests (with the possible exception of the Paper Form Board) are increasingly drawing upon the abstraction, judgment, reasoning, and vocabulary learned in school, we can then say that the results reported support the view that lower class children are handicapped primarily in Burt's fourth level of intelligence.

Even more tenuous inference is necessary to reach this conclusion with regard to the 13-year-olds in this community (Havighurst and Breese, 106) who were given the Thurstone Primary Mental Abilities Test; all abilities correlated with socioeconomic status, but the highest correlations were attained with numbers, verbal comprehension, and word fluency, whereas space ability, reasoning, and memory showed a lesser relationship to social class. Even if we assume that the subtests measure what they purport to measure, we would be hard pressed to demonstrate that the highly correlated abilities involved a consistently higher level of abstraction than the lower. Similarly, Britton (27) administered several intelligence tests to 232 children aged 9 to 11, and one year later administered the Goodenough Draw-a-Man Test to the same children; whereas the intelligence tests correlated significantly with social status, the Goodenough did not. Again, we are forced to make assumptions about the level of abstraction and the kinds of intellectual skills required for performance on the Goodenough; the kinds of assumptions made will determine whether or not the results of this study will support our hypothesis. This is at best dubious scientific procedure, and serves well to point up the complete inadequacy of studies into the "why" of the progressive failure of lower class children in school and on tests as they grow older.

The most direct and the most ambitious attack on this problem to date was made, again at Chicago, by Allison Davis and Kenneth Eells. Their premise, stated in the manual for the Davis-Eells Games (56), is as follows:

> The fact is that there is no satisfactory objective criterion of true mental capacity, and therefore no possibility, at least at present, of constructing a satisfactory test of intelligence by purely objective means. It is necessary for the makers of intelligence tests to construct items which appear to require the main types of intellectual problem-solving behavior (p. 7).

Furthermore, in the course of the numerous studies of intelligence test performance undertaken by the Chicago group it was established that, to a degree not previously realized, children tended to give correct answers to analogies, and to other questions involving reasoning, on a basis different from that 'which the test constructor had in mind. By thus producing the right answers for the wrong reasons they made test scores even more unreliable and difficult of interpretation.

In an attempt to remedy the difficulties they perceived, Davis and Eells devised a group test, the Davis-Eells Games, administered with verbal instructions, which presents the child with a series of problems presumably familiar to anyone living in an urban environment in the United States. Three alternative solutions to each problem are presented in a comic-book format with verbal instructions and questions, the child being asked to select the one most effective or appropriate. The authors feel that the problems are typically encountered by children of all social classes, but warn that, although the test is applicable to American children in any city or small town, "scores for children from homes where a foreign language is spoken, and scores for children from strictly rural areas, should be interpreted with caution" (56, p. 1). They did not expect that the Index of Problem Solving Ability derived from the test would correlate highly with standard achievement tests because of the lack in the Davis-Eells of emphasis on memory and efficient work habits. They actually found the mean coefficients of correlation with various achievement tests administered in urban schools to be: reading, .43; language, .40; arithmetic, .41; and spelling, .24.[17]

Davis and Eells characterize their test as "culture-fair" in order to distinguish it from the so-called "culture-free" tests we will be considering later. This designation gives recognition to the fact that no test can avoid favoring certain kinds of cultural experience over others; the authors feel that their test does avoid social class bias within the limits of English-speaking urban children in the United States. Since this presumption rests upon *a priori* considerations it cannot be proven to be true, but at the same time there are no immediately apparent grounds for disputing it. However, a serious question must be raised as to the utility of the test, as applied to children in general and to retarded children in particular. Put more directly, if we have an Index of Problem Solving Ability (*IPSA*) on a child, what can we predict about the child from this index?

Earlier in this chapter we cited the comments of Stenquist (263) on the research which led up to the Davis-Eells Games, to the effect that until teachers, the public, and others cease the practice of effectively equating "intelligence" with the ability of a child to handle schoolwork there is little purpose in devising a test which will measure intelligence in any way other than the recognized *IQ*. Davis and Eells state explicitly that the *IPSA* is not the same thing as the *IQ,* but are not prepared to say exactly what relationship obtains between the two. Geist (84) attempted to explore this point by administering the Davis-Eells and the Stanford-Binet Form *L* to 50 children, 10 each from Grades 2 to 6, divided into upper, middle, and lower class. He found the two tests correlated within the three class groups with Pearson *r*'s of .00, .67, and .78 respectively. Even if one disregards the

---

[17]Compare the similar correlations found by Zweibelson (Table 3).

small size of the sample, these results are inconclusive and can be interpreted in several ways. One conclusion might be that children with educational advantages can bring different specialized skills to each kind of test, whereas deprived children respond in the same way to all tests, thus explaining the lack of an upper class correlation and a high lower class correlation. This does not, however, permit any conclusions as to what the *IPSA* actually measures even in the lower class. Another kind of observation we might make is that if the Davis-Eells is designed to correct the unreliability and undue difficulty of standard intelligence tests for lower class children, why should it be in this class group that the *IQ* and *IPSA* correlate most closely? Viewed in this way, the Davis-Eells appears to perpetuate the disadvantages of the Stanford-Binet without improving on its predictive value in the higher social levels. However, all we can really say is that the Geist study tells us nothing positive about the predictive value of the Davis-Eells and perhaps increases our doubts as to its utility.

A similar ambiguity exists with regard to the findings of a study by Rosenblum, Keller, and Papania (222). They administered the Davis-Eells Games, Stanford-Binet Form *L*, Wechsler Intelligence Scale for Children, and California Mental Maturity Test to 30 lower class, non-organic, retarded children at the Wayne County Training School; these children were equally divided between white and Negro, and averaged 12 years of age and 2.6 years in the school. The mean *IPSA* score of 64.6 was lower than that attained by these children on any other of the tests, the highest being on the Wechsler Performance Scale (72.7). Since all of these tests are standardized to yield a median score at 100 on a "normal" population, it is clear that the Davis-Eells offered the children no better opportunity to show what they could do than any other test. The authors felt that this might perhaps be due to the fact that the tests were administered by middle class people and hence mobilized the hostility of the children to all the tests; this would not, however, account for the probably significant difference between the highest and lowest results. They also noted, more significantly, that these retarded children appeared very concrete in their approach to the Davis-Eells problems with little ability in abstraction, and that they were exceedingly poor in providing correct or appropriate reasons for the selection of particular problem solutions, whether these were correct or not. This, of course, is the very criticism levelled at the standard tests of intelligence by the Chicago group, and suggests that at least for these retarded children (who had a mean *IQ* of 67.6 on admission, range 55-75) the Davis-Eells comes no closer than standard tests to providing a true measure of mental ability. Finally, although this point is not mentioned by the authors, it should be borne in mind that many of the neighborhood activities of play, shopping, etc., portrayed in the Davis-Eells Games are not likely to fall within the experience of children institutionalized in a training school, making the test not "culture-fair" for children who have resided for some time in an institution.

Angelino and Shedd (9) undertook to evaluate the culture-fairness of the Davis-Eells Games by administering the test to two groups of children in Oklahoma City, 152 of lower class and 155 of upper class, utilizing the class criteria employed by the Chicago group. Approximately equal numbers were taken from each of the first six grades of two elementary schools. With the exception of the second grade, the differences in mean scores exceeded 15 points, and *all* the differences were significant at the one per cent level. Surprisingly enough, however, whereas the differences favored the upper class in Grades 2 through 6, in the first grade the lower class children were markedly superior to the upper class. This first grade result reflected a very low score (78.0) for the upper class rather than unusually high performance by the lower class children. Although it is impossible to determine the meaning of the first grade reversal, one is forced to agree with the authors that this study strongly suggests that the Davis-Eells is probably still contaminated with cultural factors. It should, however, be noted that no mention is made of the language spoken in the home of the children tested. Although the care taken by the authors to conform in other respects to the requirements established by Davis and Eells presumably was extended also to language, in the absence of a specific statement the possibility exists that some children speaking Spanish or some other language—presumably in the lower class groups—may have affected the results.

A similar comparison of children divided into upper and lower class groups was made by Altus (4) in the elementary schools of Santa Barbara County, California. She confined herself, however, to drawing only on fourth grade children, and also had some reservations as to the accuracy of placement of some children with respect to social class on the Warner Index. As did Angelino and Shedd, she found the Davis-Eells *IPSA* favored the upper class children, who averaged 106.4 as against the lower class mean of 97.9. Altus also administered the California Test of Mental Maturity to the same children; the *IQ* derived from the *CTMM* closely paralleled their *IPSA*'s, the means falling at 113.1 and 95.6 respectively. Of the total of 168 children, 46 showed differences between *IQ* and *IPSA* of 20 points or more. Of those with a higher *IPSA* than *IQ*, the great majority as might be expected came from the lower half of the socioeconomic scale, 14 as against two. However, there were also 10 lower class as against only four upper class who had *IQ*'s 20 points or more higher than their *IPSA*'s. The culture-fairness of the Davis-Eells Games is thus again in question—the findings of this study seem to suggest the Games are almost as biased by social class as a standard intelligence test. However, the criterion of upbringing in an urban environment is not well met in Santa Barbara County; most of the county is rural agricultural and Santa Barbara, the only real city, is of medium size (about 50,000 population) and spread out over a considerable area.

We have engaged in a rather extended discussion of the Davis-Eells Games here as well as in Chapter XI because this test represents the first systematic effort to control the social class factor in the measurement of intelligence, and thus has raised real hopes of providing a basis for more realistic estimates of the ability of children to cope with their over-all environment. Thus far, unhappily, we do not have evidence which would suggest that this hope has been realized. It is clear that for the test to be "culture-fair" the children tested must have shared in reasonable degree in the "typical" urban American culture. This means, among other things, that it is likely to be less fair for the more retarded children whose restricted life does not necessarily include as many opportunities to go shopping, ride street cars, participate in free play groups, work with tools, handle money, and so forth. This does not mean that the test is inappropriate for all retarded children, but it does mean that for any child, retarded or not, some knowledge is necessary of the range of social experience to which the child has previously been exposed. Without this information on each child who takes the test we become to an indeterminate degree more uncertain in any predictions we may make on the basis of *IPSA* scores.

But even if we are concerned with an urban American child from an English-speaking home who we know has had the experiences typical for his background, what can we actually predict from the Index of Problem Solving Ability? We know that the standard *IQ* is the best available single predictor of the usual sorts of school performance, being in effect validated against this criterion, and that the *IPSA* is not intended to measure the same thing as the *IQ*. Therefore it is to be presumed that the Davis-Eells is not the most useful instrument to employ in determining fitness in the classroom. It may help to identify the child who is sufficiently "bright" but who for some other reason cannot adjust to school, but unless we can identify and deal with the other impediment we have gained little, and the Davis-Eells is not designed to identify extraneous emotional or cultural factors.

Nevertheless, there is value in having a means of being more certain that we are dealing with a potentially adequate child whether or not he does well in school. Even if he never overcomes his school difficulties, there is good reason to suppose he will be in the vanguard of those many adolescents who proceed from a school career of consistent retardation to an adult life of adequate and sometimes superior social and occupational performance. Intelligence, when not tied to a circular definition in terms of the *IQ*, is usually considered to involve the ability to solve problems, and in particular those problems relevant to the successful performance of the individual in all the normally expectable cultural settings. Clearly this is the ability which the Davis-Eells Games undertakes to test and, despite the questions raised by the studies discussed above and in Chapter XI, it has yet to be demonstrated that it is not a fair test of this ability provided it is used on the population for which it was designed. When we say that we do not know what sorts of real-life performance the *IPSA* predicts we are in effect saying that we are not equipped to capitalize on intelligence unless it is adapted to the school situation. Viewed in this way the "uselessness" of the Davis-Eells reflects not so much a failure of the test constructors as a lack of flexibility in our culture—the inability to develop alternative ways of preparing those children for adult life who are not able to profit from conventional schooling. This is a point of view to which we will return in the next section.

C. Ethnicity

Here we are concerned with the relationship between test performance and what used to be referred to loosely as "racial" origin, embracing nationality, cultural-religious entities such as Jews or Arabs, and more properly racial groups such as American Indians or Negroes. As we observed in the chapter on heredity and environment, studies in this area have employed the premise, implicit or explicit, that differences in intelligence are somehow inherently associated with ethnic origins. This genetic premise appears firmly rooted in our folklore although, as we saw, it as yet lacks any scientific basis. However, despite the inconclusiveness of research on the influence of ethnic origin on intelligence, there have been a sufficient number of studies with this particular focus to warrant separate attention to at least a selected few. The majority of these are early, concentrated particularly in the early 1930's.

As we have mentioned before, a rather large number of studies have demonstrated that children, particularly of school age, of different ethnic groups perform differently on intelligence tests even when age, social class, and the like are held constant. Correspondingly, of course, there are differences in the incidence of mental retardation. There is furthermore some consistency to these findings, which suggests that Jews come near the top of the list in average test scores, Negroes and Italians near the bottom, and others fall in between although with less consistency in rank order. The difficulty of course arises when we try to discover what factors are operative to produce these gross differences. Some studies, therefore, have been undertaken to break the problem down into more manageable components.

One approach has been to test children of mixed Indian-white or Negro-white blood to determine whether more white blood regularly raises the *IQ*. In 1933 Garth (81) published the most careful of the several studies done on children of Indian-white parentage. He administered the Otis Classification Test to 1022 children in Grades 4 to 9 of government schools in Oklahoma and South Dakota, classifying each in accordance with the proportion of white blood in his ancestry. On purely sociocultural grounds one would expect the degree of white blood to show some relationship with intelligence and school achievement, because a white parent would be more likely to draw a child away from traditional Indian culture and therefore more into the white environment where he would be exposed to the kinds of stimuli and experience necessary for successful test performance. (As we shall see later, a closer tie to Indian culture does in fact appear to hold down the *IQ*.) Even this expectation was only slightly realized; the degree of Indian blood correlated with intelligence score and achievement score respectively only .19 and .11. In contrast intelligence, achievement, and school grade intercorrelate .67, .68, and .81, with little change in coefficients when degree of Indian blood is partialled out. In other words, intelligence and achievement are much more intimately related to the amount of schooling received than to the amount of white blood. Of course it could then be argued that only the children with more white blood were capable of handling higher grades of school, but here we find that degree of white blood and school grade correlate only .12—i.e., there is only a slightly greater amount of white blood in the ancestry of children in higher grades than lower.

There are several facts to be borne in mind in assessing the significance of Garth's study. First is the size of his sample, large enough to assure statistically reliable results. Second, the majority of Indian-white mixtures are of sufficiently recent date to provide reasonably confident genealogical determinations. Third, the European and Indian populations which met in North America comprised breeding populations kept genetically, geographically, and culturally separate over many centuries if not millenia. And fourth, there is ample evidence that in most American Indian groups white admixture carries with it a strong implication of acculturation toward a white way of life and abandonment of Indian values and patterns of thought and action, leading us to expect that with more white blood Indian children would be likely to be more acculturated and thus to perform better on tests devised for white populations. In view of these facts the relationships found by Garth between school-related factors and degree of white admixture are if anything surprising in being so low. As with so many other approaches to the nature-nurture problem in intelligence, this study cannot disprove the existence of inherent ethnic differences but it puts the burden of proof very heavily on those who would claim such genetic differentials are real.

In 1936 Witty and Jenkins (298) undertook a critical survey of the more numerous studies dealing with the relationship between proportions of Negro and white blood and the IQ. They found that the preponderance of evidence pointed toward a lack of relationship. This result was probably to be expected if for no other reason than the variety of factors which make the study of persons of Negro-white ancestry considerably less clear cut than is the case with Indian-white admixture. Intermixture of Negroes and whites on a large scale has been going on for much longer than with Indians, and generally more covertly, so that genealogical records are vague in the extreme and degree of mixture is often estimated on the very unreliable basis of appearance. Genetically, the separation of the populations of Europe and of Africa has not been nearly as complete as in the case of Europeans and American Indians. Within the mixed group a selection process has taken place through the "passing" of individuals who combine lighter skin and, perhaps, a superior ability to adapt to different behavior patterns. On the other side, however, the likelihood of a cultural correlate of admixture is less for Negroes, thus providing greater a priori credence to a genetic basis for any correlation which might be found with degree of white blood. One reason for the lesser cultural difference is that, although there are subcultural differences relevant to intelligence test performance between general Negro culture in the United States and white culture, this difference is not nearly as dramatic as that obtaining between Indian culture and European culture. Furthermore, whereas a "halfbreed" Indian is in somewhat different social status than a pure Indian, a Negro of mixed ancestry is still socially all Negro. The cultural factor in ethnic mixture of Negroes is thus less strongly weighted in favor of showing a correlation between IQ and amount of white blood, but it is by no means eliminated and simply makes it even more difficult to determine which differences, if any, shall be considered genetically significant. This, combined with the difficulty in obtaining genealogical data, makes the study of Negro-white mixtures a singularly unpromising line to pursue in the study of ethnic differences in IQ.

The remaining studies to be considered in this section may be discussed more briefly. Several point up various possible pitfalls of research in ethnic correlates of IQ. In 1928 Klineberg (156), after administering the Pintner-Paterson Performance Tests to a number of Indian and Negro groups, concluded that they scored lower than the white norms primarily because they could not meet the time criteria, but when given adequate time to complete the test they could reach the norm level of accuracy. This finding raises the question of whether time-limited tests, of which there are many in use, are appropriate for use with any subcultural groups who do not place a premium on speed. Put another way, if members of ethnic subgroups are able to solve problems correctly and live in a setting which does not require that problems be solved with great rapidity, is it justified to view test results which are lowered by a speed factor as indicators of inferiority, whether inherent or learned?

Smith (253) administered some special tests, one of them non-verbal and the others intended to test comprehension of written and spoken English, to children of representative ethnic groups, aged 10 to 15, in Honolulu in 1924, and then readministered the same tests to comparable groups 14 years later in 1938. He found that although the rank order of the various ethnic groups had not changed over the years, mean scores for each group had risen substantially. This outcome is probably to be expected in view of the gradual Americanization of the polyglot population of the Hawaiian Islands. It of course indicates the need for caution in interpreting results of testing of ethnic groups at different points in time, or of separate groups in differing stages of acculturation. But, more importantly, it shows such test results to be at least as dependent upon the historical flux of opportunity as upon any inherent capability of different groups. A similar outcome, for example, was reported by Wheeler in isolated Tennessee communities in a study discussed in Chapter X.

We discussed in the section on heredity and environment Pasamanick's (202) findings that subcultural influences affecting intelligence should be traced back to conception and even earlier, particularly as these affect diet. He has criticized the work of others who make ethnic comparisons (e.g., his 1951 critique of Carlson and Henderson's (37) study of Mexican children, 201) without due regard for these early environmental studies. However, he also found (200) that if it is possible to control the prenatal and perinatal environment, at least approximately, the effects of the postnatal influences are not apparent until early childhood. He made a careful study of 53 Negro and 99 white infants born after full term pregnancies in New Haven and found that, with prematurity ruled out, the differences known to exist later do not appear before the third year of life. This implies that whatever the prenatal as well as postnatal influences may be which later become effective in depressing test performance, they do not have any detectable influence on motor ability or other developing capabilities at least until the child of a minority ethnic group has reached an age of talking and otherwise interacting socially with others.

Jenkins studied several groups of highly superior Negro children, drawn primarily from the public schools of Chicago (Witty and Jenkins, 298; Jenkins, 134, 135, 136). He found that gifted Negro children, including some of apparently pure Negro ancestry, cover the range of intelligence all the way up to the highest levels reached by white persons and that their backgrounds are in general comparable to those of gifted white children, including a large proportion of middle class and professional parents. However, Jenkins found that the proportion of Negro children who are gifted, with high IQ's and school grade advancement, is considerably smaller than among white children. As he observes (136, p. 401): "The abstract mental tests that contribute to psychometric intelligence do not measure the factors of personality and motivation that largely determine success in life."

Turning now to the influence of ethnicity in children definitely adjudged retarded, two studies are of particular interest. In one of these Gibson and Butler (85) selected from the files of their institution for retarded children in Ontario, Canada, 200 cases admitted over a 10-year period. These were selected to include only cases in two groups, one in which a hereditary etiology was diagnosed and the other comprising cases in which no medical basis for retardation could be found. These cases were then determined to have been either of foreign parentage or from homes in which the parents were native born to the United States or Canada (French Canadians were excluded entirely). An estimate of adequate or poor home environment was also made. They found that in the group with identifiable hereditary etiology the distribution of nationality and home environment corresponded approximately with that of the surrounding community at large. This was largely true also of the group of undetermined etiology whose IQ was under 50. However, those admissions with an IQ over 50, a level at which neurological complications are generally considered to be less likely, showed a far higher proportion both of foreign parentage and of poor home environment than in the other groups or the general population. In the undetermined etiology group, for example, the IQ-over-50 group of 33 had 70 per cent foreign parents, whereas in the 59 cases with IQ below 50 only 30 per cent of the parents were of foreign origin, a difference significant at the .001 level. Comparable differences were found with respect to home environment within the undetermined group. These findings strongly suggest that at the borderline level where pathology, hereditary or otherwise, is less likely to be operative, ethnic handicaps as well as socioeconomic deprivation can depress a child's performance sufficiently to push him over the line into an institutional status.

A different approach to ethnicity in institutionalized children was taken by Shotwell (242) with results closely congruent with those of Gibson and Butler. She selected 80 Mexican and 80 American children of comparable ages from the Pacific State Hospital in California. Their Binet IQ's ranged from 50 to 79. She administered to each of these children the Arthur Performance Scale tests and compared their Arthur scores with their Binet IQ's. The American children averaged five points higher on the Arthur than on the Binet, but the Mexicans averaged 22 points higher. In no case did a Mexican subject have an Arthur score more than five points below the Binet score, whereas $22\frac{1}{2}$ per cent of the American children had Arthur scores more than five points below. Of the Mexicans, $27\frac{1}{2}$ per cent had Arthur scores 30 or more points *above* Binet. Thus members of the ethnic minority were institutionalized with low IQ's based on a verbal intelligence test, but when these same children were given a non-verbal performance-type test which presumably was less handicapping they obtained scores in or near the normal range. Although a low IQ does not automatically lead to institutionalization, it can often play a crucial rôle in such a decision. Taken together these studies in Ontario and California cast strong doubts on the validity of the customary intelligence test results as criteria for placing a child of a minority ethnic group in an institution, and lead one to wonder how many of the ethnic children in our schools for the retarded may not have a potential for fairly immediate return to the community. Of course one could raise a similar question regarding many non-ethnic children also, but Gibson, Butler, and Shotwell force us to realize that it is a question particularly appropriate to ask regarding members of at least some ethnic minority group members.

To sum up, the studies reviewed here which are concerned with the influence of ethnicity on *IQ* return us to the conclusion implied at the outset, that is, that differentials in intelligence test performance by members of various ethnic groups are, as far as the evidence we have available goes, primarily cultural in origin, compounded doubtless of motivation, thought, and habit patterns, and differences in language. Because language appears to loom so large in this whole problem, we shall turn to this next.

D. LANGUAGE

The relationship between language facility and intelligence, particularly intelligence measured by a test score, has been a major focus of interest for many years and has attracted some excellent researchers. Two aspects of the problem have received primary emphasis. First, both historically and in amount of study devoted to it, is the assessment of language skills or handicaps as they affect performance on the verbal types of intelligence tests which comprise the bulk of the standard tests—the Stanford-Binet, Wechsler-Bellevue, etc.—which, among other things, provide one of the primary diagnostic criteria of mental retardation. Since the groups most conspicuously handicapped in this regard are those of foreign ethnic origin, the majority of studies in this area have been concerned with bilingualism. Regardless of the direction from which this problem is attacked, one is constantly confronted with the close association of the three phenomena of ethnicity, bilingualism, and retardation, each interlinked with the other in a vicious circle of cause and effect. We see this in the French Catholics of the Northeastern United States, the Spanish-Americans of the Southwest, Italians and Puerto Ricans in New York and other big cities, and in American Indians scattered throughout the country.

The second and more recent focus of interest reflects the intimate relationship between language and culture, language being the primary medium of cultural learning and itself reflecting the categories of experience stressed within the culture. The presumption here is that a person retarded in language development will therefore be handicapped also in learning the other aspects of culture which are important to his over-all functioning in the society and to his performance on any sort of intelligence, performance, or aptitude test. For example Nisbet (194), in a study discussed in some detail in Section X, reaches the conclusion that differential language facility is a major factor in determining the inverse correlation of *IQ* and family size.

Among the several "firsts" which can be claimed for the study by May

Bere (17) in 1924 of Italian, Bohemian, and Jewish school children in New York City is the systematic examination of the effects of bilingualism on test performance. She pioneered many of the procedures used repeatedly by later researchers, including assessing the effects on test scores of differing degrees of bilingualism (in this case based on the amount of the foreign language spoken in the home), comparing the performance of bilinguals on verbal versus non-verbal tests (using the Stanford-Binet and the Pintner-Paterson Performance Tests), and evaluating the relationships between all of these factors. Her findings also anticipated much of the ambiguity of results which has characterized research in this area. She found, for example, in partialling out such factors as father's occupation, length of residence in the United States, and the like that some correlations showed significant relationships, including amount of foreign language spoken in the home, but none of these correlations were consistently significant for all groups. Similarly, she divided her subjects into those whose Stanford-Binet score was higher than their Pintner-Paterson score, and those for whom the reverse was true. She found significant differences between the ethnic groups on this basis, but the differences one might then expect between these subgroups in regard to the amount of foreign language spoken in the home failed to materialize.

Similar inconsistencies, and failures to find statistically significant relationships between variables in some populations where other studies would lead one to expect them, have characterized research in bilingualism ever since. Conveniently, this is a field which has been subject to periodic and exhaustive reviews of the literature, including those by Arsenian (11, 12) in 1937 and 1945, Spoerl (258) in 1942, and Darcy (52) in 1953. Arsenian's 1945 review is probably the most penetrating of these and is therefore worth citing at some length:

> In general the pattern of these investigations has been to administer tests of intelligence to bilingual and monoglot children and to compare the results. Some of the investigators have used only verbal tests of intelligence, others only non-verbal or non-language tests, and still others have administered both verbal and non-verbal tests to the same groups of children. These investigations have been conducted on from nursery school and kindergarten to the college and university levels, with most of the studies covering the elementary school period. Both individual as well as group tests of intelligence have been used, and in a few instances the verbal intelligence test has been administered in the two languages of the bilingual child. The determination and the measurement of the degree of bilingualism of the child has been variable: in some instances the performance of the bilingual child has been compared with

that of his monoglot contemporaries of his own natio-racial group, at other times with a different or a mixed group.

A few of the studies are longitudinal—the observations and the testing having been made on the same child at different periods of growth, most of the studies are cross-sectional—the observations and testing having been made at one point in the child's development. A few investigators have used the correlational technique in seeking the relationship between degrees of bilingualism and intellectual ability, most researchers have satisfied themselves with a comparison of averages and variabilities and the statistical significance of differences between bilingual and monoglot groups.

Because of these circumstances the results of these studies are not uniform, however, after examining nearly 100 investigations in this country and abroad the following summary of the findings can be made:

1. Bilingual children as compared with monoglot children of the same age and environment are neither retarded nor accelerated in their mental development. This conclusion is especially evident when the two groups are compared on non-language tests of intelligence.

2. When verbal tests of intelligence are used for comparison in the majority of cases, the bilingual children fall short of their monoglot contemporaries, this disparity being greater the more verbal the content of the test is. This generalization must however be limited by two observations:

   a. On the whole, the older the bilingual child and the higher the level of his educational attainment, the smaller is the discrepancy between his verbal intelligence test performance and the performance of a monoglot of the same age or educational attainment.

   b. The verbal intelligence tests show that the apparent retardation of bilingual children varies from place to place and from group to group. Bilingual children in urban areas, like the Welsh children in the cities and the Jewish children in London or New York, show either no retardation or a slight superiority to the norms of monoglot children, while in rural Wales the Welsh children, and in the southwest of the United States the Spanish-speaking children according to these verbal intelligence tests show a serious handicap.

This summary points to the conclusion that bilingualism neither retards nor accelerates mental development, and that language handicap is most likely the factor responsible for the discrepancy between the performances of bilingual and monoglot children on verbal tests of intelligence.

Bilingualism and Language Development

Several individual studies of language development of bilingual children have been made by parents. The classical study in this field, and the most careful, is that of Jules Ronjat. In 1913 Dr. Ronjat (220) reported in great detail on the linguistic development of his bilingual son, Louis. From the time of Louis' birth, his father spoke French and his mother spoke German invariably in the presence of the child or in speaking to him after he was able to talk. According to Ronjat, Louis' accent, pronounciation, and knowledge of the two languages were not retarded in any way because of his bilingualism. In 1923, 10 years after the publication of his monograph, Dr. Ronjat in a private communication to Dr. Michael West was able to confirm his earlier statement regarding the normal development in the two languages of his son, Louis.

Several other developmental studies of this type summarized by Spoerl (258) seem to indicate that whenever the sources of the two languages were kept distinct and the manner of presentation remained consistent during the early developmental period the situation was normal. However, when the process was interfered with, as when the mother spoke sometimes German and at other times English, or when the child was moved from a bilingual to a unilingual environment, or vice versa, difficulties arose, such as refusal to talk in one of the two languages learned, or some confusion and retardation in language development, at least temporarily. In this connection one should bear in mind the situation in numerous second generation immigrant homes in the United States, where the parents speak English to the child while the grandparents consistently use the language of the old country, with no permanent illl effects on the child's language development.

Two studies of the language development of preschool children give somewhat divergent results. McCarthy (178), studying children from foreign language homes in the United States, concludes: ". . . the hearing of a foreign language in the home does not seem to be a handicap in linguistic development as it is measured by the mean length of response, which when applied to larger groups has proved a very reliable index."

Smith (251), studying an extensive sampling of children in Hawaii from Chinese, Filipino, Hawaiian, Japanese, Korean, and Portuguese-speaking homes, finds serious language handicap in children from two to six years of age. Two of her conclusions are pertinent:

"The children in Hawaii were compared with a monolingual white American group previously studied. They are found to use more exclamatory and slightly fewer interrogative sentences, and to make much less frequent use of complex and compound sentences. Sentences that serve merely to name an object or person continue to a later age than with monoglot children. However, age trends are found to be similar, for exclamatory and naming sentences decrease; questions, answers, and complex and compound sentences increase with age.

"The evidence, although insufficient, suggests that pidgin English is more responsible for incorrect English and bilingualism for the overuse of interjections, short sentences, immature type of questions when classed as to meaning, and lack of complex sentences."

While the difficulties encountered by the bilingual child in his early period of language development are of interest, and must be provided for in an educational program, it is of greater interest to know whether or not these difficulties are permanent. . . .

It is necessary, therefore, to canvass the studies of the language development of bilingual children on successively higher educational levels. Most of such studies cover the elementary school period. There are a few on high-school level, and very few indeed on the college or more adult levels. The usual method in these studies has been to compare the vocabulary size of the bilingual child with that of his monoglot contemporary. . . .

The results of these studies are not uniform. Certain of the studies, notably those in Puerto Rico, in the southwest of the United States, and in rural Wales show rather serious vocabulary handicap for the bilingual child in both languages. Other studies, notably those in urban centers of the eastern part of the United States, show equality with monoglots, or in a few instances even a larger size of vocabulary in the English language by bilinguals as compared with monoglots. The explanation of these apparently contradictory findings is to be sought in the following:

1. The higher we go on the educational level the more opportunity does the bilingual child have to catch up with the monoglot in his knowledge of the vocabulary of the dominant language. Terman's finding is of great interest in this connection. He discovered that for the bilingual student, vocabulary is lower than mental age up to the third or fourth grade, but that after 12 years of age vocabulary is equal to mental age. This result receives some corroboration in the findings of Decroly in Belgium, and Saer in Wales.

2. The higher we go on the educational level the greater the selection of bilingual students, since, as the New York Regents inquiry shows, a larger percentage of bilingual children leave school than of monoglots. Intelligence and language facility are probably two of the factors in this selective process.

3. There is truth also in the statement of the Canadian committee appointed to inquire into the conditions of the schools attended by French-speaking pupils, namely, that proficiency in the use of one language is assuredly no barrier to securing equal proficiency in the other if proper methods of organization and instruction are followed.

On the whole, these studies show a language deficiency for the bilingual child. However, the extent and period of such deficiency seem to depend on certain factors, such as the extent of educational opportunities, the intelligence of the bilingual children, and the methods of organization and instruction in schools.

Bilingualism and School Achievement

The bilingual's deficiency in language reflects in his school perform-ance, especially on the elementary school level. Studies reported from Belgium, Czechoslovakia, Canada, the Philippine Islands, Puerto Rico, and a number from this country are almost unanimous in showing lower performance by the bilingual child. This deficiency of the bilingual is most apparent in verbal subjects, such as reading, history, and geog-raphy; and is much less apparent in non-verbal subjects, such as arith-metic and science. On the high school level—there are few satisfactory studies—the differences seem very slight, and on the college level they apparently disappear. The most satisfactory investigation on the college level is that of Spoerl, who equated two groups of Freshmen—bilingual and monoglot—as to age, sex, socio-economic status and intelligence, and compared their performances on the Nelson-Denny Reading and the Purdue English Placement tests, in addition to examining their school grades and progress. Dr. Spoerl (260) concludes her study with the following statement:

"Summarizing the conclusions based on the various tests which were administered, it becomes clear that at least at the college level, there are no continuing effects which stem from a bilingual childhood and which show themselves in the academic records, vocational choices or English ability of bilingual students. Neither does binguality seem to have a significant effect on the performance of college age students on a verbal test of intelligence. If there were a bilingual handicap in their childhood, it has certainly become stabilized by the first year of college."

It must be borne in mind that in the studies regarding school achieve-ment, especially those made in the United States, the language situation is such that the student is in the process of losing one language—his vernacular, and of learning another—the dominant language. A truly bilingual situation where the two languages are on equal footing is not encountered. Fortunately one study exists, that reported by Professor Bovet (23), where the latter situation obtains. M. E. T. Logie, the di-rector of a school in the Union of South Africa, by special permission from his government, conducted an experiment in his school as follows. The pupils in his school were given bilingual instruction, the same lesson being taught in Afrikaans, and then recited in English, or vice-versa; the same teacher taught the subject in both languages without favoring either one or the other. It was also seen to that the children in playing games were mixed rather than divided into linguistic groups. The affec-tive as well as the purely language learning factors were therefore constant for the two language groups. After four years of this experience the children were tested as to their knowledge of the mother tongue and of the second language, both, also in arithmetic (this subject being se-lected as a test for logical thinking), and in geography. The results of these tests were compared with the results of the same tests taken by pupils in unilingual English and Afrikaans schools. On none of the tests were the bilinguals shown to be inferior to their unilingual contemporaries. This experiment, more crucial than any others, shows that bilingualism per se need not be a cause for school retardation even in the elementary school. . . .

Bilingualism in Relation to Personal and Social Adjustment

In most bilingual situations the two languages involved do not carry equal social prestige; one of the languages is usually more dominant, carries greater social approval, is the representative of the "superior" culture. This situation obtains especially in countries of immigration and colonization. The question arises whether in such situations the bilingual person does not suffer from a sense of inferiority or inadequacy, whether or not he is socially frustrated, how well he is able to accept himself and his social group, how securely anchored he is in the two cultures represented by the two languages.

There are many speculative claims but little experimental evidence. A study by Darsie using teachers' ratings as measures of pupil adjustment finds the Japanese children more stable emotionally than the American children in the same schools. Pintner and Arsenian report zero correlation between degree of bilingualism as measured by the Hoffman Scale and school adjustment as measured by the Pupil Portraits Test. The population in this study consisted of 469 native-born Jewish bilingual pupils of the 6th and 7th grades in a New York City public school.

The most noteworthy study in this field is that of Dr. Spoerl (259). She equated two groups of college freshmen on mental ability, age, sex and socio-economic status and then studied intensively the personal and social adjustments of the bilingual and the monoglot groups using a number of good measuring and analytical devices of adjustment. These were: the Allport-Vernon Study of Values, the Bogardus Test of Social Distance (modified), the Kent-Rosanoff Association Test (modified), the Bell Adjustment Inventory, and the Morgan-Murray Thematic Apperception Test. Her conclusion of this study is worth quoting at length:

"Our conclusion, then, is that the emotional maladjustment of the bilingual student, insofar as it expresses itself in terms of reactions to social frustration, and particularly in terms of family disharmony, is the result of the culture conflict to which the native-born children of immigrants are subjected. But this culture conflict is complicated by the bilingual environment. Thus it is that bilingualism enters into the situation, not in its intra-personal aspects, but rather as a symbol of one of the environmental factors converging upon the second generation. Most of the emotional maladjustment of the bilingual student is environmentally determined, and is not the result of mental conflict engendered by the complexities of thinking or speaking in two languages. This is true of the social mal-adjustment, the lack of harmony in the home situation, and the lack of identification with the present environment (coupled with a rejection of the cultural background of the parents), all of which tend to characterize college students who are bilingual.

"One finding remains, however, which does not fit into this culture-conflict complex. That is the finding, primarily from the Association Test, of a significantly larger number of reactions on the part of bilingual students in terms of the act of speech to the word language; and in terms of the act of understanding to the word understand. These suggest that, although at the college level bilingualism, as such, is not affecting the student's expressive power (as evidenced by his control of English, his almost equal vocabulary, and his academic performance) there is in his mental organization a residual effect of the emotional turmoil and mental effort which must have been present in the early days of his school career when English was not, for him, a facile medium of expression."

The social psychology of bilingualism is most interesting as well as most important because of the following facts. Language is the medium of culture; in addition to being a code it is also a tradition; it embodies in itself the sufferings as well as the aspirations of a nation. As language represents one of the most potent forces of national existence, its encounter and struggle with another language calls forth an interplay of emotional forces which result in the pathos and drama of human life. Here we are dealing not merely with the acquisition of two languages in place of one, but with the complex psychological and sociological phenomena of a culture conflict. . . . (pp. 73-80).

It is clear from the above discussion that although for the otherwise well-advantaged child bilingualism need not be a handicap, in the majority of cases it does result in retardation in school and inferior performance on the verbal tests which are the mainstays in assessment of school-age children. Inasmuch as most bilingual children come from ethnic minority families, the conflict in cultural rôle identification discussed by Spoerl is undoubtedly a strong contributing factor to the poor school performance and adjustment of bilinguals revealed in statistical surveys, although this point is seldom explicitly recognized. It would, however, be almost impossible reliably to estimate the amount of deficit introduced by emotional as against intellectual obstacles in the development of ethnic bilingual children.

The necessity of learning two languages simultaneously must create additional obstacles to learning for a child, however effortless or successful the process may appear. The maintenance of a normal developmental curve, at least during the first years of school and before, is almost certainly accomplished in spite of, rather than because of, the additional language. In the first place, the sheer number of words and grammatical rules which must be learned to reach a certain level of proficiency in two languages is obviously nearly double that required to reach this level in only one. Smith (252), for example, tested the vocabularies of 30 Chinese children aged 3 to 6½ years born and raised in Hawaii, and found that whereas two-fifths of her sample exceeded the norms of monolingual children, when words of identical meaning were counted only once instead of twice only one-sixth exceeded the norm.

More important than the quantity of learning required is the complexity. In discussing the results of his study of monolingual and bilingual children in Belgium, Toussaint (274) pointed out that during the early years when children learn primarily in terms of concrete one-to-one associations between words and perceptual stimuli, the necessity for learning two words for each stimulus and remembering which word to use in a given context can present a very substantial obstacle. As Arsenian pointed out above, if there is consistency of persons or contexts for the use of each language, the choice and ambiguity are reduced, although not eliminated. However, the restriction of one language or the other to use only in certain contexts can result in poor performance when the child is forced to use one of his languages in a situation in which he usually uses the other. Keston and Jiminez (152) administered the Stanford-Binet to 50 bilingual Spanish-American fourth graders in Albuquerque, each being tested with both the regular English version and a Spanish translation, half receiving the English first and half the Spanish first. They found a correlation with school grades of .62 for the English test, but of only .11 for the Spanish. The authors concluded that, although Spanish was the mother tongue of these students, all their schooling had been in English and it was in school that they learned the kinds of skills required for performance on this test. This conclusion forces one to question the usually-heard opinion that bilinguals should not be tested in their second language lest they be unfairly handicapped. Unfortunately, however, the Spanish translation of the Stanford-Binet used in this study was one which had been prepared in Madrid and therefore employed Castillian Spanish, which differs substantially from the idiom spoken in the American Southwest. It is impossible to determine how much of the variability in the Spanish test scores bears on the conclusions reached by the authors and how much is a result of the use of an unfamiliar form of Spanish. This ingeniously designed study should be replicated using a more appropriate translation.

Two interesting but not immediately explicable findings emerged as a by-product of the study by Altus (4) of Santa Barbara County fourth graders referred to earlier in the discussion of ethnicity. Her sample included 31 bilingual children, primarily Spanish-American and lower class. Although their scores on the California Test of Mental Maturity were lower than those of their monolingual lower class schoolmates (language *IQ* 86.7, non-language *IQ* 93.8, versus 95.6 full-scale *IQ* for all lower class) their *IPSA*'s on the Davis-Eells Games were almost identical with the lower class mean (bilingual 97.7, lower class as a whole 97.9). Although this finding is not statistically significant, should it be duplicated in larger studies of more typically urban children it might lead to the suggestion that the Davis-Eells, whether or not it is "culture-fair" for children of all social classes, is "language-fair" for bilingual children. Should this prove to be true it would provide an unexpected but valuable addition to the tests useable for bilinguals; we say "unexpected" because the authors of the test specifically exclude its use on children in whose homes English is not the primary language. Secondly, it is interesting to note in this study that whereas the bilinguals averaged only a seven-point difference in their language and non-language scores, the total sample had a 10-point difference (97.2 versus 107.4), quite the reverse of what one would expect of a putatively linguistically handicapped subsample. Altus apparently overlooked this comparison (in fact suggesting that the 10-point difference might be due to the inclusion of the bilinguals) so we do not have information as to possible reasons for this paradox, nor can we determine whether it is statistically significant.

Bilingualism is of interest to us here because it is one of the important factors contributing to subcultural mental retardation. Studies of bilinguals are also important to us for the light they shed on general learning and use of language as this affects test and school performance of all retarded children, whether they know one language or several. The bilingual child is primarily handicapped because of his inadequate facility in one or both of his languages, and his problem therefore probably has much in common with that of any child whose language development is below the norm. This larger group would include children with a variety of speech and hearing defects, and probably also a large proportion of lower class children. Schulman and Havighurst (237), in one of the few studies of this aspect of language abilities, found in their research on 9th and 10th graders in a Midwestern community that vocabulary size correlated .46 with socioeconomic status, although there was considerable overlap between the status groups. Also, some of the children may themselves have been bilingual, but were tested only for English vocabulary.

In considering the significance of this correlation between vocabulary and social status it is important to bear in mind that the IQ also correlates with social status. This is of course true of IQ's based on verbal tests, and we have just noted that such tests are considered unfair for children with language handicaps, but it is also true of non-verbal test IQ's, albeit in somewhat less degree, as the University of Chicago studies cited earlier in this section have shown. Although there is no obvious and direct relationship between language handicaps and performance on non-verbal tests, there is increasing recognition that a child with retarded language development lacks the ability properly "to incorporate his environment, and increase progressively in the power to handle it" (McCandless, 177, p. 679). In other words, intellectual development is an important part of general learning of one's culture, and since language is the primary modality of such cultural learning, it readily follows that an impairment in language can be expected to affect all areas of intelligence.

Perhaps because this relationship between language and intelligence is so obvious very little research has been done to explore in more detail how the process operates. One early study by Robson (218) in 1931 is worth mentioning. He administered a word-association test to three different groups of children within the age range of 7 to 13: 16 children from a poor industrial district in England, selected by their teachers for backwardness, 18 English-speaking children from South Africa, similarly selected, and 20 institutionalized retarded children, selected for high intelligence. Sixty per cent of all these children failed to respond to the meanings of the words given at all, offering words which rhymed or sounded alike, or merely repeating the word or staying silent instead of producing a semantically related word. We do not know the degree to which the subjects were inhibited by the test situation itself or were otherwise prevented from best utilizing their abilities, but we can probably agree with Robson that at least some of the children reflected in their inadequacy in using words a "relative inability to interpret other people's behavior and consequently to share their experience" (p. 135).

A more recent study by Wellman and McCandless (283) makes quite clear the importance of language in developing the skills necessary for test performance. They administered the Stanford-Binet Form L and the Smith-Williams Vocabulary Test to 34 preschool children aged three to five in the fall and spring of one school year. They found that whereas those children who in the fall had a higher vocabulary age than mental age gained an average of 7.6 *IQ* points through the year, those whose vocabulary age was lower than their mental age gained an average of only 0.6 *IQ* points. We may conclude from these results that those children best equipped to profit from the stimulation and learning opportunities of preschool were those with the greatest language facility, although we must also bear in mind the possibility that in some cases the teachers may have been talking "over the heads" of all but the most linguistically adept children and thus not giving the others a fair learning opportunity.

These studies, although useful in supporting the commonly assumed relationship between language facility and intelligence, provide little insight into the more detailed mechanisms whereby the relationship is implemented. Much more research is needed in exploring the verbal tools necessary for the development of rational and abstract thinking, particularly in order that we may be better prepared to give the retarded child the essentials he may need to develop his intellectual skills in closer conformance with his true capacity.

E.   Rural-Urban and Regional Differences

A large number of studies are available which consistently show that persons, both children and adults, who live in cities are more "intelligent" than those who live in rural areas. These findings are based in general on three kinds of data: test results on school children, entrance tests for college students, and rejection rates for draftees.[18] Equally consistent results have been reported with respect to regional differences, particularly the analyses of intelligence test performance and rejection rates for mental deficiency of draftees in both World Wars. The outstanding work in this area is that of Ginzberg and Bray (87) on World War II and Korean War data; their book is discussed at some length in Chapter X and needs no additional consideration here. It may simply be observed that, in the United States at least, regional differences in intelligence correspond rather closely to regional differences in urbanization, and most of the conclusions we may reach regarding rural-urban differences can therefore be generalized to the regional level. It should be noted that in the South and Southwest, which showed the highest

---

[18]Typical studies are those of Hauch (104) on Silesian 12-year-olds from rural and industrial districts; Wheeler (289) on Tennessee mountain school children; Smith, (249, 250) on University of Kansas freshmen; Nelson (192) on State College of Washington freshmen; and Hyde and Kingsley (126) on draftees from the Boston area. Armstrong (10) compared the test performance of "rural" children from Bedford, N.Y., with children from New York City, matched for school grade and father's occupation, and found no difference; this unexpected outcome probably results from the fact that Bedford is an upper middle class suburban community, not rural in the usual sense of the word.

draftee rejection rates for mental deficiency, not only is a larger proportion of the population rural, but also there are proportionately fewer large cities, and those studies of rural-urban differences which have also taken into account the size of cities have shown a consistent correlation of this factor with test scores.[19]

Obviously the mere concentration of people in a limited area is not in itself enough to account for the increase in measured intelligence with urbanization. The explanations for this phenomenon which are generally advanced fall into three major categories: (1) the ability of cities, with a more concentrated tax base and more children available as students, to build better schools, attract better teachers, and assign students to classes all of whose members have approximately equal levels of performance; (2) "selective migration," by which is meant that the more capable people in a rural area or small town will be the ones most likely to have the resources, initiative, and motivation to improve further their status by moving to the city, leaving their duller fellows behind; and (3) the city, through the stimulation and competition induced by a larger number of interpersonal relationships, and through the wider range of experiences available, provides a better opportunity to develop the skills important for an intelligence test or in school—intellectually, emotionally, and in specific knowledge.   Looked at in one way it might be said that the first of these explanations—better schools—is but one aspect of the generally superior intellectual opportunities of the city; however, schools reach only those who are brought up in the cities, whereas the other urban effects are at least theoretically operative at any age.   Another reason for maintaining a distinction between school-age children and adults in this context is well stated in the words of caution with which Lemkau, Tietze, and Cooper (166) introduce their data on mental deficiency in the Eastern Health District of Baltimore:

> The definition of mental deficiency was originally based upon social competency, but with the development of applied psychology, diagnosis has become more and more dependent upon the results of tests designed to evaluate the so-called intellectual functions of the personality. The rapid popularization of intelligence tests, based on the demonstration of their usefulness, especially in the field of education, has tended to make

---

[19]As was pointed out in Section II, the great majority of draftees rejected for "mental deficiency" would actually come under our designation of mentally retarded, many undoubtedly because of membership in a subcultural group, because those with identifiable neurological or other pathologies resulting in mental deficit are likely to be screened out on medical grounds before they come up for testing.

mental deficiency an inability to perform certain set tasks, rather than an inability to discharge the responsibilities of living in society.

This change in definition, from terms of social competency to terms of *IQ* or its equivalent, has extended beyond the instrument that made it possible. The tests of intelligence generally used in this country are not properly standardized for use with adults. Nevertheless, they are so used, and the results are directly compared with those secured from children of the age groups for which proper standardization has been made.

Persons who are now in school, or who have recently been in school, in large centers of population have almost all been tested, and mental deficiency, as the term is applied to this group, means, all too frequently, failure in tests. Social competency continues to be the basis of definition for most older adults, those who were out of school before the widespread use of testing. However, in the case of these older persons also, tests are often used to substantiate observation and to reduce the estimate to quantitative terms. This situation must be kept in mind constantly in evaluating statistics on mental deficiency (p. 278).

To this we need only add that their observations regarding older people apply in only slightly lesser degree to persons taught in small country schools, where there is little need for classifying large numbers of students by levels of ability and psychological services are often not available for this purpose even if the need were felt.

Many educators feel that more favorable opportunities exist for developing an effective curriculum in an urban as against a rural setting. The argument for this point of view runs as follows. Large schools with large numbers of students close at hand permit not merely separate classrooms and teachers for each grade, but often a division of the grades on the basis of the capability of the various students. The "four-track" system recently introduced in the Washington, D. C., public schools was accomplished essentially by reassignment of the available children and teachers; were it attempted in a country school with at best only one teacher available for the basic curriculum at each grade level such a system would require a substantial increase in staff. Experience in the District of Columbia and elsewhere has shown that this specialization of curriculum permits not only the gifted children to advance more rapidly, but also the slow ones. It also helps reduce the stigma often associated with special classes with their implication of a separation of the "subnormal" from the "normal" children. Another advantage lies in the opportunity to employ more teachers of specialized subjects such as music, shop, foreign languages, and the like. Extra-curricular activities can be organized and directed by persons trained in a variety of fields, and pupil personnel services are provided to help students with remediable handicaps. Furthermore, although the rapid growth in urban population has unquestionably created serious problems of overcrowding, it should be borne in mind that it has also resulted in the building of large numbers of new school buildings whose architecture and facilities are generally superior to the older country schools. All of these factors combine to afford the child better educational opportunities and at the same time to provide a more satisfying environment for teaching, thus helping to attract more and better teachers irrespective of salary differentials.

Rural schools also have more attendance problems. Bringing children in from a distance can be seriously impeded by weather and other factors which have little effect on city schools. In agricultural areas, particularly in the South, children are often taken out of school, even to the point of closing the schools, to help in the fields at certain seasons. Davis (60) found that in a state-accredited Negro school in the South, whereas children completing the eighth grade were supposed to have had 72 months of schooling, the children in this school averaged only 53.5 months. Their IQ's were generally low (range 55 to 105, median 78) and showed a significant positive correlation with the number of months of actual school attended.

The arguments favoring specialization and differentiation in the organization of necessarily large school systems are certainly persuasive. However, the small—even one-room—country schools also have their champions. Large schools can only judge success in the education of large numbers of students on an essentially statistical basis. This means in effect that they must rely primarily upon quantifiable measures closely related to the immediate curriculum objectives: school grades, promotions, and test results. As the data to be presented in the next section will attest, academic performance is not necessarily a reliable predictor of the ability to cope with the social, occupational, and other problems of life in our society. Through the more individualized teacher-student relationship of the small school, this broader preparation can often be realized more effectively. Furthermore, even a "platoon" system such as that mentioned above in the District of Columbia depends for its initial assignment of pupils largely on test results. Yet we know that even when predicting academic performance intelligence and achievement tests are far from being 100 per cent valid. Although a readiness to watch for and reassign students who appear to have been misplaced can compensate somewhat for these deficiencies, it can well be argued that the teacher in a small school, working continuously with her students as individuals, is better able to recognize their latent abilities and to perceive the steps necessary to bring these abilities to fuller expression. This individual work with children can be more rewarding to at least some of the kinds of people who enter the teaching profession, so that the superior qualifications of the teachers attracted by the inducements of city schools may be partially offset by the limitations imposed upon them through the standardization of curriculum and teaching techniques required in operating a large-scale educational facility. We do not know how many students benefit from this more intimate relationship with the teacher to the degree that they obtain a higher IQ than would otherwise have been the case, nor whether their numbers are sufficient to invalidate the explanation of rural-urban IQ differences in terms of the richer educational facilities in cities. We will discuss more fully in the next section the matter of preparation for broader life problems outside of the school and have mentioned the subject here only to indicate that even this seemingly certain explanation of rural-urban differences can be questioned.

The concept of selective migration, which accounts for rural-urban differences in intelligence by assuming that the brighter people leave the country and go to the cities, has also acquired a somewhat controversial flavor. This apparently results from a tendency to phrase the concept as a general law, applying to all situations. Actually, there is quite conclusive evidence that in some instances selective migration does take place, whereas in others it perhaps does not. Schmidt (236) followed up the graduates of a rural school near Berlin, and found that the people who had had the higher grades in school were the ones who generally gravitated toward the metropolis, while those ranking lower in grades stayed in the country. Brugger (31) found a similar tendency in four districts in Switzerland, but less pronounced due apparently to the smaller contrast in way of life between villages and cities in Switzerland; however, there was a marked preponderance of more gifted men (although not women) who emigrated out of the country. Husén (124) analysed the results of large-scale administration of a Swedish Army group intelligence test and found that migration from lower to higher population density areas was significantly more frequent among those with high test scores, and that the migrants generally had scores comparable to the average for the higher density area into which they moved. These tests were, however, administered at indeterminate periods after migration, and the new environments may have altered the subjects' test capabilities. Similarly Fairbank (70) compared a "normal" and a "subnormal" group 17 years after they were first studied in Baltimore and found that the normals, more frequently than the subnormals, had the initiative and resources to move to other parts of the city in search of more varied employment opportunities. Gist and Clark (89) conducted a carefully controlled follow-up of 2544 high school students from rural communities in Kansas. These people were tested at the time of their graduation from high school in 1922-23, and then in 1935 their places of residence were compared with their IQ's at graduation. There was a progressive increment in average intelligence among those resident in 1935 in each of four categories of cities graded by increasing size, the highest scorers living in metropolitan centers or emigrating out of the state entirely.

Evidence of this sort, pointing clearly to the operation of selective migration among some groups, was readily coupled with regional differences in Negro scores found on the Army Alpha and Beta tests of World War I and led to the conclusion that the urban centers of the North were draining off all the capable Negroes from the South. Klineberg (157) tested this hypothesis among Negro children who, with their parents, had moved to New York City from the Southern cities of Nashville, Birmingham, and Charleston during their school years. He compared their school records before moving with those of other children whose parents had not moved and found no significant differences, demonstrating that whatever the reasons which prompted some people to go North while others remained behind, these were not reflected in the school performance (and therefore presumably IQ) of their children. From these findings he concluded "that the Negro who leaves the South for the North is not on the average superior to the Negro who remains behind, and that the present superiority of the Northern over the Southern Negro may be explained by the more favorable environment, rather than selective migration" (p. 62). This conclusion, although very possibly correct, does not appear necessarily to follow from his data. The parents, not the children, were the ones who took the initiative in moving, and we do not have IQ's or any other measures of intelligence for them. To conclude that the movers were not superior to the non-movers we have to assume (a) that the children's school records reflected accurately what their IQ's would have been had they been tested, and (b) that the parents' IQ's are close correlates of those of their children. Both of these assumptions have some a priori validity, but taken together they introduce a sufficient number of unknowns to make Klineberg's rather sweeping conclusions appear somewhat tenuous. In addition, it should be noted that he studied only children who had come North from some of the largest of Southern cities; this was probably necessary in order to prevent the cost of data-collection from rising to prohibitive levels, but his sample was by the same token in no way representative of the total influx of Southern Negroes into New York City, for many come from rural areas in the South. The possibility therefore remains that among Southern Negroes the same trend obtains as demonstrated elsewhere—i.e., that migration is selective for higher intelligence from rural areas both to Nashville, Birmingham, etc., and to the North. We cannot say that this is so, but Klineberg's data do not demonstrate that it is not. To prove this point conclusively either way would probably require a very large scale survey and follow-up, whose cost would have to be weighed against the possible gain to be derived from having such knowledge. Whether or not the North is skimming the cream of Southern Negro society there is little or nothing anyone can or necessarily should do about it.

The important fact is that the Negroes, and particularly the Negro children, who arrive in the cities of the North are intellectually inferior to those born or long resident there, but with the passage of time, and in particular with continued attendance in Northern schools, this deficit is largely made up. In connection with the study discussed above, Klineberg also tested a number of children who had moved from the South into New York City schools and found that *IQ* showed a fairly high correlation with years of residence in New York. Before this McAlpin (176) and Long (170) had conducted similar studies with identical findings in the District of Columbia; Long also concluded that the *IQ* increase of his immigrants as compared to that of his controls who were born in Washington stabilized after about 8½ years of residence in the District of Columbia. Lee (163) replicated these studies in Philadelphia and reached comparable conclusions; his findings were more conclusive because he had available not only the length of residence in Philadelphia for each child, but also the results of tests administered at the time of first admission to the local schools. In this way he was able to appraise the actual improvement in the children rather than just knowing that the ones who had lived there longer tested higher. He had available, as did the earlier researchers, a control group of Philadelphia-born Negro children.

The rise in *IQ* of these Negro children who moved into Northern cities can fairly readily be explained on the basis of the schools available to them in the North, which were superior to those they had previously attended. The greater possibility for job advancement in return for good school grades undoubtedly also increased the motivation toward schooling for some. But it is probable also that living in these cities, particularly for those children who came from rural areas, provided specific experiences which increased their ability to cope with the sorts of problems posed by intelligence tests. Shephard (239) for example administered a battery of tests to two groups of children, matched for parental occupation, age, sex, and United States citizenship, from rural communities in Kansas and from New York City. He found the rural Kansas children significantly superior in mechanical ability and the urban New York children in verbal ability and speed. These differences doubtless reflect motivation as well as content of experience, but would appear to support his general conclusion that: "From the results of this study there is an indication that the common assumption that one regional group is intellectually superior or inferior to another is unjustified. Rather, the performance of the different groups should be evaluated in terms of the degree to which they possess specific traits and abilities" (p. 462). In connection with a larger study of social class and intelligence Havighurst and Janke (109) administered a similar battery of tests to 110 ten-year-olds in a Midwestern community with closely comparable results. Even though this was a relatively small community (10,000 population) those children classified as urban did better in all the tests than the rural children, with the exception that the rural boys were superior in mechanical ability. The mechanical skills (measured by the Minnesota Mechanical Assembly Test) displayed by the rural children in both these studies undoubtedly were acquired through experience with farm equipment.

In a somewhat similar earlier study, Jones, Conrad, and Blanchard (138) found that a group of rural New England children, although performing much lower on the Stanford-Binet than a comparison group of gifted urban children, surpassed the urban group when given a special formboard test which involved deliberately rural content. Although it can justifiably be said that the special test was biased in favor of the rural children in this case, it should be borne in mind that the majority of the children in the standardization populations for most intelligence tests are drawn from urban areas. Since we know that urban and rural children perform differently, establishing test norms in this way constitutes a bias in favor of the urban child. We must constantly bear in mind that the Stanford-Binet and other standard tests of intelligence measure only one special set of skills. As with the mechanically gifted farm boys, we are seeing here children who, even though the commonly accepted criterion of the Stanford-Binet would classify them as *below* average in "intelligence," can sit down in a testing situation and use their minds with *above* average effectiveness with respect to a different, but for them highly relevant, set of skills.

The study of rural-urban differences, and particularly of children and adults who leave the country and arrive in cities with an apparent intellectual deficit, has great research promise for the exploration of subcultural mental retardation. We now know that many of these people are, in terms of the usual test criteria, retarded on their arrival, even though seldom very severely, and that they appear rather consistently to improve intellectually to a level of parity with their new neighbors. Careful longitudinal studies, starting with a precise evaluation of the areas in which their deficits lie—knowledge, mental skills, and motivations—and following on with study of the processes whereby these deficits are remedied, could tell us much we do not know about techniques and emphases to use in corrective education. Not only is this a readily available population for study, but it is one in which many of the variables which normally plague designers of research in subcultural groups are already controlled. Whether we are dealing with Southern Negroes who move to Harlem or the children of white farmers who move to the Bronx, we are studying people who blend with their neighbors in appearance and language—even though at first they may differ a little in dress or accent. They also share the values and knowledge of a single basic culture and are handicapped only in certain segments of experience. For the very reason that their problems are not so all-encompassing, we cannot apply our findings directly to the education of, for example, Puerto Ricans. But we can chart out some facts and generate hypotheses in an area which has thus far scarcely been touched. We are able to identify a large array of subcultural groups whose members are handicapped on intelligence tests and in other ways often to the point of being considered mentally retarded, but we can say very little about the actual processes whereby these handicaps are either created or corrected. The migrants who constantly flow into the cities appear to provide one excellent and relatively simple group upon which to begin.

F. SEX DIFFERENCES

There is little that can be said regarding differential performance of boys and girls on present day intelligence tests, for it is customary in developing and standardizing these tests to eliminate those items upon which the two sexes consistently perform differently. Although statistically significant sex differences have from time to time been reported within normal populations, particularly when the analysis gets down to subtests or individual items, the findings do not conform to a consistent pattern. If enough groups are tested it can be expected by chance alone that in some cases differences will be found which appear significant within the data for a single group. Insofar as chance is not operative, we can only conclude that the test-makers have failed in their intention to eliminate items to which boys and girls respond differently.

The effort to avoid discrimination between the performance of the two sexes can be understood historically, particularly in the United States, by recollecting the era of uncritical enthusiasm for intelligence tests when they were felt to tap in each individual his inherent and unchanging mental capacity. It was at this time that Terman undertook his revision of the tests devised by Binet and Simon, with little evident concern over the doubts which plagued the original authors as to what they were really measuring. Within Terman's premises, a test which differentiated consistently between the sexes would thereby be demonstrating the inherent inferiority of one sex to the other, a wholly unacceptable proposition. Since that time it has become widely recognized that the *IQ* is not constant over time and therefore cannot be measuring purely inborn characteristics, that it is affected among other things by a host of cultural and emotional factors, that it is intimately related to academic experience, and that people can therefore perform differently on intelligence tests without necessarily being better or worse in the absolute sense envisaged by Terman. However, despite this sweeping reorientation to the meaning of intelligence tests psychologists continue to adhere closely to the precepts of test construction laid down in the original Stanford revision of the Binet test.

Thus there is still not available any test of over-all "intelligence" which will permit except accidentally of differential performance by the two sexes, although it is readily apparent that boys and girls of normal upbringing in our society have different sorts of experiences and we have different expectations of them, even in the schools. It is not likely that an item would be dropped from a mechanical assembly test because girls performed less well on it than boys, yet the intelligence test-constructors will not permit us to discover whether there are important differences we should know about in the intellectual functioning of the two sexes. No rationale has been offered for this ever since Terman simply stated that he eliminated tests which would be "relatively less fair to one sex than the other," seeing no need for further justification at the time. As Pastore (203) observed, would it not have been equally appropriate to eliminate items on which there was differential performance by Negro and white children? Davis and Havighurst (59) show some exasperation over Terman's procedure:

> How can a mental test be "less fair" to boys than to girls? It involves

no organic sexual differences, so far as we know. There is here no question, apparently, of different cortical structure, or glandular secretion. Clearly, then, if a question is unfair to boys, as compared to girls, it must be that their social experience is different, on the average. Their training as males or females in the family, school, and play group differs, and therefore the amount of experience they have had with various types of mental problems differs. Their social motivation, as boys or girls, to learn how to solve such problems must also differ. Terman certainly did not believe that girls were genetically superior to boys in mentality, or vice versa.

Thus, upon what must have been a purely social and cultural basis, that is, upon the conviction that any problem was "less fair" if either sex proved "superior" to the other sex in solving it, Terman eliminated all such problems from his test.

Upon exactly the same principle as Terman used to control sex bias in tests, one might throw out all problems in which any socio-economic group proves superior. . . .

The continuing attempt of test makers to obscure differences in performance by boys and girls runs counter to the constant and conscious effort of parents, teachers, and society at large to instill in growing children the very different attitudes, motivations, and behaviors expected of each sex. It is of course clear that the philosophy of test construction, tied as it now is to the criterion of school performance, reflects little sophistication in the realities of our culture as a whole; but even if one were willing to accept a limitation on the applicability of intelligence tests strictly to school use this would not justify the obliteration of sex differences. Certainly by high school, and in reality well before, the curricula and educational expectations of boys and girls are differentiated. It follows that if they are to learn different things they will need to draw upon different kinds of intellectual skills in order to do so, and a test which fails deliberately to discriminate between these skills must necessarily suffer a concomitant reduction in predictive accuracy. Furthermore, educational achievement as represented for example by a high school diploma is viewed by most teachers as more crucial for a boy than for a girl, since every boy must be prepared to get a job—preferably, in the teachers' value system, a white-collar job—whereas this is a matter of individual choice for girls. Thus, whether it is explicitly recognized or not, the standards of performance and the expectations a boy must meet tend to be higher than those applied to girls.

If the elimination of sex difference discrimination from intelligence tests makes little sense with respect to "normal" children, it represents a grave shortcoming when the tests are applied to retarded boys and girls. Here the sex differences are striking, important, and little understood. The Onondaga County survey (193) found, as have earlier studies, that roughly twice as many boys are referred for mental subnormality as girls.[20] Lemkau (165) has suggested that this may be "due primarily to two characteristics of the male that are well recognized; first, his retardation in comparison with the female as regards communication skills and second, his greater aggressiveness that tends to lead to lower grades in deportment, reflecting his greater capacity to 'make trouble' and thus have his defect discovered in the course of a fundamentally unrelated investigation. These two factors are not themselves uncorrelated, as any remedial reading teacher can testify."

Other explanations than those offered by Lemkau are equally plausible. The higher expectation of boys discussed above is probably at least partially responsible, for more concern is likely to be shown toward the possible academic failure of a boy than a girl, and he will therefore probably be referred for attention—and tested—more consistently than in the case of girls. Also, as we shall see in the next chapter, in some lower class groups a boy who does well in school is considered to be trying to curry favor with the teacher and is therefore rejected by his group, whereas this stricture does not appear to apply to girls. Two important things are to be observed about these and other possible explanations for the greater number of boys than girls who are found in the higher categories of subnormality. One is that they are speculative. We do not know, and given the present nature of intelligence tests it is hard to see how we can know, what significance we should attribute to the kinds of test performance characteristic of retarded boys as against retarded girls.

The other is that we also do not really know whether the true incidence of mental retardation of boys and girls is different—i.e., whether screening methods and agreed-upon psychometric or other criteria would reveal the differences discussed above. The data we have, of which those derived from

---

[20] The effect of possible differences in the incidence of organic disorders leading to mental deficiency is not clear. In the Onondaga survey, the sex ratio in referrals below the age of five with a clear organic diagnosis showed a marked preponderance of boys, but the prevalence of organic cases over five years was about equal for both sexes. One can speculate as to the significance of these differences, but for the purposes of this report it is probably sufficient to note that organic cases contributed only about one-seventh of the total referrals in Onondaga County. Their numbers would thus not be enough materially to affect the striking two-to-one ratio found in the total sample. Our discussion here is therefore concerned essentially with sex differences in referrals for non-organic mental retardation.

the Onondaga County survey are the latest and best, are concerned with cases reported or referred by a variety of agencies. We thus do not have data on how many children are actually retarded, but rather upon those about whose retardation someone saw fit to take action of one sort or another, thus bringing cases to attention.[21] This is an unfortunate situation from several viewpoints, but at the same time may not be as serious as it would appear. Mental retardation is a social and cultural phenomenon as well as a medical and psychological diagnosis. Children are identified as retarded in terms of culturally defined criteria, and it is equally as important to know about the characteristics of this total group which has been rejected by society as it is to isolate those who fail to meet a given single criterion such as obtaining an *IQ* over 80. We might find that there are no significant sex differences in the distribution of *IQ* throughout the lower end of the range and we would still be concerned with knowing what factors differentiate the larger group of boys who are socially designated as retarded from the smaller group of girls. The *IQ* simply does not provide a sufficient basis for gauging the numerical extent or nature of the retarded population as it presently exists, but a test of adequate sensitivity *should* be able to discriminate between various possible forms of intellectual deficit which have contributed to the retarded designation.

If the items on tests which differentiate between the sexes were not so systematically discarded, patterns would emerge from the intelligence test performance of normal children which we could say were characteristic of the respective sex rôles. We would then have some standard against which to compare the test profiles of retarded boys and girls and thus perhaps obtain some idea whether we should look first at intellectual, emotional, or cultural aspects of the problem in search of a cause and therefore correction and prevention. However, the existing tests will not permit of this, nor can they provide a test of any hypotheses our speculations might generate.

G. CULTURE

Everything we have said thus far in this chapter could readily be sub-

---

[21] Jastak, whose contributions to the theory of intelligence are discussed in Chapter XII, undertook such a survey of the population of the State of Delaware with the objective of determining not only the prevalence but the nature and significance of retardation; unfortunately the analysis and publication of his material appears to be in abeyance, thus depriving us of a very rich source of factual information as well as the exploration of a series of highly challenging hypotheses. A preliminary report (Jastak and Whiteman, 133) does not deal with sex differences.

sumed under the heading "Culture" in its usually accepted meaning. Intelligence tests measure—and attempt to predict—learning, yet learning and culture are but two sides of a single coin: culture provides the content and technique of learning, and learning is the medium for both continuity and change in culture. With respect to intelligence testing and measurement Davis and Havighurst (59, p. 301) have said: "The crucial problem raised by the attempt to compare scientifically the capacity of any two individuals to learn is that of finding situations with which the two individuals have had equal experience"—whether these two individuals are identical twins or live on different continents. And again (p. 303): "The sociologist and social anthropologist have been convinced, through studies of a great many human societies, that cultural learning runs through nearly all the 'mental' behavior of human beings. Social anthropologists therefore strongly doubt that cultural behavior can be eliminated from any intelligence-test response."

Despite our obvious agreement with this point of view we have elected thus far to treat social class, language, and so forth separately for two reasons. One is that it has been traditional to do so and one finds the literature naturally falling into one category or another. The failure thus implied to perceive that each of these factors is but part of a total cultural context, whose effects are interrelated and often cumulative, has been responsible, we feel, for much of the futile repetitiveness and sterility of research in this area. Nevertheless by confining ourselves here to a review of existing research we have had little choice. The second reason is that by attempting to carry each line of attack as far as we can toward an adequate conclusion we have, we hope, demonstrated the necessity—even the inevitability—of taking into account the total cultural context of even such a specialized form of activity as performance on an intelligence test. The effects of bilingualism, for example, cannot be assessed merely in terms of the psychological problem of learning two languages, but must also take into account conflicts in cultural identification, values associated with the two cultures and languages, and often also minority group membership. Similarly social class has its correlates in level and kind of aspiration, in kinds of thinking which are encouraged or discouraged, in ethnicity, in language facility and in a host of other factors in addition to the primary fact of differing levels of economic resource.

We have until now been concerned principally with the results of testing done within our own cultural setting. Therefore the differences we have discovered should properly be called subcultural, because the people who have been sorted out for study into various kinds of groupings share in common

much of our total cultural system. Viewed against the shared totality of
their cultural experience, the differences between them appear minor when
compared with, for example, the difference between any one of them and an
Eskimo north of the Arctic Circle or a Bushman on the Kalahari Desert of
Southwest Africa. Nevertheless these relatively minor differences are enough
to affect test scores significantly and therefore are of importance to us.

As we now turn to examine studies done in cultures strikingly different
from our own we find researchers sharing, explicitly or implicitly, the common goal of determining the degree to which various sorts of tests really
measure intelligence in the abstract as against the more circumscribed array
of skills considered important in our own culture. Even this, however, is an
objective culturally bound by our own value systems. As we shall see in the
next section not all peoples place a high valuation on intelligence, and certainly not on the "intelligence" we measure with tests, nor are persons mentally
subnormal even by local standards necessarily ostracized or otherwise penalized. However, even though other peoples may not be concerned with the
minor variations in IQ which cause so much distress in our own society,
their test performance, in light of their radically different cultural backgrounds, may be able to give us some additional perspective on our own
smaller subcultural differences.

But here again a word of caution is in order. Motivation is an important
factor in any sort of performance, and it has been given substantial—although
even then probably not adequate—attention in the literature of psychometric
testing of retarded as well as normal children. But this attention has been
focused primarily on motivation as it is specific to the testing situation: competitiveness and the desire to excel, anxieties over failure, the valuation
of speed, etc. There has been little consideration of the broader implications
of the label of retardation in our society. McCandless (177, p. 684) makes
a useful distinction in discussing the development of subcultural mental
retardation:

> First, the environment from which the subcultural mentally defective
> person comes is one providing minimal opportunity for the learning of
> the skills which are subsumed under the term intelligence.
> Second, the environment from which the subcultural mentally defective
> person comes is one in which he has maximum opportunity to learn "self-
> defeating" techniques—e.g., loosely defined, expectancies of failure, ab-
> solute as opposed to relative thinking, concrete as opposed to abstract
> thinking, belief in his essential worthlessness, etc.

Although we might argue that the kinds of thinking referred to under the second heading more properly belong with the skills referred to under the first, we find here clearly stated the separate aspects of the problem: on the one hand the different strictly intellectual learning processes characteristic of various subcultures, and on the other the more pervasive personality disorganization felt by retarded persons generally in our society. We can compare people who obtain low test scores in our society with those in another culture on the first dimension, but not necessarily on the second.

Most testing of non-European peoples has been done with performance tests of one sort or another. Although, as we have seen, many researchers have failed to perceive the handicap introduced by verbal intelligence tests when administered to subcultural groups in our own society, the language barrier is so obvious among less civilized peoples that few attempts have been made to utilize tests which require any language skills outside of the oral instructions. Two studies can be mentioned briefly to document the fairly self-evident implications of the use of verbal tests. Sparling (256) administered the Stanford-Binet and the Porteus Maze to 32 Indian children aged 8 to 17 institutionalized in Canada; their mean Binet *IQ* was 75 (range 54-101) while the Porteus Maze mean was 108 (82-142), suggesting that if a non-verbal test had been used initially none of them might have been institutionalized. Rohrer (219) in contrast administered the Goodenough Draw-a-Man Test and the Otis Test of Mental Abilities to Osage Indians in Oklahoma and found their scores at or above the norms for the tests; many Osage, through oil revenues, have fared very well economically and enjoy equal opportunities with their white neighbors. Thus we see that American Indians are not necessarily handicapped at all in test performance if they are fully acculturated, but seriously handicapped on verbal tests if they have been living the life of Indians.

Turning to performance tests, one of the most searching and thoughtful studies on record, and also one of the few wherein the subjects had had practically no experience with Western schooling, was completed over 20 years ago by Nissen, Machover, and Kinder (195). They administered a variety of performance tests to 50 children of the Sousou tribe in French Guinea, a part of French West Africa from which many of the slaves were taken who contributed to the Negro population of the United States and the Caribbean. There were 42 boys and 8 girls, aged 5 to 14. As might be expected the Sousou performed consistently below the norms, but this was more evident on some tests than on others.

Without attempting a thorough-going analysis of the functions underlying the tests, we may say broadly that tests which have pictorially representative content, which involve symbolic material, and which require
combinative activity based on the perception of part-whole relationships,
produced the poorest results when applied to our subjects; these tests
include the Digit Symbol, the·Ship Test, the Manikin and Feature Profile
and the Healy 'A.' At the other extreme, tests which involve imitative
functions, immediate memory, perception and retention of visuo-kinaes-
thetic cues and which, besides, are practically without representative
content, yielded the best results; these tests were the Cube Imitation,
Adaptation Board, Pyramid, and Paper Folding. . . .

When the results on the separate tests are compared with each other
. . . it is noted that as the content and activities involved in each correspond more to specialized experience in a civilized environment, they
provide greater difficulties for our culturally primitive subjects. Conversely, as the content and activities involved in each correspond more
to the common matrix of universal experience they provide less difficulty
for our subjects. Without implying that the elements of native capacity
underlying any of the tests have received optimal developmental stimulation in our subjects, we may therefore suggest that in general the higher
the median score achieved on a test and the greater the variability of the
scores, the less have the capacities underlying that test been restricted by
the absence, in the environment of our subjects, of the features present in
the environment of the standardization groups. The order of the tests
in the list, in addition to revealing any unevenness of native capacity,
would be indicative to a considerable extent of the relative degree to
which the development of the capacities underlying each of the tests has
been specifically affected by the differences between the West African
and American environments. The tests would naturally follow the same
order as to appropriateness for measuring primitive capacities.

The marked differences among the separate tests with respect to the
effectiveness with which they were handled by our group of subjects
as a whole appears to us to have implications of fundamental importance
for the use and interpretation of tests in clinical practice. In the application of the tests of this series to mental defectives we do not find
the consistent discrepancies which are a part of the results of this study.
It is particularly impressive, therefore, that a series of tests, co-extensive
in normative range as standardized and clinically regarded as being
comparable, should have yielded such disparate results when applied to
our culturally primitive subjects whose environmental homogeneity is
probably not exceeded anywhere. This is not a result of special abilities
or disabilities for individual subjects; the unevenness which the results
show is distinctly a group phenomenon. While from a practical clinical
standpoint, where the disposition of individual cases is an ever-present

preoccupation, tests may be regarded as being normatively comparable, our results suggest that for more fundamental interpretations a more analytical approach is required. Rather than the multiplication of statistical data, we feel the need of investigations directed toward the phenomenological aspects of tests and their relation to training, culture, environment and race (pp. 338-339).

In the interpretation of any data in the field of racial psychology, it is essential to recognize the limitations inherent in the standards of comparison which are used. Even though proficiency in the tests used may be a significant measure of the abilities required by the highly specialized culture and environment of the standardization groups, we are not warranted in assuming that it would be equally a measure of abilities encouraged by or suited to the quite different culture and environment of our subjects. The selection of features of our own civilization as a basis for measuring the inferiority of individuals of other cultures is obviously arbitrary and artificial. Our particular culture may, and probably does, emphasize certain aspects of "intelligence" to the neglect of other aspects. Furthermore, we have, as yet, no adequate measures of intensity of feeling or of the capacity for experiencing and expressing emotion; we have no standards for study of individual or social integrity. The tests which we have used take no account of these matters, and the civilization out of which the tests have developed seems to consider them relatively unimportant. It is conceivable that under a culture which would place greater emphasis upon affective experience, there might be correspondingly less concern with matters which seem to us of major importance (p. 352).

Particularly significant in this analysis is the realization that tests can be biased not merely by their content, but also by the perceptual and rational tasks required, some of which may involve processes of a kind not familiar within the culture—in this case those requiring "combinative activity based on the perception of part-whole relationships." The present writers found a very similar difficulty in their study of the natives of Truk, an island group in the Western Pacific (Gladwin and Sarason, 90). This study will be discussed more fully in the next section, for it attempted among other things to set "intelligence" within the broader framework of affect and personality in the manner urged by Nissen, Machover, and Kinder, but our experience with a performance test is worth noting here:

The Kohs Block Designs, normally administered as part of the Arthur Point Scale battery, were selected for use on Truk with the hope that this test which requires no explicit verbalization might provide some measure of intelligence comparable to American standards. The test consists in arranging a number of identical colored blocks in patterns to conform to a series of increasingly difficult designs printed on small cards; the designs are geometric and linear and thus conformed in general to the types of design found in published works on Trukese material culture prior to leaving for the field. Unfortunately, it soon became evident that performance on this test correlated fairly closely with the amount of schooling to which each subject had been exposed. As the ability to see the content of photographs and other pictures appeared also to be a function of experience gained in school, it was concluded that the indigenous training of the Trukese leaves them poorly prepared to discern the field and ground relationships upon which successful performance in this test rests. Scoring of the test results along conventional lines, which would give data comparable to those for which the test was standardized in the United States, would in the case of the Trukese present a picture of doubtful significance. For this reason although the test was administered to all subjects in the interests of conformity no attempt will be made here to present an analysis of the results (p. 213).

Although not directly relevant to intelligence testing, it is interesting to note that in interpreting the protocols of the Bender-Gestalt (a psychodiagnostic test dependent upon the perception of spatial and field-and-ground relationships) Dr. Bender (in Joseph and Murray, 139, p. 142) found that among the natives of Saipan to the north of Truk, "Gestalt patterns corresponding to those found in confusional states appear to represent norms." She apparently did not realize that the diagnostic norms of the test were vitiated by the different perceptual modes of the Saipanese. Living in our own culture, with virtually universal and constant exposure to pictures—three-dimensional forms projected on a two-dimensional surface—it is difficult to comprehend the difficulty experienced by some people in reversing this projection to separate subject from background.

Klineberg (156), Steggerda (261), and others have attempted to set down systematically all the factors their experience in intercultural testing led them to believe need be controlled in order to assure a valid measure. These included the obvious variables of language and cultural content, and particularly the attitude toward speed of performance. Many researchers have found to their frustration that "beating the clock" is not necessarily rewarding to peoples in cultures other than our own. Klineberg, after administering the Pintner-Paterson performance tests to several groups of Indian and Negro children in the United States, concluded that "there is evidence that the superiority of white over Indian and Negro children in performance tests is largely, if not entirely, a superiority in scores for *time*. There is no superiority, and in some cases an inferiority, in the scores [of white children] for *accuracy* of performance." One can either disregard the time limitations on the ground that a person who is not trying for speed is not having his ability in this regard validly tested, or else take the position that all of the performance criteria of the test are essentially those valued in our own culture and the time criterion should therefore remain in force as a logical part of the whole.

Other factors mentioned are the ethnic identity and relative status of the test administrator, whether the testing is done in a native or foreign setting, whether chronological age (denominator in the IQ) can be determined with any accuracy, group versus individual performance as a function of cultural attitudes (Clements, 48), and the amount of exposure of the natives to Western culture and in particular schooling. A surprising number of researchers, presumably preoccupied with determining the intelligence correlates of "race," have failed to record or take into account the amount of schooling their subjects have had. When this variable is included, as for example in the extensive study of Arthur Point Scale performance by Havighurst and Hilkevitch (108) of 670 children from six different American Indian tribes, it appears that schooling materially affects test scores. The effects of schooling are not, however, confined merely to the content of test questions. Leighton and Kluckhohn (164) found that 23 Navaho children who had some schooling achieved a mean IQ on the Arthur Point Scale (a combination of several separate performance tests) of 102.5, whereas 41 completely unschooled children averaged only 79.8. The authors concluded from this testing experience that "it would be incorrect to claim that schooling makes the children more intelligent: rather it helps them to mobilize their own ability so that they can do well on the Arthur test." Only in school do they have real experience with pencils and toys and "familiarity with being told by a strange white person to do an apparently senseless task" (p. 153).

Numerous efforts have been made to produce tests more appropriate for cross-cultural applications. These range from such minimal modifications as the direct translation of a standard test into a foreign language to the construction of completely new tests. The two best known instruments to emerge from the latter activity are the Porteus Maze Test and the Cattell Culture-Free Test. The Porteus Maze, as its name implies, consists in a series of mazes the subject is asked to trace through. Although this would appear to be a rather esoteric form of activity the test has actually been administered to a very large range of peoples with little apparent difficulty or misunderstanding of instructions. It was included in the Arthur Point Scale battery until its 1947 revision, and Porteus himself (208) has used the test widely among tribes in Africa, Australia, and Southern Asia, as well as in Hawaii and other less remote regions. Porteus, as well as others, administered a variety of other performance tests along with the mazes, with variable results.

The fact that some people score higher and others lower on the mazes than on other tests does not, however, of itself prove anything about the validity of the test. Each test presumably measures a particular aspect of mental ability which will be favored by the cultural milieu of one group and inhibited by another. Thus we come back to the essential dilemma of cross-cultural testing: lacking any constant criterion of intelligence, or even in many cultures a high valuation of intellectual skill, there is nothing against which to validate any test, nor any means to assure that any given test "makes sense" to the people taking it within a particular culture. This is the same dilemma we saw with the Davis-Eells Games, but greatly magnified. If exposure to Western schooling improves performance on a test, we can probably conclude at least that experience exclusively in the native culture does not equip the individual to do the best he could with the tasks presented—the point made above by Leighton and Kluckhohn. Porteus is in effect saying the same thing when he remarks that "the effect of schooling on performance tests is not related to the test content but rather to the whole test situation" (p. 215). Nevertheless, the Porteus Maze Test appears to be one of the "easiest", perhaps for some reason the least strange, for people of other cultures to work with. Havighurst and Hilkevitch found this to be true in their study of American Indian children cited above, and its wide use in cross-cultural testing would suggest that others have had the same experience.

But this does not mean that the mazes provide the magic key to comparisons of the innate mental capacity of different cultural groups. Porteus was the first to admit this: "A warning should be given, and emphasized, that the Maze is by itself far from being a satisfactory measure of intelligence. All we can say of it is that the complex of qualities needed for its performance seem to be valuable in making adjustments to our kind of society" (p. 257). Elsewhere he suggests that these qualities may include "prudence, foresight, and mental alertness" (p. 234). Its virtue, then, lies in the fact that many sorts of people can feel comfortable working with it, rather than in freedom from cultural bias.

The Cattell Culture-Free Test has not been utilized nearly as widely as the Porteus Maze and we cannot therefore judge as readily the degree to which it presents a comprehensible format to people of widely different cultural backgrounds. The premise implied by its name that it is free of cultural bias, its results reflecting individual capabilities but not differences in cultural experience, appears completely insupportable. The test comprises combinations of geometric figures, devised and arranged in various ways for the following subtests: series relationships, classification (identifying odd items), first and second order relational matrices, sequence matrices, and mirror images. The designation of these tasks as "culture-free" rests upon a series of a priori assumptions or rationalizations which would strike any anthropologist as naïve, employing as they do a stereotype of "primitive" culture seemingly derived more from Longfellow's *Hiawatha* than from any adequate sampling of the ethnographic literature on the diversity of cultures of the world. We may comment on a few examples of such reasoning contained in Cattell's (39) description of the test. Working with series relationships "has natural interest and connects with natural happenings, e.g., growth" (p. 169). In the test series the geometric figures are of a constant size and develop through the addition of component parts, precisely the opposite of animal growth, and scarcely comparable to plant growth. Even if this were arranged in a fashion comparable to actual growth, the transition from a three-dimensional living being to black lines printed on a white two-dimensional sheet of paper would be difficult indeed for many "primitives." With regard to classification, Cattell says: "Picking out the odd item . . . has a certain intrinsic fascination, and resembles operations known to primitives (e.g., picking out the odd animal from the herd)" (p. 171). Only a very small fraction of the peoples of the world are herdsmen, and they generally know each animal individually rather than identifying them by color or other general class characteristics. Furthermore, anthropologists are often frustratingly aware that the bases for classification in other cultures—the determination of what kind of a difference makes a difference—can be very different from our own. To some people it may simply not make sense, for example, that a series of figures of the same size, shape, and blackness are to be considered "different" simply because of a few little lines within their borders are differently arranged. On mirror images: "The images are mirrored about a horizontal axis, in order that the universal experience of seeing reflections in a pool may be utilized in the instructions" (p. 175-176). Mirror-imaging in a pool requires that (*a*) the countryside have pools, (*b*) the body of water be small and protected enough to be completely calm, and (*c*) there be sufficient backdrop to provide subject for reflection. These conditions are far from universal. Aside from people who live by the constantly moving ocean, by swift rivers, or on the desert, one wonders how many children reared in our own cities have the opportunity to become familiar with this phenomenon.

The experience of psychologists does not encourage one to consider the Cattell test culture-free either. Eells (67) observes that:

> If by a "culture-free" intelligence test is meant one in which the "intelligence" of a child is somehow measured entirely apart from the impact of any cultural experiences on the child, the term is practically a nonsense term. . . . The very fact of requesting the children to work with material that looks meaningless to them introduces problems of culturally-determined work habits and attitudes (p. 292).

Similarly Anastasi and Cordova (6) administered the test to Puerto Rican children in Harlem (finding they performed consistently below the norms) and concluded:

> No test can be completely "culture-free," or even "culture-constant," since the content of any test will tend to favor one or another culture. The elimination of specific culturally limited information from a test is only a partial and superficial solution. Each culture stimulates the development of certain abilities and interests, and inhibits others. The resulting psychological differences will inevitably be reflected in test performance, as in any other behavior of individuals reared in diverse cultural settings. In the Cattell test, for example, the items consist almost exclusively of abstract geometric forms and patterns; and the test is, of course, of the paper-and-pencil variety (p. 6).

The Cattell test, then, is simply not culture free. It has been standardized against other widely-used intelligence tests in our own culture and could therefore presumably be used as a substitute for them, in our culture, but this would have to be viewed as a convenience, not an improvement. We have no basis whatever for believing that this test is any more fair for a subculturally retarded child than is any other.

In concluding this discussion we must seek to answer two questions: First, What validity, if any, is there in the administration of tests across cultural lines? And, more importantly, What have we learned from this survey of cross-cultural testing that is relevant to the problems of subcultural mental retardation?, since it is clear that in many of the non-European peoples where testing has been done they do not view retardation as a serious problem, or indeed a problem at all. With respect to validity, it is safe to say at present that no test exists which can approximate to a measure of inherent mental capacity irrespective of cultural experience, or which can measure differences of intelligence between individuals of a different culture than our own along dimensions they themselves consider most important. It is also extremely likely that such a test or tests will never be successfully constructed, if for no other reason than that the very concept of testing is itself at home in only a few cultures, principally our own.

Presumably one could design a test for a given culture which would be a measure of intelligence as it is viewed by the participants in the culture, and thus differentiate between individuals, but this would be unique to that particular culture. Furthermore, since many peoples do not have an abstract concept of intelligence as such, one would find that one person is considered very intelligent because of his knowledge of folktales, another because of his knowledge of animal trails, and yet another because he can stalk or paddle a canoe silently. It would be hard to test for all of these at once, and if one did so it would be likely that one would then find that the people who told the best folktales did so because they were related to the teacher of folktales and he would not pass them on to others, and so on. The more specific a test becomes the more likely it is that day-to-day performance will reveal as accurately as the test whether a person possesses the skill in question.

On the other hand if one is concerned with identifying in a native population those individuals who would be the best prospects for schooling or for administrative or commercial jobs, that is for rôles in which our cultural values become important, tests appropriate for our culture are appropriate for them also. But in testing for this purpose we still do not wish to have the test itself create any more artificial stumbling blocks than necessary, which leads us to consider which tests are intrinsically most easily handled by non-European peoples. As we have seen, performance tests are more readily comprehended than verbal tests by non-European people, and among these there is some reason to feel that the Porteus Maze is the least threatening of all. Whether it would be adequate to predict, for example, school success among persons who had had no schooling at all remains to be demonstrated, but the evidence would suggest that this test would be a good one to try first.

The parallel between testing of non-Europeans and of subculturally retarded children in our own society is obvious, and thus brings us to consideration of the second question above. Let us take lower class ethnic children as an example. We already know that many consistently do poorly on standard intelligence tests, and also frequently in school. This failure on tests probably results from a combination of specific test content which is unfamiliar, of the demand for kinds of thinking for which they are ill-prepared, and of their motivation and attitude toward tests and school. If we wish simply to reconfirm this finding any standard intelligence test will do. But if we wish to correct their deficiencies, and particularly to concentrate on those with the most promising prospects, we are facing the same problem suggested above with respect to the selection of likely candidates for schooling or jobs among a native population. Granted we want to discover their potential for performance along lines *we* value, whether they do or not, but in testing them we wish the test itself to present a minimum of obstacles. In other words we wish that as far as possible the child taking the test will not find it strange, anxiety-producing, or intellectually formidable and hence hopeless. We also want to reduce to a minimum the specific content which we already know he has not mastered because of his subcultural upbringing. For this reason, with retarded children as with non-Europeans, performance tests should be viewed as superior to verbal tests. This is already recognized by many psychologists.

But practically no research has been devoted to discovering which of the many available performance tests *appear* least threatening to such retarded children. Surely there must be a difference, as there seems to be among tests administered to non-European peoples, and it is of real importance to discover the causes of this difference. Many of us can still remember the chill of despair which descended when the first question on the final exam turned out to be on a topic we had failed to review. How then must a child, who realizes a test may make a major difference in his future, feel when he is faced with an array of tasks many of which appear impossible? If he sees and at once understands a task he believes he can tackle he will undoubtedly perform more nearly at his best level. This may be the greatest virtue of the Porteus Maze Test for non-Europeans, and this virtue could well prove equally lustrous in the field of subcultural mental retardation. The whole question of how much anxiety is generated in the perception by a retarded child of one test as against another, to which a review of cross-cultural testing has directed us, has been almost completely neglected. Attention has instead been devoted to the appropriateness of content (e.g., verbal versus performance tests) and to comparison of scores on tests and subtests as though each of these scores reflected capability irrespective of differential anxiety and attitudes.

In sum, then, if we accept the fact that we cannot at present materially change the culturally determined standards of adequate performance, and that most intelligence tests will do little more for the retarded child than to confirm existing suspicions of inadequacy, we must turn our attention to determining which test or tests best differentiate among retarded children between those who have more promise and those who have less, and in what directions the assets or liabilities of all of them lie. To do this we must find which tests interfere least with the expression of those abilities which the child does possess. Reverting to the Davis-Eells Games described earlier in this chapter, we might wonder in terms of our present discussion whether the reason why even this test appears to penalize some lower class children is not because of unfamiliar content but rather that the choices between alternate solutions are perhaps sufficiently close or ambiguous that they seem hopeless and induce despair in the child who is intellectually unprepared for this kind of problem. This is pure speculation, but represents a line of research which should hold great promise of reward. It is certainly clear that in its present state of development psychological testing of retarded children contributes little either to our theoretical knowledge of the problem or to their personal dilemmas. Perhaps if we explore the emotional impact of various tests as such on retarded children this situation will improve.

XV. INTELLIGENCE AND CULTURE

A. Problem-Solving Ability in Subcultural Groups

In the preceding chapter we have considered at some length the cultural implications of performance on intelligence tests for persons at both normal and subnormal levels of mental functioning. Intelligence tests, however, are but one of several criteria usually employed in assessing the capabilities and prospects of both normal and subnormal persons in our own Western society, and are of minimal or no consequence in this regard in many other cultures. So in this chapter we will look at intellectual processes in a broader cultural framework, seeking to determine what factors influence the development of various modes of attacking problems, and what kinds and levels of problem-solving ability are acceptable and approved in different sorts of cultures. For this purpose we have to pay attention not merely to the mechanics of the thinking process and how it is learned, but also motivations and attitudes toward intellectual achievement as these affect both children and adults. With respect to problem-solving, we will be concerned with the levels of ability (both high and low) the culture can accept, and in addition with the question of what kinds of problems are considered worth solving at all, and in what ways it is allowable to seek solutions. In other words, whereas in the preceding section our focus on tests forced us to remain largely within the limits accepted in our middle class culture for definitions of intelligence, here we may take a broader view of what intelligence and normality mean to people living in other cultures and within subcultural groups in our own society. In attempting to apply the results of existing cross-cultural research—or of that which we might suggest should be done—to the problem of subnormality in our society, we must bear in mind that the solutions found in other cultures are not necessarily applicable to our own. The fact that in another society physical ability is more highly valued than mental, and that all but the most severely mentally deficient persons are therefore not particularly penalized or even noticeable, will not help us to find a place for similarly handicapped persons within the framework of rigid intellectual demands characteristic of our social environment. Nevertheless cross-cultural research can provide us with valuable insights and perspectives on our own problems, can illuminate the causes and perhaps some solutions for retardation within subcultural groups in our society, and can make an important contribution to our understanding of the etiology of identifiable pathological conditions the occurrence of which follows different patterns in other cultural settings.

278

Unfortunately there are practically no systematic studies of subnormal functioning in non-European cultures, so this chapter necessarily must offer more hunches and hypotheses than facts. This meager prospect is relieved by one outstanding exception, the study of the Hutterites by Eaton and Weil (65). Because it is virtually unique in its field and because it will provide a setting against which a number of problems may be raised in the remainder of this chapter, a fairly extensive review of those aspects of Eaton and Weil's study which bear on mental subnormality will provide an appropriate starting point.

The Hutterites form an autonomous cultural group with a theocratic social system residing in the north central United States and southern Canada. The following is a partial description of Hutterite culture:

> Hutterites believe in the communal ownership and control of all property. Like the Catholic orders, they live under economic communism in the classical and nonpolitical sense. Christ and the Bible are their ideological guides. Hutterites expect the community to assume a great deal of responsibility for each member. It is the community which buys clothing, doles out pocket money to each person, and pays a traffic ticket. No wages are paid. Each person is expected to work to the best of his ability. He eats his meals in the community dining room; the meals prepared by different women in rotation. If he is sick, the colony pays for all necessary care. In case of male death, widows and dependents have no financial worries; the loss of a breadwinner never means the loss of bread. The Hutterite way of life provides social security from the womb to the tomb. The religious creed of the group gives the members a further guarantee of security beyond the tomb. It promises absolute salvation to all who follow its precepts.
>
> The average Hutterite baby is delivered at home with a midwife in attendance and by "natural childbirth." Ultimately he will have between ten and eleven siblings. Children are generally wanted. Birth control practices are considered sinful; violations of this taboo are extremely rare. There is much communal co-operation in the care and education of the children. Infants are looked after by the mother for the first two months after birth. Then the mother must work part of each day in the community kitchen or garden, and an older girl, not necessarily a relative, helps out. After the age of two and a half, all healthy youngsters attend a communal kindergarten, where they stay most of the day. When they reach school age, they continue to spend many of their waking hours as a group, often under the supervision of a Hutterite religious teacher. He is responsible for much of the discipline outside of the hours when the children attend public school. Since both mother and father work for the colony at least part of each day, older siblings assume much of the care of their younger brothers and sisters.

In general, young people do a great deal of their growing up within a stable and closely-knit group of peers. The process of socialization and development depends greatly on "horizontal" identification with their peer group. Imagination and expectations are influenced considerably by other children of similar physical and mental development. The Hutterite nuclear family performs fewer functions than is general in American society, but there is strong emphasis on kinship ties in all social relations. The cultural pattern of growing up to become a Hutterite adult varies little from colony to colony, but as in every human group, there are important variations in the emotional relationships between parents and children. Two mothers may be equally determined to teach an eight-year-old daughter to be an efficient caretaker of the baby and resist the temptation to run off in the yard to play with boys of her age (who have no such similar work expectations to live up to); but where one mother may teach and discipline with patience, humor, and love, another may be vindictive and infantile, almost forgetful of the fact that an eight-year-old girl is still a child.

Virtually all Hutterites leave school on their fifteenth birthday, the day which marks their assignment to an adult job. Full membership status is acquired after baptism, between the ages of 18 and 25. Very few people remain single. Several decades ago parents and community leaders exerted some influence on the choice of marriage partners; at present, however, this is rare. After marriage men tend to acquire more prestige and are given more responsible work assignments. They are put in charge of the carpentry, welding shop, horses, pigs, or some other department of the large-scale community farm enterprise. Women begin to raise a family. They also acquire more prestige in the informal discussions which precede all formal community decisions. Women can retire from regular community chores at the age of 45; retirement for men takes place later. No one is pushed to exert himself much beyond what he himself regards to be his capacity. "Do the best you can" rather than a competitive slogan, is characteristic of the entire life cycle.

All Hutterites live in small and nearly self-sufficient settlements in which social relationships are generally informal or primary. They have an average of 92 members, with 16 family units. There is virtually no movement from one to another, except for women at marriage when, with few exceptions, they move to the husband's community. Most members of the sect spend their entire life within the same group. When a community grows too large through natural increase, new land is purchased and another village is built. Half the membership, chosen by lot, "swarm" to form a new "hive," as Hutterites like to refer to this process of binary fission. In each of the 93 settlements there are individual differences in prestige, which are largely a function of age, sex, and work. However, this society comes as close to being classless as any we know (pp. 27-30).

In the study the fields of sociology, anthropology, psychology, and psychiatry were represented. What is unusual in this study is that a serious attempt was made to screen the entire Hutterite population. "There was no sampling; the entire population of 8,542 persons living in a large geographical area, including parts of South Dakota, North Dakota, Manitoba, Alberta, and Montana, was screened for cases of mental disorders. The staff visited 84 of the 93 colonies in existence at the time the field work was completed; the remaining nine colonies were screened through a variety of informants" (p. 230). Before presenting the findings of this study it should be pointed out that Hutterites are "quick to recognize severe or moderate forms of mental deficiency" (p. 149).

Of the 51 cases diagnosed as mentally defective, 15 were severely defective, being unable to talk or walk normally and frequently unable to feed themselves. Four of these were mongoloid, two of basal ganglion disease, two of Little's disease, two of hydrocephalus, one of dwarfism, and four of epilepsy (cases of epilepsy not associated with mental deficiency were considered separately).[22]

Twenty of the 51 cases diagnosed as mentally defective were considered as moderately defective. "They could dress themselves . . . and could do simple work under supervision. . . . They could all qualify for admission to an institution for mental defectives" (p. 151). The remaining 16 patients were diagnosed as mildly defective. "They generally had some schooling and

---

[22]The data on mongolism presented by Eaton and Weil raise some intriguing questions. Although these were not explored by the authors, they illustrate the kinds of opportunities cross-cultural research in mental deficiency—i.e., in organic disorders which result in mental subnormality—can provide. The cases of mongolism reported for the Hutterites yield a prevalence rate not notably different from that found in our own culture, but the mothers of these children averaged 29 years of age at the time of delivery whereas in our culture the average age is 41. Investigators of this disorder have frequently emphasized both the advanced age of mothers and so-called reproductive exhaustion; in the case of the Hutterites the first of these explanations does not appear applicable. Should we then conclude that reproductive exhaustion is the more crucial etiological factor? Or are there perhaps differences in diet, care of mothers during pregnancy, protection against heat or cold, or any one of a multitude of other possible cultural factors we should investigate? We would not venture an answer. The point rather is that we have here a population similar (as far as we know) to ourselves in a biological sense yet differing with respect to a frequently cited aspect of mongolism and at the same time experiencing—much more uniformly than we—significantly different culturally determined relationships with their environment. The investigator with a hunch or hypothesis regarding external factors in the etiology of mongolism would do well to inquire whether it fits the situation of the Hutterites—or of any one of the hundreds of non-European cultures available for study—before accepting a proof or disproof based only on evidence from our own society.

knew the rudiments of reading and writing. They participated in the work of their colony and as adults had a regular work assignment which required little initiative or skill" (p. 151).

Although Eaton and Weil felt they had located virtually all the moderate and severe cases, they recognized that they had probably failed to enumerate many cases which should have been diagnosed as mildly defective. There were several lines of evidence pointing in this direction. In the first place, in those settlements personally visited by the staff in which all members were examined the rates were 10 per cent higher than in the population as a whole. Secondly, on a rating sheet filled out by the Hutterite religious teachers and also by the non-Hutterite public school teachers, the public school teachers rated more children as "dull" than did the Hutterite teachers—a finding which did not become known until the field work was over so that these children could not be diagnosed by the research staff. Finally, 70 per cent of all cases diagnosed were of severe and moderate degree—i.e., presumably reflecting pathology rather than learning deficits—whereas other populations studied have shown a much higher proportion of mild degree. We may therefore conclude that if intelligence tests or other diagnostic criteria utilized within our culture were applied to the Hutterite population more cases of mild deficit would probably be found, although we cannot predict with confidence what the prevalence rates would be. The explanation for this discrepancy is almost certain to be found in the observation by Eaton and Weil discussed below that the Hutterites show a high level of social acceptance of mentally deficient persons, and thus might be able to absorb into the normal population without special attention persons who could not meet the sharply drawn levels of tolerance characteristic of our culture. This point deserves some emphasis, not because we wish to raise doubts as to the prevalence rates cited by the authors of this study, although these have been criticized, but because it makes clear the hazards involved in attempting to determine epidemiological statistics in other cultures with regard to mental subnormality. A diagnosis of mental deficiency or retardation is compounded in our culture of medical, psychological, social, and cultural considerations (implicit or explicit), and a setting in which the relevance of any one of these is different will produce a different distribution of individuals identified as subnormal by the members of the society under study.

There is an unusual amount of in-group marrying among the Hutterites, a fact which led Eaton and Weil to ask: "Is there evidence to support the widely held assumption that inbreeding in a population necessarily leads to deterioration in the germ plasm of a population, which shows up in a high frequency of mental deficiency?" (p. 152). The apparently moderate rate of mental deficiency among the Hutterites is sufficient basis for answering this question in the negative. However, Eaton and Weil did not report geneologies for the diagnosed cases of mental deficiency. In addition, we do not have clinical descriptions which would allow for a possible etiological classification. Consequently, we cannot evaluate the specific rôle of genetic factors in those cases which are reported. Neither can we ascertain whether certain types of mental deficiency (e.g., phenylketonuria) occur at all among the Hutterites. At one point Eaton and Weil (p. 152) state: "None of the defective adult women could find a husband, but four men married and had families. They had a total of 22 children in 1951, two of whom were moderately defective." Since we do not know the clinical picture either of the fathers or the two defective offspring, we cannot evaluate whether two defective offspring (which could be only from one or two of the four fathers) is an inordinately low or an expected number. In a community that can be as comprehensively studied as the Hutterites much valuable data on genetic factors in mental deficiency could be obtained—perhaps obtained more quickly than through similar studies in our own culture.

An important finding of the study is that none of the defectives has ever been institutionalized, although the Hutterites are not opposed to commitment.[23]

> There is considerable social acceptance of mentally defective persons among the Hutterites. Once a child's retardation is recognized, he is usually taken to a doctor to determine if there is any medical remedy for the condition. If there is none, the child and his limitations are accepted fatalistically. The community provides the family with additional help, if needed, to give optimum physical care to the youngster. In some families the mother will turn the child over to a sister or her mother, who may have more time and patience. Feelings of rejection by the parents exist, but they are usually well repressed. Other children are punished if they ridicule or take advantage of the afflicted child. Defectives who reach adult life are encouraged to work.
>
> Defectives are not thought to be morally responsible for what they do. Those who engage in antisocial activities are punished only if they show sufficient insight to be affected by punishment. The community keeps them in line by watching them carefully. In two cases where mildly defective individuals violated a number of religious rules, the community "cancelled their baptism" rather than excommunicate them. By can-

---

[23]Even in the case of the psychoses institutionalization among the Hutterites is rare.

cellation of their baptism they were reduced to the status of children, who
are thought to be incapable of sinning and therefore can attain salvation automatically (p. 157).

One cannot find a greater contrast between Hutterite and American culture
than in regard to institutionalization: in our own culture available institutional facilities are overtaxed, more facilities are in the planning stage, and
the end is not in sight. More important than the staggering financial burden
of the situation is the unhappy fact that institutionalization frequently raises
as many psychological problems as it resolves (225). These are problems which
the Hutterites, as well as people of many other cultures, do not have to
resolve.

Granting that Eaton and Weil, focusing primarily on the neuroses and
psychoses rather than on mental deficiency, did not provide us with clinical
descriptions, genealogical charts, or other appurtenances of an ideal study
of subnormality, yet they have documented some of the most important of
the cultural implications of mental retardation. Particularly, it is clear that
among the Hutterites—however they may appear to outsiders—the intellectual preparation provided within the culture is adequate to meet the needs
of adult life within that setting. Furthermore, the standards of adequacy
set by the culture appear to be wide enough to embrace most people who
function at anything but a pathologically deficient level, a fact strikingly
reflected in the very small proportion (compared to our culture) of the
population identified as subnormal which falls in the "slight deficiency" category. Finally, the Hutterite society is so organized that it can take care of
all persons, whatever their level of functioning, within itself without resort
to special institutional or other devices. In all these respects the Hutterites
conform much more closely to the patterns characteristic of the non-European cultures of the world than they do to the standards of our own society
which surrounds them.

A more concrete comparison is perhaps in order. On the one hand we
may cite the Trukese, studied by the present authors (Gladwin and Sarason,
90). In this island society in the Pacific inadequacy in intellectual functioning is simply not viewed as a problem except for a scattering of obvious
pathological cases; people of both sexes appear to fall readily into productive
activities they are fully competent to perform. Younger men, however, often
seek employment at the American administrative center, sometimes at the
garage where trucks and other vehicles are maintained under the supervision
of Americans.

These jobs were eagerly sought after, under the impression that one could thus quickly learn the facility in working with machinery which the Trukese greatly admire in Americans. These youths were anxious to learn and within the limits of their understanding of English followed carefully the instructions they were given. But if what they had been taught did not work they were helpless. An American boy interested in mechanics is soon inculcated with the idea that every new piece of equipment is a challenge; if he does not know how it works, much less what may be wrong with it, he should take it apart, find out how it works, and then fix it. This approach was incomprehensible to the Trukese; even when given an old engine to practice on, their only solution to a problem was to ask someone who knew (p. 142).

Compare this with the following description:

She is cheerful, inclined to be quarrelsome, very active and restless, very affectionate, willing, and tries; is quick and excitable, fairly good-tempered. Learns a new occupation quickly, but requires a half-hour or twenty-four repetitions to learn four lines. Retains well what she has once learned. Needs close supervision. Is bold towards strangers, kind towards animals. Can run an electric sewing machine, cook, and do practically everything about the house. Has no noticeable defect. She is quick and observing, has a good memory, writes fairly, does excellent work in wood-carving and kindergarten, is excellent in imitation. Is a poor reader and poor at numbers. Does fine basketry and gardening. Spelling is poor; music is excellent; sewing excellent; excellent in entertainment work. Very fond of children and good in helping care for them. Has a good sense of order and cleanliness. Is sometimes very stubborn and obstinate. Is not always truthful and has been known to steal, although does not have a reputation for this. Is proud of her clothes. Likes pretty dresses and likes to help in other cottages, even to temporarily taking charge of a group (pp. 7-8).

This is Goddard's (92) description of Deborah Kallikak, a girl of 22 who had spent the last 14 years of her life in an institution, presented by him as a classic example of mental deficiency. It is clear that the Trukese, completely adequate intellectually when operating within their own culture, perform no better than Deborah when faced with a problem from our culture which calls for rational thinking and logical induction. It should also be borne in mind that a garage mechanic in our society is viewed as a laborer—albeit skilled—and not an intellectual or professional.

Why do the Trukese develop such a concrete and limited approach to problem-solving? The answer must, as in our own society, be sought in childhood, the period when a person learns from the preceding generation the multiple facets of the cultural heritage to which he is born. Childhood for a Trukese is a period of freedom with almost complete lack of supervision by adults except for occasional, and inconsistent, reprimands and punishments. Children play in groups together and are given practically no systematic positive instruction. They are viewed by adults as irresponsible and, being unable to do responsible and useful work, not worth instructing. The word for "child" in the Trukese language in fact means "does not comprehend."

This freedom and lack of supervision or direction, although it might be looked upon as utopian by a middle-class American child, provides a very poor climate in which to learn effectively and efficiently to cope with problems or to profit from the wisdom of past experience contained in the culturally defined solutions to such problems. In this connection we can recall the differences in amount of freedom noted by Davis and Havighurst (57) between lower and middle class children, with associated differences in intelligence test scores. This freedom can also leave an individual drifting, uncertain, and without emotional support, a thesis developed at length for our own European society by Erich Fromm (77). The Trukese child suffers under these handicaps until he is close to adolescence, when he begins to be perceived as having a potential for usefulness and receives practically his first positive and systematic instruction of any kind.

> Having at first been told practically nothing, and later what not to do, now, finally, he is told what he should do. At long last he is given a guide by his parents for behavior, at least of certain kinds, and a more positive status in the household. He begins to learn that there are "right" ways as well as wrong ways of doing things for his parents. Set against the background of ambiguity which has surrounded his attempts to determine what his parents expected of him thus far in his life, these rather specific instructions take on more importance than one would otherwise anticipate. They are, in effect, likely to be overevaluated, not in the sense that the child would throw himself with overenthusiasm into his work, but rather that he would tend to take very literally and concretely his instructions, attempting to perform his tasks exactly as he had been told. Concreteness in following directions and a tendency to accept situations in their most literal sense is a characteristic of children even in our own society, and appears to be a means of responding to new situations for which past experience and immediate guidance is barely adequate. It is the "safest" way to react when one is unsure of the full significance of the total situation. If children in our society who are given consistent positive as well as negative guidance and instruction practically from the time they say their first words tend to respond concretely, it is small

wonder that the Trukese child takes literally these directions which he finally receives for the first time in the latter part of his childhood. He has been left largely incapable of dealing with new situations both by the generalized anxiety he has learned to feel toward any interpersonal situation as a result of his unpredictable childhood relationships and by his failure to distill out of his inadequate attempts to identify with his parents any over-all guide for behavior which would permit him to respond to his problems in any more generalized sort of way. Just as his relations with people are inherently superficial, so he looks in a new situation for the most superficial and obvious aspect which bears any resemblance to what he has encountered in his past experience, and interprets the situation in these terms.

Unlike Americans, however, the Trukese in general never lose this concreteness of response. It is a by-word among Americans that the spirit of the law is more important than the letter, and the ability to recognize this distinction in dealing with his problems is a measure of an American child's growing maturity. The Trukese, on the other hand, tend always to see the letter of the law and even as adults are seldom able to approach a situation with the more abstract view implied in seeing the spirit of it. Thinking in abstract terms involves a measure of ambiguity, a weighing of alternatives in terms of personal value judgments, which is an inherently more hazardous approach than simply to be literal and concrete, taking the situation at its face value and using its most obvious external signs as cues for behavior and response. By hazardous we mean that there is implicit in the abstract approach the possibility that one's opinions and reactions will not coincide with the interpretation of the situation made by one's fellows. If all situations are interpreted in the simplest and most literal terms the possibility of disagreement is reduced to a minimum, although the flexibility and creativity of the individual who habitually responds in this fashion is of course reduced. We see, then, why any child will tend to approach his problems literally and concretely: being faced by a constant succession of new problems with which he is more or less inadequately prepared to deal, he plays it safe and responds in a minimum fashion to all of them. The Trukese, however, lives out many of his formative years without really beginning to acquire the knowledge or experience which will equip him to approach his life situations in a well-rounded sort of way. When he finally does begin to learn, he responds in a fashion which American children at a corresponding age are beginning to grow out of, and for the rest of his life is seldom able to improve upon this type of performance.

This does not mean that because after all these years the Trukese finally receives in late childhood some actual positive instructions, he takes them literally and adopts this approach to problems for the rest of his life out of sheer relief. Undoubtedly there is a measure of truth in this statement, for the security he feels in finding a mode of behavior which is indubitably "right" after a childhood spent in doubt and confusion is not likely soon to be forgotten. More important than the relief he now feels, however, are the years which have gone by, years during which he might have been learning how to deal with his parents and other people in a confident and effective manner, and how to express his opinions freely without fear of making some small misstatement and with it bringing down about him what little security he has been able to find in a generally hostile and unpredictable social environment. By the time the Trukese child has, at an age of perhaps nine or ten, begun to learn how he really should behave he has acquired a fundamental mistrust of his fellows and a lack of confidence in the adequacy of his own resources as a means of coping with his social problems; as we have discussed in some detail in the preceding pages, his response to this sense of social inadequacy is to attempt not to offend anyone, particularly his relatives. It is for this reason that he seeks the "safest," the least provocative, and therefore the most conventional and literal response he can find to every problem he faces. This conservatism and concreteness, rooted in the uncertainty and inconsistency of his childhood, he carries with him throughout his life. As long as he can structure a situation so that there is but one correct solution he feels secure; but if the situation demands of him initiative, responsibility, or assuming a position of eminence and authority, he feels anxious and withdraws (pp. 269-271).

Hogbin (118), in one of the very few available descriptions of children's learning experiences in non-European cultures, describes a similar outcome of intellectual concreteness and rigidity resulting from a very different kind of learning process among the Wogeo of New Guinea. They are a people geographically in the same corner of the world as Truk, but culturally quite different. The Wogeo believe that everything valuable in their culture was handed down from mythical hero-ancestors and, being a traditionally oriented people, they are conservative and opposed to latter-day innovation and initiative. In keeping with this they provide children, much earlier in their lives than do the Trukese, with instructions and explanations "so detailed that the need for seeking additional information seldom arises, and 'why' questions, the everlasting bane of parents in our community, are rarely heard" (p. 285). The implications of these two very different sorts of learning process for the development of adult personality and for individual and cultural adjustment in the face of changing conditions are of major consequence, but the important aspect of both for our present discussion is that they each produce by different means an intellectual set toward the solution of problems characterized by concreteness and a severe limitation in the ability to contemplate an array of alternatives before reaching a solution. It would be safe to predict that a normal and adequate native of Truk or Wogeo, even though equipped with the necessary knowledge of language and formal cultural content, would do very badly indeed on the Stanford-Binet or in the fourth grade of school.

B. Cultural Learning and Intellect

The fact that so similar and—by our standards—meager intellectual development can be produced in such divergent ways in two cultures immediately raises the question whether the consistent intellectual inadequacies found in children of our lower class groups, ethnic minorities, etc., may not actually have very different origins in one group as against another. This is a question for which we do not have an answer, and even a guess would probably not be justified. We have been aware of subcultural mental retardation ever since regional differences in intelligence test scores were established on the basis of World War I data, yet the 30-odd years which have intervened have been devoted almost entirely to determining the nature and extent of subcultural differences, not to seeking their causes, outside perhaps of identifying broad differences in the quality of school systems. We know, especially through the work of the Chicago group discussed in Chapter XIV, some of the ways in which lower class children, for example, fare in school and the handicaps under which they suffer, but we do not know what it is in their preschool and extracurricular experience which has equipped them so poorly for this task. This is a—perhaps *the*—crucial question to answer with respect to retarded children of all sorts who do not show pathologies, but we have scarcely scratched the surface of exploring the group characteristics which must provide the background and basis for comparison in individual cases.

Cross-cultural studies can be helpful in suggesting the range of variables which should be examined, but much needs to be done within our own society right now. Studies of non-European societies have the disadvantage that often their members perceive no need for superior intellectual skills and can therefore afford to inhibit, as the Trukese and Wogeo do, the development of mental ability even in those individuals who for some reason tend in this direction. In our society, however, the rewards for intelligence combine with opportunities for mobility to assure that most persons can capitalize at least in some degree upon those intellectual tendencies which their inherent

nature and their experience bring forth.   Furthermore, few people in our society will deny the advantages of being intelligent and resourceful, even
though they may vary widely in the amount of effort they are willing to
devote to developing these qualities in themselves or in their children.   In
other words, the kinds of intellectual development valued in our society as a
whole (the lack of which comprises mental retardation) can be assumed to be
viewed as at least somewhat worth while by members of any subcultural group
within it, something we cannot assume for many non-European peoples,
and the values of his own subculture will not be likely severely to penalize
an individual whose development is above average, thus assuring a full range
of mental ability within the limits set by the opportunities offered within
the given group.   There will be exceptions, of course, such as adolescents
who consider any boy who does well in school to be a teacher's pet (Margolin, Roman, and Harari, 183), but limitations are far less likely to stifle
possibly superior children when they know or believe that society at large will
offer rewards for their efforts.   There is a truly urgent need for this kind
of research.   We have a surfeit of testing and the derivation of ethnic and
social class IQ's.   What is needed now is a more exploratory anthropological
type of approach to the values and processes governing the learning situation for children.

In view of the long-standing concern of anthropologists with culture and
cultural transmission, it is difficult to explain the small amount of attention
they have paid to the mechanics of this transmission.   How early, and particularly how consistent, is instruction?   Who assumes responsibility for
instruction, not merely of formal skills, but also in the subtler aspects of
values and social relationships?   Who is available and recommended for
emulation?   Of great importance, what happens when a child asks, "Why?"—
is he rewarded or punished, answered or not, answered in terms of logic or
of tradition or is he told he is too young, is he encouraged or discouraged to
think about it himself, etc.?   What kinds of skills are presented as valuable?   If
these include mental skills, are they rational, memory, or what?   What
means are used to foster their acquisition?   These, and a host of others, are
the questions which must be answered if we are to understand how learning
takes place, and how the intellectual tools for further learning are acquired.
Persons studying non-European peoples should seek answers to them, and
they are equally at the core of the problem of mental retardation in our own
society.

In the absence of any detectable pathology there is at present available no valid explanation of a child's retardation except a deficit in learning. Furthermore, since all or most children in a given group are exposed at least formally to the same classroom environment, yet some do well and some do not, we must assume that the deficit results from the foundation of skills, attitudes, emotional sets, and social and intellectual habits the child brings to that environment. This foundation is built in the cultural and individual milieu of his home and peer group. Until we can identify those factors which are relevant to the building of a foundation for learning, and establish some norms with respect to these, we have nothing against which to evaluate individual experience and opportunity. For this purpose we have available in our society not only the "average" middle-class children of old American ancestry, but a variety of subcultural groups in which we know the children are less well prepared to learn the intellectual skills demanded by the larger culture and within which research should be able to isolate significant and important differences in the process of learning and preparation for further learning. Once some of these are identified and assessed more systematic means of observing and perhaps measuring them can be devised, and individual studies as well as surveys can have more meaning. We know that neither present intelligence scales nor any other single instrument can be expected reliably to predict subsequent failures when administered to preschool children, and therefore certainly cannot be used to identify those aspects of a child's experience which are helping or hindering his learning at the time. The study of learning in children from subcultural groups, whose later performance our present knowledge permits us to predict will in many cases be below average, can reveal at least some of the factors necessary to fill this large gap in our knowledge of mental retardation.

As we suggested in the preceding section, we may find that lower class Italian children—who consistently average low in *IQ* and often do poorly in school—are expected to do many tasks around the home strictly in the manner they are told, without inquiring as to the reason for doing these tasks in a certain way or as to why the tasks need be done at all. This might be expected to produce some rigidity in their approach to problem-solving, and hence a low intelligence test score. If this is so, are German children—who usually score higher and do better in school—assigned their tasks differently, and if so, in what way is the process different? Or if not, both being treated inflexibly in this regard, what makes the later difference? We may then find that the Italians tend more toward the common non-European thesis that manual skills are more important than mental, thus lowering the motivation of children toward school. Or perhaps Italian children during school years are expected to do some of their household jobs in the morning, and thus arrive at school (where most testing is also done) tired whereas German children do not—not a profound difference, but if it exists, important to know. These examples are speculative, but suggest the kinds of avenues which need exploring. They also reflect variations which can be expected to appear on an individual basis in middle class families; the findings of such research would by no means be applicable only to the particular groups studied.

Some beginnings have been made in exploring the subcultural differences in learning experience of the sort discussed here. The work of Davis and Havighurst (57) and of Sears, Maccoby, and Levin (238) on social class differences in child rearing discussed in Chapter XIV is of course highly relevant, although the primary focus of both studies is on emotional development and any conclusions we may reach about the effect of the differences found on intellectual development are largely inferential. The exploratory nature of their approach, guided by theory in the kinds of questions asked but otherwise taking little for granted, is however precisely what is needed at this stage in the study of learning processes.

McClelland and his associates have done considerable work in the study of motivation, using as a starting point an achievement score derived from stories told by the people tested (McClelland, Atkinson, Clark, and Lowell, 179); the procedure is similar to that used in the Thematic Apperception Test except that the stimulus material is verbal rather than pictorial and the test situation is structured to be variously relaxed, neutral, and achievement-oriented. The stories are then scored for achievement motivation in accordance with a special set of criteria. Winterbottom (179), in connection with this study, established a series of 13 aspects of independence training of children, determining that those mothers who sought to have their children reach these goals of independence at an early age were those who also had high achievement scores. In other words, the mothers appeared to project their own achievement motivation, be it high or low, upon their children in terms of seeking early or later independence training. McClelland, Rindlisbacher, and deCharms (180) administered questionnaires regarding the desired age of independence training to a series of parents aged 30 to 50 who had at least one child, utilizing those items found by Winterbottom to correlate highly with achievement score in mothers only. Dividing the parents on a religious basis, the means for all items and both parents were as follows, each figure representing the age at which they hoped their children would become independent in the 13 types of activity: Protestant, 6.64; Jewish, 6.59; Irish Catholic, 7.66; and Italian Catholic, 8.42. On the basis of these findings the Catholics could be expected to push their children's development less hard than the others; at the same time the difference between Italian and Irish Catholics makes it clear that religious affiliation is but one aspect of broader subcultural differences which are at work. With respect to education of the parents, parents who did not graduate from high school hoped for an average independence age of 7.81, those graduated from high school but not college, 7.43, and college graduates 6.75. We cannot of course tell here whether educational level itself creates a desire to push the children along, or whether both reflect social class or perhaps ethnic differences. Finally, they found that mothers were more eager than fathers, the means being 6.88 and 7.77 respectively. We do not know what this means, but the plausible explanation comes to mind that independent children give more independence to their mothers than to their fathers. This ingeniously contrived series of studies can provide, in themselves and in the further exploration of this method, many fruitful hypotheses. Unfortunately for our purposes, however, they fail to examine the crucial variable: the intellectual and motivational development of the young children of these parents, and how it is affected by the aspirations of their parents for them.

Other studies in intellectual motivation, although dealing with the children themselves, do not focus on the preschool years. However, insofar as motivation during school is subculturally determined it is affecting the performance of children in these groups at the time when differences between subcultural groups become most apparent. A number of studies have demonstrated that motivation for academic achievement is less in lower social classes (Hollingshead, 119; Girard, 88). Rosen (221) found this reflected in the projective achievement score described in the preceding paragraph. He established scores for 427 boys, aged 8-14, in New England, identified by ethnicity, religion, and social class. Although the ranking of motivation (from high to low) in the total sample followed the expected order—Greek Orthodox, Jews, white Protestants, Catholics (French-Canadian and Italian), and Negroes—when middle class groups only were compared the white Protestants were highest and the Negroes not significantly different from them, higher than any other group. An analysis of variance indicated that social class was a stronger over-all determinant of motivation than ethnicity.

A questionnaire survey of the mothers of these boys ranked them on their vocational and educational aspirations for their sons in slightly different order, the Jews being highest, closely followed by the Greeks, and the French-Canadians lowest.

There is some agreement that the social class impact on intellectual motivation results at least in part from the lesser rewards, tangible and intangible, received by lower class boys from middle class teachers who find children of their own class more acceptable (Davis, 54; Abrahamson, 1). This probably provides some realistic basis for the already noted opinion of some lower class boys, particularly with behavior problems, who attribute school success of their companions to currying favor with the teacher (Margolin, Roman, and Harari, 183; Glueck and Glueck, 91). We do not know to what degree these attitudes are derived from parents, and how much they are based on the perceptions and resentments generated within the peer group of children themselves. Some indication of this is, however, found in a study by Stendler (262) in which she interviewed 250 mothers of first graders. She found that whereas the mothers' aspirations for (and preparation of) their children increased with higher social class, criticism of the school's handling of their children showed no relationship to class position. If these findings were found to be generally true they would suggest that the level of aspiration is determined at least partially by parental attitude, but that the resentments or satisfactions are derived from the children's own experience.

Another aspect of motivation emerges from studies of the disparity between level of aspiration and level of performance. A greater disparity between aspiration for occupational and social achievement on the one hand and test or academic performance on the other seems to be characteristic of minority groups. Beckham (15) and Boyd (25) found this to be true in testing Negroes as compared to whites. We do not know to what degree these findings are affected by the social class differences in Negro motivation noted by Rosen. Gould (95) concluded from a study of Columbia College students that those in which the discrepancy between present and expected future achievement was greatest belonged in more cases to minority groups: lower class, foreign parentage, and/or minority religions. All three of these studies, however, applied to urban populations who were presumably maximally exposed to the philosophy of personal success which permeates our culture. In contrast to this Lewis (168) found white children in the Cumberland Mountains of Tennessee attending poor schools with no encouragement from their parents and with no personal aspirations, in most cases, other than to remain as they were and where they were.

It is clear from this brief review of the motivational aspects of learning that important differences in both parents and children exist within the subcultural groups of our society, and that the origins of these differences are complex and probably often multiple. The examples of Truk and Wogeo, as well as other cultures for which intellectual motivation is more sketchily described, suggest that the differences are even greater when we look at non-European peoples. Undoubtedly motivational factors, subcultural and individual, play a major rôle in precipitating mental retardation and deserve careful attention in assessing individual cases. Outside of fairly crude value judgments, however, we do not have any basis for determining how much and what kinds of motivation are really beneficial for learning. Low motivation will undoubtedly in most cases lower achievement, but it may also lower frustration if a discrepancy between aspiration and attainment might otherwise exist, and through better emotional balance lead ultimately to more effective social and even occupational performance. Too much pressure from parents may lead to withdrawal, and, as Kanner (147) suggests, even to autism. At present we really know very little of the manner in which motivation is dynamically related to learning, or which aspects of motivation deserve most attention.[24] Yet motivation is the one factor in the learning process on which we have any information which is at all adequate regarding subcultural or cultural differences.

If we turn from research in the motivation for learning to seek subcultural differences in the intellectual processes of learning—ways of thinking and attacking problems—we find virtually no studies available. We do know from the many studies referred to in the preceding section and in Section II that highly significant and consistent differences do exist between the school and test performance of children in various subcultural groups. But we cannot tell where the determinants of these differences lie. The effects of social class, ethnic subcultures, language, etc., are confounded together. We do not even know as a starting point how much should be attributed to different ways of thinking as against different motivations for thinking. The data cited from non-European cultures suggest that we should look for differences between groups in our own society in the mode of attacking

---

[24]Although not concerned directly with retarded children, a ten-year longitudinal study of school children conducted by the Committee on Human Development of the University of Chicago in coöperation with community of Quincy, Illinois (Bowman, DeHaan, Kough, and Liddle, 24) may provide a large body of controlled data relevant to the problems under discussion here. However, the study is only at its midpoint now, so several years will elapse before any extensive findings will become available.

problems, a conclusion supported by the very few studies of American children in which subcultural differences in subtest profiles have been analyzed. Haggard's (101) analysis of test results of high and low social status Midwestern school children pointed in this direction. Brown (29) reported a study of second generation Jewish and Scandinavian kindergarten children in Minneapolis which suggests that even identical over-all *IQ* averages may mask differences in problem-solving approach; this study is of particular interest due to the young, essentially preschool, age of the subjects. There were 324 Jewish children and 323 of Scandinavian extraction. Although the *IQ* varied in both groups with social class, ethnicity alone created no significant difference in average total scores. However, when performance on subtests (of the Stanford-Binet) was compared for both sexes the Scandinavian children excelled on tests involving motor coördination (draw a square, copying diamond, and ball-and-field) and patience, whereas the Jewish children excelled in counting pennies, distinguishing right from left, comprehension, naming coins, giving the date, and repeating four digits backwards. These findings are reminiscent of the rural-urban differences discussed in the last chapter, in which rural boys somewhat older than Brown's subjects do better on mechanical assembly tests and urban boys better on intelligence tests.

Paradoxically, although we have been pressing our contention that research should be devoted to cultural and subcultural differences in intellectual development in order to shed light on the causes of mental retardation, studies of the intellectual environment of severely retarded children, regardless of cultural affiliation, provide our most graphic picture of the importance of differences in the context of and stimulus for learning—in these cases characterized by extreme impoverishment. One of the present writers has already reviewed this subject (Sarason, 225, Chapter 6) so it will be necessary here only to cite material illustrative of the kinds of factors involved. Skeels, Updegraff, Wellman, and Williams (247) have provided us with a striking description of the effects of an orphanage environment (coupled with generally bleak earlier experiences) on the intellectual functioning of a group of 21 children, aged 18 months to five and a half years, who were enrolled in a special preschool training project in an otherwise typically understaffed and poorly equipped orphanage in Iowa:

> Language and speech were greatly retarded. Not only was the vocabu-
> lary meager and based upon very limited experience but the sentence
> structure was far below that ordinarily expected. Coupled to these two

serious handicaps were such faulty enunciation and poor speech habits that the language of the children was in the great majority of cases either entirely or practically unintelligible. Although children who were already acquainted were able to make each other understand some few simple interchanges, any constructive conversation seemed out of the question. Voices were unpleasantly monotonous, mumbling was common. With little provocation, talking voices would become loudly demanding. Finally, and of great significance in the teaching situation, was the fact that these children were not accustomed to listening to the words of adults or of other children in order to acquire ideas. Words as a medium of communication were poor commodities in this environment. In fact, the urgency for communication seemed to confine itself to situations of extreme discomfort (anything looked upon as discomfort by the child seemed to him extreme) and in such situations a loud crying was the favorite resort. On the other hand, there was a considerable amount of what might be called "verbalization," which consisted of imitation of the sounds of words of others, more with the idea of filling space than with definite communicative purpose. A phrase or word said by one child would be repeated by several not as a game, not in hilarity, but more as an activity arising from nothing and resulting in nothing.

The attitude toward adults was a strange mixture of defiance, wish for affection, and desire for attention. It was rather startling to find that there was little desire for the teachers' approval; the children seemed to crave attention but whether that attention was due to disapproval or approval mattered little. There seemed to exist what might be termed a feeling of the individual against the world, expecting no quarter and giving none. That a promise or consequence would follow simply because its prospect was stated seemed not so much to be disbelieved as to be ignored. There were few reactions which indicated a recognition of individual differences in adults. Strangers and visitors were objects of curiosity and overwhelming attention but the children's reaction would probably have been the same to wax figures. In other words, interest in clothing and appearances was uppermost and conversations were limited to a few stereotyped questions such as "What's that?" and "Who are you?" with little attention to or understanding of replies (pp. 23-24).

It might be added that the efforts of the staff to communicate with and help these children were heroic, and in many cases notably successful, as was a different experiment reported by Skeels and Dye (244) in which one- and two-year-olds from the same orphanage were placed under the supervised care of adolescent retarded girls in a training school. In both cases, of course, the children were suffering from severe emotional deprivation as well as from a lack of educational opportunity, but they provide us with some understanding of the nature of at least one kind of intellectual deficit as such, and the means whereby it can be remedied once a child has become emotionally accessible.

The unsatisfactory characteristics of the institutional environment will not necessarily be improved upon if a child is left at home with a mother who is herself retarded. Town (275) has forcefully described the environmental factors which can readily produce generations of Kallikaks.

> Without any assumption concerning why certain families are apparently foci for feeblemindedness, the simple, unelaborated fact that they are has far-reaching social implications. It means that in these families there are "blind leaders of the blind"; it means that feebleminded mothers, mere children in common sense, are rearing and caring for children, many of whom present problems that might well daunt the wisest of mothers; it means that children sicken and starve because their mothers are incapable of preparing their food and serving it at regular intervals; it means that babies die because their feebleminded mothers see not that they are ill; it means suffering, squalor and starvation of body and spirit (p. 1).

There can be little question as to the validity of this characterization; it would be seconded by any caseworker who has visited severely retarded mothers with children in their homes. It is even confirmed in a series of descriptions by Goddard of visits to the homes of Kallikaks (92, pp. 70-100) although he failed to perceive that he was thereby describing an environment in itself sufficient to explain the deficiencies of the Kallikaks without recourse to the hereditary deficit whose existence he believed he was documenting.

But if the effects of being reared by a retarded mother are so devastating, how can we account for the outcome of the Skeels and Dye experiment mentioned above? Here we have the example of 13 retarded orphanage children who were placed on the wards of a home for feebleminded girls, usually one to a ward, where their IQ's increased an average of 27.5 points over a two-year period while their companions left in the orphanage were dropping an average of 26.2 points. Granted that the physical needs of the experimental children were better met than in the homes Town describes (although this was also true of the orphanage control group) and that the institutional girls were perhaps not quite as severely handicapped as Town's (or Goddard's) mothers, but these factors alone would not account adequately for the completely opposite outcomes. Skeels and Dye concluded that their substitute parents, although performing well below the norms for their ages, were nevertheless sufficiently ahead of their young charges to be able to provide them with an apparently rich (for babies) dose of intellectual stimulation. It is only reasonable to assume a similar capability is also present in the mother who keeps her child at home. Aside from matters of physical care, the important difference appears to lie in the fact that the institutional girls were living a life devoid of excitement or any particular focus of emotional interest; they were able and delighted to shower upon the babies in their care endless affection and attention along with the minimal but adequate intellectual stimulation which created the increase in *IQ*. At home on her own, however, the feebleminded mother is already overwhelmed by problems and activities with which she cannot cope and has nothing left over to give her child. What we are saying in effect is that whereas subcultural differences which result in higher rates of slight retardation are compounded of motivation and of patterned differences in approaches to problem-solving, in severely retarded families motivational deficits appear to be primary and result in reduced *amounts* of problem-solving activity rather than necessarily in different *ways* of solving problems.

Nevertheless if we take as our objective the determination of the full range of relationships between kinds of learning situation and kinds of thinking and problem-solving which result from this learning, the plight of the child of severely retarded parents or in an institution can be illuminating and is worthy of more research. At present this is the only group, distinctively different in intellectual development from the "typical" middle class child, on which we have any real information with regard to thinking processes as distinct from motivation for thinking. Furthermore, in the severely retarded group we know about both intellect and motivation and can see the relationship between them. The only systematic studies of subcultural differences in intellectual motivation—those discussed above based on McClelland's work—do not have corresponding data from their subjects on intellectual achievement, so that we cannot assess the effects of one on the other. This seriously limits the applicability of this body of research to the problems with which we are here concerned.

We do of course know a good deal about the adverse effects of some sorts of emotional maladjustment which block intellectual development. This, however, is a different problem from that of motivation for learning; its resolution is to be sought in personality theory and in psychotherapy and counselling. We recognize that it may often be difficult in the individual case to determine immediately whether we are dealing with a child who has never developed any real motivation to learn or whether his motivation has been blocked by other factors. This difficulty probably has played a large part in the failure of all the behavior sciences to give adequate attention to the positive aspects of intellectual motivation and their effect on cultural learning. If, however, we are concerned as we are here in determining the bases for research in the etiology of mental retardation we must make such a distinction very clearly in our research thinking. Differences in intellectual motivation and in intellectual process appear to affect large groups of people fairly uniformly, although they are at present little understood; emotional blocks, on the other hand, are more idiosyncratic in origin and have been and are being fairly extensively studied. Both contribute heavily to our population of retarded children and both equally deserve extended study. Intelligence is an integral aspect of personality, and there is no reason why, for example, anthropologists studying the relationship between personality and culture should not devote as much attention to the learning process as they do to weaning. In fact, since as we have already pointed out learning is the mechanism of cultural transmission, perhaps they should place learning near the head of their list of research priorities.

Before leaving the problem of learning to turn to the life situations for which this learning is the preparation it may be well to summarize what little we do know about subcultural aspects of the learning process. Because our data are thus far very fragmentary, we can express only impressions rather than conclusions. We can at least be fairly sure that the learning process, both in mechanics and in motivation, differs between subcultural groups whether these are defined on the basis of social class, ethnic origin, rural-urban, or other criteria. Of these various groupings we will hazard the opinion that, taking Western Europe and North America as a whole, social class probably exerts the most decisive effect—in other words that a lower class Frenchman is more like a lower class American along the dimensions with which we have been concerned than he is like a middle class Frenchman (88). There are of course differences, even if of a lesser order, between the two lower class groups also, with the result that when lower class Europeans emigrate to the United States they are doubly disadvantaged and thus contribute more than their share to the retarded population.

As to the nature of the differences we are still quite uncertain. We hope that this problem will become more manageable when research employing factor analysis and related approaches tells us more about the organization of intellect, and these findings have been applied to diverse segments of the population. It is here that we feel particularly acutely the interruption in the work of Jastak on the verge of his analysis of data from the state of Delaware, for his theoretical position is very close to that which we urge repeatedly in our report, and his is the first study of subnormality in our society to be based on a probability sample which can be expected to yield true prevalence data rather than merely rates of referral. The work of Guilford (99) and of Hebb (112) is promising, but has yet to be applied to subcultural differences. Meanwhile, we do know that there are some subcultural differences with respect to the motivation for intellectual achievement, although we cannot define the effects of these differences other than inferentially, and we also know that level of motivation correlates generally with higher social class.

With respect to kinds of thinking process, the continuum from concreteness to abstraction in thinking appears the most fruitful to explore until our tools become more refined. We know this dimension is important with respect to school and test performance, and it seems reasonable to assume that it is relevant also to total life experience. However, the fact that many school failures do not lead to lifelong failures requires that this projection be made with caution. Again, there is evidence that concreteness is particularly limiting to the intellectual ability of lower class children and probably adults, and perhaps also rural residents, but we cannot locate any ethnic differences along this continuum unless we wish to do so entirely by inference from IQ's. This about sums up the extent of our knowledge. Yet every time we refer to a limitation we are speaking also of a disproportionate contribution to the population of retarded children; viewed in this light it becomes urgent that we add to the very meager store of knowledge on subcultural intellectual differences we have summarized here.

C. Intelligence and Social Functioning

We have repeatedly stressed the fact that mental retardation or mental deficiency (in other than severe cases), regardless of cause become problems only insofar as they interfere with the ability of an individual to function as a member of his society. We have had in Section II the example of our society rejecting as unfit vast numbers of its "uneducated" members, and in contrast to this we saw the Hutterites finding no difficulty in utilizing fully the energies of people often referred to by non-Hutterite teachers as "dull." The contrast becomes even more dramatic when we turn to non-European cultures, of which Wogeo and Truk have already been cited as examples. These comprise total populations all of whose members would probably be classified by our standards as markedly subnormal in intellectual functioning and, if we may accept the findings of cross-cultural intelligence testing reviewed in Chapter XIV as a valid indicator, this outcome would probably be true also for many other non-European peoples.

One should not conclude from this that all these "primitive" cultures are characterized by extreme simplicity and a rather vegetative sort of existence. The Trukese, for example, have a complex social organization and an often intricate technology. To cite but one aspect of the latter, they build sailing canoes which are as notable for their hydrodynamic efficiency as they are for craftsmanship, and possess skills in open-ocean dead-reckoning navigation without the use of either compass or chronometer greater than any other people in the world. The Australian aborigines, who lack clothing and use only the crudest of tools, are all able to regulate their social relationships within a system of kinship so complex that it required the efforts of two generations of anthropologists to unravel its subtleties. These people have intelligence and use it very well; it is simply that they do not use it in the same ways we do, or perhaps we should say more properly that they do not define intelligence in our terms—if indeed they treat it as a separate conceptual entity at all. It is for this reason that we remarked earlier that knowledge concerning the intellectual requirements for functioning in cultures other than our own can be of little practical utility in the solution of our problems. It is the demands of our own society which are critical in determining who shall be rejected from our midst, and we must therefore have knowledge primarily of our own culture in order properly to define our task.

Cross-cultural comparisons do, however, provide us with some perspective for this task. We have noted in the non-European societies mentioned thus far that mental retardation appears generally to be no serious problem, and even the comparatively few mentally defective persons who may be found have to be fairly severe in degree or defect before they require special attention; these observations could be extended to most of the other cultures upon which we have any information at all. Yet we have also noted that the members of these societies have to possess considerable mental ability, even if this does not coincide with our definition of intelligence, in order to fulfill their culturally defined rôles. Furthermore, such societies seldom offer anything approaching the bewildering array of occupational and social choices we find in our own highly diversified culture, which means that within limits a person in a non-European society has to fit a certain set of requirements or else be unable to function—a plight an American college graduate would undoubtedly find himself in for a long time if he tried to become a member of Australian aboriginal society. Why, then, are there so few intellectual misfits, and most of these a result of organic disorders? The answer appears to be that practically all non-European children learn ways of thinking and behaving which are consistently appropriate to the requirements which will be placed upon them by their culture as adults. The conclusion is then inescapable that this is true in far fewer cases in our own culture.

We have already considered the first half of the equation, the learning of intellectual skills, and were forced to conclude that we are at present able to isolate for study only a very few of the doubtless many variables in the learning situation which affect a child's preparation for later life, and that we know very little about the effects of even those few factors we have identified as relevant, particularly as these factors affect groups rather than just individuals. If we look at the other side of the equation, the functional intellectual requirements of our society, the harvest is equally sparse.

One fact does stand out prominently, however, and that is that the criteria customarily used to define mental retardation are not adequate to predict social and occupational success or failure except at the extremes. We are fairly safe in predicting that even a borderline case will never reach the higher categories of professional-intellectual status, and we can be reasonably certain that a severely retarded individual will never be able to function fully independently in society. But between these extremes prediction becomes very doubtful. Several lines of evidence support this conclusion.

One of these is the age-specific prevalence of referred mental retardation, best and most recently exemplified in the Onondaga County survey (193) mentioned in earlier sections. At each age level we see the reported prevalence of retardation rising steadily, until at the age at which compulsory school attendance is no longer required an abrupt decrease is evident to a reported rate lower than for any of the school-age years. This means that children who have actually been considered retarded and intellectually inadequate in almost two out of three cases cease to be so identified as soon as their school obligations are outgrown, and can therefore be presumed to have made some sort of satisfactory adjustment.

The nature of this adjustment is suggested by a number of follow-up studies which have been done in various parts of the United States on persons who some years before had been judged as children, largely on the basis of *IQ*, to be morons, subnormal, defective, or the like (40, 70, 151, 189). With relatively few exceptions, the individuals in all of these studies were found to have made a social adjustment which would have to be considered at least adequate, the great majority of them being self-supporting, and when retested showed a consistent rise in *IQ*, often to dull normal levels or higher. Compared to individuals earlier judged "normal" who were used as controls, the formerly retarded persons have slightly higher divorce and minor civil offense rates and somewhat lower grades of occupations with lower standards of living. They are therefore not spectacularly successful, but can scarcely be called failures, inadequate to cope with the requirements of social living.

Further support comes from studies of occupational placement with respect to *IQ*. Hegge (113) examined the employment records of 177 boys who were paroled from the Wayne County Training School to meet war manpower shortages in 1941-42; they averaged 17 years of age with a mean *IQ* of 71.8. Eighty per cent of these obtained jobs, but the striking finding is that although these jobs covered a wide range of activities, including many in skilled categories, there was no significant correlation between the *IQ* at time of parole and the wage level obtained. A more extensive study by Himmelweit and Whitfield (117) points in the same direction. They related the scores of 10,000 British Army recruits on a 10-minute paper-and-pencil test which gave a rough approximation of *IQ* to placement of these recruits in 39 selected occupations. Although there was a tendency for persons of higher intelligence to enter into the higher grade positions, in all but the highest grades of work the full range of intelligence scores was found. In other words, persons of the lowest intelligence levels were able to perform successfully in all but the highest level jobs. Also in England, O'Connor (196) examined the ability of a group of 47 "feebleminded" (*IQ* mean 70, range 65-79) adolescents to obtain employment in the two years preceding Army service and found it no different than that of a control group who had normal *IQ*'s (mean 99.5, range 94-106) although the normal group generally obtained more skilled jobs.

The most systematic research on this problem has been undertaken by Jastak. Although, as previously noted, the analysis of his data has unfortunately been interrupted, he has published with Whiteman (133) some preliminary findings on the social adjustment of the individuals in his sample who were classified as retarded. They comprised approximately five per cent of a random probability sample which included slightly over one per cent of the population of the State of Delaware. The criteria used for a definition of retardation were as follows: (*a*) an *IQ*, based on the combined results of 15 different tests, (*b*) an altitude score, representing the highest standard score attained on any of the subtests, (*c*) a schooling achievement index (number of grades achieved divided by the average number of grades achieved by his age group), and (*d*) an occupational achievement index based on the intercorrelated variables of skill level, salary, increase in salary from preceding job, whether or not he supervised others, mobility from his father's occupation, and mobility from his own first job. A person was considered retarded if he fell into the lowest 25 per cent of the distribution for each of the four criteria—in other words, although 25 per cent of the sample was for example considered low in *IQ*, only about one in five of these was also low enough on all of the other three criteria to be classified retarded. After examining the social and occupational adjustment of this retarded group Jastak and Whiteman concluded:

> One cannot help but be struck by the many similarities between the retarded and non-retarded in many areas of adjustment. The lower degree of intelligence of the retarded group does not prevent a sizable number of them from working gainfully, with a good deal of stability and satisfaction. Marital adjustment reveals no gross signs of disharmony. The retarded do not impose a disproportionate load upon community resources either in the form of legal infractions or excessive demands for social service. They are distinguishable from the non-retarded mainly by their dissatisfaction with educational experiences, by their absence from formal social participation, and by their dependence in choosing leisure time activities.
>
> Mental subnormality, it appears, need not connote an inability to fill an acceptable social rôle (pp. 66-67).

If one does not have to be mentally "normal" in order to fill an acceptable social rôle, what significance does the line dividing "subnormality" from "normality" really have? Certainly we would reject the suggestion that the jobs requiring lesser skills which these people (along with many "normals") fill are somehow fit only for outcasts of our society. It is in fact clear from the evidence presented that there is no criterion of culturally acceptable performance which most retarded individuals cannot meet, even if minimally, with one glaring exception. Were it not for this exception our society would probably have a problem of retardation little greater than that of the Hutterites or the Trukese. The exception is of course school performance, and the *IQ* concept which is a part of the same complex of standards and values.

Because of the hurdle of school, when we think of retardation we think of retarded *children*, and rightly so because it is only at school age that prevalence rates reach alarming proportions. We have already discussed in sufficient detail in this and the preceding section the various experiences and handicaps which a retarded child encounters in school under the screening of middle class criteria of behavior and performance. We do not need to repeat the discussion, and for our purposes here will only draw attention again to the emotional impact upon a child in his formative years of being segregated because of mental subnormality. Although we know very little about the nature and magnitude of this impact, it must be substantial, particularly in the areas of motivation for initiative and ambition which are so vital to occupational and social success in our society. No amount of intelligent dedication on the part of teachers of special classes can erase the fact that their pupils have been declared unfit to participate with their peers in an activity which society inflexibly demands of all its members of a certain age.

Worse off than those who are merely emotionally damaged by school failure are those who are institutionalized needlessly as a result of this failure. Happily the proportion of subcultural or "garden variety" retarded children in institutions is constantly decreasing, for the great majority of these can be expected on the basis of our present knowledge to be able with some help to make an acceptable social adjustment if they are not kept too long in the institutional environment described earlier in this section. Quite probably some of the children with milder degrees of organic defect who now go to institutions could also make an acceptable adjustment if they were pointed in this direction throughout their developmental years without regard to school standards. This is of course the objective of many special classes, but it is often implemented only after the child has tried and failed to cope with a normal curriculum, with all the damaged hopes and disillusionment of parents and child which this implies.

What is needed is a battery of scales which will predict to some degree at least the ability to develop social and occupational skills adequate for social living, scales which will be divorced as far as possible from the *IQ* concept. There are of course available tests of motor coördination, mechanical aptitude, social maturity, and the like which can be used with fairly young children, but their relationship to adult adjustment has been little explored, so we do not really know whether they will predict this or not. Here again we must return to Jastak's research. His data include the results of administering a large number and variety of tests and scales to persons of a wide range of ages and levels of social and occupational achievement. Although he cannot perforce supply longitudinal information leading from childhood tests to adult performance in a single individual, his research otherwise comes closer than anything undertaken thus far to determining the relationships between test variables of all sorts and the intellectual functioning required by our culture for adult non-school social adequacy in a broad range of activities. If we had the results of this study, and of others which it would undoubtedly stimulate, we would be much better prepared to advise parents on courses of action they should take, to help teachers of special classes for retarded children in establishing curricula, and to evaluate the importance of subcultural differences in learning with respect to social living as a whole rather than just school performance. We might even be able to make some suggestions to school administrators—who are after all trying to do the best job they can—as to what the elements of a realistic curriculum might be instead of just criticising them for being unrealistic. Although it is quite correct to say that teachers belong to the middle class and therefore teach in terms of the values and standards they have learned, it is scarcely just to hurl the middle class label at them as an epithet without even being able validly to propose other ways of teaching which might be more valuable for certain purposes and certain pupils.

In speaking of social adequacy we must not assume that this is an absolute standard or level of performance, common to all situations, or we will fall into many of the same fallacies which plague us when we try to interpret the meaning of the IQ. At the same time we must not so particularize the concept that we fail to take into account the variety of day-to-day activities in all of which an "adequate" individual must be competent within a given social setting. What we are referring to rather is the presumption that the different intellectual habits which we know are learned in different subcultural environments must reflect in some degree the criteria of normal mental ability demanded in these various settings. This is comparable to saying that the thinking patterns learned by the Trukese, although different from our own, are appropriate, adequate, and normal for functioning in Trukese society. The lower IQ's characteristic of the rural South doubtless reflect different ways of thinking and levels of adequacy for those who live in that part of the country, as compared to the Northeast for example. It is important that we should know what these differences are. But at the same time we should not assume that these standards are permanent, or even adequate for all the individuals who are members of a given group at one time. Both individual mobility and over-all social change can alter requirements. People move up and down the social scale between classes, children of immigrants move out of their ethnic enclaves, people move from the rural South to the urban North, and even the South itself is becoming industrialized and more like the North. A person who is adequate at one time and place may later prove inadequate, or the reverse, but we can neither predict nor advise in these matters until we know much more than we now do about the intellectual requirements for social adequacy. This is another area in which we know much more about emotional factors, and particularly emotional impediments, than we do about the equally crucial cognitive factors.

D. CULTURAL STEREOTYPES OF RETARDATION

We should mention briefly the usually negative reactions conjured up in many people in our society by the idea of mental retardation and particularly mental deficiency. These range perhaps from the gamut of "happy moron" jokes to real anxiety over the kind of social blight envisioned in Goddard's Kallikak study. The Kallikaks had their share of criminals, and they are often linked with the Jukes, who had even more. The presence of such unfounded stereotypes greatly aggravates the entire problem. It can be very damaging to the self-perceptions of retarded children and of their parents, and is likely to launch the child into any new social situation with two strikes against him. It generates unwarranted pressures within our society to get rid of the problem through the self-defeating device of institutionalization (in remote places) and through sterilization. And it undoubtedly has much to do with the lack we have so repeatedly noted of interest on the part of competent researchers to work in the field.

As we have already noted, many non-European peoples are, like the Hutterites, very accepting of even severely defective persons, caring for them patiently, often affectionately, and even sometimes striving to discover even one skill or attribute they can admire (cf. Bogaras, 21, p. 43; Hawes, 110, p. 250; Joseph and Murray, 139, p. 285; League of Nations, 162, p. 126). This information does not, however, help us to deal with the problem in our own society. It is essentially an educational problem, and there is little doubt that the virulent stereotypes are already gradually weakening. But a systematic social psychological study of the origins and strengths and distributions of these attitudes in our culture could provide a valuable educational tool for accelerating the present scattered progress in growth of understanding. The techniques and personnel for this kind of study are readily available and the price would be small compared to living longer in a climate of damaging public stereotypes.

E. Cross-Cultural Research in Organic Disorders

Although we have concluded that there are serious limitations to the practical application of cross-cultural research on either learning processes or criteria of social adequacy, just the reverse is true of the possibilities for research into the etiology of organic disorders resulting in mental deflciency. We know that diet, blood chemistry, heredity, and a variety of environmental factors play a part in at least some of these entities. Yet in our society we find extreme genetic heterogeneity coupled with usually very inadequate genealogical information, diets which vary widely between individuals and places and even from day to day, and extensive artificial manipulation of the environment from drinking water to air temperature.

Many of these factors are far more constant and determinate in non-European cultures, even those which have been subject to considerable foreign impact. Many of these peoples pay much more attention to preserving genealogies than do we; although in many cases the system of reckoning kinship may leave some of the geneticist's questions unanswered, the available data are still far superior to those provided by our sloppy practices. At the same time breeding populations are likely to be more stable, even though never completely isolated; this is particularly true of islands widely separated from each other. The research currently being conducted on Guam in amyotropic lateral sclerosis (*ALS*) is an example of the possibilities offered by such a population showing comparative genetic homogeneity.

Dietary patterns are often nearly uniform throughout large areas, particularly if regular supplies of imported foods are not available, and variations occur predictably with the seasons. This applies not only to the kinds and quantities of food eaten, but to methods of preparation. At the same time adjacent tribes may often be found who eat the same kinds of foods but prepare them differently, thus permitting controlled comparisons.

Although all cultures have means for controlling the external environment, this control is usually much less complete than it is in ours. The introduction of foreign clothing and housing, of public health services, and a variety of other factors are closing the gap slowly, but it remains wide, leaving non-

Europeans more directly exposed to environmental effects. It should be remembered that the major theoretical frontier established by the study of sickle-cell anemia had its beginning in observations made in the malarial regions of Africa, among non-European peoples.

If for example societies could be discovered in which mongolism did not occur and others in which it did, and it is our impression that both exist, hypotheses which involved blood chemistry or diet or environmental factors could readily be tested by a study of conditions obtaining in these societies and their members. There is also the possibility that a genetic hypothesis, if one were developed along some new line with respect to mongolism, could receive a more definitive test in a non-European culture where the disorder occurs. Furthermore, if it is possible to survey the entire population as Eaton and Weil attempted with the Hutterites we need not confine ourselves merely to presence or absence of a disorder, but can perhaps determine changes in incidence under measurable changes in external conditions.

The opportunities of cross-cultural research into the etiology and epidemiology of a variety of metabolic and other disorders, not merely those affecting mental capacity, are almost limitless and have been little utilized. Yet we know enough about a sufficient number of cultures to provide a basis for planning carefully controlled studies. Furthermore, anthropologists and other scientists often go out to study other cultures and conditions; with a little additional training they might well be prepared to undertake exploratory investigations before a major investment was made. This is one research area in which we feel cross-cultural research, as against studies of the cultural variations within our own society, can pay off handsomely.

XVI. THE SEVERELY DEFECTIVE INDIVIDUAL

A. Psychosis and Mental Deficiency

The relationship between psychosis and subnormal functioning is a research problem about which a fair amount has been written over the years. At different times comprehensive reviews of the literature and critical discussions of the problem have appeared (18, 28, 35, 97, 98, 111, 115, 128, 141, 198, 204, 206, 207, 209, 278, 291) which, with almost no exception, have made a plea for a systematic study of the problem. Unfortunately, as with so many other research problems in subnormal functioning, this theoretically and socially important problem has not attracted the attention of more than a few researchers. It would seem appropriate, therefore, to summarize briefly some of the things that seem to be known about the relationships between psychosis and subnormal functioning.

1. Psychosis is found at all levels of subnormal functioning. Even in the case of idiots marked and dramatic psychotic-like changes in behavior have been noted—in some cases, apparently, the behavior is episodic while in others it is followed by deterioration.

2. Psychosis occurs in cases with no discernible organic pathology as well as in those with marked pathology.

3. Practically every major psychotic symptom which has been described in the non-defective patient has also been noted in many of the defective cases. There appears to be little justification for the generalization that when psychosis occurs in a mentally defective individual it is necessarily less "complex" than when found in the non-defective individual. There is also little support for the equally sweeping generalization that psychosis or psychotic-like behavior in the defective individual tends to be of short duration.

4. As a result of work in the last 20 years on childhood schizophrenia, there is little doubt that many children who were committed to an institution for the mentally defective were in fact misdiagnosed and misplaced. Kanner's (142, 143, 144, 147, 148, 149, 241) now classic descriptions of the autistic child provided further evidence that our institutions contained cases in which personality or affective rather than intellectual maldevelopment was the primary factor. While one would like to believe that our institutions are admitting far fewer of these cases, there is no evidence that this is the case.

311

5. The schizophrenic type of reaction is the most frequently found psychosis among the mentally defective.[25]

6. The incidence of mental illness among the mentally deficient appears to be much higher than in the general population.

The theoretical and research implications of the above summary statements—which undoubtedly are not of equal status in terms of scientific validity—cannot, in our opinion, be discussed without serious consideration of the problems to which we now turn.

B. THE PROBLEMS OF DIAGNOSIS AND INCIDENCE

When we are confronted with the possibility of the diagnosis of psychosis in a non-defective individual, several questions are routinely asked:

How does the individual view and experience his environment and how deviant is this from the way in which we (or others in his particular cultural group) describe that environment? What is his conception of himself (e.g., ability, powers, attractiveness, usefulness, worthfulness) and how is this related to his conceptions of others in his environment? In asking these questions one is interested not only in the contents of an individual's views and experiences but in the kinds of thought processes which they indicate: the bases of his conceptualization, the nature of his associative processes, the degree and nature of fantasy, the rôle of language in communication, etc. Put most briefly, these questions are directed to answer the question of the nature and adequacy of the individual's interpretation of reality.

What is the nature and rôle of emotions and feelings in the individual's adjustment and thinking? How are these factors related to the questions raised above? What may be inferred about the rôle and adequacy of the defensive reactions associated with strong feeling and emotion?

What light is shed on the above questions from an examination or recon-

---

[25]In Pollock's (206, 207) study of mental disorders among mentally defective first admissions to the state hospitals of New York, approximately 40 per cent of the cases were of the episodic variety. The cases in this study probably are made up of individuals who resided in the community and those who were transferred from institutions for the mentally defective. It seems reasonable to assume that the chronically psychotic, mentally defective individual who has made some kind of adjustment in the community or institution would not be sent to a state hospital. The episodic variety—which may be characterized by excitement with depression, paranoid trends or hallucinatory attacks—usually present such supervisory problems to the community or institution that they are likely to be sent to the state hospital. If a more representative sample of the mentally defective population were studied, it would not be surprising if the proportion of chronic cases would be more than 20-25 per cent reported by Pollock.

struction of the life-history? What are the experiences (e.g., separation, trauma, failure) or types of relationships (e.g., social class, ethnic) which influenced the development of the individual and are reflected in his current life adjustment?

The above are certainly not all the questions that are asked when one is faced with the diagnostic problem of psychosis or, for that matter, understanding the personality of *any* individual. But we think we have listed enough of the questions to substantiate the conclusion that the diagnostic process is a searching comprehensive investigation which has the understandably ambitious aim of attaining understanding of another person's "psychology"—*that* individual's way of thinking, feeling, and acting. *Rarely, if ever, is the mentally defective individual studied or viewed in this way.* We think it would indeed be an interesting research project to obtain and evaluate diagnostic folders in the files of institutions for the mentally ill and the mentally defective. The important point for our present discussion is that since the mentally defective individual is rarely studied in the way indicated above, we cannot at all be secure in accepting available statistics on the incidence of psychosis in the mentally defective population. The absence of adequate and appropriate diagnostic procedures suggests that available statistics are probably largely based on the obviously psychotic individual and that the less flagrant case goes unnoticed or his "peculiar" behavior is blamed on his *IQ*. (When an individual with an *IQ* of 180 behaves peculiarly we do not assign cause to his *IQ*, but should an individual with an *IQ* of 50 behave similarly we usually point to the *IQ* as the etiological agent.)

It should not be thought that if one could carry out adequate diagnostic procedures with a representative sample of the mentally defective population, the true incidence of psychosis would be easily established. One of the most thorny diagnostic problems involves the lower grades (i.e., idiot and imbecile) of mental deficiency. In many of these cases language is either nonexistent or inadequate for communication, the establishment of rapport difficult, and a wide variety of organic pathologies present. In short, the conditions which ordinarily allow us to understand the covert reactions and experiences of another person are present minimally with many of these cases. It is usually when marked and dramatic changes in the overt behavior of such individuals are observed, that we can deduce that some kind of corresponding change has taken place in the covert aspects of behavior. The following cases from Greene (97) are examples of this:

In regard to the symptomatology of psychoses occurring in even the Low Grade Mental Defectives, it is a very common expression heard among the laity and I frequently hear it from the medical profession, including psychiatrists, that such and such an individual is an "insane idiot." Just what is meant by this term, I do not comprehend fully or fully understand what they comprehend by making such a diagnosis and think it a rather loose terminology, for certainly all idiots are not insane, neither all insane, idiots. It is my belief, however, that we do have actual psychosis appearing in the very low-grade mental defective and they do deteriorate. The following is an example of psychosis in an individual who might be definitely classified from the standpoint of mental defect as an idiot.

S.M., Chronological Age, 37 years; Mental Age, 2.6; IQ 16. This individual is the youngest of seven children, two of whom have been patients at this institution, both feebleminded. Other than sibling's history of mental defect, there is no other family history of note. Physically, she is under-height but generally well-nourished, with rough coarse skin, dissimilar ears of simple pattern and with adherent lobules. She has a high-narrow palate, facial asymmetry rather marked, otherwise no marked stigmata. Developmental history indicates that she began to walk at the age of one year and to talk at three years, but uses only phrases at the present time. According to developmental history, in childhood, she was obedient, apparently good-tempered and able to learn to do simple errands. Admitted to this school at the age of 14, she immediately began to show marked emotional instability in laughing one moment and crying the next, apparently without external stimulus; always exhibited a tendency to collect bits of rubbish and articles of clothing which she secreted about her person and this habit has continued to increase. Had long periods of crying at the age of 27 without apparent causative factors and at this age had to be excluded from the physical training classes because of her noisy and erratic behavior. She shows increasingly frequent periods of restlessness, sleeplessness, wandering and running about the house in an aimless manner between periods of sitting motionless under a piano or lying under a bed. During these excited periods she refuses to go to the dining room for meals and will tear her clothes in order to avoid it. She continues to cry without reason almost continually and must be coaxed and wheedled to do those things which she formerly performed without question. She has lost the ability to do tasks which she used to accomplish well, such as bed-making.

These episodes of excitement are usually accompanied by loss of weight. Between attacks, she seems to be in good physical condition, eats well and is generally quiet. The attacks of excitement are becoming more frequent and lasting for longer periods. In this case, the individual presents the differential diagnosis from the usual idiot in that she has episodic psychotic attacks, loss of weight, emotional instability, excitement and depressions, refusal of food, collecting of purposeless and useless rubbish, sleeplessness, and furthermore, she has deteriorated.

The following is an example of a low-grade imbecile with psychosis.

J.B., Chronological Age, 42 years; Mental Age, 4.6; IQ 28. This boy is a sturdy imbecile with the cyanotic hands, dissimilar ears, and facial asymmetry so often associated with mental defect. In addition, it is recorded that his eyes are dissimilar in size and shape; his speech is clear, and there is a peculiar twitching of head and extremities. He is somewhat under average height, with a very good muscular development.

The family background is very poor,—the mother mentally deficient and a patient in the department for the insane at the Tewksbury State Infirmary, and the father a chronic alcoholic. The patient is the last of six pregnancies, five having died,—four of hydrocephalus and one of phthisis.

There is very little definite information concerning early development, but the history states that the peculiarity was evident from birth. He has never learned to dress or undress completely, and though indolent, has always been obedient and amenable to discipline. When admitted to the institution he knew neither colors nor numerical combinations, could not be trusted to do the simplest errand or any sort of useful work.

Since his admission, most of the time has been spent at the farm colony, where he has learned some of the rudimentary tasks in connection with farming, but his work is not entirely satisfactory, for he is clumsy, erratic and undependable. His customary good nature has been increasingly interrupted by periods of violent excitement. During these episodes he exhibits the stereotyped attitudes and jerky, monotonous speech characteristic of Dementia Praecox. In 1926 these traits became more bizarre in character; he began to talk to himself and developed a rather elaborate ritual in regard to eating. The matron reports that at times he would remove his clothing and rush out of doors, irrespective of the weather; again, would pour hot liquid food over his head, and several times deliberately leaned against hot steam pipes.

There is a regular periodicity about these attacks,—the patient being quiet and well behaved for two weeks and disturbed and violent for the succeeding two.

These episodes became so increasingly severe that it was necessary to remove him from our farm colony and care for him in the infirmary of the institution proper and at the present time, he has changed from a pleasant, agreeable, rather talkative imbecile to one who wanders around by himself, rolls his head from side to side, has an anxious, apprehensive expression, talks to himself, has had an entire change of disposition. He exhibits erratic behavior, and instead of being able to help in the usual routine, requires constant supervision in order that he may be even clothed. He is very untidy in his habits, profane and obscene in his language, queer in his mannerisms about eating, each spoonful of food that he takes from his plate has to be passed under his knee and into the other hand before being put in his mouth. He is now a muttering, suspicious, erratic and depressed individual, with deterioration, and was committed April 23rd to a mental hospital.

Perhaps the most extensive clinical investigation of psychosis in the lowest grades of mental defect was that by Earl (64) who described what he called the "primitive catatonic psychosis of idiocy." From a study of 135 male idiots he differentiated a group of 38 cases whom he thought fitted this category. The following behavioral descriptions are from Earl:

Signs of deterioration

A general deterioration of behavior and of adaptation is constantly present. Speech fades out, toilet habits are lost, and the patient becomes apathetic, inaccessible, degraded, and destructive. Reliques of former abilities can often be demonstrated in grossly deteriorated patients. Thus several cases in this series show an understanding of speech quite out of keeping with their apparent mental level. Others can dress or undress or perform some simple task: two of the cases can play simple ball games well, though they are quite untrainable and require every nursing care and attention. Even on the purely neurological level these people often show a degree of co-ordination and control complexity of movement quite beyond the pure profound idiot.

Many of the symptoms of deterioration of behaviour can be analysed into catatonic manifestations or signs of emotional dissociation, and will be discussed under these headings. It seems probable, however, that a certain degree of permanent loss of potential ability is always present.

Signs of catatonia

Catatonia is a marked feature. The cases may be roughly divided into two groups—the stuporose or cataleptic, and the excited or hyperkinetic. There is no sharp line of demarcation between the groups; it would be more accurate to speak of a series, with the completely apathetic and the completely excited cases at either end. Twenty cases were mainly cataleptic and 18 mainly excited in type.

Catalepsy. That loss of motor initiative described by De Jong and Baruk in their experimental animals is well seen in the cataleptic group. These patients stand about in the typical posture of schizophrenic stupor, with bent head and semiflexed knees—hands hanging idly by the sides. The patients take little or no notice of threatened danger, but they will move when ordered to do so and, having once started, they will continue at a familiar simple movement. Thus they may be herded round a ward, or even engaged in very simple tasks such as cleaning spoons.

Automatic obedience. Echolalia is not uncommon but is rarely marked. Occasional echopraxia is also seen, and the understanding of words can sometimes be demonstrated in a patient who is allegedly "incapable of speech or of understanding speech"—for a sharp command, unaccompanied by gesture or facial expression, may be at once obeyed.

Muscular catatonia. The actual muscular catatonia varies. It could be demonstrated in 23 patients. It is commonest in the simple cataleptic group. In the hyperkinetics negativism is the rule, and muscular rigidity difficult to demonstrate.

The irregular type of stretching reactions described by Claude, Baruk, and Nouel was very well demonstrable in many cases. During passive extension of the flexed arm, the biceps tendon can be felt to resist, to contract, to move easily, even to anticipate movement; each for a moment in turn and quite irregularly. In some of the cases the anticipation of passive movement was obvious and the flexed arm extended itself in advance of the movement of the examiner. Lastly, in five cases after passive flexion and extension of the forearm, rhythmic repetition of the movements was set up which lasted for several minutes.

The degree of muscular catatonia present does not correlate exactly with the degree of psychosis present. This was well seen in one case in which the rhythmic repetition was continued for some minutes during which time it was possible to persuade the patient to attend to and even to reply to questions.

Autism is seen in all the cases, and is sometimes marked. The patients are not interested in their surroundings; and are often solitary, sometimes morose, refuse to mix with others and tend to conceal themselves under tables or in corners. The head is often bowed, or the coat pulled over the face; or the boy may sit in the 'intra-uterine' position.

Mutism. Some degree of mutism is always found. It varies from one patient to another and sometimes from day to day in the individual patient. Some patients will answer questions; some have a few stereotyped words and phrases; some remain quite mute. This mutism seems to be largely an autistic or negativistic feature rather than a true loss of ability. And here we have evidence that, in some cases at any rate, the mutism cloaks the degree of knowledge of, and contact with, reality. Thus one boy of 12 years who had been grossly psychotic since his second year, who had been partially mute for years, and who had spoken no word during the three months he had been under observation, managed to exasperate an attendant into threatening to smack him; to which he replied with great emphasis "No! you bloody well won't" . . .

Signs of emotional dissociation

Variability. The emotional abnormality shows itself in various forms, some of which have already been described under other headings. A rather wide variation in the general reaction to life frequently occurs;

a matter of months or even years at a time. More obvious is the occurrence of so-called 'episodes' or 'mental turns' lasting for a day or a week. These episodes may take the form of excited periods or states of depression, weeping or apathy, or vague anxiety. One of the hyperkinetic cases will weep steadily for two days at a stretch; another has days on which he is almost somnolent; whilst some of the mildest of the cataleptic group have their days of excitement and activity.

These episodes may be very early signs and may occur as the only emotional abnormality seen in otherwise fairly 'normal' idiots. They are possibly analogues of the psychotic episodes which occur in some high-grade aments, and which, when frequently recurring, sometimes presage the permanent installation of a psychosis.

Impulsiveness. Sudden outbursts of general excitement sometimes occur, lasting a few minutes or more, often accompanied by hyperkinesis and occasionally by manifestations of fear, rage or pleasure.

These outbursts are closely related to the hyperkinesiae, as are also the sudden flashes of impulsive violence which occur in these patients, who will suddenly scratch, bite or strike out at a nurse or a fellow-patient, sometimes in response to some trivial annoyance, more often without visible cause. Outbursts of excitement occur in nearly all the cases, being more dramatically striking in the cataleptics: violence is almost confined to the hyperkinetic group . . .

Mannerisms and attitudes. These are found almost only in the hyperkinetic group, just as in the experimental animal they occur in the stage of hyperkinesis. Some of these patients tend to assume the 'intra-uterine' position, and other strange postures. Thus one boy will sit for hours with his neck fully hyperextended; another assumes the 'crucifixion' attitude; another throws back his head and extends one arm and hand in a gesture of imperious command. One patient insisted on keeping all his fingers rigidly outstretched at times, even when concentrating quite well on a Wallin's peg board during a mental test.

Self-injury. Self-injury is frequent, occurring in 13 of the cases. Its usual forms are striking the head, tearing the skin with the nails, or biting the hand. One boy bit a large hole in his lower lip. Self-injury is, of course, not uncommon in simple profound idiocy, but there it is usually either the result of long-continued slow movements of auto-erotic type or else a part of a rage reaction. In the catatonics the action is sharp and energetic, is not a response to an external stimulus, and is accompanied by varying emotional expressions; sometimes weeping, occasionally pleasure, and in two cases no emotion of any kind.

Causeless weeping. A most important sign of emotional abnormality is the occurrence of weeping or laughter without cause. This occurred in 16 cases, and the writer has never seen it in a case which did not at the time or subsequently develop signs of psychosis. The periods vary in length and frequence, and the causeless weeping is sometimes accompanied by self-injury . . .

Depth. The depth of the psychosis is not easy to estimate; the clinical picture is confused by the profound intellectual deficiency. Generally speaking, the stuporose cases are surprisingly accessible to external stimuli, and though they quickly sink back, one cannot easily distinguish between the withdrawal of stupor and the mere apathy of idiocy. The writer has only seen one case of profound stupor—the case is not included in the present series. The hyperkinetic cases are less accessible, or respond only by exhibiting further abnormal psychomotor phenomena. In both groups, and particularly in the cataleptics, there is a definite day-to-day variation which is rarely seen in the stupor reactions of the intellectually normal.

A variety of clinical types were represented in Earl's series of cases:

'Simple' primary oligophrenia	10 cases
Mongolism	2 cases
Epiloia	5 cases
Acquired organic cerebral lesion	8 cases
Dementia infantilis	2 cases
Unknown	11 cases

Earl points out that because of inadequate case history data the exact age of onset of the psychosis could not reliably be determined. In the large majority of cases, however, the psychosis was already "definitely established" before the age of 10 years. It is worthy of note that Earl states that in this series "no case of congenital profound idiocy occurred." In each of these cases, apparently, the original level or potential was above the level of idiocy Earl found at the time of his study.

It has been argued by some that the undisputed fact that psychotic-like, particularly schizophrenic-like, symptomatology is frequently observed in the lower grades of mental defect is no basis for assuming that psychologically we are dealing with the same condition as when these symptoms are observed in the intellectually normal person or even the high grade type of mental defect. According to this argument the schizophrenic symptomatology—particularly some of the bizarre and repetitive motor phenomena—is a more or less direct reflection of the organic pathologies which so many of these cases have. Although organic pathology certainly cannot be considered a fortuitous factor, there has been no convincing demonstration of the nature of the relation between organic pathology and the behavioral symptoms—nor does the organic pathology seem capable of explaining either the episodic or the chronic nature of the motor and emotional symptomatology.[26]   It is our opinion, which we will more fully discuss later, that the state of our present knowledge is such that we cannot rule out the possibility that psychological factors play a rôle in the psychotic-like behavior of many severely defective individuals.   Until the kind of clinical investigation exemplified by Earl's work is combined with adequate life-history material—the kind of material which Earl recognized he did not have in his (institutional) cases—the question of the rôle of psychological factors in the psychotic-like behavior of the severest grades of mental defect must remain an open one.

---

[26]Dementia infantilis, originally described by Heller (100, 123), is a specific example of the problem, even though it is traditionally not included among the mental deficiencies. These are cases in which the child is apparently normal up until three or four years of age at which time a variety of behavioral changes are observed, the child deteriorating to a point whence he is frequently indistinguishable from many "conventional" defectives of the idiot or imbecile level. Some workers reported that they found the pathological anatomical basis of this condition and therefore excluded them from the schizophrenias. Others could not corroborate these pathological findings and considered it a variety of schizophrenia. As with the severe grades of mental deficiency, the inaccessibility of these cases makes the usual psychological and psychiatric diagnostic modes of study almost impossible. It is our opinion that it is unlikely that a specific pathological brain condition will explain the complex behavioral changes described in these cases. This is not to say that brain pathology may not be an etiological factor but rather that it interacts with psychological factors which also play a determining rôle in the course of the condition.   We would agree with Earl's (64) conclusion about the etiology of psychosis in idiots: "The etiology of the condition is a subject for further study. The present evidence would appear to indicate the causal importance of physical rather than of experiential factors. The final decision cannot be reached until much more is known, both of the behaviour patterns of idiocy and of their physical correlates."

XVII. THE SEVERELY DEFECTIVE INDIVIDUAL (CONTINUED)

A. Performance and Potential

In previous sections of this report we emphasized the importance of observing the non-test as well as test behavior of the individual. It was our opinion that if we could observe the individual in other life situations, we would be better able to understand discrepancies in level of functioning between test and non-test situations and, perhaps more important, to evaluate more validly the potentialities of the individual. In those sections we were primarily concerned with problems of the nature and measurement of intellectual processes. We feel that the same point of view may be of help here in indicating some direction in which research on personality organization and functioning of the mentally defective might take. It is our opinion that such research would be of relevance to the problem of psychosis among the mentally defective population.

The tendency to view the defective individual from the standpoint of a test score is probably most true in the case of those labelled as idiot or imbecile. With such individuals the intelligence or developmental quotient has not only exempted them as subjects of psychological research but it has also served as an effective barrier against innovations in training and treatment. This situation is all the more surprising in view of the findings of some of the psychological research that has been done. For example, in 1931 Aldrich (3) described a study of the problem-solving behavior of idiots:

> The first problems of this series involved box-stacking as a means of obtaining a lure. The child was brought to the room by the experimenter, who then remained outside, observing the child's behavior through a one-way vision screen. The lure was suspended from the ceiling, at a height proportionate to the number of boxes to be used and the height of the child. The problems increased in difficulty until they were beyond the range of the child's ability to solve them. The circumstances which accompanied success or failure were carefully recorded.
>
> The second group of problems of this series involved the use of implements. These problems were likewise arranged in order of complexity. The lure was placed in a pen six feet square, made of palings four feet high. The implements were sticks which could be used either singly or combined, according to the problem.
>
> The solutions of the problems both with boxes and sticks depended upon self-initiated activity. There were no verbal directions and no adults or other children to depend upon for cues or encouragement. The child was in the room alone, and success in the problem could only be

expected when there was sufficient incentive value in the lure to bring
about a spontaneous response in the child's behavior. This fact led to
experimentation with the lure itself as a means of studying the effect
of incentive on the individual performances.

The first lure was a ball, which in no case failed to attract the child's
attention and bring about at least a reaching response, the most primitive
form of adaptive behavior in such situations. Then a ball and a cookie
were presented, and finally a banana.

As judged by the amount of activity induced in the subjects and the
number of successful responses, the ball, although an eagerly accepted
toy held less incentive value than the cookie, while the banana surpassed
either of these. Tommy, for example, piled two boxes together for the
ball and cookie, but absolutely ignored the third box. However, when a
banana was substituted as the lure he immediately stacked three boxes
together. Such an observation leads to the speculation that ability cannot
be determined until stimulation is maximal.

Billy was obviously afraid of standing on three boxes after he had
stacked them together. He attempted it several times when the ball was
suspended above his head, and each time gave up. When the banana was
used, however, he immediately stood on the same three-box structure,
displaying no overt fear reactions. Incentive in this observation seemed
definitely associated with the elimination of an emotional obstacle to
success.

Many responses in the situations revealed personality differences of
much importance. For example, when the child was taken to the room
and the door shut between him and the experimenter, there were many
kinds of reactions. One child cried at being left alone, and he continued
to do so until it was necessary to take him from the room. Others
whimpered when their attempts failed, and still others showed evidence
of discontent and anger under such circumstances by stamping or banging
on the door with their fists. However, the latter displays accompanied
failure and not mere discontent at being alone.

The reactions of the children during the momentary presence of the
experimenter at the beginning and end of the trial also suggested personality differences.

For example, Sammy began his solution of the problem the minute the
door was open for him. Carl waited until the door was closed, with the
experimenter outside, while Jimmy waited until the end of the trial
period, when the experimenter had re-entered the room, before beginning
any activity toward the ball, and then looked constantly for approval and
assurance.

These personality differences displayed according to the presence or
absence of the observer, suggest important considerations with respect
to adult presence and attention in a training program. Obviously we

must treat every child individually, encouraging those who respond best to encouragement and isolating those who develop best in self-initiated activities.

Distractibility was sometimes prevalent and in some cases associated with failure. George, who has very low intelligence and meagre adaptability, was hyperactive upon seeing the ball, and reached for it repeatedly. But he did not use the boxes at all until the experimenter placed them directly under the ball. George then became engrossed in climbing up and down, and completely ignored the ball. In this case the solution iself was a distraction in obtaining the end result.

Binet mental age within the limits of the group was not a good measure of a child's ability to solve these problems. The three who failed the simplest problems were of the lowest mental ages. However, the seven subjects who ranged in mental age from two to three years did not seem to be sufficiently differentiated by the tests to account for their varied ability in these situations.

These and similar observations of the idiot's activity in problem situations at the borderline of his ability suggested incentive, emotional makeup, and individual personality reactions as well as mental age as influential factors in idiot behavior and trainability.

Although Aldrich employed a "test" situation, it obviously differed in important respects from the formal testing situation—in fact, level of performance between the two situations was not highly correlated. Although the following statements are contained in the above quotation, we think they are deserving of restatement:

1. Under conditions of strong motivation, some severely defective individuals are capable of directing and sustaining their attention to the external environment, their level of problem solving in the process being surprisingly good. If we knew more about the everyday behavior of these individuals, this conclusion might take on added significance.

2. From Aldrich's description it would seem that some of these individuals were responding in more than a concrete fashion. One hesitates to ascribe to these individuals the capacity to reflect and organize but it seems to us difficult to square the descriptions with the assumption that these cases could respond *only* in a concrete, passive, unreflective way.

3. There are marked personality differences among severely defective individuals—suggesting that the kinds of interpersonal relationships which they have experienced were not identical. Put in another way: the factors to which we ordinarily attribute importance as a source of individual differences may be operative even when dealing with severely defective organisms.

There are a number of grounds on which one might question these conclusions. One might say, especially in regard to the second conclusion, that these cases were not "true" idiots but individuals who had in effect regressed from a higher level of functioning. But what are the personality dynamics and external conditions associated with such regression? If one invokes some organic pathology, how is one to understand the resulting individual differences? One need not resort to a construct of regression, embedded as it is in a theory of personality, and simply state that some of these cases were just not given an opportunity to develop what capacities they had—they were given a label and then handled in a manner considered appropriate to it. This is in effect saying that some of these individuals suffered from *understimulation*, an argument rarely advanced with the severest grades of mental deficiency. Firm conclusions from Aldrich's study cannot be drawn, although similar findings have been reported by Gardner (79).[27] The point that seems least questionable is that even in the severe grades of mental deficiency individual differences *in behavior and personality* exist. This is but another way of saying that we are dealing with individuals whose behavior is not due to static factors but to a dynamic interaction between internal and external forces which reflect previous experiences—in short, these dynamic interactions have a history. From this viewpoint it should not be surprising, therefore, that personality changes over time should be noted in some of these individuals, even some of the marked and dramatic changes noted in the previous chapter. The research problem is not so much what we label some of these changes (e.g., psychosis) but understanding their psychological basis and implications for training and treatment.

---

[27]In 1948 McPherson (182) presented a comprehensive review of experimental studies of learning in subnormal individuals, several of the studies being concerned with the severely defective cases. It is not surprising that McPherson concluded: "The outstanding impression gained from this review of learning in the subnormal is one of lack of information. The actual experiments have been few, the number of subjects small, the tasks to be learned heterogeneous within a narrow range, and the motivational factors inadequately controlled. The results of this review serve not so much as an aid to the technician in meeting clinical problems but as a reminder to the experimentalist." However, the following conclusions did seem to be supported by findings of more than one investigator: (*a*) changes in incentives or motivation resulted in increased learning and (*b*) there is a lack of relationship between learning behavior and intelligence test score.

Recent studies in England by Clarke and Hermelin (47), Gordon, O'Connor, and Tizard (93, 94), Loos and Tizard (171), and Tizard and Loos (272) certainly are in line with the conclusions and findings given above. Clarke and Hermelin concluded: "It seems that the limits to the trainability of imbeciles are very much higher than have been accepted traditionally either in theory or in practice." A recent book by O'Connor and Tizard (197) has summarized most of the English studies.

B. Significance of Itard's Study

It is something of a commentary on our contemporary knowledge that the best description yet made of the behavior of a severely defective individual is that by Itard (127) on the *Wild Boy of Aveyron*. For the purposes of our present discussion the following should be said of this classic:

1. At the time that Itard took Victor, the Wild Boy, under his wing there was no reason to believe that the boy had ever functioned at a higher level. Itard was viewed as something of a fool for attempting to work with the boy. We make this point because we think it not unlikely that were someone today to give as much time to an idiot or imbecile child as Itard gave to Victor, he probably would be viewed not as a fool but as someone with a curious penchant for wasting time.

2. Although Itard was disappointed that he could not make Victor into a normal youngster, what he did accomplish with the boy can be appropriately labelled as phenomenal. Over the long period of training one could see the development of various ego functions, the capacity to delay responsiveness—in short, one saw the development of a surprisingly complex personality.

3. Perhaps the most important conclusion that could be drawn from Itard's work is that even in severely defective individuals the quantity and quality of interpersonal relationships is an important variable in determining the level of complexity and efficiency of psychological functioning. Put in another way: even in the severely defective child the measurement of intellectual performance and potential cannot be meaningfully done without consideration of environmental opportunity and stimulation.

C. Significance of Research With the Severely Defective Individual

Thus far in our discussion we have concentrated on the severely defective individuals because, in addition to the research implications already noted, there are other considerations which make psychological research with these cases important. For example, it has been noted by Lemkau (165) and others that the distribution of intelligence may not be a normal one because the number of idiots and imbeciles is apparently significantly greater than one would expect from the normal probability curve. On the basis of our above discussion we think it not unlikely that such a conclusion may be a function of the practice of using test scores which reflect performance rather than potential.[28]   If in some of these cases we are dealing with personality regression, in others organic deterioration, while in others inadequate training and stimulation have not allowed for full development of potential— if these conditions occur among severely defective individuals, statistics about the incidence of idiots and imbeciles (as identified by test scores) cannot be considered as being very meaningful.

As soon as one seriously considers the possibility that even in severely defective individuals the quantity and quality of interpersonal relationships are important variables in development, the rôle of parent-child relationships must be evaluated.   In recent years we have become aware of how the severely defective child affects the lives of parents and siblings but little or no attention has been given to the influence of parent upon child.   In fact, when one considers the psychological disruption which frequently occurs in families with a severely defective child, it is difficult to avoid the conclusion that the child in some way is affected by it.   That this possibility has been little discussed, let alone studied, is probably due to the implicit assumption held by most professional workers that the severely defective organism has no personality or intellectual potential to speak of and therefore one need not be concerned about psychological consequences.   We have no doubt that in some cases such an assumption is warranted, but we also have no doubt that in some cases the assumption is without foundation.

The following question may have occurred to some readers of this report: assuming that what has been said so far has some merit, how can one justify the expenditure of time, money, and personnel for research with individuals who will always be in need of the closest supervision, even in the institutional setting?   This question can be answered in several ways.   On the most practical level one could say that to the extent that such research increases our psychological understanding of these individuals the problems of care and training would be correspondingly decreased.   If such research would serve to enable us better to help parents in the handling of these children, it would represent an important social contribution.   Again on a practical level: although the knowledge we may gain from such research may never enable us to help the severely defective individual as much as one would like, it may be of great value when applied to the less severely defective individual.   If by our increased understanding of the severely defective individual we can

---

[28]It is interesting to note in this connection that Earl (64) concluded that none of his psychotic cases of the idiot level were "congenitally profound idiots" as their behavior at the time of the study might have suggested.

learn how to modify his behavior and increase his range of adequate responsiveness, however small such modifications and increases might be, then we would have reason to expect that similar endeavors with the less severely defective individual would be more productive.

D. THE PROBLEM AND NEED OF THEORY

Perhaps the greatest significance of research with the severely defective individual is the challenge it presents to psychological theory and practice. How adequate are our psychological theories for understanding the problems we have thus far discussed in this and the previous chapter? The fact that most psychological theorists have never been concerned with problems of subnormal functioning is less important than the fact that we cannot assume that their theories would be at all adequate to cope with these problems. By adequate we mean that a meaningful research program, derived from a systematic theory, could be set up which would show promise of illuminating the kinds of problems we have been discussing. It should not be overlooked that the idiot and imbecile are human beings, and any theory which purports to be a theory of human behavior should be able, if not to give satisfactory answers to the problems which the behavior of these individuals present, *at least to indicate how to go about finding the answers*. The problem of theory is basic because we all operate, implicitly, or explicitly, on the basis of some theory of human behavior. It is only through the process of scientifically *testing* our theory that we can evaluate its adequacy as a basis for our practice. It is because psychological practice must be based on some theoretical conceptions that concern with psychological theory cannot be viewed as a luxury.

To our knowledge there has been but one attempt to view mental deficiency (particularly of the severe grades) from a systematic, theoretical position. We refer here to Clark's (42, 43, 44, 45) attempt to view the problem from the standpoint of psychoanalytic theory. There is much one can question and disagree with in Clark's ultra-orthodox psychoanalytic formulations. Aside from the fact that he was employing analytic theory of the 1925 variety, the major difficulty one encounters in reading Clark is his completely uncritical acceptance of the validity of the theory in all its aspects. The quotation which follows is less open to these weaknesses, and can serve to illustrate some of the points we have attempted to make (44, p. 36):

If we say that mental deficiency consists of some failure in the processes of acquiring, absorbing, and using knowledge for an adaptive mastery of reality, what are the specific defects which lie behind this failure? In many instances, brain lesions and organic injuries or defects have been indicated as the basis for a mental arrest. Other investigators have referred to "a pathologic variation in the germ cell," which makes complete mental growth impossible. Another plausible explanation for mental deficiency is advanced by those who hold that there is a defect or arrest in the development of the neurons. Each of these points of view would seem a reasonable attempt to determine the basic cause of mental arrest. Each consists of a formulation which the observed data frequently appear to warrant. Yet we feel that none of these theories can indicate just how the fundamental cause leads to the difficulties which the ament is seen to have. Nor do they contain possibilities for understanding the individual in such a way as to help him in his problem of getting along in the world.

Our belief is that even in cases where a definite organic injury is present, there are dynamic or psychological factors which play a prominent part. The ego, as we view it, is not only an organization of character-patterns and abstract capacities, but also is made up of the sum of the physical elements constituting the human body. The total "self" would consist of the individual's body, his mental impressions from it, and his co-ordination of the somatic, as well as the psychic elements referring to it. Any wound to the physical structure must be reflected in the ego's efficiency and in its sense of power to govern the total organism in its approach to reality. Especially must a handicap result, if the injury is to that portion of the machine which is most sensitive and most needed in the process of guiding or directing. A lesion in the brain, therefore, or an injury to the central nervous system would greatly impoverish the weapons by means of which the ego carries out its appointed tasks. Furthermore, a physical injury of this nature results in a severe psychic wounding of the ego. The sense of self-assurance and confidence is deeply hurt, for the ego misses some part of its feeling of completeness. In a sense it has been castrated, and it automatically seeks some emotional compensation. Case-studies have suggested that the ego's need for love is greatly emphasized in such instances; that there is an added impounding of libido within the personality, as a narcissistic agency for psychic healing and soothing. An injury coming early in life might thus serve to inbind a more solid formation of primary narcissism, and the extra narcissistic need might well inhibit the full ingestion and absorption of identifications. In other words, a lesion might cripple mental development, not directly but through its burden of handicap upon the ego and the libidinal processes necessary for mental growth and functioning. We must grant to organic factors, wherever present, a share in the causation of mental enfeeblement; but we hold that it is mainly through its effect upon the ego and upon the distribution of available energies that a physical defect exerts its mental crippling. If we regard the problem in this way, it seems to bridge the gap between an atypical organic "cause" and a "result'" in the realm of mental functioning. . . .

We should prefer to summarize these basic crippling factors and recognize them simply as constituting a fundamental ego-defect. Whether this be in the germ cell or in the development of the neurons, we may at least say that the total ego is without some degree of its usual endowment for meeting reality. In dealing with amentia, whatever more remote etiologic data may be held responsible for its inception, our major concern practically is with the imperfections noted in the ego's functioning. Here we must leave concrete, physical representations and turn towards capacities which have to do with definite mental processes. Our point of view is that the ego's defect lies within such capacities as perception, memory, ideation, judgment, and reasoning. These are specific phases of its endowment, necessary for mental grasp and adaptation or mastery of its surroundings. They may be originally handicapped from some physical lack in the elements which go to make up the ego (germ plasm, neurons, etc.) ; they may be crippled at some time as a result of organic injury (lesions, etc.) ; or they may be innately defective themselves as capacities forming part of the patterns which the ego inherits. Whatever the ultimate, basic cause, the important fact is that these capacities are the defective elements most typically observed; and these functions are the ones which need helpful understanding if development is to be brought up to the highest possible level of individual usefulness and happiness.

Our opposition, therefore, is not against the scientific investigators who indicate organic or constitutional defects as the basis of mental arrest. Rather, we take issue with those who infer from these findings that "therefore nothing can be done about it." Our opinion is that a recognition of certain unchangeable, irremediable factors in an individual is absolutely necessary, but that within the limits imposed by such physical or deeply ingrained handicaps there is much that can be better understood and more constructively dealt with.

It is for this reason that we emphasize the dynamic elements in the problems of amentia. They are the moving forces of energy which must be used in the actual functioning of whatever capacities the ego does possess. They are the vitalizing powers which are necessary for advancing mental development as far as inherently possible, and for directing this development into the channels of greatest individual efficiency. We refer specifically to instinctual energy, for it is from the libido and from the destructive impulses that the driving force for all contacts with reality seems to come.

Thus the main, immediate problem in mental arrest seems to concern the aspects of ego-development and the uses to which emotional energy is put. If we are to understand and help retarded individuals, we need to study the formation of primary narcissism and its effects upon the capacity for making identifications. It will be pertinent to investigate the manner in which oral-libido is used with the destructive impulses for an ingestion of knowledge from the outer world. We must get a clearer insight into the development of secondary narcissism, its advantages in supplying the urge towards grasping reality, and its disadvantages in obstructing the full absorption of what is taken in. Our understanding of the ament will be further advanced if we can observe the extent to which he has attained objectivity, by means of which he can reproject and use his acquirements for adaptive purposes. And finally, we may better appreciate his difficulties in attaining a social adaptability and in adhering consistently to moral codes when we see more deeply into the formation of the super-ego.

These are the factors we feel are all-important in any theory of mental arrest which strives to deal with backward individuals as living beings. They are the elements which seem to influence the ament's functioning in everyday life and his possibilities for a restricted but at least a further elaborated development.

The above quotation can serve as an example of how theory can direct our attention to problems ordinarily unnoticed. An important problem in analytic theory concerns the process whereby the dependent infant, whose behavior appears almost exclusively determined by *his* experience of pleasure and pain, becomes capable of directing attention and interest to another person and responding in a way so as to obtain "pleasure" from that person—the transition from a state of primary to secondary narcissism. It is assumed that this transition takes place by means of a process of identification with an external figure and that this process already reflects certain intact ego functions (e.g., perception, memory, increased control of motility). When these ego functions are defective in the very young children, it becomes much more difficult, if not impossible in some cases, to make the transition from a state of primary to secondary narcissism. What is important in Clark's formulation is that he raises the possibility that the defective ego functions may have the effect of reinforcing or fixating behavior on the primary narcissistic level, and that an *unusual* amount of attention and understanding would be necessary if the child were to begin to make the transition. From this theoretical formulation, therefore, research interest becomes focused on the psychological development of such children and the external conditions necessary for facilitating maximal development of potential.[29] Put in another way one could say that this formulation suggests that the behavior we observe in these cases, even in the severely defective ones, may not be representative of what they could do under other conditions of rearing and training. It is not surprising that Clark makes special reference to Itard's work and attributes the changes observed in Victor to the unusual amount of attention, love, and stimulation which Itard and the governess gave to him. It should also be noted that in the two severely defective boys whom Clark described, and with whom a therapeutic approach was attempted, support for the above formulation is found. In these two cases, however, the amount and quality of attention given does not begin to compare with that described by Itard.

There are several things which should be emphasized about Clark's theoretical formulations in order to illustrate the fruitfulness of viewing specific problems from the viewpoint of a general, systematic theory. First, it directs our attention to the earliest phases of development and emphasizes the importance of special handling *at those times*. It also makes us aware of how little interest has been shown in describing and understanding the ways in which the defective infant or very young child is reacted to and stimulated by parents.[30] Second, the theoretical formulation suggests a course of action. The process of testing the theoretical formulation involves attempts to change the behavior of the patient. In the work of Clark, as well as that of other analytic work (2, 41) with defectives, the course of action has basically in-

---

[29]Despite his formulations Clark, strangely enough, never gives what we would call a case history for any of the children he describes. Nothing is said about the parents or problems and methods in rearing the child—nothing about the earliest phases of development which are so crucial in his theory.

[30]This statement may not adequately convey the complexity of the problem. For example, there is probably great variation in when the diagnosis of severe mental deficiency is made or communicated to parents, so that these children differ in the amount of time they were responded to as normal children. We do not think one can assume, without further evidence, that to be handled and reacted to like a normal child can only be "good" for the severely defective child. In addition we do not know what changes take place in rearing practices after the parents know of the child's condition. We think it would be more than worth while if studies could be made of (a) the *specific* advice which parents are given in relation to ways of handling the infant or young child, (b) the justification which the physician can give for such advice, (c) and the adequacy of such advice when viewed in light of the everyday problems which such children present. It is our impression, which one of us (225) has elaborated on elsewhere, that the very nature of the diagnosis, the way in which it is frequently communicated to parents, and the vague or too general advice given to parents about details of rearing the child often produce marked psychological disruption in the parents. It would be doing violence to any psychological theory of child development to assume that the child, even the severely defective, was not in some way affected by such disruption.

volved the establishment of an interpersonal relationship and the subsequent use of this relationship to increase the range and adequacy of the individual's externally directed behavior. Even with the severely defective individual, as described by Clark and Itard, this type of relationship can frequently be established.

Following the completion of this section an article by Benoit (16) appeared which deserves mention because it is one of those rare efforts to discern the practical significances of a systematic theoretical position. In this instance, it was Hebb's (112) neurophysiological theory of brain function which was employed. The present writers are not competent to evaluate either Hebb's theory or the manner in which it is employed by Benoit. However, there is no doubt in our minds that the problems to which Benoit's attention has been drawn are important and one can only hope that they give rise to a formal research program.

1. Hebb's theory has been concerned (among other things) with the problem of the adverse effects of stimulational privation in early life.

> It seems appropriate to inquire into how the theory might illuminate and make possible a more effective control over the learning process in the mentally retarded. For one thing, there is a tendency for parental attention to shift to some extent from training in self-help and other activities to excessive care when reactions and general behavior are seen to deviate from normalcy; and there arises the question as to whether this inclination to overprotection might not have a destructive or stunting effect on the development of the child, over and above any neurological impairment that may occur. Furthermore, because the evidence gathered from animal studies seems to support the claim that stimulational privation in early life produces adverse effects even in late maturity, one is prone to wonder whether a conscious effort to lay more emphasis on training with reference to both amount and degree of adaptivity might not result in raising the achievement level in all the major spheres of performance (16, p. 500).

Benoit's focus on parental handling of the subnormal infant, and the possibility of understimulation in these instances, coincides with the speculations of the writers earlier in this section.

2. "The key element in the learning process is attention. In the Hebbian framework, the control of attention is assumed to be achieved through the delivery of facilitation from one organizational structure to another. Accordingly, in order to ensure attention, structures that may logically be presumed to be appropriate antecedents to any given response must be activated;

that is, a set must be established." Benoit points out that the establishment of appropriate sets in the defective organism may be made impossible or interfered with because of that organism's incapacity to handle or organize the variety of stimuli which impinge upon him. "One may infer that the successful production of new learning may require the elimination of irrelevant stimulation. When learning is very imperfect a complex situation may elicit mass activation, which obviously results in diffuse thinking. Accordingly, the theory suggests that the teaching situation be made more effective by simplifying contexts. By diminishing the volume of stimulation, there is less chance of disturbing a given organizational structure while it is in process of being reinforced with a repetitional series." This conclusion is very similar to that of Strauss and Kephart (267). Both Benoit, as well as Strauss and Kephart, discuss the problem of the control of irrelevant stimulation primarily in terms of the older, defective child. It would be our suggestion that equally (or more) important is the study of this problem in infancy and very early childhood, not only because they are the periods of initial learning but also because they are the times when the parents of the defective child receive the least guidance in training procedures. The significance of these early periods is central to Hebb's theory as the following statement by Benoit indicates:

> Finally, Hebb strongly urges that active concern with intellectual training begin early. On the face of it, a new organizational structure can be formed at any time in the life of the individual, provided the necessary maturational level has been achieved. Actually, however, the situation is not so simple. As a person ages without opportunity for new experiences, without acquiring new knowledge or new organizational structures, learning sets weaken or become relatively ineffectual, owing to the reversibility of the growth process that gives rise to the structures that mediate learning; in other words, behavior becomes permanently constrained within the limits of primitive habits. There is considerable evidence to the effect that providing the young with abundant suitable environmental stimulation greatly affects the course of their development right on into adulthood, whereas the same advantage later in life produces much less startling results.

In our opinion, Benoit's article not only underlines the importance of theory as a guide to problems and practice but also emphasizes the need for closer study of the experiences and training of the defective child in his earliest years.

E. BOURNE'S PROTOPHRENIA

In 1955 Bourne (22) reported a study of severely defective individuals which because of its implications requires special mention. His subjects, all with *IQ*'s below 50, were 154 young children admitted consecutively to an English hospital.

> Of the 154 cases, 138 had an evident organic cause and 16 had none. The distinction was based on clinical investigation and a medical history derived from several sources. The chief source was standard history forms completed by the hospital's social workers in each case, and in 74 by the outpatient consultants as well. Also there were 330 medical reports—an average of two per patient in the larger group and three in the smaller—specially requested from hospitals attended previously. Many of these were really plural reports, concerning more than one admission, or coming from independent departments, or referring to other members of the family too; in 100 of the cases, including 14 of the smaller group, the pregnancy and labour were described. In 34 cases I interviewed relatives—mostly at their wish, but in a few cases to get extra details.
>
> There were 36 deaths, all in the larger group, 31 coming to necropsy, and in all of these organic disease was found.
>
> . . . At the Fountain Hospital, with 600 beds for mentally defective children, almost all under 5 years old on admission, the processes causing severe mental defect are relatively recent and thus unusually accessible. It will be shown that clinically, as well as at necropsy, most of the severe cases can be explained by organic brain disease, and that heredity seems much less significant than is sometimes believed. There remains a small group of children, lacking any apparent organic or familial pathology, who appeared to me to display notably both a curious pattern of abnormal behaviour and a background of appalling misfortune. It was postulated that in such cases a faulty upbringing might cause failure of mental growth.
>
> . . . The information was gathered from the sources mentioned for the medical history, the standard forms ensuring certain items uniformly for all cases, and the reports from other hospitals supplying occasional psychiatric accounts of near relatives; in addition, there were 209 reports from outside social agencies, mainly local-authority workers.
>
> Where occasional discrepancies were met, an obviously less reliable report was discarded, or further inquiry was made. My judgment replaced that of others in a single instance:
>
> All accounts referred to a mother as mentally defective because she had been certified as such in prison and spent years in a colony. As her letters were far too fluent for this diagnosis, she was interviewed. She proved to be a psychopath, of at least average vocabulary and

literacy, from a criminal family, and now the prosperous young widow of an engineer who had died "suddenly." If she was defective, it was in morals and not intelligence.

For statistical treatment, the social histories compiled in this way were tabulated, the items extracted for this falling into some fifty categories. The two groups were then compared statistically, item for item, mainly by the X^2 test with Fisher-Yates correction, required because one group was numerically small.

Because the number of mongols in the organically affected group was large, it was necessary to prevent unknown factors that might be peculiar to them from influencing the comparisons, either by swamping real differences or by creating misleading ones. As a precaution, every calculation had to be repeated with mongols treated as an isolated group. In the event, this turned out to have been superfluous, uncovering nothing otherwise overlooked, and indicating only the differences to be expected between mongols and the rest of the organic cases.

We shall not go into the details of Bourne's findings. Suffice it to say that his data indicate that the small group with no organic pathology came from backgrounds which, both before and after their birth, could be described as psychologically unhealthy in the extreme.

The outlines of the condition isolated now emerge. The young child, though physically healthy, will present severe backwardness evident from about the second year, with curious behaviour disorder and a history of perverted mothering in infancy. In his first two years he will either have been reared by an extremely disordered person, commonly a psychopath, or else deprived for long and repeated periods of the mother or her substitute; usually he will have suffered both misfortunes. None here were simply reared in an institutional setting—of three so reared from the age of 18 months or less two first endured terrible neglect by unstable mothers, one passing later through five institutions, while the 3rd went from foster-mother to institution to institution.

Clinically these children's backwardness is uneven; despite an *IQ* about 40, their early milestones are not much delayed, and they lack the clumsiness and impoverished expression of other imbeciles—some, indeed, are very graceful and attractive. At times they appear extraordinarily remote and even deaf, tending to monotonous mannerisms, banging their heads, and tearing their hair out; many also have intolerable propensities for screaming and destructiveness.

Of those I have observed in hospital for a year or two beyond their 5th birthday, some become docile imbeciles, and others burnt out and dilapidated ones; yet others do not change.

The condition described here must be of great social interest since it cannot be rare, it is probably preventable, and it may initially be treatable.

At the Fountain Hospital about 10 per cent of severe aments seem to be in this category. Admissions are from a big area and without any selection, and this figure must be fairly representative of extreme defectives under hospital care. The condition may therefore be responsible for many thousands of people occupying hospital beds in this country. Moreover, this is a restricted estimate confined to psychogenic defect in apparently pure culture. This condition may be even commoner for the following reasons: (a) Milder emotional undernourishment or damage, or an equal degree in a more resistant victim, may account for some of the less extreme defectives in the community, and even more of those in institutions. (b) Some mental defectives of organic aetiology may have been reduced to the institutional level by such trauma, additionally. Possibly these children are less equipped to overcome indifferent rearing and very liable, by virtue of physical deformity, to elicit it.

The histories of these cases monotonously disclose how little realisation still exists among social agencies, doctors, and hospitals that a small infant is a social being who needs more than food alone to grow up. For example, the digestive difficulties, failure to thrive, and napkin rashes common in these infants, and a crying illustration of maternal incompetence, led to their spending weeks at a time in hospital, always to be discharged "recovered," and always to relapse with another complaint, but never led to serious probing of the mother. Even when backwardness was obvious, the exclusion, often recondite, of physical disease left inquiry exhausted; in all five cases in this series where the child was under one hospital while the mother was under another for psychological treatment no communication appears ever to have passed between the two.

. . . It will have become apparent that these children may superficially resemble adults with chronic schizophrenia. However, similar behaviour does not mean identical psychopathology, and merely to label these defectives as psychotic deprives the term of any precise meaning. Generally, psychosis designates disorders where ego functions disintegrate, where the person ceases to be himself. These children have no such disorder, and far from presenting disintegration, with two exceptions, they achieved integration at no time at all, their disruption being presumably of primitive infantile processes assembling towards an organized personality. The early distortion of those unintegrated processes that survive may account for the curious behavior which characterises these patients.

Protophrenia seems to me a suitable name for this condition, implying an aborted organization of the personality as distinct from disorganization, to which psychosis refers, and from undistorted retardation accompanying organic cerebral defect, which, by itself, seldom produces autistic behaviour disorder, to judge from the material here.

It is uncertain how protophrenia is related to the syndrome of "early infantile autism." There seem to be differences in that a proportion of the cases here are not autistic and in that only some of Kanner's cases were regarded as mentally defective and none are described as having behaviour disturbances apart from lack of emotional relationship to people and monotonous adherence to some daily routine. The background of his cases was different too, containing an excess of socially and intellectually superior forebears.

Protophrenia can be regarded as a psychogenic failure of ego formation. Its study must be relevant to that of pathological ego formation, generally, where early emotional trauma is at all important. This includes the fragility underlying adult schizophrenia and child psychoses, and the maldevelopment of psychopathic adults and problem children. The present arrangement whereby mental deficiency, child guidance, and adult psychiatry are practised in almost complete isolation from one another can only impede understanding of the common processes basic to each.

As Bourne recognized, the number of cases is small and the study requires replication by others. In such replications it would be recommended that the reliability of clinical judgment concerning organic pathology or no pathology be determined in order to evaluate unwitting bias due to knowledge of case history data. In his study Bourne did both the clinical examinations and analysis of background data. Bourne was aware of this source of contamination of judgment and seemed studiously to try to avoid its effects. But the methodological problem remains and should be squarely met in future studies. We would agree with Bourne that his findings are potentially of great significance and demand further study.

An important question raised by this study may be put as follows: Why is it that some children who have been subjected to the kinds of experiences and relationships which Bourne describes do *not* develop the picture of severe subnormality he calls protophrenia? It probably would not be difficult to find children who have been subjected to even worse experiences and relationships but who do not manifest such an extreme picture. We are here raising the possibility that there is a predisposing factor which selectively determines the degree to which a child will be affected by certain untoward experiences or relationships. We shall return to a consideration of this problem following a discussion of the idiot savant and infantile autism. At this point we wish merely to state that while it has been obvious that there are temperamental and behavioral differences among children from the earliest days of life, and it has been assumed that such variations are important in some way in atypical development, the problem has been little studied.   As we hope to indicate later, however, certain clinical observations reported in the past decade or so allow one to think more specifically about the nature and varieties of predisposing factors.

F. The Idiot Savant and Infantile Autism

Although the idiot savant has been described and discussed many times over the years, it was not until 1945 that a really penetrating and comprehensive review and discussion of the problem appeared.   In that year Scheerer, Rothmann, and Goldstein (235) published their monograph, a work which has not received the attention it merits.   The reader is urged to read this monograph from which we give below the authors' summary statement:

> L, an 11-year-old boy with behavioral peculiarities has been studied over a period of 5 years and a reliable record of his previous development obtained.   L showed distinct musical aptitude—he played melodies on the piano by ear—and was remarkable in verbal retentiveness.   His skill in rapidly manipulating simple numbers was also unusual, and he performed so-called calendar calculations amazingly well.   Numbers he remembered with the same ease as occurrences which to his mind had once become connected with them, so that he volunteered dates, names, places, and times of events at the slightest provocation.
>
> In spite of all this, L's general information was surprisingly subnormal, and, with the exception of the just mentioned aspects of his surrounding, nothing aroused his interest.   He never absorbed or learned in a normal fashion, nor could he attend a regular school.   He was retarded in the mastery of many skills commensurate to his age, and he was lacking in social awareness with a limited repertoire of social responses.   L had an IQ of 50 which classifies him technically an "idiot-savant."
>
> An investigation of L's personality structure was carried out with specially devised experiments, with standard tests and with careful exploration of his spontaneous behavior in everyday life.   An analysis of all data and of the findings in multiform performance fields failed to disclose an individual segmental defect or several specific defects. Instead, his various deficiency symptoms pointed to a functionally common disturbance, a general impairment of abstract capacity (e.g., in the semantic use and ideational understanding of language, of social contents and relations; in reasoning, in the grasp of causation, of logical meaning, of symbols, of conceptual number relations; in the cognitive structuring of visual performances and visuo-motor tasks).   This picture of general abstract impairment was corroborated by the experimental evidence that L succeeded in his own performance-specialties without having a genuine understanding of their meaning as to content and im-

plication. Further exploration of his thinking, learning, and social behavior revealed an abnormal concretization. He could only grasp and learn what made situational or tangibly patterned sense to him. Otherwise, if he retained at all, it was in an automatic, associative manner by habituation.

A positive evaluation of his successful performances, abilities, and skills was attempted. After having experimentally ruled out other alternatives, it was found that L possesses an initial endowment in the acoustic and audio-motor sphere, probably supported by kindred imagery. This endowment expressed itself particularly in his sensory motor receptiveness for melodies, i.e., for acoustic "Gestalten" and for verbal patterns. On this basis his musical performances, his verbal and tonal memory (absolute pitch), and his aptitude for serial grouping became explicable (e.g., his rapid oral counting and spelling, forward and backward, his large digit span and his calendar performance).

Further analysis of his procedure in the utilization of this endowment revealed however, that it did not operate in a normal manner. It was bound to an abnormally rigid concreteness and functioned in a sterile, bizarre, and undiscerning form. Symptomatically, in music he could not develop his talent through study or practice. His performances were desultory, depending on specific circumstances and his interest ranged from obsession with a special phonograph record to appreciative enjoyment of opera arias or Handel's "Largo" on records and indifference to *any* radio music. Correspondingly anomalous function of his talent was manifest in his excessive tendency to count indiscriminately, and to resort to an enumerative verbalization and inane speech clichés whenever he was confronted with a task that overtaxed his power.

We find then that an individual who is handicapped in abstraction and endowed in a particular field of performance shows a *sub*normal intelligence and an *ab*normal canalization of his endowment. In interpreting this personality picture we concluded: owing to his impaired abstract attitude, L cannot realize his remaining potentialities in a normally integrated manner. He is therefore driven in an abnormal degree and direction to exercise those functions which nature permits him to develop, because these are the only performances through which he can actualize himself and come to terms with his surroundings. The least impaired function thus becomes a coping mechanism of adjustment, but, since it can only operate on the level of concrete reactions, it becomes canalized into atypical forms of expression. This result seems to point to an organizational interdependence of basic psychological functions. Certain pertinent implications with regard to normal personality structure and with regard to the problem of idiot savant are discussed and the following generalizations considered:

(1). How an endowment operates and develops, depends upon the organization of the person as a whole.

(2). There exists a functional interrelation between abstract capacity, intelligence, and special endowment.

(a). The abstract capacity is essential for the normal functioning of intelligence. The bearing of this on the association theory of intelligence is followed up.

(b). The abstract capacity is conditional for the normal functioning and development of an endowment, although the latter may be anchored in concrete processes, e.g., of Gestalt type.

(3). The term idiot savant is a misnomer. Idiot savants are talented aments who possess an amented talent.

In order to test these conclusions a comparative study of other reported cases of idiot savant was undertaken and various explanatory hypotheses of other authors were critically examined. The evaluation of this case material seems to confirm our interpretation, since no cases were found in which a talent functioned normally in an individual with abstract impairment. These led to the establishment of certain criteria for the psychological identification of a talented ament.

In studying the reported superior abilities in aments two phenomena invited particular attention because they posed an intriguing psychological problem. These were (a) the relative frequency of number manipulation and retention, and (b) unusual features of memory.

(a). The analysis of the psychological processes involved in these number performances laid bare their origin in concrete perceptual counting procedures with specific limitations. A comparison between this stage of primitive, concrete grouping and the initial procedures in arithmetical prodigies showed basically common characteristics. It became clear, however, that the arithmetical prodigy who developed further towards a cognitive understanding of mathematics outgrew this original stage of concrete dependency in his number operations, because he could increasingly adopt an abstract approach. In contrast the abstract impairment prevented the talented ament from passing beyond the initial stage of concrete grouping procedures.

(b). The striking retention of numbers or of outlandish and irrelevant data, as, e.g., railroad tables or an entire newspaper column, is all the more surprising as in most every instance the retained material is not understood by the ament in a normal way. A psychological appraisal of the changes in figure-ground organization as experienced during pathological concreteness led us to set forth a new explanation of these peculiar memory processes. The observations on the cases studied indicate that a defective organism will cling tenaciously to those aspects of a situation and those features of material which make concrete palpable sense to him, i.e., with which he can deal successfully. These aspects are thrust into the foreground of the phenomenal organization as the "figure." Such a difference in perceptive centering in the abnormal's coming to terms with the world of the "normal" leads to a different centering of performance. Therefore, these aments retain easily what may appear senseless or peripheral or irrelevant to the normal observer. To the aments in question, however, this is the only "sense" possible and pivotal in the experienced contents. This explanatory attempt is tested on diversified case material. Finally, comparing abnormal concreteness in aments with stages of concrete reaction in normal children the following question is raised: Does the atypical memory organization in a subnormal child represent a lawful modification of a normal development phase which has become pathologically "eccentric" and conditioned as a coping mechanism?

It has indeed been a rare event in psychology and psychiatry when clinical problems which have been considered rather different are brought in relation to each other. For this reason we give the following from Scheerer, Rothmann, and Goldstein (235, p. 57):

> Recently Kanner has discussed 11 cases of personality deviation in children in terms of "autistic disturbances of affective contact" which he considers a special syndrome. Pointing to the misplaced eagerness of parents to promote precociousness in their children he states: "Their excellent rote memory, coupled with the inability to use language in any other way, often led the parents to stuff them with more and more verses, zoölogic and botanic names, titles and composers of Victrola record pieces and the like. Thus, from the start, language, which the children did not use for the purpose of communication—was deflected in a considerable measure to a self-sufficient, semantically and conversationally valueless or grossly distorted memory exercise. To a child 2 or 3 years old, all these words, numbers, and poems (questions and answers of the Presbyterian Catechism; Mendelssohn's violin concerto; the twenty-third Psalm, a French lullaby; an encyclopedia index page) could hardly have more meaning than sets of nonsense syllables to adults. It is difficult to know for certain whether the stuffing as such has contributed essentially to the course of the psychopathological condition. But it is also difficult to imagine that it did not cut deeply into the development of language as a tool for receiving and imparting meaningful messages."
>
> Kanner's behavioral observations in these children represent new valuable material for mental pathology. Since his case histories show many parallels to those here presented it may be in order to make some comparisons between his interpretation and our hypothesis on the rôle of concreteness in defective children and their retentivity.
>
> According to Kanner "the outstanding, 'pathognomic,' fundamental disorder is the children's *inability to relate themselves* in the ordinary way to people and situations from the beginning of life." He explains all behavioral abnormalities found in these children from their *affective*

disturbance, from their "desire for aloneness and sameness." To Kanner the inconsistent picture of intellectual ability, the obsessive repetitiousness, the shock reactions to loud noises and moving objects, and the "truly phenomenal memory" in these children is accounted for by their emotional resistance against change in the outer situation—the insistence upon "identical spatial or chronological order." In following Kanner's impressive observations in support of his view, it appears nevertheless as if Kanner has neglected the qualitative nature of the intellectual abnormalities in this picture. The case histories abound with instances of compulsive concreteness in thought and action. In our opinion this is only explicable on the basis of an impairment of abstract attitude which is intimately bound up with the affective disturbance. To mention only a few problems, it is hard to see how an affective disturbance alone can account for what Kanner calls the "literalness" in these children, their inability to use "yes" as a *general* symbol of affirmation, detached from the specific situation in which it had been acquired; their inability to understand prepositions in the abstract sense. (Asked to put something down, the child puts it on the floor—understanding the word only in the originally acquired situational sense.) It is hard to follow Kanner when he makes the affect-anomaly responsible for: "the absence of spontaneous sentence formation and the echolalia type of reproduction, which in every one of the eight speaking children has given rise to a peculiar grammatical phenomenon. *Personal pronouns are repeated just as heard.* The child once told by his mother 'now I will give you your milk' expresses the desire for milk in exactly the same words. Consequently he comes to speak of himself always as you and of the person addressed as I." We have encountered this reversal of pronouns in three cases here presented all of which showed pronounced impairment of abstraction.

This peculiar "grammatical" phenomenon appears to be more than a mere grammatical one or a purely mechanical echolalia. The child hears himself addressed as "you" and the other person speaking of himself as "I." Only on a concrete level of thinking is the literal application of the word "you" to the child himself and "I" to the other person explicable, because the child cannot detach the words from their experienced "belongingness" in the actual situation and reverse this belonging in terms of a relational symbol. (The corresponding phenomenon in normal children is their frequent use of their first name or the third person in referring to themselves.)

Is the child's inability to shift the word "you" from himself to the other person, and the word "I" from the other person, is this inability to grasp the relational meaning of "you" and "I" in the abstract, merely the result of the affective disturbance or is it not a symptom of impaired abstraction and limitation to the concrete as well?

In discussing their peculiar memory Kanner speaks of parrot-like repetitions of heard word combinations, of "delayed echolalia."

As in the case of *L*, "the children had learned at an early age to repeat an inordinate number of nursery rhymes, prayers, lists of animals, the roster of presidents, the alphabet forward and backward, foreign (French) language lullabies . . . even long and unusual words were retained with remarkable facility." Yet in contrast to these recitals, their spontaneous language-development and understanding was retarded. In Kanner's concepts it is the need for "sameness and autistic aloneness" that sufficiently accounts for both, this semantic retardation and for the abnormal retention of verbal material, which latter he characterizes as completely senseless for the children. This makes it quite difficult to understand *why* they so eagerly and readily absorbed and reproduced such material, and even liked to spell out words. Is perhaps the fact that the children did not grasp the meaning of language in the normal way the motive for their heightened responsiveness to and their tenaciously obsessive reproduction of phonetic sound patterns? In the light of our own case-material it seems highly probable that these children excelled precociously in verbal memory for the same reasons as we outlined in our hypothesis. And the question may arise, whether the disturbance in affective human contact they suffered is not secondary to the defect in abstraction or parallel to it. Perhaps this hindered a normal grasp of the semantic aspect of language and impelled these children to cling to that aspect of speech which was concretely sensible and apprehensible for them in terms of auditory motor patterns (235, p. 57).

The similarities between the autistic child and the idiot savant are indeed striking. We feel, however, that there are several questions which seem to pose difficulties for an explanation based primarily, if not exclusively, on an impairment of abstraction.

How is such an explanation to explain (or to be integrated with) the impression, reported by Tredgold (276) and supported by our own review of the literature, that the large majority of idiot savants are males? There also seems to be a preponderance of males among the reported cases of infantile autism.

There appear to be no grounds for doubting that there is an impairment of abstraction in both the idiot savant and the autistic child. When Scheerer, Rothmann, and Goldstein cautiously suggest that in these cases we may be dealing with a lawful modification of a normal development phase which has become pathologically "eccentric and conditioned as a coping mechanism," at least two questions arise. Is the coping mechanism always a response to the impairment of abstraction—that is, is the impairment of abstraction always the *etiological* factor "forcing" the child to develop atypically? Is development normal up until that phase when the organism should be able to respond abstractly? To answer either question in the positive would certainly conflict with the experience of those clinicians who report having discerned the characteristics of autism well before the period when abstraction as an intellectual characteristic normally becomes manifest (174, 213). In other words, factors other than intellectual seem, in some cases at least, to be primary.

To explain the idiot savant and the autistic child primarily in terms of an impairment in abstraction would be more plausible if these were cases with demonstrable central nervous system pathology. In the published literature many, if not the large majority, of these cases have no such discernible pathology. Because these conditions can and do appear in the presence of positive neurological evidence of brain injury does not allow one to assume that where such evidence is lacking it is because of the crudity of neurological procedures. This may be the case but the burden of proof would seem to be on those who make the assumption. Because schizophrenia can follow alterations in the central nervous system does not mean that all schizophrenia can be explained in this way.

Perhaps our most serious reservation to Scheerer, Rothmann, and Goldstein's discussion of the idiot savant and the autistic child concerns their failure to consider the possible ways in which familial personalities and organization either interact with or cause or exacerbate the impairment of abstraction. For example, Kanner, who has reported the largest series of cases of infantile autism, comes to the conclusion that the personality of the parents and their techniques of child rearing are not irrelevant factors in attempting to understand the autistic child. It may be that Kanner's sample is in some ways a biased one but until this is demonstrated one cannot dismiss the possibility that factors external to the autistic child are important in the development of the condition. In this connection it might be pointed out that in the case of the idiot savant which Scheerer, Rothmann, and Goldstein describe there is practically no discussion of the possible rôle of parental personality on the child. We point this out because of our impression that what little is contained in the monograph on parental personality and behavior suggests similarities to Kanner's descriptions of the parents of his cases. Unfortunately (but not unexpectedly) in the entire literature of the idiot savant there is not a single acceptable personality description of the parents. We are here not contending that parental personality and behavior is the etiological factor—for reasons to be discussed later we feel such a statement to be unjustified on theoretical grounds. However, for similar reasons, we are contending that any explanation of behavior which is based exclusively on factors "inside" the individual is likely to be a very incomplete one.[31]

If one were to assume that the kinds of cases we have been discussing were in some way primarily a function of non-environmental factors (e.g., brain-injury, genetic, constitutional, etc.) then one would expect that they would occur in any culture, e.g., the so-called primitive ones. There is no evidence that this is the case. However, since anthropologists have not been interested in these types of problems, and are not trained to pick them out, the absence of evidence in this instance means little or nothing. We would suggest that cross-cultural studies of infantile autism and idiot savants might be fruitful regardless of the direction of the evidence which would emerge.

In summary, Scheerer, Rothmann, and Goldstein have made an important contribution in pointing out and discussing the similarities between the autistic child and the idiot savant. There is little doubt that in both these conditions there is an impairment of abstraction. In raising questions about the adequacy of such an impairment for explaining these conditions, we have tried to suggest that such an explanation does not seem to cover what apparently are certain facts—particularly the sex difference in the incidence of the two conditions. In addition, we expressed the opinion that discovery of those factors which antedate and are related to the impairment of abstraction may be of vast importance for our understanding of the early development of intellectual functions—their nature, course, and relation to the external environment. The importance of these cases to the development of a science of psychology would seem to be vastly beyond what their relatively rare occurrence in the general population would suggest.

We hope it is clear from the previous discussion that we are dealing with conditions the etiology of which is very ambiguous. These cases are certainly not homogeneous in terms of presence and degree of organic pathology. It is also impossible to do other than grossly speculate about the possible rôle of environmental factors. It seems fair to say, then, that neither in the case

---

[31]In their discussion of very young autistic children, Ritvo and Provence (213) state: "We do not in our thinking neglect the part the mother's attitude plays in this condition. We believe that the child's disturbance sets in motion a circular process with child affecting mother and mother in turn affecting child. We would like to conclude with a remark made by the mother of one of these children when told of her child's need for continued stimulation from her: 'Why should I pick him up when he doesn't even smile at me?'"

of infantile autism nor in the idiot savant can one justifiably ascribe the con-dition to either environmental or organic pathological factors. It would indeed be surprising if the ultimate explanation required knowledge of but one of these factors—the conditions seem far too complex to hold out hope for such simple explanations.

There is one variable, however, which seems not to have been given the attention in theory and research which it seems to deserve. We might begin our discussion of this variable by posing a question we raised earlier in relation to Bourne's "protophenia" (see page 337) : Why is it that some children who have been subjected to the kinds of experiences and relationships which Bourne describes do *not* develop the picture of severe subnormality he calls protophrenia? It probably would not be difficult to find children who have been subjected to even worse experiences and relationships but who do not manifest such an extreme picture. Assuming that there is a relationship in Bourne's cases between certain environmental factors and extreme deficiency, we are unable to explain why more children do not develop this condition. We are faced with the same question of selectivity of occurrence with the idiot savant and infantile autism, regardless of whether one assigns primary importance to organic or environmental factors.

While we would agree that the organic and environmental factors have to be viewed in relation to each other, the variable we have in mind is perhaps independent of both, at least in the earliest months of life. We are here referring to something akin to what Bergman and Escalona (19) have called "unusual sensitivities in very young children":

> It was several years ago that the authors were first struck by the observations to be reported here. Some very young children possessed unusual sensitivities manifesting themselves in several, if not in all, sensory modalities (visual, auditory, tactile, etc.). Colors, bright lights, noises, unusual sounds, qualities of material, experiences of equilibrium, of taste, of smell, of temperature, seemed to have an extraordinarily intensive impact upon these children at a very early age. They were "sensitive" in both meanings of the word: easily hurt, and easily stimulated to enjoyment. Variations in sensory impression that made no difference to the average child made a great deal of difference to these children. They were also characterized by a certain precocity, though this was very unevenly distributed among the diverse functions of their personality. The first impression which some of their reactions and abilities gave was that of unusual giftedness such as might be observed in the budding of a genius. Further observation, however, suggested comparison with individuals suffering from a traumatic neurosis,

or a psychosis, and even with feebleminded children. Closer study and follow-up then made it appear that childhood psychosis was the fate of these children, though we are not sure yet that all children of the type to be described eventually develop a clear psychotic picture. . . .

If we examine more closely those facts that impressed us as bespeaking unusual sensitivity in the described children, we become aware that they differ from each other in several respects, and can be grouped accordingly. We find that we have observed facts pertaining to many parts of the sensorium, i.e., to visual, to auditive, to tactile, to olfactory, to gustatory, to equilibrium, and to temperature experiences. Some of the children reported on reacted very sensitively to light or colors, to noises and music, to materials that came in contact with their skin, to smells and perfumes, to foods, to rocking and swinging, to cold air or cool objects. Thus, one obvious principle of grouping our observations is furnished by the sensory modality.

Then we find that what impressed us in some observations was the reaction to the intensity or quantity of stimulation, while in other cases the observation is more easily understood as a reaction to quality. Thus if any kind of slight sound seems to awaken a sleeping infant, or arouses a reaction from the waking one, we will consider that he reacts to the intensity of the stimulation, in fact here to a very low intensity. But if certain sounds or combinations of sounds attract a child, while other sounds or combinations of sounds of equal loudness repel him, it seems plausible to consider this a reaction to quality. Other reactions to quantity that we find in our material are, e.g., reactions to light of a certain brightness, reactions to normally imperceptible (or at least not usually reacted to) amounts of odor, reactions to slight disturbances of the equilibrium, to slight impressions on the feeling of temperature. On the other hand, observations pertaining to certain colors, certain materials, specific odors, foods, we can group with reactions to quality. Whether a special fondness of rocking should be grouped with reactions to quality or to quantity may be debatable. With some sensory modalities this distinction does not seem to make much sense. We would not be able to say, e.g., what a reaction to quality would be like in the modality of the sense of temperature.

Bergman and Escalona go on to point out that unusual sensitivities in young children may result in premature defensive reactions which are inadequate in the face of later trauma. "The hypothesis will be offered that the infant who is not sufficiently protected from stimuli either because of a 'thin protective barrier,' or because of the failure of maternal protection, may have to resort for such protection to premature formation of an ego. When this premature ego breaks down, possibly as a consequence of a trauma, the psychotic manifestations are thought to set in."

Bergman and Escalona's clinical observations and conclusions allow one to raise several questions: (a) To what extent do autistic children have a history of unusual sensitivities?—a question which Bergman and Escalona raise but which existing studies cannot answer; (b) To what extent would the histories of idiot savants indicate unusual sensitivities preceding the appearance of unusual intellectual behavior?; (c) To what extent do the children described by Bourne have unusual sensitivities? *Perhaps of more significance than these questions is the assumption that the crucial factor in these types of atypical development is the interaction between unusual sensitivities, on the one hand, and environmental factors, on the other hand.* Whether the infant with unusual sensitivities develops atypically may be a function either of parental handling of these sensitivities or fortuitous organic conditions or some combination of both.[32]   In other words, not all children with unusual sensitivities would be expected to develop atypically. Similarly, objectively similar environments or organic pathologies would have differing effects on individuals who differed in terms of the unusual sensitivities described by Bergman and Escalona.   For example, the "protophrenics" described by Bourne may be those who had unusual sensitivities, while other children with similar or worse experiences and relationships but who did not show such extreme subnormality may not have had such sensitivities.

It is reasonable to assume that sensory hyperreactivity is but one of several ways in which the young child may be unusual.   Put in another way: the very young child can be viewed in terms of various behavioral continua, and extreme placement on any of these continua, as in the case of unusual sensitivities, may be the predisposing factor which when interacting with environmental or organic factors has untoward effects.   The work of Fries (74, 75, 76, 175) on "congenital activity types" supports the contention that the study of temperamental variations in the very young child may pro-

---

[32]The occurrence in the same child of an unusual sensitivity and an organic pathology does not, of course, mean that the two are causally related, although this may be the case in certain instances. The presence of an unrelated organic pathology may make it more difficult for the child (and parent) to cope with the sensitivity. For example, Frankl (72) described a case of severe autism in a child with tuberous sclerosis. Although most cases of tuberous sclerosis are severely defective, there are some whose intellectual functioning is less, or not at all, affected by the condition (277, p. 278).   In any event, extreme autism is not a marked behavioral characteristic of these cases. The extreme picture of autism which Frankl describes need not be related, in its initial phases at least, to the central nervous system pathology. It is conceivable that their origins are independent but that the central nervous system pathology exacerbates the autistic tendencies.

vide at the least a partial answer to the question why different children are differentially affected by similar external events or similar organic conditions. This is clearly not a problem of peculiar significance to the area of atypical development but one which is truly basic to our understanding of normal development, the nature and range of the earliest individual differences in relation to rearing and educational techniques.

G. LIGHTNER WITMER

If only for historical reasons we feel compelled to say something of Witmer's work. Psychologists, psychiatrists, and educators of today may know of Witmer's name in connection with the fact that he organized the first psychological clinic in this country in 1896 at the University of Pennsylvania. What has been forgotten, unfortunately, is that in the early years of this century he was concerned with and wrote most illuminatingly about the differential diagnosis between mental deficiency and childhood psychosis. Years before the autistic and schizophrenic young child was described and recognized by American psychiatrists, Witmer published his "orthogenic" case reports in which the major characteristics of this type of child were delineated. To be sure, Witmer's descriptions are not as sophisticated or complete as those of today, but the serious reader who studies Witmer's writing will probably agree that he must be considered one of the real pioneers of American child psychiatry.[33]

Aside from his awareness of the importance of differentiating between mental defect and childhood psychosis, the significance of Witmer's work lies in his therapeutic approach to and success with these instances of differential diagnosis. We give below excerpts from one of his reports (296):

> At the age of two years and seven months this boy responded to every test like a feebleminded child and he was diagnosed by competent experts as feebleminded. Today he is a normal boy, not quite seven years old, reading, writing, and doing the number work of the second school year. Either he was not feebleminded and the diagnosis was a mistaken one, or feeblemindedness can be cured. What is feeblemindedness—a performance level or an irremediable mental defect? Don's response to treatment shows that he had grave but not irremediable de-

---

[33]In 1907 Witmer started the journal called *Psychological Clinic*. It is no longer in existence. Some of his case reports (292, 293, 294, 295, 296, 297) are more concerned with subnormality than others. Throughout the journal will be found similar cases by his students. As would be expected, there is much in the journal which is now outmoded, but the serious student of the problem will gain much by scrutiny of all the volumes.

fects. His arrest of development was nearly complete, the results of disease and the psychosis which accompanied the disease.

When a normal adult becomes insane we observe a marked change of character. "He is no longer himself," we say, and a prominent symptom is a reduction of mental level called technically "dementia." Autointoxication, disease and shock may cause insanity. Let us suppose that one or all of these causes affect a child in his first or second year. We shall not be able to observe much change in the child's mentality except that his mental development will be arrested. I maintain that one type of feeblemindedness, better called arrested development, is due to the same causes which produce insanity in an adult, and that in some cases the psychosis or mental disorder can be cured and the child restored to completely normal condition, provided the case be taken in hand early enough.

Except to the very observant eye of an experienced expert, these cases look more like feeblemindedness than insanity. Nevertheless, they are a species of feeblemindedness or insanity, whichever name we choose to apply, very different from the congenital imbecile, one of the mongolian type, for example. The mental disorders of children which cause arrest of development and apparent feeblemindedness are as diverse as the mental disorders observed and classified by the alienists. A child may be either feebleminded or insane, or he may be both feebleminded and insane. Some of the Orthogenic Cases reported in the earlier numbers of the PSYCHOLOGICAL CLINIC, notably Orthogenic cases Nos. 4, 6, 12, and 13, are not primarily cases of congenital defect, but cases of mental disorder in which there is a greater presumption of possible cure than in the cases of the child who is both qualitatively and quantitatively feebleminded.

. . . He was five years old last July, and so I entered him the following autumn in a near-by school, where he is the youngest of a group of first-grade children. His teacher says that he reads better than any of them and, except that he is poor in handwork, she considers him as competent as the other children.

"Terence," said he to his pal, the gardener, who was taking him to school the first day, "don't call me Donnie when we get near the school; don't call me Donnie or Don; call me Donald, which is right."

I saw Donald for the first time when he was two years and seven months old. His father carried him into my office, and deposited him, a soulless image, absorbed in the inspection of a card which he held in his pudgy hands, as regardless of his father and mother as of the new objects about him. While his gaze moved over the card, he scratched the back of his teeth; and then again he made a crooning, humming sound with which it is his habit to lull himself to sleep.

He paid no attention to a rattle, to a bright-colored ball or to a picture book which I held before him, but every effort to remove the card from his hands he resisted. His face, already crimson, became empurpled. His physiognomy took on an expression of angry hostility; and I retreated before the approaching storm, leaving him again to his absorption in the card.

"He is fond of music," his mother said; but the liveliest strains of the talking machine were powerless to distract him from his chosen preoccupation. In the months to come I was to discover that by prefererence he would sit or lie in bed for hours, looking attentively at the object which he happened to be holding in his hands. It appeared to be persistent, concentrated attention, that most difficult and valuable of mental powers to cultivate.

From two to six years the child has the flitting attention of a monkey. "How do you select your monkeys for training?" a trainer of animals was once asked.

"I hold a lighted match before them," he replied, "and picking out as the easiest to train those that look longest at the burning match."

Donald would look at nothing but his card. One could not guess what lay behind those dull blue eyes. Was it interest, or only emptiness of mind—the dreamy listlessness with which the corner loafer looks at the passing world?

"What are those abrasions about the mouth and ears?" I asked.

"When he gets angry," his mother said, "he will scratch and tear at them."

"What else can he do?" I asked, not venturing to break in upon this obstinate immobility by trying to get him to perform the simple task which might, perchance, reveal some hidden mental ability.

"Can he walk?"

"A little, but he only began about two months ago," she replied. "Until he was over two years old he hadn't even crawled; and he only learned to crawl by his nurse taking hold of his knees and advancing them one after the other."

As the flower blooms, the fish swims or the bird flies, so the child crawls, walks and talks. It is the unfolding of his own instinctive impulses. But this child had to be taught to crawl and to walk, and even yet he could only toddle about uncertainly. If he fell upon his face he would lie helplessly crying with his nose to the floor. Either he did not have the strength to change his position, or he did not know how, or he was unwilling to make the effort.

He never uttered a word spontaneously, and he could repeat at command only a few words like "Kitty," "Mama"—eight words in all. His understanding of language seemed to be limited to pointing to his head, eyes, ears and nose when these words were spoken. Even a chimpanzee of the same age as this boy, if brought up in human surroundings, will give evidence of understanding more of spoken language than this boy did. He could not feed himself. A much younger child can hold a cup or a spoon, but this boy could not even close his lips upon a cup when it was offered to him. He was still in diapers, and weeks were to pass before he could be safely clothed like the normal boy of two years and a half.

At two years and seven months Donald was doing no more than many a child does at twelve months, no more than every child should do at fifteen months. No one who saw him needed to consult an expert before deciding that he was subnormal. You had only to look at the large head—"top-heavy Bill" one of his teachers called him—the fat red face, the expressionless eyes and the helpless body to arrive instantly at the conviction that "this child is feebleminded."

And feebleminded I thought him—of such low grade that I refused at first to accept him for educational treatment in my school. With reluctance I finally yielded to the parents' pleas. He was the youngest child I had ever accepted for psychological treatment, and apparently the most hopeless.

The expert, like the parent, bases his opinion on the child's appearance, behavior and history. But even more important than these is the *"attempt to teach."* In doubtful cases I do not like to express an opinion until after I have observed the results of attempting to teach the child something new. This can often be done at the first examination, but I could not even begin to teach Donald.

"I should like to see him walk," I said. But when he was lifted from the couch, put upon his feet and made to walk, he burst into a paroxysm of rage. His eyes became bloodshot; even his gums bled. When he was put back upon the couch he returned to his contemplative absorption in the card. Offered a block, he made no effort to take it. He even closed his eyes, as though the very sight of it and me were more than he could endure.

When I took the card away, so as to secure his undivided attention, he had another paroxysm of rage. From this, however, I derived a little hope, for passion and rage may be an expression of strength. The child at least had energy at his disposal. His violent resistance evidenced resolute determination. Obstinate children are better material for training than the overpliant sort. I looked at him, sitting impassive, but always bolt upright, and this too, I thought an encouraging sign.

"He is a very easy child to neglect," one of my teachers entered in her report soon after he came to the school. "If you let him alone he will sit or lie in bed for hours and give no trouble. It is only when you try to do something with him, to dress him, or bathe him, even at times to feed him, that the trouble begins."

It takes some time and care to adjust a child to new surroundings, so I considered it no great misfortune that Donnie promptly got the measles. For a couple of weeks it was necessary to isolate him in the care of a trained nurse. This probably helped to make him less resistant to strangers. Perhaps there also awoke within his soul some responsive feeling of gratification when the soothing hand of the nurse or the doctor brought him relief from his distress of body. One month after Donnie's arrival I began his education.

"What to do," and "How to do it" are two puzzling questions confronting teacher and parent at every turn. To answer the first question is to present the aims of education. In the early years of education the three R's are the chief objective. The answer to the second question, "How to do it," will determine our method of procedure.

Educational aims and practice are commonly the outcome of theory. For example, an interesting and important theory of recent origin is the Montessori method. It aims to develop a child's natural abilities. It also has a theory of educational practice. It emphasizes and, in the opinion of many, relies exclusively upon appealing to the child's natural inclinations and desires. Deprecating the use of constraint and force, it throws the reins over the neck of the horse. Several children have been brought to me for examination and educational treatment who were nearly ruined by too close adherence to this supposed Montessori method.

I hold that constraint and liberty have equal value. At one time constraint, at another liberty, will bring the best results. The wise employment of constraint and force calls for greater intelligence and judgment on the part of teacher and parent than the leaving of the child free to work out his own salvation and development.

I try to approach the problem of educating a child like Donald without any preferred theory. More than twenty years of experience has led me to see that there is some good in most theories. A few are fit only for the scrap heap. One guiding principle, however, has stood the test of time and use: "The first task of teacher and parent is to gain and hold the child's attention by giving him something he *can* do, and after that something he *can't* do"—this in general is my method.

My educational aim is to develop attention by choosing tasks which develop it. Whether a child be one year of age, or two years, or six, whether he be in high school or college, the guiding principle of the educator should be to gain and hold attention first, and then to cultivate concentration, alertness, persistence, and endurance, all of these being attributes of attention.

For the rest, I feel my way. I watch the child to discover what he does with interest and with ease, and from here I get him to take a step forward in the direction best calculated to bring him to what I am aiming at, "the next higher level of attention." Montessori provides the child with stimulating objects—her didactic material—and leaves it with the child to make the next step forward. This is doubtless an acceptable procedure; but suppose the child refuses to take a step in any direction. He must be shoved.

To shove a child in the direction you want him to go is easy if the child is pliant and submissive. If he is a fighter like Donnie, and if, like him, he has no desires except to be let alone, the development of attention and the enforcement of obedience must go hand in hand.

When you have a trout on a hook at the end of a thin line, the only way to land him is to play him. He is lively and vigorous. He has desires which conflict with yours. If you use too much force you will break the line. If you use skill, yielding and yet constraining, you will in time get him into your basket. In this way the skillful teacher "plays" the child. The hook of attention is attached to the line of obedience, and then she watches the child's every move to insure his advance in the required direction. Shall she coax or force him? On the lee short of this question many a gallant education craft lies shipwrecked.

You can coax most children, some of the time at least, by appealing to their interests and desires, even as the hunter entices the deer to come within gunshot by appealing to its curiosity. But some children can't be coaxed, any more than you can wheedle a trout into your basket.

For example, take Donald. He did not have a keen desire even for food. He would not eat prunes, apparently because he disliked their appearance, and so they had to be mixed with his cereal in order to get him to eat them. He would not drink milk or water from a transparent glass. It must be offered to him in a cup. In the early days, indeed, he declined to drink water at all, and got his only liquid in the shape of milk or soup.

He declined to accept a sugarplum offered as a reward of merit; and if you took away the object he so fondly clasped in his hands, and then yielded to his ragings and returned it to him, he would very likely throw it violently across the room. He disliked to be dressed. He disliked to be taken out of bed and put on the floor. He disliked to be taken for a walk.

All these things aroused angry resistance; and in his passion he went so far as to do himself bodily injury; but as long as Donald held something in his hand there was peace and quiet.

"What to do with him?" He could not be bathed and dressed in this happy state of calm contemplation. Take away what he held and his hands went up to his ears and mouth, tearing at them till they bled. Tell him to keep his hands down, they went up just the same; perhaps he only scratched himself a little more strenuously. Put mittens on him, as his former nurse did, and he still went through the motions.

Smack his hands, anger and passion intensified the violence of his resistance. The only thing to do was to hold his hands. Could he be compelled to keep them down after they were released? The historic battle lasted for an hour and a half. His hands were held while his teacher spoke to him from time to time: "If I let your hands go, will you keep them down?"

He raged, he stormed, he grew apoplectic, but the hands were firmly held. At every lull in the storm they were released, and up they went again. In the end he gave in. Ninety minutes showed remarkable endurance, determination and consistency of purpose, qualities which might be successfully employed in his educational development later.

Never again did Donnie hold out for so long on this or any other issue. My records show that though he raged at intervals during the ensuing twelve months, the longest period of resistance lasted for ten minutes only. He had learned his lesson. There was an inevitable persistence that would outlast his own. He might as well give in first as last.

The subsequent development of this boy under Witmer's supervision was both dramatic and heartening. That Witmer was an astute observer who did not allow dramatic change in the patient to cause him to overlook problems and weaknesses may be gleaned from Witmer's concluding remarks:

If I began my work without a theory and without understanding Donnie's mental status, I am far from that position now. I have unraveled much of the mystery, and I find the understanding of this one child of important value in interpreting the behavior and progress of other normal children. I believe that Donnie was at the start dominated by fear, which plays still an important rôle in his behavior. His concentration on the card was in the nature of a defensive reaction. He disliked to get out of bed because he was afraid to get out of bed. He disliked to walk and talk because he was afraid—perhaps of failure.

It was noted on one occasion that when taken outdoors he would not stop screaming even after he had been put on the back of a pony. I know now that this was the worst thing that could have been done to him. Donnie is afraid of all animals. He takes kindly, however, to little creatures and has often alarmed his teachers by bringing them caterpillars and worms.

One day Donnie, while seated at a table playing with a train of cars, had his attention called to the fact that a little gray kitten was in the room. He was mortally afraid of it, so he would not turn his head to look, but kept moving the train back and forth, saying, "Ppff! Puff!" in the same absorbed concentration which was characteristic of him at the beginning. He was ignoring the kitten just as he used to ignore people he disliked by closing his eyes when they came into the room.

He was afraid to look down a well, he was afraid of a doll, of a soft rubber ball, of a balloon, a loaf of bread, a spinning top. He was afraid to go on a sailboat the first time, but the second time he went with joy. He took a fearful pleasure in trains, for he loved them as moving things, and yet they terrified him. He would say: "Let us go to town in the three trolleys"; but when you asked him why he would rather go in the trolleys than in a train he would never tell you.

He has never verbally admitted that he is afraid of anything. "Won't hurt you," he very early exclaimed whenever he was frightened by anything; and this was one of his first spontaneous reflections. "Don't have to pat the pony," he would reiterate during the many weeks required to get him to overcome his fear of the school pet. The effort to take him out driving in a little pony cart, which it was thought would entertain him, only succeeded after a period of two months. But then, as was usual with him, he couldn't get enough of driving behind the pony.

Even yet he is afraid. "I like dogs," he declared lately, as he started on his way to school. "Nice kind dogs which don't bite," he added thoughtfully. Nevertheless, he managed unobtrusively to place his companion between himself and every dog. "I like to pat dogs," he boasted; but when one appeared unexpectedly he excused himself tactfully: "I don't like them that color."

So, while Donnie is fearful, he is not a coward. He is doing his best to overcome his fears, and he has worked out his own method of doing this. He had no fear of dark or of the supernatural.

Fears and desires are the two greatest motive forces of mankind. No problem is more perplexing and none so absolutely fundamental as the proper treatment of fears and desires so that these motive forces may excite the actions desired. As I understand Donnie now, he had no desires, but many fears. We compelled him to do those things which he feared. As soon as he had done the fearful thing, the fear, in many instances, disappeared and desire took its place. Donnie is now afraid chiefly of what surprises him.

Donnie's obstinacy measured the intensity of his fear, but in part it measured also the intensity of his desires. Always, from the very beginning, Donnie has known just what he wanted. Never was there any wobbly uncertainty of choice. He either desired it or he didn't desire it. This, to my mind, is a strong and valuable trait of character if you can turn it to the right use.

The desire for possession gives rise perhaps to his keenest pleasure. He held on to his card, not only because it enabled him to ignore the fearful things of the world about him, but he held on to it because here was something "all his own." Not until recently has he been willing to share any of his possessions with others. For a long time he not only clung passionately to his own possessions, but appropriated the playthings of all the other children as well, so much so that his room was known as the "Robber's Den." He is now so far advanced on the road to generosity that he will give away his second-best toy.

He has always shown the same concentration of attention which he showed at the beginning. One day recently he wore to school a necktie which he had borrowed from the gardener, Terence. The teacher could do nothing with him that day because he persistently explored the attributes of his new possession. He met Terence, who came to take him home, with the matured fruit of his morning's work: "Terry, can you see the top of *your* necktie?"

His first craze was for automobiles, and then for sailboats, bicycles, trains and cars—anything that moved. As he learned to talk, he went through the magazines. "It's an automobile, see the automobile," he kept reiterating. When he grew fond of excursions abroad, "Are we going out, Agnes?" he would say, "Agnes, are we going out?" a thousand times until he threatened to drive his nurse to distraction. No child can have a better endowment for future accomplishment later than this power of persistent concentration.

Donnie's traits of character are therefore positive traits. He has a definite array of abilities, keen desires, self-dependence. Even from the first he preferred to walk alone, though in constant fear of falling, rather than hold someone's hand. He only sought the hand if a terrifying object came in view. With strong desires and fears, strong likes and dislikes, Donnie has an equal capacity for happiness and great unhappiness, for success and failure. He can be sweet-tempered or angry and resentful. His emotional balance is easily disturbed, and he still requires very careful handling.

Of the cause of Donnie's mental condition when he came to us, and which led several experts to diagnose him as feebleminded, I cannot be sure. He had an illness after birth, which I now believe left his brain so devitalized that it permitted fear to gain the upper hand over desire. Of one thing I am certain: If Donnie had not been given the painstaking and expert training to which we subjected him he would by now have fallen into a state of irremediable feeblemindedness.

Although today the term psychotherapy refers to a variety of techniques and interpersonal relationships, it is most likely that no "school of psychotherapy" would advocate Witmer's initial handling of this boy. It would be quite wrong, obviously, to view his initial approach as a punitive one (although from the standpoint of the boy this was the case) in the sense that it reflected Witmer's feelings and did not stem from any theoretical conceptions. By focussing on the boy's inability or unwillingness to respond to an external figure, Witmer was deliberately attacking in a direct and dramatic manner the most blatant symptom, i.e., the autistic-like way of relating to the external world. Equally important, we think, is that this child was placed in what was essentially a therapeutic-educational milieu in which all phases of his behavior were under scrutiny, supervision, and stimulation. One gets the impression of a total push situation which went far beyond what today takes place in individual psychotherapy with these kinds of cases (on those relatively rare occasions when such treatment is attempted). The fact that the above case is but one among many reported by Witmer and his students would seem to have implications for current attitudes toward the treatment (or, more frequently, the non-treatment) of the very young, withdrawn, autistic-like, and defective-like child.

There are two things which impress one in Witmer's work. First, Witmer seemed to employ therapeutic effort as a way of deciding between one or another diagnostic possibility—most frequently between normal or defective potential. Second, the fact that the child with whom he was working was subnormal, and in some cases apparently severely defective, did not seem to influence the intensity of Witmer's therapeutic efforts. One gets the impression from his writings that Witmer, like Itard, was not discouraged by outward appearances and was possessed by a fierce determination to demonstrate that in the most hopeless case there was unrealized potential which could be made manifest under proper guidance. Such an attitude may be a mixed blessing and result in failure and harm to others. But when in the case of people like Itard and Witmer such an attitude is combined with brilliance and creativity—and a remarkably painstaking attention to detail and method—one gets the kinds of results that shed real light on human potentialities. Research reports like the present one are far less needed in the area of subnormal functioning than people like Itard and Witmer. Freud did not need somebody else's research report to make his now recognized contributions to psychology and psychiatry and, in their own fields of interest, neither did Itard and Witmer.

XVIII. THE HIGHER GRADES OF MENTAL DEFECT

Most psychological research in subnormal functioning has utilized the so-called high grade cases of mental defect. This research has tended to be of two kinds: (*a*) that which has been concerned with a particular type of mental defect (e.g., cerebral palsy, minimal brain injury), and (*b*) that which has been concerned with a particular procedure (e.g., psychotherapy) or personality characteristic (e.g., rigidity). In this chapter we shall be discussing both kinds of research; our choice being determined by the amount of previous research done on a problem as well as our opinion about the potential significance of the particular problem.

A. CEREBRAL PALSY[34]

In 1949 one of the writers (225, p. 186) stated:

> In reviewing the psychological work which has been done with the cerebral palsied, one is struck by the paucity of studies. Aside from the pioneer efforts of Lord and Doll, the psychological problems, practical and theoretical, presented by the cerebral palsied have not been attacked. What studies have been made indicate that while psychological procedures are an indispensable part of the diagnostic armamentarium, there are wide gaps in knowledge concerning the intellectual and emotional growth of the cerebral palsied child; especially with the very young child is there need for refined procedures which will make early diagnosis valid and reliable. There has not been a single study in which a sizable group of cerebral palsied children has been followed from infancy to maturity. If such a study should be done, the factors making for individual variations in rate of development would probably become clearer. In setting up such a study it would be necessary for the psychologist to focus some attention on parent-child relationships. In the past the presence of the severe motor defect has obscured the fact that the cerebral palsied child is being responded to and stimulated by people whose behavior in turn is affected by the severely handicapped child. Although many cerebral palsied children are severely limited in exploratory and locomotor activity, it seems reasonable to assume that parental behavior may either accentuate or lessen the deleterious effect of such restrictions. Case studies by Thorne and Gesell demonstrate that parental attitudes toward and the handling of the cerebral palsied child can be important factors in intellectual growth. It must

---

[34]Many cerebral palsied cases are characterized by a severe degree of mental deficiency. We have put our discussion at this point in the report because there has been some psychological interest in the high grade cerebral palsied child whereas little or none has been shown in the severe cases. The present discussion is relevant, we think, for most cases of cerebral palsy regardless of level.

be concluded that the nature of the growth of intellectual behavior in
the presence of a severe motor handicap existing from birth remains a
fertile area for research. Until the relation between capacity and functioning is better understood, the clinician must be cautious in interpreting
the significance of test findings.

In 1955 Cruickshank (50) presented a survey of the literature on the
psychological aspects of physically handicapped children and many of the
studies he discussed concerned cerebral palsied children. It is our impression from his review that, while a little progress has been made in understanding some aspects of the functioning of these children, particularly in
the perceptual area, there still has been little or nothing done along the lines
of a *longitudinal* study of such children. There are several reasons for our
emphasis on the longitudinal type of study:

1. It is our experience that when one groups cerebral palsied children
on the basis of degree of physical or motor impairment, there is wide variation within any one group in personality organization and intellectual level
and efficiency. Variation in these respects still obtains when one compares
mildly with severely handicapped cerebral palsied children. It is by no
means rare to see a quadraplegic whose functioning is discernibly better than
many hemiplegics. It is our clinical impression that *one* source of such
variation is parental reaction to and handling of such children. This is
probably not a very revealing statement and by it we mean nothing more
than that we have been impressed by how certain parents seem to have been
able to respond to their child as if his physical handicaps were merely an
obstacle which they had to help the child circumvent to whatever degree was
possible. It is as if they were truly able to conceive of the child as a unique
and developing individual. This is in marked contrast to many parents who
seem fixated on the child's physical handicap and their own frustrations and
disappointments. It goes without saying that parents *should* be expected to
respond to the birth of such a child with feelings of frustration and disap-
pointment, but many parents are unable to overcome these feelings to the
point where they can gain satisfaction from their interaction with the child.

2. In the early study conducted at Vineland by Doll, Phelps, and Melcher (63), they noted a tendency in some of their subjects for test scores to
increase over a longer period of time than is characteristic of an institutionalized, mentally defective population. In commenting on this finding
one of the present writers stated (225, p. 176):

One of the most interesting findings in this study concerns the concept of delayed development. If the validity of this finding should be confirmed in studies with larger numbers of cases, it would mean that the clinician working with the younger cerebral palsied would have to exercise caution in predicting the course of a patient's intellectual development. From a theoretical standpoint it would be of significance to determine why some cases show this delayed development and others do not. The unpredictable relation between the focus of the brain lesion and the intellectual level indicates that anatomical factors may not be sufficient to explain the differences in the rate of intellectual growth. When one considers the possible effects of the presence of a cerebral palsied child on family structure and relationships, the influence of these factors cannot be disregarded. Not all parents react to the cerebral palsied child in an accepting, warm, consistently affectionate manner. The effects of such a child on the emotional stability of the parents are considerable, as Lord noted in her study. It seems reasonable to assume that parents of the cerebral palsied child react more realistically and less emotionally to his limitations and deformities when he is older than when he is younger. The number of parents who never "accept" their child is probably considerable. It is interesting to note that the children displaying delayed development in the Doll, Phelps, and Melcher study showed this growth after they had been admitted to the Vineland Training School. Although preadmission test data were not available, one might speculate about possible differences in the handling of the child at home and at Vineland and their differential effects on rate of development. The very high standard of care and individualized training for which Vineland is noted may well have been a factor in the delayed development of some of these children.

In light of the absence of longitudinal studies we do not feel justified in speculating further on the rôle of psychological factors on the intellectual development and personality organization of the cerebral palsied child. We are of the strong opinion that until these children are studied longitudinally— with the degree of attention to familial factors which psychological theory indicates—our understanding of these children will not be enhanced and our handling of them will not change in any fundamental respect. When it is remembered that we are dealing with individuals who vary markedly in degree of physical handicap, that these variations are psychologically effective or limiting at different phases in development, that methods of rearing and external stimulation must take such variations into account, and that the parents must understand the significance of all these factors and be able to respond to the psychological needs of the child—when the problem is stated in this way one soon becomes aware of how little we know, how inadequate our advice to parents must be, and the pressing need of research in this area. In our opinion, the need for this type of research is further emphasized by recent studies (50, p. 319) which, in contrast to earlier ones, indicate that the bulk of cerebral palsied children are either mentally retarded or defective—at least insofar as test scores are concerned. It is highly improbable that research confined only to the site of lesion and degree of motor involvement or physical handicap are sufficient to explain either such over-all findings or the individual differences in functioning which are always found.

Mention should be made here of some ongoing but unpublished research being carried out with cerebral palsied and other groups under the direction of Kirk at the University of Illinois. Starting with Osgood's (199) theoretical analysis of the language process, Kirk and McCarthy (155) and Sievers (243) developed tests with the aim of determining as specifically as possible where in the complicated communication process an individual's difficulty could be pinpointed. If this difficulty could be pinpointed there would then be the possibility of being able to develop more adequate training or remedial procedures than is now the case. The following is an illustrative case:

> John was referred for a diagnosis because of delayed speech development. He was diagnosed at several medical clinics with contradictory results. Neurological and *EEG* examinations were essentially negative. Due to poor motor coördination, delayed speech and behavior, it was suspected that he was brain-damaged.
>
> John did not speak in words and sentences until the age of four. Individual speech correction was tried at this time with little results. A teacher of the deaf worked with him at the age of five and obtained results in speech development.
>
> The language test was administered to him at the age of 6-8. . . . Although his language was quantitatively below that of the average child of his age (language age 3-11), his major deficits were in the association process at the grammatical or sequential level. His association at the semantic level was relatively superior to his other processes and levels.
>
> To check his general development other tests were administered. On the Stanford-Binet he obtained a mental age of five years and five months with an *IQ* of 73. On the WISC Scale he obtained an *IQ* of 76. An analysis of the subtests of the intelligence tests confirmed the profile on the language test. For example, in repeating sentences, which utilizes association at the semantic level, he was superior. In the repetition of numbers, which represents the association processes at the sequential (non-meaningful) level, he was inferior. In a reading readiness test his lowest score was in rhyming, which represents association at the

grammatical or sequential level. In other words, when meaning was dominant he scored high; when the tasks involved putting together sequences or patterns with little or no semantic components he scored low.

In a conference with the parents they informed us that this boy never went through the babbling stage. As a consequence, he did not imitate. It appears that language in this boy developed by a circuitous route. He did not babble (cause unknown), hence did not develop the decoding, association, or encoding processes at the integration level. This defect resulted in retarded imitation—which is decoding, associating, and encoding at the grammatical level. Speech was delayed. Meaning was established without the benefits of babbling and imitation. Instead, the language process had to await a decoding, association, and encoding process at the semantic level, a later stage of development. Even at the age of six and one-half he was still defective at the grammatical level. . . .

Because this case was of great interest to us, a tutor was hired and a special remedial program begun, aimed at training in sequential skills. Assessment after five months of training showed he had made 3.5 months gain at the grammatical level in the visual-manual and audio-vocal channels, respectively.

This case illustrates the ability of the test to differentially diagnose communication dysfunction in psycholinguistic terms for an individual child. It illustrates how the underlying language theory may be used to suggest a course of remediation.

Initial results with these language tests suggest that the underlying theoretical rationale has some validity. Kirk, *et al.*, are well aware of the defects of the tests as now developed and work is under way to refine their procedures. What we feel at the present is most significant about this work is (*a*) the recognition of the utility of theory in focusing on and illuminating new aspects of an old problem (i.e., language and the communication process); and (*b*) the attempt to integrate meaningful psychological test results with remedial program planning—an attempt which, as we shall see below, is all too rare.

B. THE DIAGNOSIS OF MINIMAL BRAIN INJURY

The value of psychological tests as aids in the diagnosis of brain injury has been of much interest to psychologists and has given rise to some controversy (225). We would agree with Goldenberg's (267, p. 164) recent conclusion, based on his review of the literature, that even those tests which seem to have the most promise will have to be much more developed before they can provide a valid criterion of brain damage in the absence of positive

neurological signs. When one considers that many high grade and borderline defective cases present thorny problems of differential diagnosis (e.g.,
between brain injury and emotional disturbance), it becomes apparent that
the accurate determination of brain injury, especially minimal brain injury,
is an important area of investigation.

There is an aspect to the problem of the diagnosis of minimal brain injury by psychological tests which deserves emphasis if only because it tends to
be overlooked. We refer to the obvious fact that cases of minimal brain injury are undoubtedly not homogeneous in terms of site and extent of lesion.
It would be expected, therefore, that different degrees and sites of lesion
would interfere with or be manifested in behavior in differing ways, as a recent
study by Morrell, Roberts, and Jasper suggests (188). Since the neurological
criteria of minimal brain injury are far from perfect, the psychologist is
comparing his test results · and interpretation to a criterion of unknown
validity. If in a particular case the neurological diagnosis is negative while
the psychological examination is positive for brain injury, one can neither
conclude that the psychologist is wrong nor right. If the neurological diagnosis is positive while the psychological examination is negative, it may be
that the particular lesion does not show up in the behavior sampled by the
tests; it may well be that the psychological examination is wrong. The point
is that when one employs an imperfect criterion—and when in addition one
assumes that different lesions probably have different effects—then unre-
solvable disagreements between the neurological diagnoses are inevitable in
clinical practice or in research in which two diagnoses are compared.

The problem may become more clear in the following example which
concerns two studies by S. B. Sarason and E. K. Sarason (227, 228) and
which have been reported in detail elsewhere. In the first study high grade
"familial," institutionalized individuals were studied. This group was divided in two according to certain psychometric criteria. One of the groups
had a test pattern considered suggestive of minimal brain injury while the
other group did not. All cases had been considered negative by neurological
examination. When EEG's were then obtained there was a significantly
greater incidence of abnormal records in the group with a test pattern considered suggestive of minimal brain injury. One thing that might be said
about these findings is that the conventional neurological examination was
far less sensitive in picking up brain disfunction than the EEG and that
the latter is a far better criterion by which to judge psychological diagnosis
than is the former. However, in a similar study of cerebral palsied chil-

dren, all of whom obviously had brain damage which was reflected in the conventional neurological examination, 9 out of 17 cases had a normal *EEG* record. One might conclude from this that the *EEG* is not as good a criterion for the psychological results as is the neurological examination. These studies strongly indicate that one of the major research problems is the unreliability of a single diagnostic procedure for brain injury. It is undoubtedly true that no single procedure is adequate for detecting brain injuries which differ in site and degree. Until multiple neurological and neurophysiological measures are utilized—much in the same way as the psychologist uses multiple test criteria—the psychologist must proceed with caution when he attributes validity to his diagnoses of brain injury.

A characteristic of most studies in this area has been the use of more than one test each of which is administered once. There is certainly nothing inherently wrong in administering a test but once as long as one is aware that one has a relatively poor basis for discriminating at least two kinds of failures or poor performance: (*a*) those cases which as a result of practice or directed instruction could learn to respond more adequately to the particular kind of problem-solving task—failures, so to speak, with the potential of relative adequacy; (*b*) cases which as a result of practice and directed instruction show no potential for improved performance. What we are in effect suggesting is that the diagnostic process be viewed as a learning one in which stimulus and instruction variations are employed in order to ascertain the conditions under which a more adequate performance is possible. If the failure group could be discriminated in the manner indicated above, it would not be surprising if more of those who showed no improvement in the course of learning would be considered brain-injured by neurological criteria than would be true of those who showed potential for improvement.

An example may clarify our suggestion. According to the 1937 standardization of the Binet, the majority of seven-year-old children are able to reproduce a diamond from a model. With decreasing age there is a decreasing number of children who can do this. These findings are frequently interpreted as reflecting the maturation of certain intellectual processes. While this is undoubtedly in large part true, it does not follow that under certain conditions of learning and motivation the majority of six and even five-year-old children could not learn to perform adequately on the task. In short, one must not confuse what a child does with what he can learn to do under altered conditions of learning. It would seem that we are dealing with a similar situation when we conventionally administer tests for

the purposes of discriminating between children with or without brain injury. We tend to assume that failure or poor performance on particular
tests is indicative of brain injury without attempting to study further the
conditions under which improved performance may be possible.

It is probably worthy of note that most investigators have been far more
interested in the problem of diagnosis of brain injury than in the significance
of such a diagnosis for the handling and treatment of the child. It is our
impression that there is too often quite a gap between the diagnosis and its
utilization in formulating a program which would minimize the adverse
effects of injury or in some way compensate for it. Aside from the obvious
benefits which could accrue to the child, we stress the aspect of program
planning because it conceivably can provide data relevant to the validity or
adequacy of diagnosis. If in a suspected or even clear-cut case of brain
injury, no particular program is planned, it is extremely difficult, if not impossible, meaningfully to relate changes in the child's behavior to the diagnosis of brain injury. If, however, program planning is based explicitly
on the nature and details of the diagnosis—if the program planning is akin
to predictions about what should happen if this particular child were handled
in certain ways—then one has a basis for evaluating the adequacy of the
diagnosis. Even here one cannot arrive at unambiguous conclusions, but particularly in instances where expected changes do not occur, such an approach
can serve as a spur to research not only on more refined diagnoses but on
the nature and behavioral implications of different types of brain injury as
well. In addition, such an approach cannot help but stimulate research on
different kinds of treatment and training procedures.

The work of Strauss (267, 268) is perhaps the best example we have
of the fruitfulness of an approach which is based on the integration of concepts in developmental neurology, diagnostic criteria of brain injury, and detailed program planning. Elsewhere one of us (225) has criticized the logic
and validity of some of the diagnostic criteria employed by Strauss. Although Goldenberg (267, p. 145) felt that these criticisms were somewhat
severe, it should be noted that they lead to a conclusion identical to his own
stated at the beginning of this section.[35] Although the validity of some of

---

[35]Keller (150), in a recent but as yet unpublished study done at the Wayne
County Training School, was unable to replicate earlier findings by Werner and
Thuma (286, 287). In these earlier studies, stimulated by the conceptions of
Strauss, significant differences were found between brain injured and non-brain
injured in the perception of apparent motion and also flicker-frequency. Keller
advances the hypothesis that unwitting examiner influence may have been responsible

the diagnoses of minimal brain injury based on Strauss' criteria can be questioned, it should not be overlooked that Strauss' conceptions have given rise to ingenious educational procedures and an environmental structuring which undoubtedly have had positive therapeutic effects. It is likely that there are cases where one would feel that a diagnosis of minimal brain injury by Strauss' criteria was unwarranted but where the child's response to the program planned for him, while it cannot "prove" the correctness of the diagnosis, certainly cannot be used as evidence against it. Unfortunately, we do not have the kind of detailed case reports which would allow one to gauge the frequency of this type of case. If we had such comprehensive case descriptions one could also get a better idea of the rôle of the "therapeutic milieu" in producing behavioral changes regardless of the presence or absence of brain injury. For example, we obviously have been impressed with the educational techniques and over-all therapeutic approach described by Strauss and Lehtinen (268). But one cannot avoid raising the following question: To what extent would children with no brain injury but with severely disabling learning difficulties and/or behavior problems benefit from the kinds of programs adapted to the presumably peculiar needs of brain-injured children? Inasmuch as the brain-injured child can be assumed to be one who also manifests personality disturbances, it is likely that some of the positive changes which occur are due to amelioration of these disturbances. This, of course, is a problem in cases where there is more than minimal brain injury, e.g., the cerebral palsied child.

Gallagher's (78) study of matched groups of brain-injured (*BI*) and familial (*F*) mentally retarded children has recently appeared. We shall quote in some detail from his concluding section for several reasons: (*a*) his results on lack of differences in perceptual behavior run counter to what has previously been found or believed, (*b*) he seems on the basis of his intensive studies to have arrived at conclusions and hypotheses similar to those discussed above, and (*c*) his suggestions about the direction of future research deserve emphasis:

> Matched groups of 24 brain-injured mentally retarded children and
> 24 familial mentally retarded children were compared on measures of

---

for the earlier significant findings, especially since the experimenters knew to which group each subject belonged and the nature of the experimental task was of a sufficiently ambiguous nature as to increase the subject's dependence on the examiner for guidance. This point, which may be or may not be correct insofar as the Werner and Thuma studies are concerned, has not been sufficiently stressed in the methodology of studies on this problem.

perception, learning aptitude, intellectual scatter, language development, quantitative ability and personality characteristics.

1. On tasks involving perceptual ability the results were as follows:

a. There were no significant differences between groups on the
Memory for Designs tests.

b. There was some suggestion that the F group produces fewer
reversals on the Copying Designs tests than the BI group although both
have reversal difficulties on Memory for Designs tasks.

c. A slight trend was found for a poorer performance by the BI
group on producing designs on a marble board.

d. Most of the BI group performed adequately on the perceptual
tasks although a minority of the group displayed definite perceptual problems.

2. Contrary to predictions, no differences were found between groups
on a test of direct and incidental learning aptitude, although a few
of the BI group were much slower in completing the learning task, perhaps suggesting some distractibility in these children.

3. No differences were found between groups on measures of quantitative concepts.

4. On the measure of language development the results were as
follows:

a. Although no differences were found on general language development, there were distinct differences between groups on their patterns of language development.

b. The BI group were superior to the F group on tasks requiring
verbal imitative responses and good speech production.

c. The F group were superior on ability to associate objects, trace
mazes and supply correctly the missing words in a sentence. These results supplied some confirmation to the notion that many BI children
have difficulty in making associations, correctly integrating verbal concepts, and using visual motor perceptual ability.

d. Both institutionalized retarded groups revealed weaknesses in
ability to produce adequate speech and verbal imitative responses.

5. Differences between groups were found on almost all personality
variables in favor of the F group. On the rating scales the BI children as a group lived up to their reputation of being hyperactive, lacking
attention, being fearful, less popular and generally more uninhibited
children than their familial pairs.

6. An analysis of successes and failures on Binet items revealed essentially no differences between groups.

7. A factor analysis of all intellectual measures revealed:

a. A high amount of variance in both groups accounted for by a
factor of general mental development.

b. The BI group produced a second factor related to poor perceptual ability.

c. General language development was found to be the second most important factor in the *F* group. The variance accounted for by both second factors was quite small.

Discussion

It makes sense to ask the question: Are the differences that can be seen between these two groups substantial enough to create recognizable differences in the total patterns of development of the children in these groups. The writer believes that this study and previous research direct an affirmative answer to this question. A second crucial question might be: Do these differences imply the need for drastically modified educational and training programs or merely slight modifications in existing programs? Here the answer is less clear and depends to a large degree on which brain-injured child you are talking about. The range of different problems and lack of problems within the brain-injured group is large enough to cast considerable doubt on the notion that plans can or should be made for brain-injured children as though they were a homogeneous group.

Practically all of the research which has attempted to describe the characteristics of brain-injured children has properly searched out areas of difference between them and groups of children without organic injury but of comparable mental status. One of the advantages of the present project is that it gave the writer a chance to observe the performance of two groups of children on a large variety of tests and ratings and thus to conclude that there are large areas of similarity between the two etiological groups as well as some differences.

Let us first examine those characteristics wherein the similarities between groups seemed to outweigh the differences.

No differences were found on quantitative ability between the groups and there seems to be little reason for making any special provision for teaching these concepts to groups of brain-injured children. Although perceptual problems were supposed to interfere with the development of quantitative conceptualization, this does not appear to have been the case. Some children in both groups did show a tendency to reverse numbers and geometric figures but this seemed to be an isolated difficulty which did not negatively influence the actual learning of grouping principles, number combinations, etc. Except in certain unique and individual cases, the rôle perceptual difficulties play in the development of quantitative concepts seems greatly overrated.

Essentially no differences between groups were obtained on the learning aptitude test which attempted to measure such important learning characteristics as memory, learning through experience, and response to the environment surrounding the learning situation. The fact that the brain-injured group seemed to learn almost as effectively as the familial children again suggests that perhaps too much emphasis has been placed on the differences between these diagnostic categories and not enough attention directed toward their similarities. Certainly it is as important for educators to realize that the *BI* group does not show inferior or unique approaches to standard learning tasks as it is to realize that *BI* children may have a tendency to turn the numeral "3" on its side.

There seemed to be general similarity in the patterns of successes and failures on the Stanford-Binet which suggested that this omnibus test (at these mental age levels) was unable to detect strong differences in intellectual approaches of the two groups. But the most surprising finding of the present study is the failure to obtain differences on a variety of measures of perceptual ability.

Although group differences were not obtained, examination of the individual cases did reveal that a minority of the children in the *BI* sample had definite perceptual problems. Conversely, it can be said that many of the *BI* children had adequate perceptual abilities in relation to their general mental development. The factor analysis on all measures, except personality ratings, did seem to suggest that perceptual difficulties play a secondary, but recognizable, part in the intellectual development of the brain-injured children but not in the familial children. However, the results of the factor analysis suggest, first of all, that general mental development is much more important in both groups than any unique and specific intellectual factors. The general mental ability factor accounted for approximately four times as much variance as did the perceptual factor in the brain-injured children. It would seem that the mental age score remains the best single piece of information an educator can have about a child although it can be made more meaningful by our knowledge of secondary patterns of factors in individual children.

Despite the rather impressive list of characteristics wherein there were no differences between the groups, there did seem to be two areas in which distinctive group differences existed. The most impressive area of difference was in the personality ratings where, as a group, the *BI* children seemed definitely inferior to the *F* group on desirable characteristics.

The fact of the difference was easier to oserve than was the underlying cause of it. One general explanation has been that the brain-injured child is not able to perceive social situations correctly or identify the correct social cues or distinguish between appropriate and non-appropriate behavior and thus becomes a behavior problem because of these deficiencies.

A second possible explanation was that the general lack of inhibition with its accompanying impulsivity and unpredictable behavior made the *BI* children socially unacceptable to peers and adults. This, in turn, produced secondary effects of fearful behavior and demands for complete attention and affection as a result of the distrust and rejection brought about by the original disinhibition.

Since this research project was not specifically designed to answer the above question, no definite conclusion can be made. Note, however, that these unfavorable personality characteristics still appeared clearly evident in the present *BI* group which did not seem to possess a large amount of perceptual difficulty. This suggested that disinhibition may have played a greater rôle in personality maladjustment than perceptual difficulties. At any rate, it presents an interesting hypothesis for further study.

The second large area of difference between the groups was their language development. It was only when the total language development scores were broken down into their component parts that these differences became noticeable. The relative inability of the *BI* group to associate objects in appropriate groupings confirmed to some extent the notion of the general difficulty they have, as a group, of developing concepts. More confidence could be displayed with this interpretation if the results on the Word Association test also had shown differences. The notion that the *BI* child has trouble placing concepts in proper association also gained some support from the poor *BI* results on the Vocal Cloze subtest which required the children to place an appropriate word in a sentence.

Strauss and Kephart have been concerned with the paradox that *BI* children can produce apparently adequate language performance even while their perceptual abilities are quite disturbed. They have considered three possible answers: The *BI* child uses language without really knowing the meaning of the words he used, he can make up for poor perception by learning about things through the perception of others conveyed to him through the medium of language, and he may learn language by listening and repeating parrot fashion. Our data supports the last of these three possibilities most strongly. The *BI* group was definitely superior on the mimicry items and also was only slightly deficient on those items which required adequate association and conceptualization.

An analysis of the language test data showed that there were tendencies for the brain-injured children to be superior to the familial children on items requiring the use of the auditory-vocal channel and inferior on items tapping the perceptual-motor channel. Although neither of these differences was statistically significant, this appears to remain a fruitful hypothesis if the measuring devices can be developed into sufficiently valid instruments.

Those brain-injured children who revealed these unique personality characteristics and language development patterns present a real challenge for educators who must develop unique teaching methods and methods of controlling environment to compensate for these differences.

It goes without saying that none of these results should be carelessly generalized to brain-injured children in the community until further investigations are made. Too many other factors such as family relationships or amount of control over behavior remain as potentially important variables in influencing personality development.

If one major difference can be pointed to in distinguishing the results of this study from previous research, it would be the lessened importance of perceptual disabilities and the increased importance of disinhibition and language development in the total developmental picture of the brain-injured child. As mentioned before, it is difficult to accept poor performance on many perceptual tasks as representing purely perceptual difficulties. Such poor performance may be due also to disturbing environmental or situational conditions which stimulate the child's disinhibitory characteristics as in the case of using confusing background patterns on a marble board test.

One important question seems to arise as a result of this study: How useful is it, from an educational point of view, to have the neurological information that a child is brain-injured? The distribution of cases, even where there were significant differences between groups, showed that many of the brain-injured children did not have the unfavorable characteristic that might be assigned to them as a group. Educational provisions made for brain-injured children on the basis of such over-all group differences would not be any more applicable to some brain-injured children than they would be to the familial children. Strauss has made the valid point that it is not necessary for everyone in a brain-injured group to be different from everyone in an organically sound group for a characteristic to be a good diagnostic indicator. The reader should not forget, however, that Strauss is referring to the use of these instruments as aids to medical diagnosis.

To ask the question another way: Does the educator not gain more information from the fact that the child is perceptually disturbed than from the fact that he is brain-injured? Brain injury is the proper province of the neurologist but the perceptual distortions, disinhibition, and problems of association that *sometimes* occur in *some* brain-injured children are the province of the educator and psychologist.

It would seem reasonable to expect the educator to make his own educational diagnosis of each child's perceptual development, personality skills or language development and make his plans accordingly whether or not a diagnosis of brain injury has been medically determined.

One thing that seems indicated is that greater attention be paid to the rôle that personality and behavior difficulties are playing in preventing many of these brain-injured children from attaining full efficiency. It is hoped that the individual training program now being tried with the

BI sample will give us some clues on the possible changes in behavior that can take place when a close personal teaching relationship is maintained with these children over a long period of time.

This leads to another question as to whether or not it is profitable to continue to do more studies designed in the same fashion as the present one. It would please the writer to believe that this study would represent the last of these attempts to obtain psychological and educational characteristics based on vague and oversimplified neurological classifications.

There would seem to be two general directions research might take from the present study. If one is interested in relating functioning behavior to the structure of the nervous system, then test results can be compared in various groups who have injuries to demonstrably different areas of the brain. If one is interested in the educational implications of such psychological characteristics as disinhibition, perceptual abilities, or language development, then these characteristics should be studied directly without being dependent upon medical diagnosis.

It is the function of science to attack one problem until it has been drained of its useful knowledge and then use that knowledge to move on to something else.

This may be the time to redirect our efforts to such complex problems as are suggested by the results of the present study and other similar research.

C. The Familial or Garden-Variety Defective

Throughout this report we have attempted to adhere to the practice of labelling as mentally defective those in whom there is some kind of central nervous system pathology. As was pointed out in Section II, there is tremendous variation within this group in degree and site of pathology and, of great practical importance, in the degree to which normal intellectual and social development are possible. For purposes of this report we have used the term mental deficiency to refer to those individuals who have demonstrable central nervous system pathology of a kind and to a degree which probably rules out normal social and intellectual functioning. These have been the individuals we have discussed in the earlier sections of this chapter, as well as in the previous one. In contrast, we have labelled as mentally retarded that large group of individuals whose retardation is not associated with organic pathology and who are able, or could become able, to maintain themselves in the community. The initial sections of this report were concerned primarily with the mentally retarded, particularly the large percentage of this group which never is institutionalized. We turn again at this point to the mentally retarded because the bulk of the "high grade" cases in our institutional population differs in no fundamental respect from those we have called mentally retarded. Parental neglect or abuse which comes to the attention of authorities, delinquent behavior, aggressive display in the school situation, lack of adequate community facilities (e.g., foster care, temporary shelters)—these are frequently the factors which determine whether or not a retarded child is likely to be institutionalized. We, therefore, think it misleading to group, as is traditionally done, the institutionalized mentally retarded with the mentally defective. Although labels frequently do not add to our knowledge, they can cause confusion. To classify the institutionalized mentally retarded child (variously called the familial, or garden-variety, or Kallikak type of defective) with the mentally defective can and has obscured in the minds of many that from the standpoint of organic pathology and cultural background the two groups are strikingly different.

In the first two sections we made suggestions about the kind of research which we felt had to be done if we were to gain an understanding of the rôle of psychological and cultural factors in the etiology of mental retardation. Sarason (225) has elsewhere reviewed the research literature and made suggestions about the direction of future research. It should come as no surprise that this research has yet to be developed. At this point we would like to indicate other areas of research which have not yet been attacked or adequately discussed.

1. From the standpoint of our society one of the most neglected research areas concerns the psychological changes which are associated with institutionalization.[36] When one realizes how many millions of dollars are spent in building and maintaining our institutions, it is surprising that very little research has been done to study the psychological changes which institutionalization brings about. Institutionalization involves a *drastic* change for the individual and there is every reason for assuming that it is experienced as a stressful one involving (*a*) separation from loved or familiar figures, (*b*) pressures to adjust to a completely new physical and interpersonal (peer and adult) environment, (*c*) confusion and resentment about their helplessness, (*d*) anxiety in relation to the future. In the case of the mentally retarded individual, who usually comes from an unfavorable family situation, we are usually struck by the material differences between home and in-

---

[36]This problem is also relevant for the various types and grades of mental deficiency. We raise the problem in connection with the institutionalized mentally retarded because they make up the large proportion of those whom the institutions consider placeable in the community.

stitution. But this is the way *we* view the change and one should not assume, therefore, that the child perceives it the way we do. What to us is a psychologically unfavorable family situation, and what may even be an unpleasant one to the child, may in the process of institutionalization be perceived by the child as his only source of security. As important as the immediate effects are those of prolonged institutionalization. It is our clinical impression that the major effects of prolonged institutionalization are four-fold: (*a*) overt conformity to the institutional culture at the expense of personal spontaneity and expression, (*b*) excessive phantasying, especially about the "outside world," (*c*) avoidance and fear of new problem-solving situations, and (*d*) excessive dependence on the institutional culture, which becomes most apparent when the possibility of leaving the institution arises. The effects of institutionalization undoubtedly vary with age at commitment. In stressing the possible deleterious effects of institutionalization we are not unmindful that we are dealing with a very complex problem. In this connection mention should be made of some interesting and unusually well-controlled studies by Clarke and Clarke (46) in England. They studied test score changes in mentally retarded individuals following institutionalization. In their published report the Clarkes present evidence for the conclusion that it was those who come to the institution from the very worst homes who showed the greatest test score changes. The ratings of home environment were made by someone with no knowledge of the test scores. In unpublished material which the Clarkes kindly sent to us further confirmation of these findings was found. In these unpublished studies "retesting was carried out by a colleague who knew neither the patients, nor their earlier test scores, nor their social ratings of early environment." Because length of time in the institution was not associated with size of test score increase, the Clarkes concluded that these changes "are more the effect of removal from a very adverse environment than of entry into a relatively better one"— a conclusion supported by their unpublished data. It is conceivable, therefore, that similar results could be obtained if this type of individual had been removed to an environment other than an institutional one. It is in no way to devalue the English studies to express the hope that research will be conducted on the personality as well as the intellectual changes which accompany institutionalization. In any event, we feel that this whole problem is a most crucial one because it bears not only on the problem of the effects of environmental change on performance and potential but on one of our society's major ways of handling the problem of mental retardation.

2. In an earlier paragraph we expressed the opinion that the bulk of the high grade cases in our institutions differed in no fundamental respect from those we have called mentally retarded but are not institutionalized. One could argue against such a conclusion on the grounds that the test scores of those institutionalized are probably significantly lower than the scores of those who are in the community and that such a difference may reflect a "basic" difference between the two groups. From all that we have said thus far in this report, it should be apparent that we do not think the grounds for such an argument are tenable. However, it should be noted that we do not have systematic studies on this problem. For example, we are not aware of any systematic study on factors associated with variations in intellectual performance *within* families of retarded children who have been institutionalized. The problems we are raising here seem very similar to that of why some children become delinquent while others in the same family or neighborhood do not. If studies of mental retardation similar to those of the Gluecks (91) on juvenile delinquency were carried out, our understanding of the problem would not only be increased but, as in the case of delinquency, we would have a more rational basis for picking out much earlier than we now can those mentally retarded children who are likely to require institutionalization.

3. In the previous chapter it was pointed out that the incidence of psychosis in the mentally defective population is apparently much higher than in the general population. The significance of this finding is obscured by the failure to break down the statistics according to etiological groups. Consequently, we do not know if the incidence rate is the same for the mentally defective and the mentally retarded. We also do not know whether the incidence rate for the institutional population is the same as for the non-institutional one. It is our clinical impression that the incidence of psychosis among the institutionalized mentally retarded is probably less than among the institutionalized, high grade defective and probably much lower than for the lower grades of mental defect. However, the recent findings by Hollingshead, Redlich, *et al.* (120, 121, 190, 210, 211, 215, 216, 234) that the prevalence of treated psychosis in lower class individuals—those to whom the mentally retarded are most similar in a cultural and intellectual sense—is much higher than for other social classes in our society suggests that the incidence rate for the non-institutionalized mentally retarded may be rather high—perhaps larger than for institutionalized mentally retarded who were not included in the survey by Hollingshead and

Redlich.[37] One might speculate that although the overprotective and infantilizing institutional environment may have deleterious effects on the personality of the mentally retarded individual, particularly if he is committed at an early age, it in some way makes the development of a psychosis less likely. These are speculations, however, which should not detract from recognition of the importance of the research problem of the relation between mental retardation and psychotic behavior.

D. PSYCHOTHERAPY

In 1955 Cowen (49) presented a comprehensive review of psychotherapeutic work with subnormal individuals, almost all of these studies being concerned with the mentally retarded and high grade defective. Cowen's excellent summary statement of the scientific status of the research on this problem follows:

> Any attempt to summarize the results of psychotherapeutic work with the defective child in a concise or confident manner must be regarded as hazardous. While there has undoubtedly been more work with defectives than with any other group of exceptional children, most authors have with good reason described their studies as exploratory. Firm generalizations would be difficult indeed to defend. It is, for example, not entirely clear why Neham, after a partial review of work in therapy with defectives concludes: "The experiments presented seem to indicate that the directive supportive method in which a warm, friendly, personal relationship is developed seems to be the best approach adapted to mental defectives." Certainly the evidence at this time is not sufficiently clear-cut to indicate that any one approach to therapy is best for mental defectives in general and even less for any specific group of defectives. There has not, in fact, been a single comparative study of the relative merits of various approaches to therapy with defectives. Similarly, one might question the basis of another of Neham's conclusions, namely that the ". . . weight of evidence indicates that high moron intelligence is necessary for therapeutic success." One must be careful to distinguish between what may appear logical and what is an interpretation of sound research. A generation ago the notion that

---

[37]In this survey a tremendous effort was made to determine the number of people in the Greater New Haven Area who were in psychiatric treatment (private, clinic, state hospital, etc.) on the arbitrarily chosen day. We think that it is a reflection of professional attitudes toward the psychological problems of subnormal functioning that individuals from the area who were in institutions for the mentally defective were excluded from the survey. To have included this large number of cases would have undoubtedly presented more than a few knotty problems for the survey but their omission does set limitations about generalizations concerning incidence of psychiatric disorders and their social class correlates.

therapy with defectives could not be successful may have seemed both logical and acceptable to most practitioners. Subsequent research has demonstrated otherwise. In the absence of comparative research in therapy with defectives at different intellectual levels, what Neham states as a conclusion should be regarded at best as a tentative hypothesis.

In a more positive vein this much can be said. Instances of successful therapeutic outcomes with defectives have peen reported from many settings by practitioners with diverse orientations. These include case reports, studies of interview therapy, reports of play therapy and expressive media, studies in group therapy, by psychoanalysts, directivists, nondirectivists and eclectics with institutionalized and non-institutionalized defectives. Though many of these reports are open to serious criticism when considered alone, together they underscore the conclusion that therapy with at least some defectives can be successful. Further, the few comparative studies of therapy with the defective and intellectually normal child offer no support for the notion that the former has a poorer therapeutic prognosis.

Although there are some instances of increases in *IQ* following therapy with competently diagnosed defectives, there is no basis for concluding that such increases are either general or typical. Most subjective evaluations of personality and behavioral changes after therapy with these children suggest that significant changes have taken place. Regrettably, diagnostic test data before and after therapy are extremely rare and are not consistent enough either to support or to contradict generalizations derived from subjective reports.

One strong indication of a growing conviction that therapy with the defective is both feasible and potentially fruitful may be found in the ever increasing number of studies being reported in this area in recent years. Unfortunately there have been few systematic attempts to analyze research problems and formulate research needs. Notable exceptions to the preceding statement include Sarason's suggestions of some basic research problems in individual psychotherapy with defectives, Cotzin's proposals for a research program in group psychotherapy, and Mehlman's analysis of methodological problems in research on therapy with the defective.

There can be little question of the effectiveness of psychotherapy with some defectives. Much needed information in this area, however, is still lacking. It is not yet clear which children in this heterogeneous group can be helped by therapy and which ones cannot, nor do we know about the relative effectiveness of various types of therapies or different therapeutic media, either with the defective group as a whole or any of its sub-groups. These are some of the important future research problems that face us. Their solution should extend the usefulness of psychotherapy to many defective children heretofore regarded as essentially unapproachable.

We shall here not attempt to review the material covered by Cowen, or Sarason's (225) review and discussion. We will at this point present certain problems and considerations not previously discussed or emphasized.

One basis for evaluating therapeutic efforts with any individual is in terms of the goals which the therapist had hoped for or anticipated, i.e., what did *he* want to accomplish at the end of his therapeutic contacts with the patient? Since most therapeutic efforts with mentally retarded or defective individuals have been over relatively short periods of time involving few contacts, it can be assumed that the goals of the therapist did not involve attempts to achieve a generalized change in the patient—the goals were specific and modest (as indeed they are in most therapeutic relationships). The fact that the evidence suggests that these individuals can benefit from brief psychotherapy is, of course, important. But what are the factors which enter into the therapist's formulation of modest goals? Very frequently practical considerations (such as available time and money) dictate the restriction in therapeutic goals. It is our opinion, however, that as important as practical consideration are implicit assumptions about the amenability of these individuals to therapeutic efforts which have as their aim a more or less generalized personality change. Put in another way: far more frequently than not the retarded individual is considered to be incapable of utilizing a long lasting and intensive therapeutic relationship in a way so as to become able to change his perception of himself and others, to effect changes in his handling of his life problems, and to narrow the discrepancy between potential and performance. We are here *not* saying or implying that the aim of such a therapeutic approach is to make the subnormal individual "normal"— or the normal person an intellectual giant. What we are trying to say is that therapeutic efforts with the mentally retarded implicitly assume that such an individual is incapable of utilizing introspection and retrospection, of experiencing insight, of examining his motivations, phantasies, and anxieties, of being able to seriously want to change his characteristic pattern of overt and covert responding—of all of these things the retarded individual is implicitly considered incapable. As soon as one considers this statement either as an injustice or as a far too sweeping generalization then at least two questions arise. First, if these statements are too sweeping, then what are the limits of the retarded in these respects? Second, what accounts for the relative absence of research with such a therapeutic approach, despite the fact that case studies have been done which suggest that such an approach may be feasible? We refer particularly to the psychoanalytically treated

case reported by Chidester and Menninger (41), a case treated in an orthodox, intensive psychoanalytic way over a period of three years. We also
refer to some of the cases similarly treated and reported by Clark (44).
As important in these cases as the degree of change effected by treatment
are the indications that the functioning of the subnormal individual always
reflects in varying degrees extremely strong neurotic conflicts stemming
from earlier experiences and relationships.[38] To what extent a condition of subnormality predisposes the individual to an exacerbation of
neurotic symptoms, or to what extent the subnormality is an effect of these
conflicts, is impossible to say. What we feel could be said is that for any
individual whose functioning is considered subnormal, we can assume the
presence of long standing neurotic conflicts which, so to speak, have added
insult and injury to whatever handicaps he may originally have had. What
is also significant about these psychoanalytically treated cases is that they
were able to learn to think about themselves, others, and the past in a way
that is ordinarily not associated with subnormal functioning.

It is our opinion that the relative absence of intensive, psychoanalytic
studies of subnormal individuals is due to at least two factors. First, as a
group psychoanalytically trained therapists are simply not interested in the
problem, in which respect they are only somewhat more delinquent than
other psychiatrists and psychologists. From time to time there has appeared
in the psychoanalytic literature case studies of "pseudo-feeblemindedness"
but these are cases, unlike those described by Chidester and Menninger or
Clark, where an initial diagnosis of mental deficiency or mental retardation
was hardly warranted. It is also our impression that when the psycho-
analyst discusses or theorizes about the problem, his unfamiliarity with the
clinical material becomes too apparent. Second there has been an encouraging increase of interest in recent years in psychotherapy with subnormal indi-

---

[38]It should not be overlooked that *therapeutic* failure does not necessarily mean
that one's efforts have been totally unfruitful. The therapy may have produced
little or no effects but one may still have gained important hypotheses about the
causes of the failure, hypotheses which may result in changes in therapeutic procedure, or stimulate research with other than therapeutic techniques, or result in
changes in type of subject (e.g., age, etiology, life situation) utilized. To obtain
any of these benefits in the face of therapeutic failure at least two factors must
be present: (*a*) the therapist must be prepared to *test* his explanations for the failure and (*b*) the therapy (its technique and underlying rationale) should contain
the possibility of obtaining data and behavior from the patient which could
shed light on factors working against improvement in therapy. It would be our
opinion that not all therapeutic techniques have equal potentiality for benefiting
from therapeutic failure.

viduals on the part of the psychoanalytically oriented (as distinguished from psychoanalytically trained) therapists. As one might expect in the development of a new area of interest, these therapists seem primarily concerned with the effects of various procedures and the methodological problems involved. While such concerns are in no way to be derogated, it should be emphasized that such concerns are not likely to shed much light on personality dynamics and structure, on the one hand, and developmental variables and experiences, on the other hand. The most durable and fruitful consequences of the development of psychoanalytic therapy (or therapies) have been less the effects of such therapy than the way it has illuminated the rôle of certain variables and relationships in the development of personality. It is because intensive psychoanalytic therapy gives us the possibility of gaining a better understanding of the developmental interaction between intellectual and personality organization that we stress its importance as a research area. We would like to make it perfectly clear that in making such a recommendation we are not in any way prejudging the therapeutic merits of psychoanalytic as against other types of psychotherapy—itself an important research problem. What we are prejudging is the superiority of psychoanalytic therapy for achieving a better understanding of the personality structure and development of the subnormal individual—an understanding which may be of inestimable value for problems in rearing, training, and parent counselling.

The above recommendation will undoubtedly be reacted to with differing degrees of scepticism and rejection, by psychoanalysts and others. Aside from the practical problem of attracting people to the problem, and making appropriate training available to them, there will be many who on theoretical and other grounds will feel such a program to be unfeasible. It would be our guess that most, if not all, who would react in this way are those who have never had intimate, day-by-day, clinical contacts with the varieties of problems and personalities which are obscured by such labels as subnormal, mentally retarded, or mentally defective. We recognize this statement to be an *argumentum ad hominem* but there are too many examples where theorizing about a problem with which there has been little or no clinical experience can prevent the acquisition of further knowledge.

Intensive, psychoanalytic therapy is certainly not the only means whereby personality dynamics and their developmental course can be studied. In this connection a study done in Belgium by Bobon (20) is worthy of note. He reported a case of a 39-year-old woman who was mentally deficient, illiterate, and who exhibited delusions of persecution. From the case history material one might question the diagnosis of mental deficiency. In light of the family background—her mother, two maternal aunts, and a cousin were considered mentally defective—one might more cautiously consider her as mentally retarded, her retardation being evident from the beginning of school. Her schizoid character was also noted early in her life but it is impossible from the material to determine the relationship between the retardation and the schizoid characteristics (e.g., gentle, timid, shy, retiring). In his report Bobon reiterates that the woman was a mental defective who later developed a full blown psychosis. Bobon's interest in this woman, who was committed to the mental hospital when she was approximately 25 years of age, stemmed from changes in her speech and use of language. We need not go into the details of these changes except to say that Bobon considered them to reflect, in part, an "intentional" or motivational factor—apparently one of which the woman was not aware. Bobon then reasoned that if a motivational factor was at work its effects on the woman's linguistic behavior would be reduced "in states of least psycho-motor activity." Various experiments done with this woman while in a state of narcohypnosis clearly revealed that she could respond more accurately and less neologistically than in the waking state. In such a state "our subject expresses herself in a generally correct way in tests of object naming. The first verbal manifestations in awakening, spontaneous or provoked, show . . . neoformations of words of the aphasic type. In the spoken language of the waking state . . . the neoformations of words of the asphasic type seem non-existent, the naming of objects is usually faulty, as are the vocabulary deformations, giving to her speech its characteristic stamp. . . . We are the first, we believe, to try to use the experimental method for this type of problem, and we again conclude: a relatively important intentional component is found in the origin of this pseudo-glossolalia."

Bobon's contribution may have, we think, important research implications for research with subnormals. It has long been known that states of narcosis may not only be therapeutically advantageous but productive of important insights into an individual's personality structure, particularly when the individual has not been amenable to conventional psychotherapeutic procedures. For research which has as its focus an understanding of the personality dynamics of the subnormal individual, the procedures exemplified by Bobon's work seem deserving of further exploration.

E. STUDIES IN RIGIDITY

The generalization has long been accepted that the subnormal individual is more rigid than the normal. This conclusion is based on anecdotal and observational data as well as on the results of some experimental studies (159, 160, 167, 285). Stevenson and Zigler (264) have succinctly summarized the basis for the generalization:

> Feebleminded individuals have been characterized as being "rigid" in numerous studies in which feebleminded children and adults and normal children have been compared. The tasks employed have been primarily of the "satiation" and "switching" types. In the former, Ss are instructed to perform a task and are allowed to repeat the task until they become satiated and no longer want to continue it. They are then instructed to perform a highly similar task and again are allowed to perform until satiated. Feebleminded Ss have been found to spend significantly more time on each task than normal Ss. This lack of influence of initial satiation on the performance of subsequent tasks has been interpreted as indicating a greater rigidity in the personality structure of the feebleminded S. In the "switching" tasks the S, after acquiring one response, is forced to switch from this response to a new response involving identical or highly similar stimuli. The smaller amount of transfer from the first to the second task shown by the feebleminded Ss has been interpreted as indicating greater rigidity.

A recent study by Plenderith (205) did not find any differences between normals and subnormals on a discrimination-learning and discrimination-reversal task. This unexpected finding has received confirmation from a series of systematic, experimental studies carried out recently by Stevenson and Zigler (264, 265) at the University of Texas. In these studies the subjects consisted of what is traditionally called the high grade, familial defective. These subjects were divided into two comparable mental age groups but differing in chronological age, i.e., a younger and an older group. In addition, a group of normal children of similar mental age as the subnormals was employed. Whereas in the earlier studies of rigidity the subject was required to perform a response *in compliance with instructions*, in the studies by Plenderith as well as those of Stevenson and Zigler, the subject was required to learn a response, i.e., the subject was required to initiate a course of action with minimal instructions and with minimal interaction with the experimenter. The following are the major findings and conclusions from these studies:

1. Neither in switching from a size-discrimination to another size-

discrimination problem nor in switching from a size-discrimination to a position-discrimination problem involving the same stimuli, were there any differences in rigidity among the three groups (normal, younger, and older high grade subjects) as measured by frequency of perseverative responses.

2. The frequency of rigid responsiveness was found to be a function of the difficulty of the problem presented. This was true for the three groups and no significant differences were found among them.

3. The discrepancy between the above and earlier findings are interpreted by Stevenson and Zigler as a function of differences in methodology employed. "In earlier studies involving tasks most comparable to the present one, S was not required to learn a response, but to perform a response in compliance with instructions. For example, in one of Kounin's studies, S was instructed to depress a lever in order to obtain marbles; following practice on this task, he was instructed to raise the lever to get the marbles. Studies such as Kounin's seem to introduce a variable which was minimized in the present study. With the present task, the correct response is acquired on the basis of the differential reinforcement S receives following each response, while in Kounin's task the response is made primarily on the basis of instructions. Differences in rigidity between normal and feebleminded Ss of the same MA in the instruction-initiated task may be related to differences in the Ss' motivation to comply with instructions, rather than to differences in a general personality characteristic of rigidity."

4. In a further study of rigidity in which the degree of supportive comments made by the examiner was varied, evidence was obtained that the subnormals who received support performed better than those who did not.

One of the major significances of the Stevenson and Zigler studies is that they illustrate that among the mentally retarded, as in the case of any other group, it is hazardous and may be very misleading to describe them as if they possess a particular characteristic (e.g., rigid) at all times in all situations. Those who have worked intensively with retarded children, as in a psychotherapeutic relationship, would probably agree that one cannot pin labels on these individuals without taking account of the stimulus conditions, the motivations engendered, and the nature of the interpersonal dynamics involved. It is probably fair to say that one of the reasons psychotherapy was for so long not attempted with subnormals was the assumption that they were too rigid to benefit from a therapeutic relationship.

The Stevenson and Zigler studies throw light on an apparent paradox involving the mentally retarded (which would include the institutionalized, high grade cases). On the one hand, it has long been the custom to regard the mentally retarded as operating best in simple, routine, monotonous situations which, so to speak, capitalized on their rigidity. This belief underlies the placement and training practices of most institutions. On the other hand, as we have discussed earlier in this report (Chapters X, XIV), many studies have demonstrated that the adult level of functioning of many individuals who in grade school were judged retarded is surprisingly good—the nature of their work and problem-solving is not compatible with the assumption that rigidity is a pervasive characteristic. The paradox resides in the fact that both conclusions (i.e., they operate well in simple situations and they also can operate well in more difficult situations) are probably true. From the standpoint of the Stevenson and Zigler studies the paradox could be resolved in the following way: if the retarded individual is put into a simple situation (e.g., vocational) in which he is instructed how to respond and in which a premium is put on compliance with instructions, the retarded individual (particularly the institutionalized one) will respond "efficiently" even though he may also impress one as rigid and perseverative. If, however, the vocational situation is one which requires a learning process, initiative in the sense of having to make judgments or choices, strong motivation, and meaningful rewards (aside from those accruing from compliance with the instructions of authority figures)—if the situation has these characteristics, then the retarded individual will perform significantly better than one would have expected from his *IQ* score. It seems reasonable to assume that in the latter instances the conditions of motivation and learning were far more similar to those of the Stevenson and Zigler studies than to the earlier studies of rigidity.

Perhaps the best observational or clinical evidence that can be cited in support of these conclusions as well as the Stevenson and Zigler studies is the work of Schaefer-Simmern (232) to which we have already alluded on page 177. It will be recalled that he was interested in the nature and development of artistic activity and in one of his studies utilized a group of high grade, familial, institutionalized cases. The artistic development and productions of these individuals were little short of dramatic, especially in light of the fact that initiative, decision-making, and criticism of one's own work was required of them. As we have said elsewhere (225, p. 320) about his work:

> Schaefer-Simmern's studies seem to have implications beyond the field of artistic activity. They corroborate a principle often neglected

in practice, namely, that the work an individual does must be of such a nature and at such a level as to engender a feeling of adequacy in relation to it and to allow him to observe his own growth process in it. Reward in the form of praise from others is important, but unless the individual receives satisfaction from his own realization of change the therapeutic effects will be temporary. Praise from others, like reassurance, is usually of small value when unaccompanied by insight. When Schaefer-Simmern's procedures are contrasted with those ordinarily employed in occupational therapy units in institutions for defectives, one wonders whether a reorientation in thinking is not indicated.

Our own experience with occupational or vocational units in institutions certainly supports the following eloquent statements by Schaefer-Simmern (232, p. 47):

> [In these occupational units] the patient may attain control over his hands, he may even learn perfect manipulation of a tool, he may become so used to this occupation that he is able to execute it without personality participation in it, he may even feel at ease in doing it, but the compulsory attention and concentration repeated over and over will throw him into a mental and emotional rigidity worse than before. He may become more or less adept at making things, but his personal relationship to them remains external because the work does not have its origin within him; it does not reflect himself. The performance is not related to the nature of his organism as a whole, as a psychobiological unity. Merely manual execution employs only a very small fraction of the total organism, and the attention and concentration it demands are not a result of the patient's inner decision. Only when the innermost core of interest voluntarily determines the applying of one's energies, when one feels that the work being done is an indivisible part of oneself (a condition which requires, of course, that it be in full conformity with one's own stage of visual conception), and when one is aware that attention and concentration are indispensable in order to realize oneself—only then does work become constructive.

One can only hope that the Stevenson and Zigler studies give rise to interest in the nature and sources of individual differences in rigidity among the mentally retarded. Given any particular experimental situation, what is the range of individual differences and what are the kinds of experiential and personality factors to which the differences may be related? In asking these kinds of questions, we are in effect suggesting that the ultimate value, theoretically and practically, of studies of rigidity (or any other single behavioral characteristic) will depend on (a) the knowledge we gain about the function of these characteristics in personality organization and (b) the antecedent factors which give rise to such a characteristic. In other words, by more or less studying a characteristic in isolation we run the risk of overlooking both its functions and development within a complex personality organization. For too long our understanding of the subnormal individual has been blocked by focusing on his intelligence as if this "thing" operated in splendid isolation from the complexity we call personality. In recent years there has been an encouraging degree of interest in the personality of the subnormal individual and we are here expressing the hope that focusing on single personality characteristics will be followed by attempts to fathom their developmental sources and course as well as their functional relationships to other significant personality characteristics.

F. Intelligence and Family Size

There have been numerous studies (194, 270), particularly in England, demonstrating a negative correlation between the intelligence test score of a child and the size of the family of which he is a member. Thomson (270), who was for long concerned with the problem, concluded that the correlation was approximately —0.25. The following illustration by Thomson may be helpful to the reader:

> I have constructed the following artificial symmetrical grid of 2,050 cases, so as to give a correlation of —0.25. It does not represent any experiment and must not be taken as giving, say, the actual range or distribution of family size. It is merely illustrative. An experimental grid would show families up to 13 and more, and the distribution of family sizes would be skew.
>
> In this grid, in which we may suppose *A, B, C, D, E, F* to be grades of intelligence and 1, 2, 3, 4, 5, 6 to be family sizes, although the tendency is unmistakable, and is expressed by the quantitative statement $r = -0.25$, there are nevertheless eighteen (14 + 3 + 1) "only" children who are below average intelligence, and eighteen members of the largest families (here families of six) who are above average intelligence.
>
> Casual observers, moreover, and even people like teachers, or journalists, or clergymen, do not see the whole population but only a selected part of it. They know secondary schoolchildren or slum children. Their acquaintances tend to belong to a class with large (or with small) families, to a certain occupational or social stratum, and so on. That is to say, they are unacquainted with the whole of the data shown in a grid [like the one below] and though, of course, they do not actually make a grid, they draw conclusions *as though* from a grid which is only *part* of the . . . [one below]. . . . Suppose we take such a part, say the top

AN ARTIFICIAL CORRELATION GRID OF 2,050 CASES REPRE-
SENTING A NEGATIVE CORRELATION OF 0.25

	1	2	3	4	5	6
A	5	18	24	14	3	1
B	18	73	114	84	28	3
C	24	114	212	192	84	14
D	14	84	192	212	114	24
E	3	28	84	114	73	18
F	1	3	14	24	18	5

left hand quadrant only, where all the families are below average in
size and above average in intelligence. That is the part of the data,
for example, which will represent the relations, friends, and acquaint-
ances of most of the readers of this memorandum. This truncated grid is

5	18	24
18	73	114
24	114	212

and gives on calculation a correlation of —0.07 only, so small as entirely to escape casual notice. Yet in the whole group of 2,050 the correlation is —0.25, and this is what matters.

In the bibliographic references given above, the reader will find discussions of the major explanations which have advanced for understanding the
negative correlation. The interested reader will also wish to refer to Anastasi's (5) recent and excellent discussion of the methodological and interpretive problems involved. For the purposes of the present report, we shall
focus on Nisbet's (194) study of the effect of "environmental influence of
the size of family on verbal ability and through it on general mental development." We choose this study because its findings and implications
seem to be very relevant for the mentally retarded individual who frequently
comes from a family the size of which is larger than that of the non-retarded
person. Our own experience with an institutional population suggests that
the incidence of large families among the high grade portion of such a population might even be higher than in the case of the non-institutionalized retarded population.

The following is Nisbet's summary of his hypotheses and findings:

The slight but definitely established tendency for intelligent children
to be found in small families and dull children in large families has
been attributed to the inheritance by intelligent children of an intelli-

gence which in their parents is associated with a smaller size of family. However, the observed tendency may be due at least in part to the fact that being a member of a large family under present circumstances depresses the environmental component of a child's test score. Predictions of the future level of national intelligence depend on how far one or the other of these causes is operating to produce the observed tendency.

The former cause is suggested by the results of previous investigations in which attempts to hold constant such factors as parental occupation or overcrowding in the home have failed to dispel the negative correlation; but such methods are not adequate if the actual family size is itself an environmental factor—if the lack of adult contact and consequent retardation in verbal development suffered by a child from a large family depresses the environmental component of his test score. Such is the hypothesis which is put forward on the basis of previous work, both on the negative association of family size and intelligence test score, and in other fields, for example, in the comparison of orphanage children and only children, in studies of bilinguals, deaf children and twins. It is not suggested that this cause alone operates to produce the negative correlation of family size and intelligence test score, but only that it contributes to the correlation to an extent sufficient with other influences to mask any possible downward trend in national intelligence and to prevent the possibility of using the testing of age-groups of children for predicting the amount of any possible decline in national intelligence level.

The hypothesis was tested by three methods: by partial correlation of family size and verbal ability with intelligence held constant; by correlation of family size and several tests with different verbal loadings; and by correlation of family size and intelligence test score at different ages.

In two groups each of some 2,500 children aged eleven plus, the partial correlation between family size and score in a test of English attainment (with intelligence test score held constant) was negative (about —.10) and significant in both groups at the .05 level. In a random sample of 200 children aged eleven, the correlation between family size and score in a verbal Moray House Test was —.30, the difference being significant at the .05 level. These results support the hypothesis that the environment of the large family constitutes a handicap to verbal development, and that this verbal retardation affects general mental development. If this were so, one would expect the negative correlation between family size and intelligence test score to be more marked at later ages when the cumulative effect of environment begins to show itself; and this prediction was confirmed with tests applied at different ages. The correlation between family size and intelligence test score in an age-group of 1,236 children aged seven was —.26; in a similar age-group of 1,270 children aged nine was —.29; and in four such age-

groups aged eleven plus was —.33. The difference between the correlation at age seven and at age eleven was significant at the .01 level,
and was not attributable to the effect of incomplete families. In a group
of 178 children who were tested at ages seven, nine and eleven, con-
firmatory results were obtained, though the difference between the correlations in this group was not significant because of the small numbers.

The results suggest that part (but not all) of the negative correlation of family size and intelligence test score such as was found in
the Scottish Mental Survey among children aged eleven, may be attributed to the environmental influence of the size of family on verbal
ability and through it on general mental development. At the same
time, in each experiment it seemed clear that the whole of the negative
correlation could not be explained in terms of this environmental influence. Others who have worked on this problem on a nation-wide scale
do not deny a certain amount of environmental influence, and would
probably wish attention to be drawn to the substantial negative correlation which remains even when the environmental influence is allowed
for.

One of the more obvious implications of Nisbet's study is the further
evidence it provides that test scores cannot be interpreted as measures of
innate ability. Less obvious, perhaps, is the implication or possibility that
language attainment is but one of many factors affected by the influence of
family size on intellectual functioning and personality organization, and that
the over-all correlation between family size and intelligence would be reduced
even further if other possible effects could be isolated. For example, Nisbet states that "words are more than mere instruments of expression but are
the very material of thought and afford a system of symbols which greatly
increases the efficiency of abstract thought." In light of this statement, one
can justifiably maintain that a test of language attainment may by no means
reflect the possibly pervasive effects of adverse factors on the development of
verbal behavior. In fact, some of Nisbet's findings may be interpreted in
this way. He found, "The correlation between family size and score in the
non-verbal Matrices test was —.20 while the correlation between family
size and score in a Moray House Test was —.30, the difference being significant at the .05 level. These results support the hypothesis that the environment of the large family constitutes a handicap to verbal development,
and that this verbal retardation affects general mental development." To
arrive at this conclusion one must assume that the non-verbal Matrices Test
does not require verbalization and the manipulation of symbols. The test does
not require articulation *but it does require sustained self-verbalization and*

symbolization. Consequently, the correlation of —.20 between family size and the "non-verbal" test may also be a reflection of the pervasive effect of handicapped verbal development. We can put the point in this way: There is probably such an intimate reciprocal relationship between the development of language and thought processes, that whatever impoverishes the former would likely have a generalized rather than an isolated effect on the latter.

Among the mentally retarded, the effect of family size on language and mental development is further complicated by the fact that they also differ culturally or in social-class terms from most of the non-retarded population. It is far more likely that these differences operate, as does family size, in a negative rather than positive fashion, especially when we are perceiving and evaluating the mentally retarded in a situation (e.g., a test or school situation) the values and language of which derive from other social class groups.

The basic question arising from this important study concerns the psychological significances of a variable like family size. Nisbet's study indicates that size of family influences language development but it does not tell us how this comes about. Is it simply that when there is a large family each child is exposed to a great deal of verbal stimulation but receives less training from adults? Is it possible that the effect of family size on language development is less a quantitative one (i.e., amount of stimulation and training) than a qualitative one in the sense of the content and style of the stimulation? These questions cannot be answered at the present time but they do suggest that a variable such as family size has implications for some of the most important developmental problems. It is easy to determine the size of a family but it is another thing to study and determine how this variable is experienced by children and affects their development. It is both sobering and instructive to note that beginning with the oft found correlation between size of family and *IQ* score, and then indicating, as Nisbet did, that the variable of language had to be considered, one soon finds oneself faced with the central problems of human development—an instance of where the more you know the more you need to know.

XIX. RECOMMENDATIONS

In various places in this report we have made suggestions about specific research problems which if pursued would, in our opinion, provide important information having both practical and theoretical significance for the field of subnormal functioning. At this point we would like to summarize briefly only those recommendations which seem to be of major import.

A. Cultural Factors

Most of this report has been concerned with what we have termed the mentally retarded individual. Such individuals, of somewhat staggering numbers in our population, come largely from the lowest social classes, or from culturally distinct minority groups, or from regions with conspicuously poor educational facilities or standards. Because the condition is so highly correlated with social class and cultural factors we have insisted on distinguishing it from mental deficiency, where such relationships do not obtain and where, in contrast to mental retardation, there is demonstrable central nervous system pathology which effectively precludes an independent social existence. Regardless of theoretical bent, no responsible investigator has denied that the level and quality of the functioning of the mentally retarded reflects social and cultural factors. *What has not been systematically studied is how these kinds of factors operate so as to have an interfering effect on development.* The question of the degree of influnce of these factors can not be answered until we understand how and when they exert their influence. There would probably be general agreement that one of the more significant impacts on the behavior sciences in the last 50 years has been made by the study of cultural variations as they affect personality development. It is because the field of subnormal functioning in general, and the mentally retarded group in particular, have in contrast been neglected or bypassed by social scientists—despite the obvious importance of such areas for these workers—that we have emphasized the importance of studying the problems of subnormal functioning in terms of social science theory and methodology. Our approach to and understanding of such areas as delinquency, alcoholism, neurosis, psychosis, and child-rearing have changed and increased in part because of the application to them of modern social science thinking and research procedures.

The field of subnormal functioning is unfortunately distinctive in its isolation from such developments, yet it is in several ways able to derive maxi-

392

mum profit from similar research orientations. Many non-European cultures provide learning situations for children which, while quite appropriate for living within those societies, render their members almost totally unfit for meeting the intellectual problems of our culture. Just as in the case of research in culture and personality, knowledge derived from such non-European cultures can give us the perspective to isolate more clearly the relevant positive and negative factors operative in intellectual development in our own culture, and will permit us to test hypotheses in this field in a wide variety of settings. Furthermore, within our own society there exist many subcultural groups many of whose currently young children we can safely predict will be rejected by the larger society as retarded during later childhood or early adolescence. We can therefore study them at an early developmental level when they are actually in the process of acquiring those intellectual attributes which will later become handicaps, and thus determine the early dynamics of some kinds of retarded intellectual development.

Culture also determines the degree and kind of intellectual ability required for adequate—including minimally adequate—performance in any society. The fact that many retarded adolescents in our society pass school age and proceed to function adequately as adults in the larger society, but some do not, points to the importance of research which will identify the necessary intellectual abilities. Virtually nothing is available in systematic form on this subject, although many persons in social work and special education are capable of making notably effective intuitive judgments as to the deficits and remedial needs of individual children.

B. Cross-Cultural Research in Pathology

Our culture has maximized control of the physical environment in all its aspects to such a degree that it often becomes very difficult to determine what dietary and other factors have impinged on a given individual even in the recent past. In contrast the usually smaller and more stable non-European societies, most of whose members live more exposed to the physical environment, prepare similar foods in similar ways, and so on, can provide populations far superior for the testing of hypotheses regarding genetic, dietary, metabolic, or other factors in the etiology of pathological conditions. These populations have received some attention from researchers in a variety of fields of pathology but not nearly to the degree that would result from a wider awareness of the opportunities available.

C. LONGITUDINAL STUDIES

When it is merely noted that there has not been a single comprehensive longitudinal study of subnormal individuals, mentally retarded or mentally deficient, it will probably be understandable why throughout this report we have discussed the need for such studies. It is as if there have been two implicit assumptions about the importance of longitudinal studies: (*a*) the subnormal child is relatively unaffected by his environment and the longitudinal study, therefore, would not be very revealing; (*b*) all behavior of the subnormal individual is explainable by his intellectual deficit—he is what he is because of his deficit and all other factors are secondary. There is no evidence for either assumption. From the standpoint of any psychological theory one would assume that the subnormal individual, even the severely defective one, *is influenced by and in turn influences* the familial and social milieu into which he is born and in which he develops. In terms of this assumption the study of the early development of the subnormal individual as a scientific problem needs no justification. Furthermore, from a practical standpoint such studies would provide empirical data which could serve as a basis for parental guidance. In the case of the defective child, for example, there simply is no available scientific basis for the guidance of parents in the rearing of the child. It is only in recent years, and largely in the case of the severely defective child, that we have begun to see how the defective infant and child affects and changes the familial environment. We have not yet gotten to the point of studying the impact on the child of the environment which he blamelessly but markedly has disrupted.

D. INTELLECTUAL FACTORS

In the past several decades there have been a few, but very important, developments in the theory and measurement of intellectual functions. These developments suggest that the variety of intellectual factors or functions is greater than had previously been thought and that our conventional tests are most inadequate for the evaluation of these factors. Despite the fact that the clinical psychologist has long been aware of the limitations of conventional tests, clinical practice in general, and in the field of subnormal functioning in particular, has been relatively uninfluenced by these newer developments. In the case of the mentally retarded, most of whom maintain themselves in the community, there is strong evidence that our conventional tests leave much to be desired both as evaluators or predictors. In part this is undoubtedly a function of the narrow range of functions which these tests presumably measure. It should be pointed out that there are surprisingly few psychologists who have been concerned with the problem of the nature and development of intellectual functions. With the exception of Jastak, we know of no psychologist who has attempted to apply such theorizing to the problems of subnormal functioning. Our recommendation (it would be better to say hope) is that as a first step an attempt be made to bring together those few workers who are primarily concerned with the theory and development of intellectual functions in order that the status of this problem area can be described in terms of varieties of theoretical approach, conflicts between theories, existing research, and the direction of future research. We would also recommend that an attempt be made at such a meeting to present to these workers, most if not all of whom have thus far not been interested in subnormal functioning, aspects of this subject which seem relevant to the development of a theory of intelligence. The publication of such proceedings would not only be a contribution to the field of psychology but could serve as an important source of research stimulation to those working in subnormal functioning. It could also serve the purpose of demonstrating to those not now in the field (or uninterested in it) the kind of productive research, theoretical and applied, which can be done.

E. PROBLEM SOLVING IN NON-TEST SITUATIONS

This next recommendation concerns what may be termed a bottleneck in the constructive use of intelligence tests. We are here referring to the practice of evaluating performance on a test either by performance on another test or with behavior and achievement in the school situation—a situation, for the mentally retarded in particular, which involves values and motivations which are different from or clash with those in their social milieu. In addition, it is probably true that the range of problem-solving situations which confronts the child in school is not representative, for the mentally retarded at least, of the problem-solving situations which confront him in non-school situations. *Many people tend to assume without the justification of research, that the level of problem-solving in a test situation is the same as that in the non-test situation.* There is evidence that this assumption is least valid for the mentally retarded and the mentally deficient. *We strongly recommend the encouragement and support of research which has as its aim the observation and calibration of problem-solving behavior in non-test and non-school situations.*

F. PSYCHOSIS AND SUBNORMALITY

The relation between psychosis and subnormal functioning involves two of the most frequent problems in our society. Although there have been a number of studies, we are far from secure in our estimate of the frequency with which this relationship occurs. Aside from the long-standing problem of establishing explicit criteria and reliable diagnoses of psychosis, the *samples* of subnormal individuals which have been studied have not been representative either of the mentally retarded or of mentally deficient populations. More important—because it reflects professional attitudes toward and handling of the subnormal individual—is that the clinical evaluation of such an individual rarely focusses on those questions which allow one to determine the presence or absence of psychotic thinking and behavior. The focus is customarily so entirely on intellectual functions and considerations of level of functioning, and only a narrow sector of these, that the concept of the "total personality" receives not even lip service. From the standpoint of management, treatment, and program planning it should make a difference whether one is dealing with consequences of an intellectual deficit or with a more complicated and pathological set of relationships. From the scientific standpoint the question is one of elucidating the *mutual* effects of intellectual and personality disfunction. Far more often than not the deviant behavior of a subnormal child is "explained" by his low *IQ*. Rarely is his level of intellectual functioning viewed as possibly being influenced, in part at least, by personality factors. In addition to recommending in a general way the systematic study of the relation between psychosis and subnormality, we would suggest that for certain aspects of the problem there might be special value in focussing on an institutional population. For one thing, within relatively few years in such a setting one can expect to find more than a few cases where the aberrant behavior has become manifest only after a period of institutionalization. Rarely does one have the opportunity to observe the development in any individual of a psychosis (or other aberrant behavior) in a setting in which events and interpersonal relationships can be directly recorded and observed. It is our hunch that this approach to the appearance of psychotic-like behavior in severely defective individuals may give us data on the rôle of external factors in pathological behavior which would have significance beyond the field of subnormal functioning. This setting also may provide an opportunity for the testing of any predictive hypotheses which may be developed with respect to metabolic or biochemical factors in psychosis. Nowhere else is available a population of presumably non-psychotic individuals among whom one can expect the emergence of a sufficient number of psychotics to justify clinical studies of the total population with the aim of obtaining valid pre-psychotic data.

G. EARLY VARIATIONS IN TEMPERAMENT

There is a problem of great significance for normal as well as atypical development which has not yet received systematic research attention. We refer here to the study in the infancy period of variations in sensory reactivity and temperament and their interactions with different types of parental personality, family setting, and social class. The study by Bergman and Escalona discussed in Chapter XVII clearly indicates the significance of the problem for atypical development. It has been suggested that infantile autism, the idiot savant, and Bourne's "protophrenia" may be instances of early and unusual reaction tendencies which have interacted with environmental factors in an adverse way. The point we wish to emphasize, however, is that the study of the early interaction between constitutional and environmental factors would seem to be of central importance (a) for our understanding of the relation between intellectual potential and functioning, (b) for the development of more discerning and comprehensive diagnostic procedures of early development, and (c) for the establishment of a base for parental guidance which would really take account of individual differences in temperament. Our recommendation that research in this problem be encouraged and supported is but one way in which we can call attention to a question the importance of which has long been recognized but which has not been the focus of very much research: how do we account for the fact that any environmental factor, or constellation of factors, has very different effects on different children?

We now turn to a series of recommendations which concern what are undoubtedly the most immediate, pressing, and crucial problems: the recruitment and training of research personnel and the establishment of appropriate settings in which they may work. The suggestions we shall make are based on certain facts and assumptions: (a) at the present time the behavior sciences (and we would include here psychiatry) are little interested in developing subnormal functioning as a recognized research area requiring special training, although it is clear from all seven of the preceding recommendations that research initially oriented toward the problems of mental subnormality will, if broadly conceived, have almost immediate importance for a wide range of pressing research areas in other fields and can thus be expected to retain the interest of those behavior scientists whom it attracts; (b) there is, to our knowledge, no research and training center where all the behavior sciences are represented and which is of such professional status so as to attract to it the best students in these fields; (c) the development in a university of a truly coördinated training program involving independent academic departments is beset with so many problems that it would be a mistake to look *primarily* to such centers for the kinds of programs which are necessary; and (d) both because of the desperate need for research personnel and the importance of insuring (to the extent which one can) that those who are attracted to the field have strong motivation for research, it would appear that the post-doctoral programs would have advantages over pre-doctoral ones.

H. RESEARCH CENTER

Our first suggestion is that an appropriate setting be found in one of the major research centers of the United States for the establishment of a fully staffed research unit to investigate the problems of mental subnormality through the full range of its medical, biochemical, psychological, social, and other aspects. Such a center can provide the leadership and focus essential to the proper development of a research program which is starting almost from fundamentals, and can at the same time attract the high quality trainees which will assure its continuation.

I. CHILD-DEVELOPMENT RESEARCH CENTERS

There are more than a few research centers in this country with a primary focus on child development. Some of these have in addition to a research program, well-developed training programs. Because of our belief that longitudinal studies in subnormal functioning are necessary if certain problems are to be better understood, an attempt should be made to set up research and training programs in a selected few of these child development centers. Such centers already have some of the necessary personnel, in some instances there is an awareness of the general significance of developmental studies in subnormal functioning, and in most cases they have available to them excellent clinical facilities. We, like many others, are of the opinion that one cannot engender interest in a research area in mature researchers by dangling large sums of money before them. However, in the case of some child research centers there is interest in subnormal functioning and their ongoing research projects are of a nature which could benefit greatly from the inclusion of different types of subnormal individuals. There would therefore seem to be a real possibility that the knowledge of *stable* financial support over a period of years would encourage them to expand their research and training programs. In our opinion these centers will have to be stimulated to such expansion by those agencies (public and private) which are ready to support program development on a long term basis—it is doubtful if such developments will come spontaneously from within. It may be profitable as a first step for a meeting to be arranged with the research and training representatives of the leading child research centers in order to determine: (*a*) the strength of their interest in expanding such programs, (*b*) the problems which each of the centers would face, (*c*) the ways in which training in atypical development could be related to current training in normal child development, and (*d*) the extent and duration of the financial support which would be necessary to initiate and maintain expanded programs.

J. Additional Training for Workers in the Field

It is disappointing but true that the quality of research being done in our institutions is poor. The psychological personnel are for the most part geographically, financially, and socially apart from their professional brethren. The disinterest of behavior science departments (psychology, anthropology, sociology, psychiatry) in the area of subnormal functioning makes the solution of the problem most difficult. We must frankly state that we do not have any bright ideas of how to begin to go about remedying this situation. On the assumption that this particular problem will not change markedly in the foreseeable future it might be profitable to consider a program which would allow the institutional worker to go for extended periods to certain centers where there is an active research and training program—a center where he can possibly learn new skills and content which he could apply to research in his own setting. *This suggestion, however, presupposes that there will be several research centers which can offer this kind of opportunity.* An increment in skill and knowledge sufficient to justify this kind of effort can probably not be attained in a one- or two-week workshop, but should rather be viewed as requiring at least a half-year or year training course.

K. Future Reports

Our final recommendation concerns what to us is a limitation of this kind of report—that is, this report was prepared by two individuals who, like the rest of the human race, have prejudices, intellectual blind spots, and limitations in knowledge and wisdom. It may turn out, therefore, that some of our suggestions and critical evaluations will be found to be in error. It may also be that some important problems have not even been raised by us. We would suggest, therefore, that after a period of time another stock-taking report be prepared by other workers. Wrong conceptions and the conclusions of faulty research have remarkably prolonged lives and the field of subnormal functioning has already suffered under more than its share of fallacious assumptions and outmoded ideas. In addition, because of its present status the field must be kept alert to new ideas and developments and their dissemination in systematic form assured.

REFERENCES, PART I

1. ADAMS, J. M., HEATH, H. D., IMAGAWA, D. T., JONES, M. H. & SHEAR, H. H. Viral infections in the embryo. *A. M. A. J. Dis. Child.*, 1956, 92, 109.
2. ADRIAN, E. D. & MORUZZI, G. Impulses in the pyramidal tract. *J. Physiol.*, 1939, 97, 153.
3. ALLEN, G. Comments on the analysis of twin samples. *Acta Genet. Med. et Gemmel.*, 1955, 4, 143.
4. ALLEN, G. & BAROFF, G. S. Mongoloid twins and their siblings. *Acta Genet. et Statist. Med.*, 1955, 5, 294.
5. ALLEN, G., & KALLMANN, F. J. Frequency and types of mental retardation in twins. *Amer. J. Human Genet.*, 1955, 7, 15.
6. ALLISON, A. C. Population genetics: the nature and causes of genetic variability in population. In *Cold Spring Harbor Symposia on Quantitative Biology*: Vol 20. Cold Spring Harbor, L. I., N. Y.: Biological Laboratories, 1955.
7. ALM, I. The long-term prognosis for prematurely born children: A follow-up study of 999 premature boys born in wedlock and of 1002 controls. *Acta Pædiat., Supp. 94*, 1953, 116.
8. ANCEL, A. La Chimiotératogenèse: Réalisation des Monstruosités par des Substances Chimiques chez les Vertébrés. Paris: Gaston Doin & Cie., 1950.
9. ANTONOV, A. N. Children born during the siege of Leningrad in 1942. *J. Pediat.*, 1947, 30, 250.
10. ARMSTRONG, M. In Etiological Factors in Mental Retardation, Report of the Twenty-third Ross Pediatric Research Conference. Columbus, Ohio: Ross Laboratories, 1956, 28.
11. BACKUS, R. C. Adhesion partitioning: intrasomatic observations on normal escherichia coli and T-2 bacteriophage. *J. Biophys. & Biochem. Cytol.*, 1955, 1, 99.
12. BAILEY, O. T., & WOODARD, J. S. Some problems in the pathology of mental deficiency with microcephaly. *Neurology*, 1956, 6, 761.
13. BAIRD, D., & ILLSLEY, R. Environment and childbearing. *Proc. Roy. Soc. Med.*, 1953, 46, 53.
14. BAIRD, D., WALKER, J., & THOMSON, A. M. Causes and prevention of stillbirths and first week deaths. *J. Obst. & Gynaec. Brit. Emp.*, 1954, 61, 433.
15. BAKAY, L. The blood-brain barrier, with special regard to the use of radioactive isotopes. American Lecture Series, No. 278. Springfield, Ill.: Charles C. Thomas, 1956.
16. BALFOUR, M. I. Supplementary feeding in pregnancy. *Lancet*, 1944, 1, 208.
17. BANG, F. B., & FOARD, M. The serology of Newcastle virus infection. *J. Immunol.*, 1956, 76, 352.
18. BASS, M. H. Diseases of the pregnant woman affecting the offspring. *Advances Int. Med.*, 1952, 5, 15.
19. BAUER, K. F., & LEONHARDT, H. A. A contribution to the pathological physiology of the blood-brain barrier. *J. Comp. Neurol.*, 1956, 106, 363.
20. BEALE, G. H. Genetics of Paramecium Aurelia. London: Cambridge Univ. Press, 1954.
21. BECKER, H. Über Hirngefässausschaltungen: I. Extrakranielle Arterienunterbindungen; zur Theorie des Sauerstoffmangelschadens am zentralnervösen Gewebe. *Deutsche Ztschr. Nervenh.*, 1949, 161, 407; II. Intrakranielle Gefässverschlüsse; über experimentelle Hydranencephalie (Blasenhirn). *Deutsche Ztschr. Nervenh.*, 1949, 161, 446.
22. BENDA, C. E. The familial imbecile or oligocephaly as a morbid entity. *Amer. J. Ment. Deficiency*, 1944, 49, 32.
23. ————. Mongolism: a comprehensive review. *Arch. Pediat.*, 1956, 73, 391.
24. ————. Mongolism and Cretinism. New York: Grune and Stratton, 1946.

25. BENDA, C. E., & FARRELL, M. J. Psychopathology of mental deficiency in children. In *Psychopathology in Children.* New York: Grune and Stratton, 1955, 56-81.

26. BERGQUIST, H., & KÄLLEN, B. Notes on the early histogenesis and morphogenesis of the central nervous system in vertebrates. *J. Comp. Neurol.,* 1954, 100, 627.

27. BERRY, H. C., DOBZHANSKY, T., GARTLER, S. M., LEVINE, H., & OSBORNE, R. H. Chromatographic studies on urinary excretion patterns in monozygotic and dizygotic twins. *Amer. J. Human Genet.,* 1955, 7, 93.

28. BERTRAND, I., & VAN BOGAERT, L. Sur les maladies démyélinisantes chez l'homme et chez l'animal: Remarques et conclusions. *Acta Neurol. et Psychiat. Belg.,* 1954, 54, 682.

29. BIESTER, H. E., SCHWARTE, L. H., & REDDY, C. H. Further studies on moldy corn poisoning (leucoencephalomalacia) in horses. *Vet. Med.,* 1940, 35, 636.

30. BLAND, P. B. Influenza in relation to pregnancy and labor. *Amer. J. Obst.,* 1919, 79, 184.

31. BONNYCASTLE, D. D., PAASONEN, M. K., & GIARMAN, N. J. Diphenylhydantoin and brain-levels of 5-hydroxytryptamine. *Nature* (London), 1956, 178, 990.

32. BOOK, J. A. Investigation of a North Swedish population with special regard to schizophrenia and mental deficiency. *Acta Genet. et Statist. Med.,* 1953, 4, 2, 345.

33. BORBERG, A. Clinical and Genetic Investigation into Tuberous Sclerosis and Recklinghausen's Neurofibramatosis. Copenhagen: Thesis, 1951.

34. BORING, W. D., ANGEVINE, D. M., & WALKER, D. J. Factors influencing host-virus interactions: A comparison of virus multiplications and histopathology in infant, adult, and cortisone-treated adult mice infected with Conn.-5 strain of Coxsackie virus. *Naval Medicine Research Institute Research Project Report,* 1955, 13, 707.

35. BORNFIELD, P., DONAHUE, V. M., & HAMBURGER, F. H. Characteristic individual electrophoretic patterns in humans. *Proc. Soc. Exper. Biol. & Med.,* 1953, 83, 429.

36. BOVING, B. G. Blastocyst-uterine relationships. In *Cold Spring Harbor Symposia on Quantitative Biology:* Vol. 19. *The Mammalian Fetus: Physiological Aspects of Development.* Cold Spring Harbor, L. I., N. Y.: Biological Laboratories, 1954.

37. BOYD, J. D. Biochemistry of the Developing Nervous System. 1954, 21.

38. BRACHET, J. Chemical Embryology. . New York: Interscience Publishers, 1950.

39. ———. The use of basic dyes and ribonuclease for the cytochemical detection of ribonucleic acid. *Quart. J. Microbiol. Sc.,* 1953, 94, 1.

40. BRAMBELL, F. W. R. A discussion on immunological tolerance. *Proc. Roy. Soc.* (London), 1956, 1, 146.

41. ———. In *Cold Spring Harbor Symposia on Quantitative Biology:* Vol. 19. *The Mammalian Fetus: Physiological Aspects of Development.* Cold Spring Harbor, L. I., N. Y.: Biological Laboratories, 1954.

42. BRAMBELL, F. W. R., HEMMINGS, W. A., & HENDERSON, M. Antibodies and Embryos. London: Athlone Press, Univ. of London, 1951.

43. BRIERLY, J. B. The prolonged and distant effects of experimental brain injury on cerebral blood vessels as demonstrated by radioactive indicators. *J. Neurol. Neurosurg. & Psychiat.,* 1956, 19, 202.

44. BRODY, T. M., & BAIN, J. A. Effects of barbiturates on oxydative phosphorylation. *Proc. Soc. Exper. Biol. & Med.,* 1951, 77, 50.

45. BROWN, M., & BRIODY, B. A. Mutation and selection pressure during adaptation of influenza virus to mice. *Virology,* 1955, 1, 301.

46. BRUEMMER, J. H., O'DELL, B. L., & HOGAN, A. G. Maternal vitamin B_{12} deficiency and nucleic acid content of tissues from infant rats. *Proc. Soc. Exper. Biol. & Med.,* 1955, 88, 463.

47. BUCK, C. Exposure to virus diseases in early pregnancy and congenital malformations. *Canad. M. A. J.,* 1955, 72, 744.
48. BUCKWALTER, J. A., WOHLWEND, E. B., COLTER, D. C., TIDRICK, R. T., & KNOWLER, L. A. ABO blood groups and disease. *J. A. M. A.,* 1956, 162, 1210.
49. ————. Peptic ulceration and ABO blood groups. *J. A. M. A.,* 1956, 162, 1215.
50. BUNDESEN, H. N. Effective reduction of needless hebdomadal deaths in hospitals: A long-term public health program in Chicago, with special reference to use of an alerter system. *J. A. M. A.,* 1955, 157, 1384.
51. CAMBIER, J. Herpetic encephalitis and meningitis in man. *Presse Méd.,* 1955, 63, 296.
52. CASALS, J. The arthropod-borne group of animal viruses. *Tr. New York Acad. Sc.,* 1957, 19, 219.
53. CATTELL, R. S., BLEWETT, D. B., & BELOFF, J. R. The inheritance of personality. *Amer. J. Human Genet.,* 1955, 7, 122.
54. CAVANAGH, J. B. Aetiological problems in experimental "allergic" encephalomyelitis. *Guy's Hosp. Rep.,* 1956, 105, 39.
55. CENTENO, P. A., WALTER, R., & THELANDER, H. E. A 5-year study of prematurity. *California Med.,* 1956, 84, 269.
56. CHANDLER, J. P., & LEWIS, H. B. Comparative studies of the metabolism of amino acids: The oxidation of phenylalanine and phenylpyruvic acid in the organism of the rabbit. *J. Biol. Chem.,* 1932, 96, 619.
57. CHEN, G., & BOHNER, B. A study of the neuropharmacologic properties of certain convulsants, anticonvulsants, and Reserpine. *J. Pharmacol. & Exper. Therap.,* 1956, 117, 142.
58. CHOWN, B. Anemia from bleeding of the fetus into the mother's circulation. *Obst. & Gynec. Surv.,* 1954, 9, 851.
59. COHLAN, S. Q., & STONE, S. M. Congenital malformation of the brain produced by exposure of the pregnant rat to rubella virus: A preliminary report. *A. M. A. J. Dis. Child.,* 1955, 90, 616.
60. CONEL, J. L. The Postnatal Development of the Human Cerebral Cortex, Vols. 1-5. Cambridge, Mass.: Harvard Univ. Press, 1939.
61. COURVILLE, C. B. Anoxemia and brain disease. *California Med.,* 1953, 79, 214.
62. ————. Commotio Cerebri: Cerebral Concussion and the Postconcussion Syndrome in Their Medical and Legal Aspects. Los Angeles: San Lucas Press, 1953.
63. CROME, L. Some morbid-anatomical aspects of mental deficiency. *J. Ment. Sc.,* 1954, 100, 894.
64. CROWE, F., SCHULL, W. J., & NEEL, J. V. A Clinical Pathological and Genetic Study of Multiple Neurofibromatosis. Springfield, Ill.: Charles C. Thomas, 1956.
65. CUMINGS, J. N. Lipid chemistry in demyelinating diseases. *Brain,* 1955, 78, 554.
66. DARKE, R. A. Late effects of severe asphyxia neonatorum. *J. Pediat.,* 1944, 24, 148.
67. DAY, M. F. Mechanisms of transmission of viruses by arthropods. *Exper. Parasitol.,* 1955, 4, 387.
68. ————. The relation of arthropod-borne viruses to their invertebrate hosts. *Tr. New York Acad. Sc.,* 1957, 19, 244.
69. DEBUSK, A. G. Metabolic aspects of chemical genetics. *Advances Enzymol.,* 1956, 17, 393.
70. DEMORSIER, G. Les syndromes vasculaires embryonnaires dans les malformations cérébrales. In *Proceedings of the First International Congress on Histopathology of the Nervous System.* Sept. 8-13, 1952, 24.

404

71. DENT, J. N., & HUNT, E. L. Radiotracer techniques in embryological research. *J. Cell. & Comp. Physiol.,* 1954, **43** (Supp. 1), 77.
72. DIECKMANN, W. J., TURNER, D. F., MEILLER, E. J., SAVAGE, L. J., HILL, A. J., STRAUBE, M. T., POTTINGER, R. E., & RYNKIEWICZ, L. M. Observations on protein intake and the health of the mother and baby: I. Clinical and laboratory findings. *J. Amer. Dietet. A.,* 1951, **27**, 1046.
73. DIECKMANN, W. J., TURNER, D. F., MEILLER, E. J., STRAUBE, M. T., & SAVAGE, L. J. Observations on protein intake and the health of the mother and baby: II. Food intake. *J. Amer. Dietet. A.,* 1951, **27**, 1053.
74. DOBBING, J. The blood-brain barrier. *Guy's Hosp. Rep.,* 1956, **105**, 27.
75. EATON, J. W., & WEIL, R. J. Culture and Mental Disorders: A Comparative Study of the Hutterites and Other Populations. Chicago: Free Press, 1955, 52.
76. EBBS, J. H., TISDALL, F. F., & SCOTT, W. A. The influence of prenatal diet on mother and child. *J. Nutrition,* 1941, **22**, 515.
77. EBERT, J. D. Appearance of tissue-specific proteins during development. *Ann. New York Acad. Sc.,* 1952, **55**, 67.
78. EICHMANN, E., & GESENIUS, H. Die Missgeburtenzunahme in Berlin und Umgebung in den Nachkriegsjahren. *Arch. Gynäk.,* 1952, **181**, 168.
79. ENDERS, J. F. The present status of etiologic discovery in viral diseases. *Ann. Int. Med.,* 1956, **45**, 331.
80. ESPLIN, D. W. Effects of diphenylhydantoin on synaptic transmission. Thesis, Univ. of Utah, 1955.
81. ESTBORN, B. Familial occurrence of multiple sclerosis. *Nord. Med.,* 1955, **54**, 1665.
82. EYLES, D., & COLEMAN, N. An evaluation of the curative effects of pyrimethamine and sulfadiazine, alone and in combination on experimental mouse toxoplasmosis. *Antibiotics & Chemother.,* 1955, **5**, 529.
83. FAJANS, S. S., & CONN, J. W. An approach to the prediction of diabetes mellitus by modification of the glucose tolerance test with cortisone. *Diabetes,* 1954, **3**, 296.
84. FALLS, H. F., & NEEL, J. V. The detection of carriers of "recessive" genes. *Eugenics Quart.,* 1954, **1**, 166.
85. FERM, V. In Etiological Factors in Mental Retardation, Report of the Twenty-third Ross Pediatric Research Conference. Columbus, Ohio: Ross Laboratories, 1956, 64.
86. FICQ, A. Localisation et dosage du lithium dans les embryons d'amphibiens. *J. Embryol. & Exper. Morphol.,* 1954, **2**, 204.
87. FINLAY, G. F. The effects of different species lens anti-sera on pregnant mice and rats and their progeny. *Brit. J. Exper. Biol.,* 1923, **1**, 201.
88. FLEICHSIG, P. Anatomie des Menschlichen Gehirns und Rückenmarks. Leipzig: VEB Georg Thieme, 1920.
89. FLICKENGER, R. A., LEVIE, E., & SMITH, A. E. Some serological experiments relating to the embryonic development of the lens. *Physiol. Zoöl.,* 1955, **28**, 79.
90. FØLLING, A. Über Ausscheidung von Phenylbrenztraubensäure in den Harn als Stoffwechselanomalie in Verbindung mit Imbezilität. *Ztschr. Physiol. Chem.,* 1934, **227**, 169.
91. FRANCIS, T. Virus problems in medicine. *Illinois M. J.,* 1955, **108**, 257.
92. FRANKLIN, R. M., RUBIN, H., & DAVIS, C. A. The production, purification, and properties of Newcastle disease virus labeled with radiophosphorus. *Virology,* 1957, **3**, 96.
93. FRASER, F. C. In Etiologic Factors in Mental Retardation, Report of the Twenty-third Ross Pediatric Research Conference. Columbus, Ohio: Ross Laboratories, 1956, 59-63.
94. FRASER, F. C., KALTER, H., WALKER, B. E., & FAINSTAT, T. D. The experimental production of cleft palate with cortisone and other hormones. *J. Cell. & Comp. Physiol.,* 1954, **43** (Supp. 1), 237.

95. FRASER, J. F. D. Fetal deaths in the rat. *J. Embryol. & Exper. Morphol.,* 1955, 3, 13.

96. FREUDENBERG, E., ROULET, E., & NICOLE, R. Kongenitale Infektion mit Coxsackie-Virus. *Ann. Paediat.,* 1952, 178, 150.

97. FREUND, J., & LIPTON, M. M. Experimental allergic encephalomyelitis after the excision of the injection site of antigen-adjuvant emulsion. *J. Immunol.,* 1955, 75, 454.

98. FRIEDLAENDER, M., MOORE, D. H., LOVE, R., BROWN, P. A., & KOPROWSKI, H. Studies with the electron microscope of virus-host relationships in Ehrlich ascites tumor cells: I. The identification and structure of anopheles A virus. *J. Exper. Med.,* 1955, 102, 361.

99. GARROD, A. E. The Croonian Lectures on inborn errors of metabolism. *Lancet,* 1908, 2, 1, 73, 142, 214.

100. GARTLER, S. M. Elimination of recessive lethals from the population when the heterozygote can be detected. *Amer. J. Human Genet.,* 1953, 5, 148.

101. GARTLER, S. M., DOBZHANSKY, T., & BERRY, H. C. Chromotographic studies on urinary excretion patterns in monozygotic and dizygotic twins: II. Heritability of the excretion rates of certain substances. *Amer. J. Human Genet.,* 1955, 7, 108.

102. GASTAUT, H. The epilepsies: Electro-clinical correlations. (Tr. Mary A. B. Brazier.) American Lecture Series, No. 204. Springfield, Ill.: Charles C. Thomas, 1954.

103. GEDDA, L. Twin studies. *Eugenics Quart.,* 1954, 1, 171.

104. GEIGER, R. Quoted in: Diphenylhydantoin and brain-levels of 5-hydroxytryptamine. Bonnycastle, *et als. Nature* (London), 1956, 178, 990.

105. GERBER, P., LOOSLI, C. G., & HAMRE, D. Antigenic variance of influenza A virus (PR 8 strain): I. Their development during serial passage in the lungs of partially immune mice. *J. Exper. Med.,* 1955, 101, 627.

106. GEYER, H. Dysplasmatisch-idiotische Kinder ovariell insuffizienter Mütter. *Arch. Gynäk.,* 1952, 181, 277.

107. GEYER, H., & SMITH, E. A. Further studies on inheritance of eye defects induced in rabbits. *J. Exper. Zoöl.,* 1923, 28, 449.

108. GIBBS, E. L., GIBBS, F. A., & GROSSMAN, H. Electroencephalographic evidence of encephalitis in children with supposedly uncomplicated childhood diseases. In *Transactions of the American Neurological Association,* 1956, 159.

109. GILLMAN, J., GILBERT, C., & GILLMAN, T. Preliminary report on hydrocephalus, spina bifida, and other congenital anomalies in the rat produced by trypanblue. *South African J. M. Sc.,* 1948, 13, 47.

110. GINZBERG, E., & BRAY, D. W. The Uneducated. New York: Columbia Univ. Press, 1953.

111. GIRI, K. V. Two-dimensional Agar electrophoresis of serum mucoproteins. *Nature* (London), 1957, 179, 632.

112. GITLIN, D., & CRAIG, J. M. The nature of the hyaline membrane in asphyxia of the newborn. *Pediatrics,* 1956, 17, 64.

113. GLUECKSOHN-WAELSCH, S. Some genetic aspects of development. In *Cold Spring Harbor Symposia on Quantitative Biology:* Volume 19. *The Mammalian Fetus: Physiological Aspects of Devolopment.* Cold Spring Harbor, L. I., N. Y.: Biological Laboratories, 1954, 41-49.

114. GODDARD, H. H. The Kallikak Family. New York: Macmillan, 1912.

115. GODENNE, M. O., & RIORDAN, J. T. Tissue culture diagnosis of poliomyelitis and aseptic meningitis. *J. A. M. A.,* 1955, 158, 707.

116. GOOD, R. A., CAMPBELL, B., & GOOD, T. A. Prophylactic and therapeutic effect of para-amino-benzoic acid and sodium salicylate on experimental allergic encephalomyelitis. *Proc. Soc. Exper. Biol. & Med.,* 1949, 72, 341.

117. GOODMAN, M., GREENSPON, S. A., & KRAKOWER, C. A. The antigenic composition of various anatomic structures of canine kidney. *J. Immunol.,* 1955, 75, 96.

118. GOODPASTURE, E. W. Virus infection of the mammalian fetus. *Science,* 1942, 95, 391.

119. GRAY, R. A. Activity of an antiviral agent from nocardia on 2 viruses in intact plants. *Phytopathology,* 1955, 45, 281.

120. GREENBERG, M. & PELLITTERI, O. Frequency of defects in infants whose mothers had rubella during pregnancy. *J. A. M. A.,* 1957, 165, 675-678.

121. GREENBERG, M., YANKAUER, A., JR., KRUGMAN, S., OSBORN, J. J., WARD, R. S., & DANCIS, J. The effect of smallpox vaccination during pregnancy on the incidence of congenital malformations. *Pediatrics,* 1949, 3, 456.

122. GREENFIELD, J. G. Maladies spontanées démyélinisantes chez l'homme et chez l'animal. *Acta Neurol. et Psychiat. Belg.,* 1954, 54, 621.

123. GREGG, N. M. Congenital cataract following German measles in the mother. *Tr. Ophth. Soc. Australia,* 1941, 3, 35.

124. GRIFFITHS, R. The Abilities of Babies: A Study in Mental Measurement. London: Univ. of London Press, 1954.

125. GROUPÉ, V., HERRMANN, E. C., JR., & RAUSCHER, F. J. Ingestion and destruction of influenza virus by free living ciliate tetrahymena pyriformis. *Proc. Soc. Exper. Biol. & Med.,* 1955, 88, 479.

126. GRÜNEBERG, H. The Genetics of the Mouse, Ed. 2. The Hague: Martinus Nijhoff, 1952.

127. HALLERVORDEN, J., & MEYER, J. E. Cerebrale Kinderlähmung (Früherworbene körperliche und geistige Defekzustände). In *Handbuch der Speziellen Pathologischen Anatomie und Histologie.* Lubarsch, O., Henke, F., & Rössle, R. (*Eds.*) Berlin: Springer-Verlag, 1956, Vol. 13, Pt. 4, 194-282.

128. HAMBURGER, V. Development of the nervous system. *Ann. New York Acad. Sc.,* 1952, 55, 117.

129. HAMBURGER, V., & HABEL, K. Teratogenic and lethal effects of influenza-A and mumps viruses on early chick embryos. *Proc. Soc. Exper. Biol. & Med.,* 1947, 66, 608.

130. HARRELL, R. F., WOODYYARD, E., & GATES, A. I. The Effect of Mothers' Diets on the Intelligence of Offspring: A Study of the Influence of Vitamin Supplementation of the Diets of Pregnant and Lactating Women on the Intelligence of Their Children. New York: Bureau of Publications, Teachers College, 1955.

131. HARRIMAN, D. G. F., & MILLER, J. H. D. Progressive familial myoclonic epilepsy in 3 families: Its clinical features and pathological basis. *Brain,* 1955, 78, 325.

132. HARRIS, H. An Introduction to Human Biochemical Genetics. London: Cambridge Univ. Press, 1953.

133. HARTMANN, A. F., PENNOYER, M. M., & GRAHAM, F. K. Anoxia at Birth. (To be published.)

134. HEGNAUER, H. Missbildungschäufigkeit und Gebäralter. *Geburtsh. u. Frauenh.,* 1951, 11, 777.

135. HEHLE, W. Isotopic labeling of viruses: III. The use of phosphorus-32 in the study of incomplete forms of influenza virus. *Tr. New York Acad. Sc.,* 1956, 18, 255.

136. HERMANN, H. The effect of amino acid analogues on the development of the explanted chick embryo. In Proceedings of conference sponsored by Association for Aid of Crippled Children, New York Academy of Medicine, June 5-6, 1952. New York: Association for the Aid of Crippled Children, 1953, 148.

137. HERNDON, C. N. Intelligence in family groups in the Blue Ridge Mountains. *Eugenics Quart.,* 1954, 1, 53.

138. HERTIG, A. T., ROCK, J., & ADAMS, E. C. A description of 34 human ova within the first 17 days of development. *Amer. J. Anat.,* 1956, 98, 435.

139. HICKS, S. P. The effects of ionizing radiation, certain hormones, and radiomimetic drugs on the developing nervous system. *J. Cell. & Comp. Physiol.,* 1954, 43, 151.

140. HOLLINSHEAD, A. C., & SMITH, P. K. Relative effectiveness of certain inhibitory chemicals on the 3 types of poliomyelitis virus. *J. Pharmacol. & Exper. Therap.,* 1956, 117, 97.

141. HONIG, E. I. An endemiological study of enteric virus infections. *J. Exper. Med.,* 1956, 103, 247.

142. HONIG, E. I., MELNICK, J. L., ISACSON, P., PARR, R., MYERS, I. L., & WALTON, M. An endemiological study of enteric virus infections: Poliomyelitis, Coxsackie, and orphan (ECHO) viruses isolated from normal children in 2 socio-economic groups. *J. Exper. Med.,* 1956, 103, 247.

143. HOROWITZ, N. H., & OWEN, R. D. Physiological aspects of genetics. *Amer. Rev. Physiol.,* 1954, 16, 84.

144. HUGHES, A. The development of the neural tube of the chick embryo: A study with the ultraviolet microscope. *J. Embryol. & Exper. Morphol.,* 1955, 3, 305.

145. HURST, E. W., SNOW, G. A., & ROBERTS, D. C. The antiviral activity of mepacrine in relation to morphological changes produced by the drug. *Brit. J. Exper. Path.,* 1955, 36, 215.

146. HUXLEY, J. S., & CARR-SAUNDERS, A. M. Absence of prenatal effects of lens antibodies in rabbits. *Brit. J. Exper. Biol.,* 1923, 1, 215.

147. INGALLS, T. I., CURLEY, F. J., & PRINDLE, R. A. Experimental production of congenital anomalies: Timing and degree of anoxia as factors causing fetal deaths. *New England J. Med.,* 1952, 247, 768.

148. JEANS, P. C., SMITH, M. B., & STEARNS, G. Incidence of prematurity in relation to maternal nutrition. *J. Amer. Dietet. A.,* 1955, 31, 576.

149. JENSEN, K. E., MINUSE, E., & ACKERMANN, W. W. Serologic evidence of American experience with newborn pneumonitis virus (type Sendai). *J. Immunol.,* 1955, 75, 71.

150. JERVIS, G. A. Excretion of phenylalanine and derivitives in phenylpyruvic oligophrenia. *Proc. Soc. Exper. Biol. & Med.,* 1950, 75, 83.

151. ———. Phenylpyruvic oligophrenia deficiency of phenylalanine-oxidizing system. *Proc. Soc. Exper. Biol. & Med.,* 1953, 82, 514.

152. JOST, A. Hormonal factors in the development of the fetus. In *Cold Spring Harbor Symposia on Quantitative Biology:* Vol. 20. Cold Spring Harbor, L. I., N. Y.: Biological Laboratories, 1955.

153. JUNG, R. Allegemeine Neuro-Physiologie. In *Handbuch der Inneren Medizin.* Berlin: Springer-Verlag, 1953.

154. JUNGHERR, E. L., SINGSEN, E. P., & MATTERSON, L. D. Nutritional encephalomalacia of chickens: Effect of treatment on the pathology. *Lab. Invest.,* 1956, 5, 120.

155. KALLMANN, F. J. Heredity in Health and Mental Disorders. New York: Norton, 1954.

156. ———. Twin data in the analysis of mechanisms of inheritance. *Amer. J. Human Genet.,* 1954, 6, 156.

157. KALTER, S. S., PRIER, J. E., & ZAMAN, H. Virus proliferation in hypoxic mice and chick embryos. *J. Exper. Med.,* 1955, 102, 475.

158. KALTER, S. S., SMOLIN, H. H., McELHANEY, J. M., & TEPPERMAN, J. Endocrines and their relation to influenza virus infection. *J. Exper. Med.,* 1951, 93, 529.

159. KARZON, D. T. Studies on a neutralizing antibody against canine distemper virus found in man. *Pediatrics,* 1955, 16, 809.

160. KEITH, H. M., & NORVAL, M. A. Neurological lesions in the newly born infant: I. Preliminary study; II. Role of prolonged labor, asphyxia and delayed respiration. *Pediatrics,* 1950, 6, 229.

161. KEMP, T. Prevalence of genetically based physical and mental deficiencies and the frequency of related genes. *Eugenics Quart.,* 1954, 1, 215.

162. KEMPE, C. H., & BENENSON, A. S. Vaccinia: Passive immunity in newborn

infants: I. Placental transmission of antibodies; II. Response to vaccinations. *J. Pediat.,* 1953, 42, 525.

163. KIRBY, W. M. M., & EVANS, C. A. Tissue culture isolation of Coxsackie group B viruses in aseptic meningitis. *J. A. M. A.,* 1955, 159, 743.

164. KIRK, S. A. Public school provisions for severely retarded children. Special report to the New York State Interdepartmental Health Resources Board, July, 1957.

165. KIRMAN, B. H. Rubella as a cause of mental deficiency. *Lancet,* 1955, 2, 1113.

166. KNOBLOCH, H., RIDER, R., HARPER, P., & PASAMANICK, B. Neuropsychiatric sequelae of prematurity: A longitudinal study. *J. A. M. A.,* 1956, 161, 581.

167. KNOX, A. W. Infection and immunity in offspring of mice inoculated during gestation with murine polio virus. *Proc. Soc. Exper. Biol. & Med.,* 1950, 74, 792.

168. KURLAND, L. T., MULDER, D. W., & WESTLUND, K. B. Multiple sclerosis and amyotrophic lateral sclerosis: Etiologic significance of recent epidemiologic and genetic studies. *New England J. Med.,* 1955, 252, 649, 697.

169. KURNICK, N. B. A rational therapy of systemic lupus erythematosus. *A. M. A. Arch. Int. Med.,* 1956, 97, 562.

170. LAFON, R., & LABAUGE, R. Le devenir des encéphalopathies de l'enfant. *Montpellier Med.,* 1956, 49, 25.

171. LAFON, R., PASSOUANT, P., FAURE, J. L., & MINVIELLE, J. Épilepsie et gémellite: Étude clinique, électroencéphalographique et psychologique de 7 couples de jumeaux univitellins épileptiques. Montpellier Méd., 1956, 49, 56.

172. LALLIER, R. Lésions de métaux lourds et le problème de la détermination embryonnaire chez les échinodermes. *J. Embryol. & Exper. Morphol.,* 1956, 4, 265.

173. LANDAUER, W. On the chemical production of developmental abnormalities of phenocopies in chicken embryos. *J. Cell. & Comp. Physiol.,* 1954, 43 (Supp. 1), 261.

174. LANDE, L. Congenital malformations with severe damage to the central nervous system due to early fetal virus infection. *J. Pediat.,* 1950, 36, 625.

175. LANDTMAN, B. On the relationship between maternal conditions during pregnancy and congenital malformations. *Arch. Dis. Childhood,* 1948, 23, 237.

176. LAPE, E. In Medical Research: A Midcentury Survey. Boston: Little, Brown, 1955.

177. LARRABEE, M. G., RAMOS, J. G., & BULBRING, E. Do anesthetics depress nerve cells by depressing O_2 consumption? *Fed. Proc.,* 1950, 9, 75.

178. LAVECK, G. D. Inapparent infection with western equine encephalitis virus: Epidemiologic observations. *Amer. J. Pub. Health,* 1955, 45, 1409.

179. LEMKAU, P., TIETZE, C., & COOPER, M. Mental hygiene problems in an urban district. *Ment. Hyg.,* 1941, 25, 624.

180. LENNOX, W. G. The heredity of epilepsy as told by relatives and twins. *J. A. M. A.,* 1951, 146, 529.

181. LHERMITTE, F. Leuco-encéphalites. Paris: Ernest Flammarion, 1950.

182. LIPTON, M. M., & FREUND, J. The transfer of experimental allergic encephalomyelitis in the rat by means of parabiosis. *J. Immunol.,* 1953, 71, 380.

183. LIU, C., & COFFIN, D. L. Studies on canine distemper infection by means of fluorescein-labeled antibody: I. The pathogenesis, pathology, and diagnosis of the disease in experimentally infected ferrets. *Virology,* 1957, 3, 115.

184. ————. Studies on canine distemper infection by means of fluorescein-labeled antibody: II. The pathology and diagnosis of the naturally occurring disease in dogs and the antigenic nature of the inclusion body. *Virology,* 1957, 3, 132.

185. LOGOTHELIS, J. A study of free amino acids in the human cerebrospinal fluid. *Neurology,* 1955, 5, 767.

186. LOWE, C. R., & McKEOWN, T. A note on secular changes in the human sex ratio at birth. *Brit. J. Social Med.,* 1951, 5, 91.

187. ————. Sex ratio of human births related to maternal age. *Brit. J. Social Med.*, 1950, **4**, 75-85.

188. LUMSDEN, C. E. Allergic encephalitis. *Proc. Roy. Soc. Med.*, 1956, **49**, 148.

189. ————. Cyanide leukoencephalopathy in rats and observations on the vascular and ferment hypothesis of demyelinating diseases. *J. Neurol. Neurosurg. & Psychiat.*, 1950, **13**, 1.

190. LUMSDEN, C. E., KABAT, E. A., WOLF, A., & BEZER, A. E. Studies on acute disseminated encephalomyelitis produced experimentally in Rhesus monkeys: Five complement fixing antibodies. *J. Exper. Med.*, 1950, **92**, 253.

191. LUTWAK-MANN, C. Some properties of the rabbit blastocyst. *J. Embryol. & Exper. Morphol.*, 1954, **2**, 1.

192. MACARTHUR, P. Congenital vaccinia and vaccinia gravidaris. *Lancet*, 1952, **2**, 1104.

193. MACFARLANE, W. V., PENNYCUIK, P. R., & THRIFT, E. Resorption and loss of foetuses in rats living at 35° C. *J. Physiol.*, 1957, **135**, 451.

194. MACMAHON, B., & MCKEOWN, T. The incidence of hare lip and cleft palate related to birth rank and maternal age. *Amer. J. Human Genet.*, 1953, **5**, 176.

195. MACMAHON, B., RECORD, R. G., & MCKEOWN, T. Secular changes in the incidence of malformations of the central nervous system. *Brit. J. Social Med.*, 1951, **5**, 254.

196. MALAMUD, N. Recent trends in classification of neuropathological findings in mental deficiency. *Amer. J. Ment. Deficiency*, 1954, **58**, 3.

197. MALPAS, P. The incidence of human malformations and the significance of changes in the maternal environment and their causation. *J. Obst. & Gynaec. Brit. Emp.*, 1937, **44**, 434.

198. MANDELBROTE, B. M., STANIER, M. W., THOMPSON, R. H. S., & THRUSTON, M. N. Studies on copper metabolism in demyelinating diseases of the central nervous system. *Brain*, 1948, **71**, 212.

199. MARSDEN, J. P., & GREENFIELD, C. R. M. Inherited smallpox. *Arch. Dis. Childhood*, 1934, **89**, 309.

200. MATHEWS, R. E., & SMITH, J. D. The chemotherapy of virus. *Advances Virus Res.*, 1955, **3**, 49.

201. MAYER, S. E., & BAIN, J. A. The intracellular localization of fluorescent convulsants. *J. Pharmacol. & Exper. Therap.*, 1956, **118**, 1.

202. ————. Localization of the hematoencephalic barrier with fluorescent quaternary acridones. *J. Pharmacol. & Exper. Therap.*, 1956, **118**, 17.

203. MCALPINE, D., COMPSTON, N. D., & LUMSDEN, C. E. Multiple Sclerosis. Edinburgh: E. & S. Livingstone, Ltd., 1955.

204. MCGANITY, W. J., BRIDGFORTH, E. B., MARTIN, M. P., NEWBILL, J. A., & DARBY, W. J. The Vanderbilt cooperative study of maternal and infant nutrition: VIII. Some nutritional implications. *J. Amer. Dietet. A.*, 1955, **31**, 582.

205. MEDAWAR, P. B. Some immunological and endocrinological problems raised by the evolution of viviparity in vertebrates. In *Symposium of the Society for Experimental Biology: Evolution*. New York: Academic Press, 1953, 320.

206. (anon.) Report of the Mental Deficiency Commission. London: His Majesty's Stationery Office, 1929, Pts. 1, 2, 3, and 4.

207. MEYER, J. E. Über die Lokalisation Frühkindlicher Hirnschaden in arteriellen Grenzgebieten. *Arch. Psychiat. u. Ztschr. Neurol.*, 1953, **190**, 328.

208. MOOLTEN, S. E., CLARK, E., GLASSER, B. F., KATZ, E., & MILLER, B. S. Blood stream invasion by Newcastle disease virus associated with hemolytic anemia and encephalopathy: Report of 3 cases. *Amer. J. Med.*, 1953, **14**, 294.

209. MOORELL, F., ROBERTS, L., & JASPER, H. H. Effect of focal epileptogenic lesions and their ablation upon conditioned electrical responses of the brain in the monkey. *Electroencephalog. & Clin. Neurophysiol.*, 1956, **8**, 217.

210. MORROW, R. S., & MARK, J. D. The correlation of intelligence and neurological

findings in 22 patients autopsied for brain damage. *J. Consult. Psychol.,* 1955, **19**, 283.

211. MULLER, H. J. Our load of mutations. *Amer. J. Human Genet.,* 1950, **2**, 111.
212. MURPHY, D. P. Congenital Malformations: A Study of Parental Characteristics with Special Reference to the Reproductive Process. Philadelphia: Univ. of Pennsylvania Press, 1940.
213. MURRAY, H. L. The immunological relationships of mother, foetus and placenta. *Liverpool Med.-Chir. J.,* 1914, **34**, 123.
214. National Academy of Sciences, National Research Council. The Biological Effects of Atomic Radiation: Summary Reports from a Study by the Academy. Washington, D. C.: 1956.
215. National Association for Retarded Children. The Viewpoint Series. New York: 1954.
216. NEEL, J. V. The clinical detection of the genetic carriers of inherited diseases. *Medicine,* 1947, **26**, 115.
217. NEEL, J. V., & SCHULL, W. J. The Effect of Exposure to the Atomic Bombs on Pregnancy Termination in Hiroshima and Nagasaki. Washington, D. C.: National Academy of Sciences, National Research Council, 1956, Publication 461.
218. NEWMAN, H. H., FREEMAN, F. N., & HOLZINGER, K. J. Twins: A Study of Heredity and Environment. Chicago: Univ. of Chicago Press, 1937.
219. New York State Department of Mental Hygiene, Mental Health Research Unit. Technical Report: A Special Census of Suspected Referred Mental Retardation, Onondaga County, N. Y. Syracuse, N. Y.: 1955, 84.
220. NORMAN, R. M., URICH, H., & LLOYD, O. C. The neuropathology of infantile Gaucher's disease. *J. Path. & Bact.,* 1956, **72**, 121.
221. NOVITSKI, E., & SANDLER, L. The relationship between parental age, birth order, and its secondary sex ratio in humans. *Ann. Human Genet.,* 1956, **21**, 123.
222. OPPENHEIMER, J. In: The Analysis of Development. Willier, B. H. *(Ed.).* Philadelphia: W. B. Saunders, 1955.
223. OSBORN, F. Preface to Eugenics, Ed. 2. New York: Harper, 1951.
224. ØSTER, J. Mongolism. Copenhagen: Danish Science Press, Ltd., 1953.
225. PARRAN, T. Nationwide need—Epidemiologists. *J. A. M. A.,* 1957, **163**, 742.
226. PASAMANICK, B., KNOBLOCH, H., RIDER, R., & HARPER, P. An evaluation of a questionnaire on infant development. *Amer. J. Pub. Health,* 1955, **45**, 1309.
227. PASAMANICK, B., & LILIENFELD, A. M. The association of maternal and fetal factors with the development of mental deficiency: II. Relationship to maternal age, birth order, previous reproductive loss and degree of mental deficiency. *Amer. J. Ment. Deficiency,* 1956, **60**, 557.
228. PENROSE, L. S. The Biology of Mental Defect, Ed. 2. London: Sidgwick & Jackson, 1954.
229. ————. On the familial appearances of maternal and foetal incompatibility. *Ann. Eugenics,* 1947, **13**, 141.
230. ————. Observations on the aetiology of mongolism. *Lancet,* 1954, **2**, 505.
231. ————. Parental age and mutation. *Lancet,* 1955, **2**, 312.
232. PETERSDORF, R. G., & BENNETT, I. L., JR. Treatment of mumps orchitis with adrenal hormones: Report of 23 cases with a note of hepatic involvement of mumps. *A. M. A. Arch. Int. Med.,* 1957, **99**, 222.
233. (anon.) The physiological basis of the electroencephalogram: Symposium II. *Electroencephalog. & Clin. Neurophysiol.,* 1953, Supp. 4, 57.
234. POPE, A. General biochemical factors in neuronal discharge. *Epilepsia,* 1952, **1**, 83.
235. POSER, C. M., & VAN BOGAERT, L. Natural history and evolution of the concept of Schilder's diffuse sclerosis. *Acta Psychiat. et Neurol. Scandinav.,* 1956, **31**, 285.
236. POTTER, E. L. Pathology of the Fetus and Newborn. Chicago: Year Book Publishers, 1952.

237. PRATT, R. T. C., COMPSTON, N. D., & McALPINE, D. The familial incidence of disseminated sclerosis and its significance. *Brain,* 1951, **74,** 191.

238. PRESSMAN, D. Current status of the tissue localization of I¹³¹ labeled anti-tissue antibodies. *Tr. New York Acad. Sc.,* 1956.

239. PUCK, T. T. In Etiologic Factors in Mental Retardation, Report of the Twenty-third Ross Pediatric Research Conference. Columbus, Ohio: Ross Laboratories, 1956, 56.

240. RASKIN, N. Antibrain antibodies in multiple sclerosis: Study of the antibrain antibodies in the blood of multiple sclerosis patients by complement fixation tests. *A. M. A. Arch. Neurol. & Psychiat.,* 1955, **73,** 645.

241. RECORD, R. G., & McKEOWN, T. Congenital malformations of the central nervous system: I. A survey of 930 cases. *Brit. J. Social Med.,* 1949, **3,** 183.

242. ———. Congenital malformations of the central nervous system: II. Maternal reproductive history and familial incidence. *Brit. J. Social Med.,* 1950, **4,** 26.

243. REED, S. C. A test for heterozygous deleterious recessives. *J. Hered.,* 1954, **45,** 17.

244. REED, S. C., REED, E. W., & PALM, J. D. Fertility and intelligence among families of the mentally deficient. *Eugenics Quart.,* 1954, **1,** 44.

245. RHODES, A. J. Recent advances in the laboratory diagnosis of virus infections. *Ann. Int. Med.,* 1956, **45,** 106.

246. RIDGWAY, L. P., & KARNOFSKY, D. A. The effects of metals on the chick embryo: Toxicity and production of abnormalities in development. *Ann. New York Acad. Sc.,* 1952, **55,** 203.

247. ROBERTS, J. A. F. Birth order, maternal age and intelligence with particular reference to a possible effect on the association between intelligence and family size. *Brit. J. Psychol. (Statistical Section),* October, 1947.

248. ROSE, N. R., & WITEBSKY, E. Studies on organ specificity: II. Serological interrelationships among thyroid extracts of various species. *J. Immunol.,* 1955, **75,** 282.

249. RUBIN, H., & FRANKLIN, R. M. On the mechanism of Newcastle disease virus neutralization by immune serum. *Virology,* 1957, **3,** 84.

250. RUCHMAN, I. Cross immunity tests in animals with epidemic keratoconjunctivitis and St. Louis encephalitis viruses. *Proc. Soc. Exper. Biol. & Med.,* 1951, **78,** 483.

251. SARASON, S. B. Psychological Problems in Mental Deficiency, Ed. 2. New York: Harper, 1953.

252. SCHICK, B. Displacental infection of foetus with virus of German measles despite immunity of mother: Analogous observations in smallpox. *Acta. Pædiat.,* 1949, 38, 563.

253. SCHINEFIELD, H. R., & TOWNSEND, T. E. Transplacental transmission of western equine encephalomyelitis. *J. Pediat.,* 1953, **43,** 21.

254. SHUMAN, H. H. Varicella in the newborn. *Am. J. Dis. Child.,* 1939, **58,** 564.

255. SCOTT, E. M., ILLSLEY, R., & BILES, M. E. A Psychological investigation of primigravidae: III. Some aspects of maternal behavior. *J. Obst. & Gynaec. Brit. Emp.,* 1956, **63,** 494.

256. SCOTT, E. M., ILLSLEY, R., & THOMSON, A. M. A psychological investigation of primigravidae: II. Maternal social class, age, physique and intelligence. *J. Obst. & Gynaec. Brit. Emp.,* 1956, **63,** 338.

257. SCOTT, E. M., & THOMSON, A. M. A psychological investigation of primigravidae: I. Methods. *J. Obst. & Gynaec. Brit. Emp.,* 1956, **63,** 331.

258. ———. A psychological investigation of primigravidae: IV. Psychological factors and the clinical phenomena of labour. *J. Obst. & Gynaec. Brit. Emp.,* 1956, **63,** 502.

259. SHOPE, R. E. Epizootiology of virus diseases. *Advances Vet. Sc.,* 1955, **2,** 1.

260. SIGEL, M. M. The influence of age on susceptibility to virus infections, with

particular reference to laboratory animals. *Ann. Rev. Microbiol.,* 1952, 6, 247.

261. SIIM, J. C. Toxoplasmosis acquisita lymphonodosa: Clinical and pathological aspects. *Ann. New York Acad. Sc.,* 1956, 64, 185.

262. SIRLIN, J. L., BRAHMA, S. K., & WADDINGTON, C. H. Studies in embryonic induction using radioactive tracers. *J. Embryol. & Exper. Morphol.,* 1956, 4, 248.

263. SJOGREN, T. Distribution of genes affecting characteristics of the population. *Eugenics Quart.,* 1954, 1, 225.

264. ————. Genetic-statistical and psychiatric investigation of a West Swedish population. *Acta Psychiat. et Neurol.,* 1948, Supp. 52.

265. SLATER, E., & SHIELDS, J. Psychotic and Neurotic Illnesses in Twins: A Study of 293 Pairs. 1953.

266. SMITH, C. A. Effects of maternal undernutrition upon the newborn infant in Holland. *J. Pediat.,* 1947, 30, 229.

267. SOUTHAM, C. M. Serological studies of encephalitis in Japan. *J. Infect. Dis.,* 1956, 98, 163.

268. Special Committee on Infant Mortality of the County of New York. Resuscitation of newborn infants: A report. *Obst. & Gynec.,* 1936, 8, 336.

269. SPERRY, R. W. The eye and the brain. *Scient. Amer.,* 1956, 194, 48 (May).

270. SPRUNT, D. H., & FLANNIGAN, C. C. The effect of malnutrition on the susceptibility of the host to viral infection. *J. Exper. Med.,* 1956, 104, 687.

271. STEPHENS, F. E. Sampling techniques available in human genetics. *Amer. J. Human Genet.,* 1954, 6, 60.

272. STERN, C. Principles of Human Genetics. San Francisco: W. H. Freeman, 1949.

273. STEVENSON, S. S., & LAUFE, E. L. Hyaline membrane syndrome. *Obst. & Gynec.,* 1956, 8, 451.

274. STIEVE, H. Die Oozytenschwäche der alternden Frau. *Zentralbl. Gynäk.,* 1951, 73, 637.

275. STREETER, G. L. Developmental horizons in human embryos. *Contrib. Embryol.,* 1942, 30, 211; 1945, 31, 27; 1948, 32, 133; 1951, 34, 165.

276. STROER, W. F. H. Studies on the diencephalon: I. The embryology of the diencephalon of the rat. *J. Comp. Neurol.,* 1956, 105, 1.

277. SUTHERLAND, J. M. Observations on the prevalence of multiple sclerosis in Northern Scotland. *Brain,* 1956, 79, 635.

278. SWAN, C. Rubella in pregnancy as an aetiological factor in congenital malformation, stillbirth, miscarriage, and abortion. *J. Obst. & Gynaec. Brit. Emp.,* 1949, 56, 341.

279. SWANK, R. L. Multiple sclerosis: Correlation of its incidence with dietary fat. *Amer. J. M. Sc.,* 1950, 220, 421.

280. ————. Treatment of multiple sclerosis with low fat diet: Result of 7 years' experience. *Ann. Int. Med.,* 1956, 45, 812.

281. SWANK, R. L., LERSTAD, O., STRØM, A., & BACKER, J. Multiple sclerosis in rural Norway: Its geographic and occupational incidence in relation to nutrition. *New England J. Med.,* 1952, 246, 721.

282. SYVERTON, J. T., BRUNNER, K. T., TOBIN, J. O'H., & COHEN, M. M. Recovery of viable virus from poliomyelitis vaccine by use of monkeys pretreated with cortisone and X-radiation. *Amer. J. Hyg.,* 1956, 64, 74.

283. TAMM, I., & OVERMAN, J. R. Relationship between structure of benzimidazole derivatives and inhibitory activity on vaccinia virus multiplication. *Virology,* 1957, 3, 185.

284. TARJAN, G., & FORBES, L. A preadmission and diagnostic service for the mentally deficient: A report on 2000 cases. *Amer. J. Ment. Deficiency,* 1955, 60, 340.

285. TAYLOR, E. S., BRUNS, P. D., ANKER, R. M., & DROSE, V. E. Correlation of uri-

nary estrogen-pregnanediol excretion with uterine motility during pregnancy. *Amer. J. Obst. & Gynec.,* 1955, 70, 894.

286. THOM, D. A. Convulsions in early life and their relation to the chronic convulsive disorders and mental disorders. *Amer. J. Psychiat.,* 1942, 98, 576.

287. THOMAS, A., & DARGASSIES, S. A. Études Neurologiques sur le Nouveau-Né et le Jeune Nourrison. Paris: Masson & Cie., 1952.

288. TOMAN, J. E. P., & TAYLOR, J. D. Mechanism of action and metabolism of anticonvulsants. *Epilepsia,* 1952, 1, 31.

289. TOMPKINS, W. T., WIEHL, D. G., & MITCHELL, R. M. The underweight patient as an increased obstetric hazard. *Amer. J. Obst. & Gynec.,* 1955, 69, 114.

290. TÖNDURY, G. Die Embryologie im Dienste der Krankheitsforschung. In *Ergebnisse der Medizinischen Grundlagenforschung.* 1956, 669-736.

291. ————. Zur Kenntnis der Wirkung der Sexual hormone auf die embryonale Entwicklung. *Vrtljschr. Naturforsch. Gesellsch.* (Zurich), 1952, 97, 12.

292. ————. Zur Wirkung des Erregers der Rubeolen auf den menschlichen Keimling. *Helvet. Paediat. Acta,* 1952, 7, 105.

293. TOVERUD, K. U., STEARNS, G., & MACY, I. G. Maternal Nutrition and Child Health: An Interpretive Review. Washington, D. C.: National Research Council, 1950, Bulletin 123.

294. TOWER, D. B. Mechanism of seizures investigated by experimental production and control of a biochemical lesion present in epileptogenic cortex. *Epilepsia,* 1952, 1, 88.

295. TURNBULL, E. P. N., & WALKER, J. The outcome of pregnancy complicated by threatened abortion. *J. Obst. & Gynaec. Brit. Emp.,* 1956, 63, 553.

296. U. S. Department of Health, Education, and Welfare, Public Health Service. Health and Demography, Washington, D. C.: October, 1956, Publication 502.

297. URNER, J. A. Some observations on the vaccination of pregnant women and newborn infants. *Amer. J. Obst. & Gynec.,* 1927, 13, 70.

298. VILLEE, C. A. (*Ed.*) Gestation Transactions of the Third Conference, March 6, 7, and 8, 1956, Princeton, N. J. New York: Josiah Macy, Jr. Foundation, 1957.

299. Conference on Viruses in Search of Disease. *Ann. New York Acad. Sc.,* 1957, 67.

300. WALLENIUS, G., TRAUTMAN, R., KUNKEL, H. G., & FRANKLIN, E. C. Ultracentrifugal studies of major non-lipide electrophoretic components of normal human serum. *J. Biol. Chem.,* 1957, 225, 253.

301. WARKANY, J. Disturbances of embryonic development by maternal vitamin deficiencies. *J. Cell. & Comp. Physiol.,* 1954, 43 (Supp. 1), 207.

302. ————. Prenatal diseases. In *Modern Problems of Pediatrics.* New York: S. Karger, 1954, Vol. 1.

303. ————. The role of congenital anomalies in the etiology of chronic diseases. *J. Chron. Dis.,* 1956, 3, 446.

304. WEBSTER, G. R. The chemistry and metabolism of the lipids of the nervous system. *Guy's Hosp. Rep.,* 1956, 105, 80.

305. WEINMAN, D., & CHANDLER, A. H. Toxoplasmosis in man and swine—An investigation of the possible relationship. *J. A. M. A.,* 1956, 161, 229.

306. WILLIAMS, C. A., & GRAYBAR, P. Immunoelectrophoretic studies on serum proteins: II. Immune sera; antibody distribution. *J. Immunol.,* 1955, 74, 397.

307. WILLIAMS, R. Biochemical Institute Studies IV. Individual Metabolic Patterns in Human Disease; an Explanatory Study Utilizing Predominantly Paper Chromotographic Methods. Austin, Texas: Univ. of Texas Press, 1951, Publication 5109.

308. WILLIAMSON, A. P., BLATNER, R. J., & SIMONSEN, M. L. Mechanism of the teratogenic action of Newcastle disease virus in the chick embryo. *J. Immunol.,* 1956, 76, 275.

309. WILLIAMSON, R. L.   A new strain of variant hog cholera virus: Preliminary report.   *J. Amer. Vet. M. A.,* 1951, 119, 382.
310. WILLIER, B. H.   (*Ed.*)   The Analysis of Development.   Philadelphia: W. B. Saunders, 1955.
311. WILSON, J. G.   Congenital malformations produced by injection of azo blue into pregnant rats.   *Proc. Soc. Exper. Biol. & Med.,* 1954, 85, 319.
312. ———.   Influence on the offspring of altered physiologic states during pregnancy in the rat.   *Ann. New York Acad. Sc.,* 1954, 57, 517.
313. ———.   Influence of severe hemorrhagic anemia during pregnancy on development of the offspring in the rat.   *Proc. Soc. Exper. Biol. & Med.,* 1953, 84, 66.
314. WINDLE, W. F.   (*Ed.*)   Neurological and Psychological Defects of Asphyxia Neonatorum.   (To be published.)
315. ———.   (*Ed.*)   Regeneration in the Central Nervous System.   Springfield, Ill.: Charles C. Thomas, 1955.
316. WITSCHI, E.   Overripeness of the egg as a cause of twinning and teratogenesis: A review.   *Cancer Res.,* 1952, 12, 763.
317. WOLF, A.   Revue des études expérimentales sur l'étiologie des maladies démyélinisantes humaines.   *Acta Neurol. et Psychiat. Belg.,* 1954, 54, 633.
318. WOOD, D.   In Etiologic Factors in Mental Retardation, Report of the Twenty-third Ross Pediatric Research Conference.   Columbus, Ohio: Ross Laboratories, 1956, 77.
319. WOODBURY, D. M.   Anticonvulsants: Basic Considerations.   Presented at the 37th Annual Meeting of the Association for Research in Nervous and Mental Disease, December 13-14, 1957.
320. ———.   Effect of hormones on brain excitability and electrolytes.   *Recent Progr. Hormone Res.,* 1954, 10, 65.
321. WOODWORTH, R. S.   Heredity and Environment: A Critical Survey of Recently Published Material on Twins and Foster Children.   New York: Social Science Research Council, 1941.
322. WOOLF, L. I., & VULLIAMY, D. G.   Phenylketonuria with a study of the effect upon it of glutamic acid.   *Arch. Dis. Childhood,* 1951, 26, 487.
323. WORCESTER, J.   The statistical approach to the study of congenital malformations.   In Proceedings of conference sponsored by Association for Aid of Crippled Children, New York Academy of Medicine, June 5-6, 1952.   New York: Association for the Aid of Crippled Children, 1953, 183-193.
324. WORCESTER, J., STEVENSON, S. S., & RICE, R. G.   Six hundred and seventy-seven congenitally malformed infants and associated gestational characteristics: II. Parental factors.   *Pediatrics,* 1950, 6, 208.
325. WRIGHT, G. P.   The dissemination of neurotoxins and neuroviruses in the nervous system.   *Guy's Hosp. Rep.,* 1956, 105, 57.
326. YANNET, H.   Mental deficiency.   *Advances Pediat.,* 1956, 8, 217.
327. YERUSHALMY, J., *et al.*   Longitudinal studies of pregnancy on the Island of Kauai, Territory of Hawaii.   *Amer. J. Obst. & Gyn.,* 1956, 71, 80-96.
328. ZWILLING, E.   The effects of some hormones on development.   *Ann. New York Acad. Sc.,* 1952, 55, 196.

REFERENCES, PART II

1. ABRAHAMSON, S. School rewards and social-class status. *Educ. Res. Bull.*, 1952, **31**, 8-15.

2. ACKERMAN, N. W., & MENNINGER, C. F. Treatment techniques for mental retardation in a school for personality disorders of children. *Amer. J. Orthopsychiat.*, 1936, **6**, 294-312.

3. ALDRICH, C. G. Experimental studies of idiot behavior. *Proceedings and Addresses of the American Association for the Study of the Feebleminded*, 1931, **36**, 282-291.

4. ALTUS, G. T. Some correlates of the Davis-Eells Tests. *J. Consult. Psychol.*, 1956, **20**, 227-232.

5. ANASTASI, A. Intelligence and family size. *Psychol. Bull.*, 1956, **53**, 187-209.

6. ANASTASI, A., & CORDOVA, F. A. Some effects of bilingualism upon the intelligence test performance of Puerto Rican children in New York City. *J. Educ. Psychol.*, 1953, **44**, 1-19.

7. ANASTASI, A., & FOLEY, J. Differential Psychology. New York: Macmillan, 1949.

8. ANDERSON, V. V., & FEARING, F. M. A Study of the Careers of 322 Feebleminded Persons. New York: National Committee of Mental Hygiene, 1923.

9. ANGELINO, H., & SHEDD, C. L. An initial report of a validation study of the Davis-Eells tests of general intelligence or problem-solving ability. *J. of Psychol.*, 1955, **40**, 35-38.

10. ARMSTRONG, C. P. A study of the intelligence of rural and urban children. *J. Educ. Sociol.*, 1931, **4**, 301-315.

11. ARSENIAN, S. Bilingualism and mental development. *Teach. Coll. Contrib. Educ.*, 1937, No. 712.

12. ————. Bilingualism in the post-war world. *Psychol. Bull.*, 1945, **42**, 65-86.

13. ARTLITT, A. H. On the need for caution in establishing race norms. *J. Appl. Psychol.*, 1921, **5**, 179-183.

14. BALLER, W. R. A study of the present social status of a group of adults, who, when they were in elementary school, were classified as mentally deficient. *Genet. Psychol. Monog.*, 1936, **18**, 165-244.

15. BECKHAM, A. S. A study of the intelligence of colored adolescents of different social-economic status in typical metropolitan areas. *J. Soc. Psychol.*, 1933, **4**, 70-91.

16. BENOIT, E. P. Relevance of Hebb's theory of the organization of behavior to educational research on the mentally retarded. *Amer. J. Ment. Def.*, 1957, **61**, 497-507.

17. BERE, M. A comparative study of the mental capacity of children of foreign parentage. *Teach. Coll. Contrib. Educ.*, 1924, No. 154.

18. BERGMAN, M., WALLER, H., & MARCHAND, J. Schizophrenic reactions during childhood in mental defectives. *Psychiat. Quart.*, 1951, **25**, 294-333.

19. BERGMAN, P., & ESCALONA, S. B. Unusual sensitivities in very young children. *The Psychoanalytic Study of the Child*, Volume 3-4. New York: International Univ. Press, 1949.

20. BOBON, J. Contribution à l'étude des phénomènes regressifs en psychopathologie. Les pseudoglossolalies ludiques et magiques. (A contribution to the study of regressive phenomena in psychopathology. Ludical and magical pseudo-glossalalias.) *J. Belge de Neurol. et de Psychiat.* (Brussels) 1947, **47**, 219-238.

415

21. BOGARAS, W. The Chukchee. Memoirs of the American Museum of Natural History, 1904, **11**.

22. BOURNE, H. Protophrenia, a study of perverted rearing and mental dwarfism. *Lancet,* 1955, Part 2, 1156-1163.

23. BOVET, P. Les problèmes scolaires posés par le bilinguisme. *Pour l'Ere Nouvelle,* 1935, No. 105.

24. BOWMAN, P. H., DEHAAN, R. F., KOUGH, J. K., & LIDDLE, G. P. Mobilizing community resources for youth: Identification and treatment of maladjusted, delinquent, and gifted children. Youth Development Series, No. 3. *Suppl. Educ. Monog.,* 1956, No. 85.

25. BOYD, G. F. The levels of aspiration of white and Negro children in a non-segregated elementary school. *J. Soc. Psychol.,* 1952, **36**, 191-196.

26. BRAY, D. W. Issues in the Study of Talent. New York: King's Crown Press, 1954.

27. BRITTON, J. H. Influence of social class upon performance on the Draw-A-Man test. *J. Educ. Psychol.,* 1954, **45**, 44-51.

28. BROMBERG, W. Schizophrenic-like psychoses in defective children. *Proc. Amer. Assoc. Ment. Def.,* 1934, **39**, 226-257.

29. BROWN, F. A comparative study of the intelligence of Jewish and Scandinavian kindergarten children. *J. Genet. Psychol.,* 1944, **64**, 67-92.

30. ————. An experimental and critical study of the intelligence of Negro and white kindergarten children. *J. Genet. Psychol.,* 1944, **65**, 161-175.

31. BRUGGER, C. Die Landflucht der Begabten. (The emigration of the gifted from rural areas.) *All. Z. Psychiat.,* 1939, **112**, 337-348.

32. BUDD, W. C. Educators and culture-fair intelligence tests. *J. Educ. Sociol.,* 1954, 27, 333-334.

33. BURLINGHAM, D. Twins, a Study of Three Pairs of Identical Twins. New York: International Univ. Press, 1952.

34. BURT, C. The Causes and Treatment of Backwardness. New York: Philosophical Library, 1953.

35. BUTLER, F. O. Psychosis in the mentally defective. *California & Western Med.,* 1937, **46**, 84-89.

36. CANADY, H. G. The intelligence of Negro college students and parental occupation. *Amer. J. Sociol.,* 1936, **42**, 388-389.

37. CARLSON, H. B., & HENDERSON, N. The intelligence of American children of Mexican parentage. *J. Abn. & Soc. Psychol.,* 1950, **45**, 544-551.

38. CASSEL, R. H. A rigorous criterion of feeblemindedness: A critique. *J. Abn. & Soc. Psychol.,* 1951, **46**, 116-117.

39. CATTELL, R. B. A culture-free intelligence test. *J. Educ. Psychol.,* 1940, **31**, 161-179.

40. CHARLES, D. C. Ability and accomplishment of persons earlier judged mentally deficient. *Genet. Psychol. Monog.,* 1953, **47**, 3-71.

41. CHIDESTER, L., & MENNINGER, K. A. The application of psychoanalytic methods to the study of mental retardation. *Amer. J. Orthopsychiat.,* 1936, **6**, 616-625.

42. CLARK, L. P. The psychology of idiocy. *Psychoanal. Rev.,* 1932, **19**, 257-269.

43. ————. Psychoanalysis and mental arrest. *Proceedings and Addresses of the American Association for the Study of the Feebleminded,* 1932, **37**, 316-325.

44. ————. The Nature and Treatment of Amentia. Baltimore: Wood, 1933.

45. ————. The present and the future outlook in the treatment of amentia. *Psychiat. Quart.,* 1933, **7**, 50-71.

46. CLARKE, A. D. B., & CLARKE, A. M. Cognitive changes in the feebleminded. *Brit. J. Psychol.,* 1954, **45**, 173-179.

47. CLARKE, A. D. B., & HERMELIN, B. F. Adult imbeciles, their abilities and trainability. *Lancet,* 1955, Part 1, 337-339.

48. CLEMENTS, F. Notes on the construction of mental tests for American Indians. *J. Soc. Psychol.,* 1930, **1**, 542-548.

49. COWEN, E. L. Psychotherapy and play techniques with the exceptional child and youth. In *Psychology of Exceptional Children and Youth.* Cruickshank, W. M. (*Ed.*). Englewood Cliffs, N. J.: Prentice-Hall, 1955.

50. CRUICKSHANK, W. M. (*Ed.*). Psychology of Exceptional Children and Youth. Englewood Cliffs, New Jersey: Prentice-Hall, 1955.

51. DANIEL, R. P. Basic considerations for valid interpretations of experimental studies pertaining to racial differences. *J. Educ. Psychol.,* 1932, **23**, 15-27.

52. DARCY, N. T. A review of the literature on the effects of bilingualism upon the measurement of intelligence. *J. Genet. Psychol.,* 1953, **82**, 21-57.

53. DAVENPORT, K. S., & REMMERS, H. H. Factors in state characteristics related to average A-12, V-12 test scores. *J. Educ. Psychol.,* 1950, **41**, 110-115.

54. DAVIS, A. American status systems and the socialization of the child. *Amer. Sociol. Rev.,* 1941, **6**, 345-354.

55. ————. Social-Class Influences Upon Learning. (The Inglis Lecture, Harvard University, 1948.) Cambridge, Mass.: Harvard Univ. Press, 1948.

56. DAVIS, A., & EELLS, K. Davis-Eells Test of General Intelligence or Problem-Solving Ability. New York: World Book, 1953.

57. DAVIS, A., & HAVIGHURST, R. J. Social class and color differences in child-rearing. *Amer. Sociol. Rev.,* 1946, **11**, 698-710.

58. ————. Father of the Man: How Your Child Gets His Personality. Boston: Houghton-Mifflin, 1947.

59. ————. The measurement of mental systems. (Can intelligence be measured?) *Sci. Mo.,* 1948, **66**, 301-316.

60. DAVIS, R. A., JR. Some relations between amount of school training and intelligence among Negroes. *J. Educ. Psychol.,* 1928, **19**, 127-130.

61. DEGROOT, A. D. The effects of war upon the intelligence of youth. *J. Abn. & Soc. Psychol.,* 1948, **43**, 311-317.

62. ————. War and the intelligence of youth. *J. Abn. & Soc. Psychol.,* 1951, **46**, 596-597.

63. DOLL, E. A., PHELPS, W. M., & MELCHER, R. T. Mental Deficiency Due to Birth Injuries. New York: Macmillan, 1932.

64. EARL, C. J. C. The primitive catatonic psychosis of idiocy. *Brit. J. Med. Psychol.,* 1934, **14**, 230-253.

65. EATON, J. W., & WEIL, R. J. Culture and Mental Disorders: A Comparative Study of the Hutterites and Other Populations. Glencoe: Free Press, 1955.

66. EDMISTON, R. W., & MCBAIN, L. C. Social and economic background affects school achievement. *Sch. & Soc.,* 1945, **61**, 190-191.

67. EELLS, K. W. Some implications for school practice of the Chicago studies of cultural bias in intelligence tests. *Harvard Educ. Rev.,* 1953, **23**, 284-297.

68. EELLS, K. W., DAVIS, A., HAVIGHURST, R. J., HERRICK, V. E., & TYLER, R. W. Intelligence and Cultural Differences: A Study of Cultural Learning and Problem-Solving. Chicago: Univ. Chicago Press, 1951.

69. Estes, B. W. Influence of socioeconomic status on Wechsler Intelligence Scale for Children: An exploratory study. *J. Consult. Psychol.,* 1953, **17**, 58-62.

70. Fairbank, R. The subnormal child; seventeen years after. *Ment. Hyg.,* 1933, **17**, 177-208.

71. Forbes, J. K. The distribution of intelligence among elementary children in Northern Ireland. *Brit. J. Educ. Psychol.,* 1945, **15**, 139-145.

72. Frankl, G. Language and affective contact. *Nerv. Child,* 1942-43, **2**, 251-262.

73. Franzblau, R. N. Race differences in mental and physical traits studied in different environments. *Arch. of Psychol.,* 1935, No. 177.

74. Fries, M. E. Psychosomatic relationships between mother and infant. *Psychosomat. Med.,* 1944, **6**, 159-162.

75. ————. The child's ego development and the training of adults in his environment. In *The Psychoanalytic Study of the Child,* Volume 2. New York: International Univ. Press, 1946.

76. Fries, M. E., & Lewi, B. Interrelated factors in development: A study of pregnancy, labor, delivery, lying-in period and childhood. *Amer. J. Orthopsychiat.,* 1938, **8**, 726-752.

77. Fromm, E. Escape From Freedom. New York: Rinehart, 1941.

78. Gallagher, J. J. A comparison of brain-injured and non-brain injured mentally retarded children on several psychological variables. *Monog. Soc. Res. Child Devel.,* 1957, **22**, No. 2.

79. Gardner, L. P. Responses of idiots and imbeciles in a conditioning experiment. *Amer. J. Ment. Def.,* 1945, **50**, 59-80.

80. Garrett, H. E. Negro-white differences in mental ability in the United States. *Sci. Mo.,* 1947, **65**, 329-333.

81. Garth, T. R. The intelligence and achievement of mixed-blood Indians. *J. Soc. Psychol.,* 1933, **4**, 134-137.

82. Garth, T. R., & Johnson, H. D. The intelligence and achievement of Mexican children in the United States. *J. Abn. & Soc. Psychol.,* 1934, **29**, 222-229.

83. Garth, T. R., Lovelady, B. E., & Smith, H. W. The intelligence and achievement of southern Negro children. *Sch. & Soc.,* 1930, **32**, 431-435.

84. Geist, H. Evaluation of culture-free intelligence. *California J. Educ. Res.,* 1954, **5**, 209-214.

85. Gibson, D., & Butler, A. J. Culture as a possible contributor to feeblemindedness. *Amer. J. Ment. Def.,* 1954, **58**, 490-495.

86. Ginsberg, A. M. Comparação entre os resultados de um teste de nível mental aplicado em diferentes grupos etnicos e socais. (Comparison of the results of a test of mental level administered in different ethnic and social groups.) *Arch. Brasileiros de Psicotec.,* 1951, **3**, 27-44.

87. Ginzberg, E., & Bray, D. W. The Uneducated. New York: Columbia Univ. Press, 1953.

88. Girard, A. L'orientation et la sélection des enfants d'âge scolaire dans le départment de la Seine. *Population,* 1953, **8**, 649-672.

89. Gist, N. P., & Clark, C. D. Intelligence as a selective factor in rural-urban migrations. *Amer. J. Sociol.,* 1938, **44**, 36-58.

90. Gladwin, T., & Sarason, S. B. Truk: Man in Paradise. New York: Viking Fund Publications in Anthropology, No. 2, 1953.

91. Glueck, S., & Glueck, E. Unraveling Juvenile Delinquency. New York: Commonwealth Fund, 1950.

92. Goddard, H. H. The Kallikak Family. A Study in the Heredity of Feeblemindedness. New York: Macmillan, 1912.

93. GORDON, S., O'CONNOR, N., & TIZARD, J. Some effects of incentives on the performance of imbeciles. *Brit. J. Psychol.,* 1954, **45**, 277-287.

94. ———. Some effects of incentives on the performance of imbeciles on a repetitive task. *Amer. J. Ment. Def.,* 1955, **60**, 371-377.

95. GOULD, R. Some sociological determinants of goal strivings. *J. Soc. Psychol.,* 1941, **13**, 461-473.

96. GRAHAM, V. T. Health studies of Negro children: I. Intelligence studies of Negro children in Atlanta, Georgia. *Public Health Reports,* 1926.

97. GREENE, R. A. Psychoses and mental deficiencies, comparisons and relationship. *Proceedings and Addresses of the American Association for the Study of the Feebleminded,* 1930, **35**, 128-147.

98. ———. Conflicts in diagnosis between mental deficiency and certain psychoses. *Proceedings and Addresses of the American Association on Mental Deficiency,* 1933, **38**, 127-143.

99. GUILFORD, J. P. The structure of intellect. *Psychol. Bull.,* 1956, **53**, 267-293.

100. GUNNARSON, S. Dementia infantilis Heller. *Acta Paediat.,* Stockholm, 1949, **38**, 209-214.

101. HAGGARD, E. A. Social-status and intelligence: An experimental study of certain cultural determinants of measured intelligence. *Genet. Psychol. Monog.,* 1954, **49**, 141-186.

102. HAGGARD, E. A., DAVIS, A., & HAVIGHURST, R. J. Some factors which influence performance of children on intelligence tests. *Amer. Psychol.,* 1948, **3**, 265-266.

103. HALPERIN, S. L. A clinico-genetic study of mental defect. *Amer. J. Ment. Def.,* 1945, **50**, 8-26.

104. HAUCH, E. Zur differentiellen Psychologie des Industrie und Landkindes. (A contribution to the differential psychology of children from industrial and rural environments.) *Jenaer. Beitr. Z. Jugend., U. Entwicklungspsychol.,* 1929, **10**, 1-65.

105. HAUGHT, B. F. Mental growth of the southwestern Indian. *J. Appl. Psychol.,* 1934, **18**, 137-142.

106. HAVIGHURST, R. J., & BREESE, F. H. Relation between ability and social status in a midwestern community: III. Primary mental abilities. *J. Educ. Psychol.,* 1947, **38**, 241-247.

107. HAVIGHURST, R. J., & DAVIS, A. Comparison of the Chicago and Harvard studies of social class differences in child rearing. *Amer. Sociol. Rev.,* 1955, **20**, 439-442.

108. HAVIGHURST, R. J., & HILKEVITCH, R. R. The intelligence of Indian children as measured by a performance scale. *J. Abn. & Soc. Psychol.,* 1944, **39**, 419-433.

109. HAVIGHURST, R. J., & JANKE, L. L. Relations between ability and social status in a midwestern community: I. Ten-year-old children. *J. Educ. Psychol.,* 1944, **35**, 357-368.

110. HAWES, C. H. In the Uttermost East. New York: Harper, 1903.

111. HAYMAN, M. The interrelations of mental defect and mental disorder. *J. Ment. Sci.,* 1939, **85**, 1183-1193.

112. HEBB, D. O. The Organization of Behavior. New York: Wiley, 1949.

113. HEGGE, T. G. The occupational status of higher-grade mental defectives in the present emergency: A study of parolees from the Wayne County Training School at Northville, Michigan. *Amer. J. Ment. Def.,* 1944, **49**, 86-98.

114. HERNDON, C. N. Intelligence in family groups in the Blue Ridge Mountains. *Eugen. Quart.*, 1954, **1**, 53-57.

115. HERSKOVITZ, H. H., & PLESSET, M. R. Psychosis in adult mental defectives. *Psychiat. Quart.*, 1941, **15**, 574-588.

116. HEUYER, G., PIÉRON, H., PIÉRON, MME. H., & SAUVY, A. Le niveau intellectuel des enfants d'âge scolaire, une enquête nationale dans l'enseignment primaire. (A national survey of primary schools—the intellectual level of school-age children.) Paris: Institut National d'Études Démographiques, 1954.

117. HIMMELWEIT, H. T., & WHITFIELD, J. W. Mean intelligence scores of a random sample of occupations. *Brit. J. Indust. Med.*, 1944, **1**, 224-226.

118. HOGBIN, H. I. A New Guinea childhood: From weaning till the eighth year in Wogeo. *Oceania*, 1946, **16**, 275-296.

119. HOLLINGSHEAD, A. B. Elmtown's Youth. New York: Wiley, 1949.

120. HOLLINGSHEAD, A. B., & REDLICH, F. C. Schizophrenia and social structure. *Amer. J. Psychiat.*, 1954, **110**, 695-701.

121. ———. Social mobility and mental illness. *Amer. J. Psychiat.*, 1955, **112**, 179-185.

122. HONZIK, M. P. Age changes in the relationship between certain environmental variables and children's intelligence. *Yearbook Nat. Soc. Stud. Educ.*, 1940, **39**, pt. 2.

123. HULSE, W. C. Dementia infantilis. *J. Nerv. & Ment. Dis.*, 1954, **119**, 471-477.

124. HUSÉN, T. Till frågan om den selektiva migrationen ur intellektuell synpunkt. (Concerning the problem of selective migration on the basis of intellectual differences.) *Studia Psychol. Paedagog. (Lund)* 1948, **2**, 30-63.

125. ———. The influence of schooling upon *IQ*. *Theoria*, 1951, **17**, 61-88.

126. HYDE, R. W., & KINGSLEY, L. V. Studies in medical sociology: II. The relation of mental disorders to population density. *New England J. Med.*, 1944, **231**, 571-577.

127. ITARD, J. M. G. The Wild Boy of Aveyron. (Trans. by G. and M. Humphrey.) New York: Appleton-Century, 1932.

128. JAMES, S. G. The relationship of dementia praecox to mental deficiency. *J. Ment. Sci.*, 1939, **85**, 1194-1211.

129. JANKE, L. L., & HAVIGHURST, R. J. Relations between ability and social status in a mid-western community: II. Sixteen-year-old boys and girls. *J. Educ. Psychol.*, 1945, **36**, 499-509.

130. JASTAK, J. A rigorous criterion of feeblemindedness. *J. Abn. & Soc. Psychol.*, 1949, **44**, 367-378.

131. ———. The endogenous slow learner. *Amer. J. Ment. Def.*, 1950-51, **55**, 269-274.

132. ———. On Robert H. Cassel's critique of "A rigorous criterion of feeblemindedness." *J. Abn. & Soc. Psychol.*, 1951, **46**, 118-119.

133. JASTAK, J., & WHITEMAN, M. The prevalence of mental retardation in Delaware. Preliminary report on a state-wide survey. In *The Nature and Transmission of the Genetic and Cultural Characteristics of Human Populations.* New York: Millbank Memorial Fund, 1957.

134. JENKINS, M. D. A socio-psychological study of Negro children of superior intelligence. *J. Negro Educ.*, 1936, **5**, 175-190.

135. ———. Case studies of Negro children of Binet *IQ* 160 and above. *J. Negro Educ.*, 1943, **12**, 159-166.

136. ————. The upper limit of ability among American Negroes. *Sci. Mo.*, 1948, **66**, 399-401.

137. JENKINS, M. D., & RANDALL, C. M. Differential characteristics of superior and unselected Negro college students. *J. Soc. Psychol.*, 1948, **27**, 187-202.

138. JONES, H. E., CONRAD, H. S., & BLANCHARD, M. D. Environmental handicaps in mental test performance. *Univ. California Publ. Psychol.*, 1932, **5**, 63-99.

139. JOSEPH, A., & MURRAY, V. F. Chamorros and Carolinians of Saipan. Cambridge: Harvard Univ. Press, 1951.

140. KALLMANN, F. J. The genetic theory of schizophrenia. *Amer. J. Psychiat.*, 1946, **103**, 309-322.

141. KALLMANN, F. J., BARRERA, S. E., HOCH, P. H., & KELLEY, D. M. The rôle of mental deficiency in the incidence of schizophrenia. *Amer. J. Ment., Def.*, 1940-1941, **45**, 514-539.

142. KANNER, L. Autistic disturbances of affective contact. *Nerv. Child*, 1943, **2**, 217-250.

143. ————. Early infantile autism. *J. Pediat.*, 1944, **25**, 211-217.

144. ————. Irrelevant and metaphorical language in early infantile autism. *Amer. J. Psychiat.*, 1946, **103**, 242-246.

145. ————. Child Psychiatry. Springfield, Ill.: Thomas, 1948.

146. ————. A miniature textbook of feeblemindedness. *Child Care Monographs, No. 1.* New York: Child Care Publications, 1949.

147. ————. Problems of nosology and psychodynamics of early infantile autism. *Amer. J. Orthopsychiat.*, 1949, **19**, 416-426.

148. ————. The conception of wholes and parts in early infantile autism. *Amer. J. Psychiat.*, 1951, **108**, 23-26.

149. ————. A discussion of early infantile autism. *Digest Neurol. & Psychiat.*, 1951, **19**, 158.

150. KELLER, J. E. The use of certain perceptual measures of brain injury with mentally retarded children. Unpublished manuscript (Wayne County Training School).

151. KENNEDY, R. J. R. The Social Adjustment of Morons in a Connecticut City. Hartford: Mansfield-Southbury Training Schools (Social Service Department, State Office Building), 1948.

152. KESTON, M. J., & JIMINEZ, C. A study of the performance on English and Spanish editions of the Stanford-Binet intelligence test by Spanish-American children. *J. Genet. Psychol.*, 1954, **85**, 263-269.

153. KIRAHARA, H. Development of intelligence and social factors. *Rôdô Kagaku* (Study in the science of labor), **1**, No. 2.

154. KIRK, S. A. Experiments in the early training of the mentally retarded. *Amer. J. Ment. Def.*, 1952, **56**, 692-700.

155. KIRK, S. A., & McCARTHY, J. J. A study of the language process of pre-school cerebral palsied children. *Progress Report to the United Cerebral Palsy Foundation*, 1950.

156. KLINEBERG, O. An experimental study of speed and other factors in "racial" differences. *Arch. of Psychol.*, 1928, **15**, No. 93.

157. ————. Negro Intelligence and Selective Migration. New York: Columbia Univ. Press, 1935.

158. ————. Mental testing of racial and national groups. In *Scientific Aspects of the Race Problem.* New York: Longmans, Green, 1941.

159. KOUNIN, J. S. Experimental studies of rigidity: I. The measurement of rigidity in normal and feebleminded persons. *Charac. & Personal.*, 1941, 9, 251-273.

160. ————. The meaning of rigidity: A reply to Heinz Werner. *Psychol. Rev.*, 1948, 55, 157-166.

161. KUIPER, T. Maatschappelik milieu, algemene intelligentie, en de selectie voor het middelbar onderwijs. (Social environment, general intelligence and selection for secondary instruction.) *Mensch en Maatschappij*, 1930, 6, 418-424.

162. League of Nations, Health Organization (Conference on rural hygiene). *Report of French Indo-China*. Geneva: 1937.

163. LEE, E. S. Negro intelligence and selective migration: A Philadelphia test of the Klineberg hypothesis. *Amer. Sociol. Rev.*, 1951, 16, 227-233.

164. LEIGHTON, D., & KLUCKHOHN, C. Children of the People; the Navaho Individual and His Development. Cambridge: Harvard Univ. Press, 1947.

165. LEMKAU, P. V. Epidemiological aspects. In *The Evaluation and Treatment of the Mentally Retarded Child in Clinics*. New York: National Association for Retarded Children, 1956.

166. LEMKAU, P. V., TIETZE, C., & COOPER, M. Mental health problems in an urban district. *Ment. Hyg.*, 1942, 26, 275-288.

167. LEWIN, K. A Dynamic Theory of Personality. New York: McGraw-Hill, 1936.

168. LEWIS, C. Children of the Cumberland. New York: Columbia Univ. Press, 1946.

169. LOEVINGER, J. Intelligence as related to socio-economic factors. *Yearbook of the National Society for the Study of Education*, 1940, 39, 159-160.

170. LONG, H. H. The intelligence of colored elementary pupils in Washington, D. C. *J. Negro Educ.*, 1934, 3, 205-222.

171. LOOS, F. M., & TIZARD, J. The employment of adult imbeciles in a hospital workshop. *Amer. J. Ment. Def.*, 1954-55, 59, 395-403.

172. LORGE, I. Schooling makes a difference. *Teach. Coll. Rec.*, 1945, 46, 483-492.

173. LURIE, L. A., SCHLAN, L., & FREIBERG, M. A critical analysis of the progress of fifty-five feebleminded children over a period of eight years. *Amer. J. Orthopsychiat.*, 1932, 2, 58-69.

174. MAHLER, M. S. On child psychosis and schizophrenia: Autistic and symbiotic infantile psychoses. In *The Psychoanalytic Study of the Child*, Volume 7. New York: International Univ. Press, 1952.

175. MALCOVE, L. E. Margaret E. Fries' research in problems of infancy and childhood. In *The Psychoanalytic Study of the Child*, Volume 1. New York: International Univ. Press, 1945.

176. MCALPIN, A. S. Changes in the intelligence quotients of Negro children. *J. Negro Educ.*, 1932, 1, 44-48.

177. MCCANDLESS, B. Environment and intelligence. *Amer. J. Ment. Def.*, 1952, 56, 674-691.

178. MCCARTHY, D. A. The Language Development of the Preschool Child. Minneapolis: Univ. Minnesota Press, 1930.

179. MCCLELLAND, D. C., ATKINSON, J. W., CLARK, R. A., & LOWELL, E. L. The Achievement Motive. New York: Appleton-Century, 1953.

180. MCCLELLAND, D. C., RINDLISBACHER, A., & DECHARMS, R. Religious and other sources of parental attitudes toward independence training. In *Studies in Motivation* (D. C. McClelland, Ed.). New York: Appleton-Century, 1955.

181. McGURK, F. C. J. "Psychological tests"—a scientist's report on race differences. *U. S. News & World Report,* Sept. 21, 1956, 92-96.

182. McPHERSON, M. W. A survey of experimental studies of learning in individuals who achieve subnormal ratings on standardized psychometric measures. *Amer. J. Ment. Def.,* 1948, **52,** 232-254.

183. MARGOLIN, J. B., ROMAN, M., & HARARI, C. Reading disability in the delinquent child: A microcosm of psychosocial pathology. *Amer. J. Orthopsychiat.,* 1955, **25,** 25-35.

184. MEAD, M. Group intelligence tests and linguistic disability among Italian children. *Sch. & Soc.,* 1927, **25,** 465-468.

185. (anon). Report of the Mental Deficiency Committee. London: H. M. Stationery Office, 1929.

186. MONTAGU, M. F. A. Intelligence of northern Negroes and southern whites in the first World War. *Amer. J. Psychol.,* 1945, **58,** 161-188.

187. MOORE, E. Our national burden: A survey of the report on mental deficiency. *Eugen. Rev.,* 1929, **21,** 117-126.

188. MORRELL, F., ROBERTS, L., & JASPER, H. H. Effects of focal epileptogenic lesions and their ablation upon conditioned electrical responses of the brain in the monkey. *J. Electroencephalog. & Clin. Neurophysiol.,* 1956, **8,** 217-236.

189. MUENCH, G. A. A follow-up of mental defectives after 18 years. *J. Abn. & Soc. Psychol.,* 1944, **39,** 407-418.

190. MYERS, J. K., & SCHAFFER, L. Social stratification and psychiatric practice: A study of an out-patient clinic. *Amer. Sociol. Rev.,* 1954, **19,** 307-310.

191. NEFF, W. S. Socio-economic status and intelligence: A critical survey. *Psychol. Bull.,* 1938, **35,** 727-757.

192. NELSON, C. W. Testing the influence of rural and urban environment on *ACE* intelligence test scores. *Amer. Sociol. Rev.,* 1942, **7,** 751-793.

193. New York State Department of Mental Hygiene, Mental Health Research Unit. Technical Report. Syracuse, N. Y.: 1955.

194. NISBET, J. D. Family environment: A direct effect of family size on intelligence. Occasional paper (No. 8) on Eugenics. London, England: Eugenics Society, 1953.

195. NISSEN, H. W., MACHOVER, S., & KINDER, E. F. A study of performance tests given to a group of native African Negro children. *Brit. J. Psychol.,* 1935, **25,** 308-355.

196. O'CONNOR, N. The occupational success of feebleminded adolescents. *Occupat. Psychol.,* 1953, **27,** 157-163.

197. O'CONNOR, N., & TIZARD, J. The Social Problem of Mental Deficiency. London: Pergamon Press, 1956.

198. O'GORMAN, G. Psychosis as a cause of mental defect. *J. Ment. Sci.,* 1954, **100,** 934-943.

199. OSGOOD, C. E., & SEBEOCK, T. A. (*Eds.*). Psycholinguistics. *J. Abn. & Soc. Psychol.,* 1954, **49,** No. 4, Part 2 (Supplemental Issue).

200. PASAMANICK, B. A. A comparative study of the behavioral development of Negro infants. *J. Genet. Psychol.,* 1946, **69,** 3-44.

201. ————. The intelligence of American children of Mexican parentage: A discussion of uncontrolled variables. *J. Abn. & Soc. Psychol.,* 1951, **46,** 598-602.

202. ————. The contribution of some organic factors to school retardation in Negro children. Paper read before the American Psychological Association, Chicago, September 1, 1956.

203. PASTORE, N. A comment on "psychological differences as among races." *Sch. & Soc.*, 1946, **63**, 136-137.

204. PEARSON, G. B. The psychoses with mental deficiency as viewed in a mental hospital: Clinical syndromes. *Proceedings of the American Association on Mental Deficiency*, 1938, **43**, 166-172.

205. PLENDERITH, M. Discrimination learning and discrimination reversal learning in normal and feebleminded children. *J. Genet. Psychol.*, 1956, **88**, 107-112.

206. POLLOCK, H. M. Mental disease among mental defectives. *Amer. J. Psychiat.*, 1944, **101**, 361-363.

207. ———. Mental disease among mental defectives. *Amer. J. Ment. Def.*, 1945, **49**, 477-480.

208. PORTEUS, S. D. Primitive Intelligence and Environment. New York: Macmillan, 1937.

209. POTTER, H. W. Mental deficiency and the psychiatrist. *Amer. J. Psychiat.*, 1927, **6**, 691-700.

210. REDLICH, F. C., HOLLINGSHEAD, A. B., & BELLIS, E. Social class differences in attitudes toward psychiatry. *Amer. J. Orthopsychiat.*, 1955, **25**, 60-70.

211. REDLICH, F. C., HOLLINGSHEAD, A. B., ROBERTS, B. H., ROBINSON, H. A., FREEDMAN, L. Z., & MYERS, J. K. Social structure and psychiatric disorders. *Amer. J. Psychiat.*, 1953, **109**, 729-734.

212. REED, S. C., REED, E. W., & PALM, J. D. Fertility and intelligence among families of the mentally deficient. *Eugen. Quart.*, 1954, **1**, 44-52.

213. RITVO, S., & PROVENCE, S. Form perception and imitation in some autistic children: Diagnostic findings and their contextual interpretation. In *Psychoanalytic Study of the Child*, 1953, **8**, 155-161.

214. ROBBINS, J. E. The home and family background of Ottawa public school children in relation to their *IQ*'s. *Can. J. Psychol.*, 1948, **2**, 35-41.

215. ROBERTS, B. H., & MYERS, J. K. Religion, national origin, immigration, and mental illness. *Amer. J. Psychiat.*, 1954, **110**, 759-764.

216. ROBINSON, H. A., REDLICH, F. C., & MYERS, J. K. Social structure and psychiatric treatment. *Amer. J. Orthopsychiat.*, 1954, **24**, 307-316.

217. ROBINSON, M. L., & MEENES, M. The relationship between test intelligence of third grade Negro children and the occupations of their parents. *J. Negro Educ.*, 1947, **16**, 136-141.

218. ROBSON, G. M. Social factors in mental retardation. *Brit. J. Psychol.*, 1931, **22**, 118-135.

219. ROHRER, J. H. The test intelligence of Osage Indians. *J. Soc. Psychol.*, 1942, **16**, 99-105.

220. RONJAT, J. Le développement du language observé chez un enfant bilingue. Paris: Champion, 1913.

221. ROSEN, B. C. The achievement motive and value systems of selected ethnic groups. Paper read before the American Sociological Society, Washington, D. C., Aug. 27, 1957.

222. ROSENBLUM, S., KELLER, J., & PAPANIA, N. Davis-Eells ("Culture-Fair") test performance of lower-class retarded children. *J. Consult. Psychol.*, 1955, **19**, 51-54.

223. SANDELS, S. Om intelligensmätningar av barn i forskolealdern enligt Terman-Merrill skala, L-formen. (The use of the Terman-Merrill scale for measuring intelligence of preschool children, Form L). *Tidskr. Psychol. Pedag.*, 1942, **1**, 65-72.

224. SARASON, S. B. Projective techniques in mental deficiency. *J. Personal.*, 1944, **13**, 237-245.

225. ————. Psychological Problems in Mental Deficiency. 2nd ed. New York: Harper, 1953.

226. SARASON, S. B., DAVIDSON, K., LIGHTHALL, F., & WAITE, R. A test anxiety scale for children. *Child Devel.*, (in press).

227. SARASON, S. B., & SARASON, E. K. The discriminatory value of a test pattern in the high grade familial defective. *J. Clin. Psychol.*, 1946, **2**, 38-49.

228. ————. The discriminatory value of a test pattern with cerebral palsied defective children. *J. Clin. Psychol.*, 1947, **3**, 141-147.

229. SATTER, G. Retarded adults who have developed beyond expectation—Part III: Further analysis and summary. *Train. Sch. Bull.*, 1955, **51**, 237-243.

230. SATTER, G., & McGEE, E. Retarded adults who have developed beyond expectation—Part I: Intellectual functions. *Train. Sch. Bull.*, 1954, **51**, 43-55.

231. ————. Retarded adults who have developed beyond expectation—Part II: Non-intellectual functions. *Train. Sch. Bull.*, 1954, **51**, 67-81.

232. SCHAEFER-SIMMERN, H. The Unfolding of Artistic Activity. Berkeley: Univ. California Press, 1948.

233. SCHAEFER-SIMMERN, H., & SARASON, S. B. Therapeutic implications of artistic activity—a case study. *Amer. J. Ment. Def.*, 1944, **49**, 185-196.

234. SCHAFFER, L., & MYERS, J. K. Psychotherapy and social stratification. *Psychiatry*, 1954, **17**, 83-93.

235. SCHEERER, M., ROTHMANN, E., & GOLDSTEIN, K. A case of "Idiot Savant": An experimental study of personality organization. *Psychol. Monog.*, 1945, **58**, No. 4.

236. SCHMIDT, J. Uber Beziehungen zwischen Landflucht und Intelligenz. (The relation between urban migration and intelligence.) *Arch. Rass. U. Gesbiol.*, 1938, **32**, 358-370.

237. SCHULMAN, M. J., & HAVIGHURST, R. J. Relations between ability and social status in a mid-western community: IV. Size of vocabulary. *J. Educ. Psychol.*, 1947, **38**, 437-442.

238. SEARS, R. R., MACCOBY, E. E., & LEVIN, H. Patterns of Child Rearing. Evanston, Ill.: Row, Peterson, 1957.

239. SHEPARD, E. L. Measurements of certain nonverbal abilities of urban and rural children. *J. Educ. Psychol.*, 1942, **33**, 458-462.

240. SHERMAN, M., & KEY, C. B. The intelligence of isolated mountain children. *Child Devel.*, 1932, **3**, 279-290.

241. SHERWIN, A. C. Reactions to music of autistic children. *Amer. J. Psychiat.*, 1953, **109**, 823-831.

242. SHOTWELL, A. M. Arthur performance ratings of Mexican and American high-grade mental defectives. *Amer. J. Ment. Def.*, 1945, **49**, 445-449.

243. SIEVERS, D. J. The development and standardization of a test of psycholinguistic growth in preschool children. Ph.D. Thesis, Univ. Illinois, 1955.

244. SKEELS, H. M., & DYE, H. B. A study of the effects of differential stimulation on mentally retarded children. *Proceedings and Addresses of the American Association on Mental Deficiency*, 1939, **44**, 114-136.

245. SKEELS, H. M., & FILLMORE, E. M. The mental development of children from underprivileged homes. *J. Genet. Psychol.*, 1937, **50**, 427-439.

246. SKEELS, H. M., & HARMS, I. Children with inferior social histories: Their mental development in adoptive homes. *J. Genet. Psychol.*, 1948, **72**, 283-294.

247. SKEELS, H. M., UPDEGRAFF, R., WELLMAN, B. L., & WILLIAMS, H. M. A study of environmental stimulation, an orphanage preschool project. *Univ. Iowa Stud. Child Wel.*, 1938, **15**, No. 4.

248. SKODAK, M., & SKEELS, H. M. A final follow-up study of one hundred adopted children. *J. Genet. Psychol.*, 1949, **75**, 85-125.

249. SMITH, M. Intelligence of university students by size of community of residence. *Sch. & Soc.*, 1942, **55**, 565-567.

250. ————. An urban-rural intellectual gradient. *Sociol. & Soc. Res.*, 1943, **27**, 307-315.

251. SMITH, M. E. Some light on the problem of bilingualism as found from a study of the progress in mastery of English among preschool children of non-American ancestry in Hawaii. *Genet. Psychol. Monog.*, 1939, **21**, 121-284.

252. ————. Measurement of vocabularies of young bilingual children in both of the languages used. *J. Genet. Psychol.*, 1949, **74**, 305-310.

253. SMITH, S. Language and non-verbal test performance of racial groups in Honolulu before and after a fourteen-year interval. *J. Genet. Psychol.*, 1943, **26**, 51-93.

254. SNYDER, L. H. Human heredity and its modern applications. *Amer. Sci.*, 1955, **43**, 391-419.

255. SNYGG, D. The relation between the intelligence of mothers and of their children living in foster homes. *J. Genet. Psychol.*, 1938, **52**, 401-406.

256. SPARLING, M. E. Intelligence of Indian children; the relationship between Binet and Porteus scores. *Amer. J. Ment. Def.*, 1941, **46**, 60-62.

257. SPEER, G. S. The intelligence of foster children. *J. Genet. Psychol.*, 1940, **57**, 49-55.

258. SPOERL, D. T. The adjustment at college age of students who were bilingual in childhood. Abstract of dissertation, Clark Univ., Worcester, Mass., 1942.

259. ————. Bilinguality and emotional adjustment. *J. Abn. & Soc. Psychol.*, 1943, **38**, 35-57.

260. ————. The academic and verbal adjustment of college age bilingual students. *J. Genet. Psychol.*, 1944, **64**, 139-157.

261. STEGGERDA, M. Racial psychometry. *Eugen. News*, 1934, **19**, 132-133.

262. STENDLER, C. B. Social class differences in parental attitudes toward school at Grade I level. *Child Devel.*, 1951, **22**, 36-46.

263. STENQUIST, J. L., & LORGE, I. Implications of intelligence and cultural differences; as seen by a test-user; as seen by a test-maker. *Teach. Coll. Rec.*, 1953, **54**, 184-193.

264. STEVENSON, H. W., & ZIGLER, E. F. Discrimination learning and discrimination reversal in normal and feebleminded individuals. Abstract of paper delivered at 1957 meeting of the American Psychological Association (New York). To be published in *J. Personal.*

265. STEVENSON, H. W., ZIGLER, E. F., & HODDEN, L. Performance of normal and feebleminded children in repetitive tasks as a function of motivating conditions. (Abstract and data supplied by authors, Univ. Texas).

266. STOKE, S. M. Occupational groups and child development. *Harvard Monog. Educ.*, 1927, No. 8.

267. STRAUSS, A. A., & KEPHART, N. C. Psychopathology and Education of the Brain-Injured Child. Vol. II, Progress in Theory and Clinic. New York: Grune & Stratton, 1955.

268. STRAUSS, A. A., & LEHTINEN, L. E. Psychopathology and Education of the Brain-Injured Child. New York: Grune and Stratton, 1947.

269. THOMPSON, C. H. The educational achievements of Negro children. *Ann. Amer. Acad. Polit. & Soc. Sci.,* 1928, **140**, 193-208.

270. THOMSON, G. H. The relations between intelligence and fertility. A memorandum in *Papers of the Royal Commission on Population,* Volume 5. London: Her Majesty's Stationery Office, 1950.

271. THORNDIKE, R. L. Community variables as predictors of intelligence and academic achievement. *J. Educ. Psychol.,* 1951, **42**, 321-338.

272. TIZARD, J., & LOOS, F. M. The learning of a spatial relations test by adult imbeciles. *Amer. J. Ment. Def.,* 1954-55, **59**, 85-90.

273. TOMLINSON, H. Differences between preschool Negro children and their older siblings on the Stanford-Binet scales. *J. Negro Educ.,* 1944, **13**, 474-479.

274. TOUSSAINT, N. Bilinguisme et éducation. (Bilingualism and education). Brussels: Lamertin, 1935.

275. TOWN, C. H. Familial Feeblemindedness, a Study of One Hundred and Forty-one Families. Buffalo: Foster & Stewart, 1939.

276. TREDGOLD, A. F. Mental Deficiency. New York: Wood, 1922.

277. TREDGOLD, R. F., & SODDY, K. A Text-Book of Mental Deficiency. London: Baillière, Tindall & Cox, 1956.

278. VANUXEM, M. The prevalence of mental disease among mental defectives. *Proc. Amer. Assoc. Ment. Def.,* 1935, **40**, 242-249.

279. VITELES, M. S. The mental status of the Negro. *Ann. Amer. Acad. Polit. & Soc. Sci.,* 1928, **140**, 166-177.

280. WARNER, W. L. American Life, Dream and Reality. Chicago: Univ. Chicago Press, 1953.

281. WASHBURN, S. L. The strategy of physical anthropology. In *Anthropology Today* (A. L. Kroeber, *Ed.*). Chicago: Univ. Chicago Press, 1953.

282. WELLMAN, B. The meaning of environment. *Yearbook Nat. Soc. Stud. Educ.,* 1940, **39**, 21-40.

283. WELLMAN, B., & McCANDLESS, B. R. Factors associated with Binet *IQ* changes of preschool children. *Psychol. Monog.,* 1946, **60**, No. 278.

284. WELLS, J., & ARTHUR, G. Effect of foster-home placement on the intelligence ratings of children of feebleminded parents. *Ment. Hyg.,* 1939, **23**, 277-285.

285. WERNER, H. The concept of rigidity: A critical evaluation. *Psychol. Rev.,* 1948, **53**, 43-53.

286. WERNER, H., & THUMA, B. D. A deficiency in the perception of apparent motion in children with brain injury. *Amer. J. Psychol.,* 1942, **55**, 58-67.

287. ————. Critical flicker-frequency in children with brain injury. *Amer. J. Psychol.,* 1942, **55**, 394-399.

288. WERTHEIMER, M. Productive Thinking. New York: Harper, 1945.

289. WHEELER, L. R. The intelligence of East Tennessee mountain children. *J. Educ. Psychol.,* 1932, **23**, 351-370.

290. ————. A comparative study of the intelligence of East Tennessee mountain children. *J. Educ. Psychol.,* 1942, **33**, 321-334.

291. WHITTEN, B. O. Psychotic manifestations of mental defectives. *Proc. Amer. Assoc. Ment. Def.,* 1938, **43**, 72-79.

292. WITMER, E. R., & WITMER, L. Orthogenic cases, XVI-George: Mentally restored to normal but intellectually deficient. *Psychol. Clin.,* 1928, **17**, 153-169.

293. WITMER, L. The fifteen months' training of a feebleminded child. *Psychol. Clin.,* 1907-08, 69-80.

294. ———. The treatment and cure of a case of mental and moral deficiency. *Psychol. Clin.,* 1908-09, **2**, 153-179.

295. ———. A fettered mind. *Psychol. Clin.,* 2, 1916-17, **10**, 241-249.

296. ———. Orthogenic Cases, XIV-Don: A curable case of arrested development due to a fear psychosis the result of shock in a three-year-old infant. *Psychol. Clin.,* 1919-22, **13**, 97-111.

297. Witmer, L., & Ambler, M. Orthogenic cases, XVII-Jack: Feebleminded or normal. *Psychol. Clin.,* 1928-29, **17**, 217-225.

298. Witty, P. A., & Jenkins, M. D. The educational achievement of a group of gifted Negro children. *J. Educ. Psychol.,* 1934, **25**, 585-597.

299. ———. Intra-race testing and Negro intelligence. *J. of Psychol.,* 1936, **1**, 179-192.

300. Woodworth, R. S. Heredity and environment—a critical survey of recently published material on twins and foster children. (A report prepared for the Committee on Social Adjustment.) New York: Social Science Research Council, 1941.

301. World Health Organization. The mentally subnormal child. World Health Organization Technical Report Series, 1954, No. 75.

302. Zweibelson, I. Relationship of pupil worries to performance on tests of mental ability. Unpublished doctor's dissertation, Teachers College, Columbia University, 1955.

303. ———. Test anxiety and intelligence test performance. *J. Consult. Psychol.,* 1956, **20**, 470-481.

INDEX

429